*Power, Politics, and Pentecostals
in Latin America*

Power, Politics, and Pentecostals in Latin America

edited by

Edward L. Cleary
and Hannah W. Stewart-Gambino

WestviewPress
A Division of HarperCollinsPublishers

Copyright © 1997 by Westview Press, A Division of HarperCollins Publishers, Inc.

Published in 1997 in the United States of America by Westview Press, 5500 Central Avenue, Boulder, Colorado 80301-2877, and in the United Kingdom by Westview Press, 12 Hid's Copse Road, Cumnor Hill, Oxford OX2 9JJ

A CIP catalog record for this book is available from the Library of Congress.
ISBN 0-8133-2128-X (HC) — 0-8133-2129-8 (PB)

The paper used in this publication meets the requirements of the American National Standard for Permanence of Paper for Printed Library Materials Z39.48-1984.

10   9   8   7   6   5   4   3   2   1

Contents

Acknowledgments

*F*ive years of preparation have engendered a number of debts for editors and contributors. Barbara Ellington has been unfailing in her support and useful advice as senior editor of Westview Press. Dorothy Windish of Lehigh University solved many problems in the course of producing a uniform manuscript.

Leading scholars in the Pentecostal and charismatic communities assisted in shaping new research and in assessing past efforts. These include Peter Hocken, secretary of the Society for Pentecostal Studies; Ken Gill, associate director of the Billy Graham Center Library; Gary B. McGee, Assemblies of God Theological Seminary; Cecil M. Roebeck and Killian O'Donnell, O.S.B., cochairs, International Roman Catholic–Pentecostal Dialogue; Donald Gelpi, S.J., Jesuit School of Theology at the Graduate Theological Union; and Cornelia Butler Flora, Iowa State University. Jeffrey Gros, F.S.C., U.S. Catholic Conference; David Barrett, editor of the *World Christian Encyclopedia;* and Samuel Escobar, Eastern Baptist Seminary, added insights into global trends.

Lehigh University, Providence College, and the Yale University Center for International and Area Studies furnished essential support at several stages of research, travel, and writing. The Overseas Missions Study Center and its director, Dr. Gerald Anderson, Calvin College's Center for Christian Scholarship, Eugene TeSalle and Vanderbilt University, and Thomas Skidmore and Brown University hosted small conferences on Latin American religion that greatly aided an interchange of ideas that was useful in the shaping of this book.

At the core of the editors' and contributors' lives are our communities and families, which have sustained us and made this volume possible.

Edward L. Cleary
Hannah W. Stewart-Gambino

1

Introduction: Pentecostals, Prominence, and Politics

EDWARD L. CLEARY

In 1986 *Newsweek* noted that Protestants, especially Pentecostal ones, were entering party politics in Latin America.[1] From then on many newspapers recorded the surprise of Catholics and the chagrin of leftists as Pentecostals became active in the public arena in Guatemala, El Salvador, Colombia, Peru, and Brazil. Political activity brought Pentecostals a notoriety that they had until then escaped. Largely ignored on the margins of society, they had grown to impressive numbers. Now journalists, the general public, and other churches found themselves faced with mysterious groups with sufficient numbers to have strong national influence.

Pentecostalism has quietly become the largest Christian movement of the twentieth century.[2] Some 400–500 million followers are spread over most of the world.[3] Their number is almost half that of the largest Christian denomination, Roman Catholicism. Pentecostalism's otherworldly style and growth by conversion and by inherited status are astonishing, given the predictions that modern times would be increasingly secular. Harvey Cox's *Fire from Heaven*[4] opened to general readers in 1995 what was barely known even in theological schools.[5] Pentecostalism is especially prominent in Latin America, where it challenges Catholic, historical Protestant, and Mormon churches, vodoun, macumba, and indigenous religions.

This book is an attempt to provide a unique view of Latin American Pentecostalism. Its contributors are seasoned Latin Americanists dealing with themes and contexts with which they have long familiarity. They examine history, looking at the roots of Pentecostalism rather than concentrating on the recent invasion of the religious right from the United States. They employ social science, especially sociology and political science, rather than polemics or speculation. They represent a mix of Pentecostal and non-Pentecostal, Latin American and

1

North American scholars, all of them highly attentive to Pentecostal perspectives. In contrast to previously published volumes, this collection seeks to present Pentecostal perspectives rather than the agendas that have dominated social science or Latin American Catholic examinations of Pentecostal growth. Who Pentecostals are and why they have taken hold in Latin America are foremost, but related questions of women in religion, ecumenism, and politics are addressed as well.

This volume has important predecessors. They include works most cited by Latin Americans, such as those of Emilio Willems, Christian Lalive d'Epinay, Francisco C. Rolim, and Jean-Pierre Bastian.[6] Willems's summary article[7] and later book, *Followers of the New Faith*,[8] became minor classics. His book, published in 1967,[9] opened a window to what *Time* in 1962 had called "the fastest-growing church in the Western Hemisphere."[10]

Willems entered the field as a pioneer, exploring. Rather than emphasizing surveys, he relied especially on repeated interviews and observation of street-corner proselytism, church services, spirit possession, and healing rites. This process resulted in a vivid picture of the conditions in which many Pentecostals lived. He believed that social dislocations among these lower-class persons produced anomie. The churches countered this moral aimlessness with a sense of purpose and a modernizing ethic capable of fitting Latin Americans into modern secular society. Willems emphasized *la tomada del Espíritu* (seizure by the Spirit) as fundamental. Seizure by the Spirit made it clear to others that one had experienced God, and on that evidence alone one was included in community worship and activities.

In a field where reputations are made by criticism, Christian Lalive d'Epinay, a young European social scientist, took a contrasting view. The title of his main work, *Haven of the Masses*,[11] captured well the thrust of his argument. The study was commissioned by the World Council of Churches, and this sponsorship and publication in Spanish as well as English gave it much wider circulation than Willems's and other studies. Lalive d'Epinay depicted Pentecostalism as a continuation of folk Catholicism, preserving the past, with the authoritarian pastor in place of the old *hacendado* or *patrón*. This explanation appealed to many, in and outside of Latin America.

Jean-Pierre Bastian represented a different strain of interpretation, one sometimes critical of Protestantism as too closely tied to liberal and North Atlantic interests. In his view, a number of Latin American Protestants "lent themselves to being true ideological vanguards of North American interests and those of the national bourgeoisie in Latin America."[12] He expressed skepticism that Latin American Pentecostalism, given its authoritarian leadership, would contribute much to democracy.[13]

Samuel Escobar, one of the most respected Latin American scholars, summarizes these studies and those of Catholic bishops, ecumenical organizations, anthropologists and sociologists in academic settings, and the mass media as displaying "an amazing inadequacy to deal with their subject."[14] Harvey Cox points to a number of "large holes" in Lalive d'Epinay's and other accounts.[15] Three studies published before 1990 should, however, be exempted from Escobar's evaluation. Cornelia Butler Flora's *Pentecostalism in Colombia*[16] was a careful study that opened the door to scholarship about Pentecostal women. Her appraisal of Pentecostal politics—"Their religious doctrine allows them to 'strip halos of sanctity' from those who occupy seats of power, and their class homogeneity allowed them to mobilize toward secular change"[17]—shed light on events that would follow. Stephen D. Glazier and colleagues received insufficient attention for *Perspectives on Pentecostalism: Case Studies from the Caribbean and Latin America.*[18] Eugene A. Nida's "The Relationship of Social Structure to the Problems of Evangelism in Latin America"[19] was a seminal contribution to the understanding of "cultural reconstruction."

For Escobar and others, a new and impressive stage of scholarship began in 1990 with the appearance of the first comprehensive works on Latin American Pentecostalism and politics and the first to appeal to a wide readership: David Stoll's *Is Latin America Turning Protestant?* and David Martin's *Tongues of Fire.*[20] Their publication opened the way for numerous commentaries, many of them opportunistic and erroneous.

Pentecostalism in Latin America is a complex development with a broad array of implications.[21] Further, Pentecostal churches do not have the same history or emphasize the same teachings as historical Protestant or evangelical churches. In a word, a good deal of discussion of Protestant history in Latin America has been irrelevant for explaining Pentecostal growth.[22]

Elizabeth Brusco, Cecília Mariz, Leslie Gill, Paul Freston, Rowan Ireland, John Burdick,[23] and others have recently completed works of unusual merit, marked by their determination to listen to Latin Americans explain religion in their own terms. Further, only recently have Pentecostal scholars been trained in social research and academic theology, and it was judged essential that their research be part of this volume. For years social scientists and journalists have ignored distinctions considered indispensable by Pentecostals.[24]

Probing into the complexities of Latin American Pentecostalism rewards readers with a surer grasp of a phenomenon that will continue to be crucial in the coming years. Without this understanding, one has an incomplete view of Latin American culture and will enter ill-prepared upon any analysis of contemporary Latin American politics.

Lack of comprehension of Pentecostalism is not limited to North Americans. By and large, Latin American politicians, Catholic church leaders, and most of the 70,000 Latin American journalists have given no evidence that they comprehend Pentecostalism. Until recently Pentecostals have been isolated, out of public view, and unreported by the media. As Philip Berryman remarks, "Secular and Catholic critics, most of whom do not seem to have ever stepped foot in an evangelical church to observe for themselves, do not appreciate what draws millions of poor people to join its ranks."[25] Pentecostals are emphasized here because they account for 75–90 percent of contemporary Protestant growth in Latin America.[26]

History and Stereotypes

To focus more clearly on the complexities that Pentecostalism presents it is useful to address next: stereotypes associated with Pentecostal history, theological achievement, distinction from latter-day cousins, and the oft-repeated charge that Pentecostalism will rend the unifying garment of Latin American culture. Because of the many false and blurred depictions of Pentecostalism, one needs to state what it is not as well as describe what it is. First, contrary to a common Latin American stereotype, Pentecostalism is not a North American invasion. It did not begin with a pervasive outside missionary effort, nor are major groups sustained by personnel or money from the United States or Europe.

In the three most prominent areas where Pentecostalism has expanded, Brazil, Chile, and Central America, outside missionaries helped to spark, not create, a Latin American institution. In the case of Chile, contributors to this volume describe North American Willis C. Hoover as accepting an invitation from Chileans to be their leader rather than characterizing him as the founder of Chilean Pentecostalism. In Brazil and Central America, as Douglas Petersen has said,[27] the "strong, determined personalities [of foreign missionaries], whose influence was more catalytic than institutional, provid[ed] models for Latin Americans who applied Pentecostal beliefs and practices to their own situations without becoming dependent or subordinate."

Missionary presence at the inception of Latin American Pentecostalism was infinitesimal. In the case of Central America, only two North American families from the Assemblies of God, now the largest Pentecostal church in Latin America, were in the region at any one time before World War II. A slight increase, ranging from two to eight missionaries per Central American country, occurred after World War II.[28] Central Americans took the initiative to organize and to staff a complex enterprise with thousands of churches and chapels and numerous projects. In Central America, Panama, and Belize the number of national credentialed pastors within the Assemblies of God alone has grown to 4,500.

Not only leadership but by far the majority of the financial support of "classical" Pentecostals comes from Latin Americans. When David Stoll published *Is Latin America Turning Protestant?* Pentecostals read it with trepidation, since Stoll had previously studied the Summer Institute of Linguistics and was highly critical of those North American missionary efforts. Stoll himself had expected to find a strong North American hand in financing Pentecostal growth in Latin America. Instead, he found that the Assemblies of God, with some 10 million members, had expended only US$20 million yearly from North America (much of it spent in the United States). More than one Pentecostal has been content to repeat Stoll's judgment that "a mere $20 million a year cannot explain these kinds of results. If evangelical churches were really built on handouts, they would be spiritless patronage structures, not vital, expanding grassroots institutions."[29]

The fundamental source of financial support for Pentecostal churches in Latin America is the generosity of individual members. Church attenders (many Pentecostals do not attend regularly)[30] give frequently and give from their substance rather than their surplus. Contributing 10 percent of income is not uncommon and is often held up as a goal. The results of this generosity are impressive. Petersen estimates that the Assemblies of God in Central America, Panama, and Belize possess combined assets of US$150 million in real estate and improvements.[31]

Is there not a North American invasion among some Protestants in Latin America? Yes, but they are not the major Pentecostal groups we are discussing. Further, Catholic critics of North American financing of Protestants frequently ignore the very large amounts of money and numbers of missionaries that the Catholic church in Latin America has received from North Atlantic countries.

Pentecostals in Latin America differ greatly from historical Protestants. Lutherans, Presbyterians, Methodists, and other such groups brought with them immigrant cultures, for example, German or British, that embodied Christianity in a different way from Latin American cultures. Pentecostals did not have to become little Germans or Britishers preferring high- or low-church liturgies. Nor did Pentecostals have to accustom themselves to the pastoral practices established by foreign missionaries as overseas extensions of their own denominations. Pentecostals were not burdened with preferences for territorial parishes, elite high schools, and expensive clinics. Nor did Latin American Pentecostals have to subordinate themselves to foreigners in high national positions. They formed rapidly multiplying small communities rather than parishes and looked to themselves for organizing rather than to central headquarters in Stockholm or in Springfield, Missouri.

But Pentecostals are profoundly Protestant.[32] Some Pentecostals exaggerate their uniqueness, and some institutional histories read almost like accounts of virgin births. Pentecostalism is deeply rooted in the Holiness and Revival traditions and in the minds of some scholars cannot be understood without knowledge of these traditions. David Martin's case for the importance of Methodism's carrying on its mission in Latin America through Pentecostal expressions may be overstated but calls attention to history's guiding hand.

The Holiness and Revival traditions grow out of a centuries-long impulse among ordinary Christians toward a deeper spiritual life, beyond mere church attendance to make contact with God. In European Protestantism after the Reformation this impulse was often guided by Pietists. They accepted as foundations the seeking of personal experience of God, commencing with a new birth by the Holy Spirit, the conviction that experience leads to reforming lives, and the idea of living within a community taking a stand against a corrupt world. Communities thus took on a *contra mundum* cast. To a remarkable degree Latin American Pentecostals mirror these characteristics.

The Pietist movement waxed and waned throughout the seventeenth, eighteenth, and nineteenth centuries. The impulse to "a higher life" took various forms. In England and the United States the tradition of John and Charles Wesley was of particular importance. Those within the Pietist tradition fought not only against declining church attendance but also against the perceived loss of religious fervor in older churches. Revivals, camp meetings, retreats, full-throated hymn-singing, and testimonies were employed.

In the United States in the nineteenth century, religious leaders were anxious about the spiritual condition of the partially de-Christianized Yankees (settled and godless) and frontier types (unsettled and godless). The Civil War was perceived as having taken its moral toll, accentuating secularism, moral decline, and indifference to religion (if not to God). Through camp meetings and revivals, circuit riders, evangelists, and pastors lead American Protestants to a fuller holiness. Since, in the view of some participants, the older (by one or two generations) churches from which they came, mostly Methodist or Baptist, had grown lifeless, innovators broke away to form new groups. After the Civil War Holiness and Revival teaching came to center upon the Pentecost event. Holiness and Revival participants used Scripture as their written guide. In their search they read the accounts of the early Christians in the Acts of the Apostles.

Perfectionist Religion

Building on Pietist backgrounds and on their reading, these innovators took for granted that every Christian was called to perfection. They increasingly focused on the notion of perfection as seizure by the Holy Spirit. Holiness preachers and songwriters spoke of the Upper-Room event. Albert B. Simpson and others in the Holiness churches preached that the gifts of the Holy Spirit, many of them bordering on the miraculous, did not cease with the apostolic age but would continue in the lives of ordinary Christians until the end of the world. In a word, Simpson and others used the standard of spiritual life portrayed in the Acts as the norm by which to measure each Christian's life. They also used it to measure the shortcomings of the churches at that time. (It is relevant here that Holiness and Pentecostal church members were critical of other Protestant churches long before judging the Latin American Catholic church lifeless.)

When Pentecostalism began in 1901 and its members experienced "a second blessing (baptism)" and spoke in tongues, its participants were hardly surprised by these events, as the Holiness movement included many elements of Pentecostalism[33] and led many participants to the doorstep of the Pentecostal experience.[34] The Holiness movement imparted more than ideas. It deeply influenced Pentecostalism's structures, mission strategies, nature of support, content, and manner of worship.[35] Latin American Pentecostals were to prove more adept at putting many theological and organizational ideas into practice than their North American or European brothers and sisters.

One of the key borrowings has been self-support generated by ministers. This was well known in Holiness circles, especially as advocated by Bishop William Taylor. Young persons went to the field (home or foreign missions) without formal backing or pledges, relying solely on faith and prayer for support. Pentecostals in Chile extended this as test or a sign—observing whether potential pastors could support themselves. Those who did not receive sufficient support were kept from advancing to higher status in the ministry.

The perfectionist character of Pentecostal churches has implications for statistics. The contributors to this volume have avoided stress on statistics, partly because they consider statistics in Latin America, especially about religion, unreliable because of inadequate surveys and lack of sustained membership. More important, many Pentecostal churches count only habitual attenders. Pentecostals are by their definition not only attenders but militants. Therefore, for many fervent Pentecostals, nonattenders are nonmembers. When Everett Wilson writes of Pentecostals in Guatemala, following pastors' reports he implies that their numbers represent about 15 percent of the population. If he had asked individual Guatemalans, the percentage would have been higher.

Theological Achievement

Pentecostalism's greatest theological achievement in Latin America is freedom of expression and the affirmation of the individual's worth within the community. These are fundamental Protestant emphases. To them may be added a call to sanctity for all members and a missionary zeal for sharing spiritual gifts with others—perpetuating the Holiness and Revival traditions and mirroring ideals of Catholic religious orders as well.

Freedom of expression in worship is the basis of a major innovation for Pentecostalism. In sharp contrast to what takes place in traditional Catholic or Protestant worship, almost anyone accepted by the Pentecostal community is allowed to interpret Scripture during worship, to moralize about the conditions of life, to preach about the changes needed in personal conduct, to pray spontaneously, to offer suggestions for the community's response to an evil world, and to vote on questions of importance such as large expenditures of community assets. All this is deeply rooted in Protestant traditions such as interpretation of Scriptures by ordinary Christians, the priesthood of all believers, and the priority of practice over dogma.

One of the marks of confusion about Pentecostal churches is calling them "evangelical." The long-standing Latin American custom of describing Protestants as *evangélicos* (sometimes with a pejorative sense of "Bible-thumpers") has led bilingual reporters to use "evangelical" as the English equivalent, overlooking its restriction to specific tendencies in Protestant history.[36] Two of the best-known depictions of non-Catholic religion in Latin America were Marlise Simons's 1982 article in the *New York Times Magazine* and a 1984 issue of *NACLA Report on the Americas* describing the offensive of conservative evangelical groups in Central America.[37] From then on, the fastest-growing groups, the most active groups, the worrisome Protestant growth groups were often referred to interchangeably as "evangelical," "Pentecostal," "conservative," and, sometimes, "fundamentalist Christian."

Pentecostals have been looked down upon by their evangelical cousins in the United States as well as in Latin America—marginalized as unreliable and regarded as theologically naive and perhaps heterodox. Evangelicals of the Billy Graham mold have typically pointed to differences between themselves and Pentecostals, who had notably lesser levels of formal education and financial support, were excessively demonstrative in worship, and placed undue emphasis upon speaking in tongues and the gifts of healing and prophecy.[38] (When the Pentecostal scholar Everett Wilson and I [a Roman Catholic] appeared on the platform at the Billy Graham Center at Wheaton College [Ill.] some years ago, we agreed that we were almost as marginal to "evangelicals" as the Jew who had preceded us on the platform.)

Missionary histories of evangelicals and Pentecostals have differed. When evangelicals such as William D. Taylor describe evangelical churches in Latin America, they presume that in evangelical churches the forms and structures and major decisions come from abroad.[39] The major Pentecostal groups have not been burdened with such a foreign character.[40] These Pentecostal groups have been largely Latin American adaptations. Their structures (such as pastorship, informal education, administrative looseness and controls) grew especially from experience in Latin America rather than being imported from Europe or North America. Their political responses were not deeply influenced by the religious right in the United States as were some evangelical churches but were fashioned as survival strategies for Latin Americans of subordinate social status. The differences were especially evident in the Central American conflicts of the 1970s.

In the course of time, however, the differences have diminished. Kenneth Gill and Robert Coote, long-term observers of Protestantism, point to the contemporary membership of Pentecostal churches within the National Alliance of Evangelicals and the inclusion of Pentecostals by that consummate evangelical, Billy Graham, within his crusades.[41] In Latin America contributors to this volume often find the distinction irrelevant in analyzing ethical or political positions.

Pentecostals, Charismatics, and Neo-Pentecostals

If Pentecostals are not Protestants of the historical traditions or evangelicals of the Billy Graham cast, neither are they charismatic or Neo-Pentecostal.[42] The mistaken identification by the media of Pentecostals with the late-arriving charismatics troubles older Pentecostal groups because of vast differences in class backgrounds, lifestyles, and political leanings. Nowhere are the differences more evident than in Guatemala, where prominent Neo-Pentecostal groups have spread across cities and countryside preaching a gospel of health and wealth, often espousing an uncritical support of military and oligarchic politics, and sweeping into their folds disaffected middle- and upper-class Catholics by the chapel full.

In brief, Pentecostals are churches founded mostly in the early part of this century. They often are connected to foundational events as Charles Parham's spiritual revival in Topeka, Kansas, in 1901 and the subsequent revival at the Azusa Street Mission in Los Angeles in 1906–1909. These are not obscure events in North American history but landmarks for many of the fastest-growing churches in the United States and the world. Classical Pentecostal groups include the Assemblies of God Church, the Church of God (Cleveland, Tenn.), the Church of God in Christ, and the International Church of the Foursquare Gospel. If readers are not yet familiar with these groups or their schools, such as Oral Roberts University and Lee College, Pentecostals are content to continue unnoticed in their counterculture, growing and changing to meet the times on their own terms.

Charismatics represent a second wave of religion attentive to the Holy Spirit and his work in individuals and churches. This second movement came to national attention in 1959 when many members of an Episcopal congregation in Van Nuys, California, and their pastor, Dennis Bennett, received what they considered baptism with the Holy Spirit. Individual members of Protestant, Roman Catholic, and Orthodox churches quickly spread a "charismatic renewal" within their traditions. By 1972 the movement had affected key figures such as Cardinal Léon-Joseph Suenens. Suenens participated in the reform movement of Vatican II and acted as mentor and integrator for the international Catholic charismatic renewal. Many independent groups outside the classical Pentecostal tradition also emerged from the religious ferment of the 1960s and 1970s.[43]

None of these distinctions would be important to many social scientists in the United States or observers of Latin America were it not for the effect of Neo-Pentecostals on public life. In contrast to the Pentecostals' asceticism and modesty, the behavior of some Neo-Pentecostals knew no restraints. They noisily entered politics, preached an ethos of consumerism, and supported or emulated the showmanship of North America's religious-right figures Jerry Falwell and Pat Robertson. In Guatemala two charismatics became presidents—one by military selection (Gen. José Efraín Ríos Montt) and the other by national election (Jorge Serrano Elías). Charismatics there supported the military's displacement and repressive control of a million internal refugees. They cooperated with government forces in pushing other churches aside, and they acted as an alternative to the progressive Catholic church for many middle- and upper-class Guatemalans. The class preferences and pro-U.S. biases of many Neo-Pentecostals earned them the enmity of older Pentecostals and historical Protestants.[44]

Latin American Culture and the Catholic Church

The Catholic church in Latin America has been largely ignorant of the indigenous character of major groups of Pentecostals.[45] As the Pentecostals' and other Protestants' presence in Latin America has increased, the Catholic church has been depicted as responding belatedly to this challenge. In fact, the Protestant "threat" has been a central theme since the 1940s and 1950s. At that time indigenous Pentecostals were growing on the margins of society, but high-profile missionary evangelical groups were coming to Latin America in notable numbers because the doors to traditional Protestant missions in China and elsewhere were closed. The first Latin American Bishops Conference noted the growing danger of Protestantism.[46]

The bishops at the 1955 conference spoke of the menace to the traditional Catholic culture of Latin America.[47] This argument has been extended to include threats to the unity of Latin American culture—the idea that Latin Americans have a Catholic soul and a Catholic culture that bind them together. Assumed in this line of argument is that Protestantism has no right to establish itself in Latin America, having its own territory in northern lands, such as Scandinavia, where it excludes Catholics as much as possible. The Protestant religion is judged incompatible with the soul and the culture of Latin America, and therefore the presence and the proliferation of non-Catholic religions cannot be considered "normal" and must be attributed to North American imperialism and disloyal, aggressive, and fanatical proselytizing.

Speaking of sects (presumably including Pentecostals), John Paul II told the bishops at the fourth Latin American Bishops' Conference in Santo Domingo in 1992, "We should not underestimate a particular strategy aimed at weakening the bonds that unite Latin American countries and so to undermine the kinds of strength provided by unity. To that end, significant amounts of money are offered to subsidize proselytizing campaigns that try to shatter such Catholic unity."[48]

Prominent North American social scientists such as Howard J. Wiarda and Glenn Dealy have developed arguments about the Catholic character of the culture of Latin America,[49] but these arguments have been criticized as deeply flawed.[50] Given the fluidity and plasticity of culture and its evident fragmentation in Latin America, I believe it impossible to maintain the fiction of a unity of Catholic culture in Latin America. No one has been clearer in taking apart the myth that Latin America has a special unity than Franz Damen, a Catholic priest performing interchurch work in Bolivia. He points to the fragmentation of religion in Latin America as part of the larger social processes occurring in the contemporary Third World.[51] He and others, such as the renowned Protestant theologian José Míguez Bonino, consider Pentecostalism an authentic expression of the Latin American ethos.[52] Damen also believes that it is becoming increasingly evident that "proselytizing methods" are not among the principal reasons for church growth.[53]

Politics and Prominence: A Map

The entry of Protestants into electoral politics began in Latin America in the 1950s,[54] was mostly episodic in Peru and Brazil, and was largely limited to Protestants who were not Pentecostal. Most of these activities were ignored until 1986, when eighteen Pentecostals were elected to the Brazilian Assembly. Until then Protestants and especially Pentecostals were praised or vilified for staying out of the public arena in terms of both social action and direct political activity. Observers strongly criticized the prohibitions on Pentecostals' entering into politics and the putative escapist ideology that served as a political opiate, as support for repressive governments, and as a denial of the major obligations of Christians to help set the world on a just and peaceful course.

Assessing politics and religion requires looking at several countries, since the character of institutions and the cultural arrangements of the countries of Latin America vary. This increases the complexity of the analysis but reduces the risk of inadequate generalizations. Here and in succeeding chapters dealing with countries, several themes, with country variations, become evident: a widening political agenda, the formation of political parties, learning experience, cycles of activism and avoidance, the role of the media, and two streams of political orientation and action.

Little research has been conducted on the details of the life of Pentecostals in the 1930s, but it seems clear that, as in Peru, Pentecostals backed parties such as the Alianza Popular Revolucionaria Americana (American People's Revolutionary Alliance—APRA) primarily as ways of breaking the Catholic religious monopoly. In more recent years political involvement has greatly widened. Prominently, Pentecostals stood for and won elections for president of Guatemala, second vice-president of Peru, and a variety of government positions in Colombia and Brazil. The range of political activity has been extensive. Pentecostals have worked in political campaigns, noisily in the case of the Alberto Fujimori campaign of 1990. Protestants—Pentecostals among them—began formulating papers on public positions.[55] They assumed a much more public role, as in El Salvador, where Pentecostals sought a harmonious church-state relationship. Even in subordinate positions such as that of Puerto Ricans in Allentown, Pentecostals have frequently protested discrimination against them.

The most basic political activity has been voting. Pentecostals have done this enthusiastically in some countries (and politicians have taken notice). Posting prominent Protestants such as Ríos Montt as candidates heading a party's ticket generates intense curiosity and even small industries tracking voting patterns. Pollsters are beginning to treat such questions as whether Protestants vote narrowly for other Protestants, "brother for brother," as some Pentecostal pastors have counseled and whether Catholics in large numbers support or avoid candidates strongly identified as Protestant. This widening political activism has led to the formation of separate political parties such as Venezuela's Organización Renovadora Autónoma and El Salvador's Movimiento de Solidaridad Nacional and Movimiento de Unidad. Although this is not a universal regional trend, separate Pentecostal or Protestant political parties have begun to appear in several other countries in Latin America. This pattern invites speculation on the fate of religious parties in secular states and parallels that of Christian Democracy, which has gradually lost much of its Christian ethical character in Latin America. Generally the religious parties are, to date, small and likely to remain so, but in contemporary politics even tiny religious parties, such as those of Israel, can hold a balance of power. Williams points out their potential role swing votes in El Salvador.

Pentecostals have clearly entered upon a political learning experience. Nowhere is this clearer than in Peru. Victor Arroyo and Tito Paredes, Peruvian Protestant social scientists, were so encouraged by events that they concluded: "The massive decisive evangelical participation in the 1990 general elections has changed not only Peru's political scene but also the characteristics of evangelical presence in the country."[56] Disillusionment set in quickly, however, and these observers' exaggeration betrays their lack of experience in political involvement.

Many Pentecostal and Protestant leaders were unprepared for larger public roles, and inexperience took its toll in political experiments. In Peru in 1980 Protestant leaders including prominent Pentecostals attempted to form El Frente Evangélico, a political movement intended to incorporate Protestants of various tendencies, but the movement failed. Arroyo and Paredes point to lack of maturity for political action, insufficiently representative organization at the national level, inadequate resources, and insufficient time for organizational evolution.[57] A larger disappointment followed Alberto Fujimori's election as president.

A leading voice in the political awakening of Protestants in Latin America, René Padilla, warns not only of entering politics without experience but of activism without a theological basis. He says that Latin American Protestantism "has a theological deficit which means that the movement runs the risk of investing its energies in fruitless or even destructive political activism."[58] But Pentecostals and Protestants have been learning quickly. The high-profile examples of Catholic activists in Latin America and, by contrast, of the North American religious right were easy to track.[59]

The relative ease with which many Protestants and Pentecostals in Latin America have entered politics has dismayed journalists and political commentators. For years they had attributed political noninvolvement to religious or theological prohibitions, depicting strong pastors as keeping their flock out of politics, with its inevitable immoral staining.[60] If this were not enough, during a crisis such as military repression pastors were seen as searching Scripture for justifying texts and consequently stressing one of Paul's comments on obedience to government authority.[61]

Pentecostals, I believe, held back from politics not primarily for the above reasons but for two others: They were mostly poor, and they were outsiders to the political process. Once they had access to people in positions of power and judged that they had the numbers and status to effect changes in the political systems, politics became a new game, open to them.[62] In effect, they entered politics *when they assessed that the benefits outweighed the costs.*

Why are religionists who emphasize spiritual experience entering politics? Because they are pragmatic. Experience is the basis of their religion and the foundation for a pragmatic, nondogmatic approach to the context in which they live. (Following the frequently cited injunction of Romans 13.1 ["Let every one obey the authorities that are over him"] was not a religious absolute but practical advice, to be followed when useful.) Hence, by the millions Pentecostals enter the polling booths and support political parties as a way of improving the environment in which they have to live.

This same pragmatism will lead Pentecostals away from politics as well. One cannot count on their remaining deeply involved in politics. Their "arrival" in politics assumes that entry into politics is a "natural" evolution. Marginal groups thus become mainstream political actors when they reach a critical size. Perhaps only an insider such as Everett Wilson could capture the character of their pragmatism. He remarks in his chapter on Guatemala in this volume that both activism and avoidance are natural to Pentecostals. They "tend to stay aloof, their independence ensuring their freedom until, with little risk of compromise, they can assert their influence." This makes political analysis and prediction precarious enterprises.

In a sense, though, Pentecostals have irretrievably lost their ability to remain out of view. As Sepúlveda and I demonstrate below, now that Chilean Pentecostals represent a significant sector of society, politicians have had to seek their views on divorce, public education, sexual questions, AIDS, and similar issues.[63] Apart from participation in party politics, Pentecostals are being thrust willy-nilly onto the public stage by the mass media.

The question is how to exploit this prominence. Will Pentecostals offer a coherent message? In contemporary Latin America organizations can seldom control communication of their moral or political positions. Television and newspaper reporters are able to ferret out Pentecostal "positions" through opinion polls, effectively circumventing authoritarian pastors.[64] And interviews for tabloids or for insatiable television news managers searching for "Pentecostal views" can typically be obtained from one or another of the hundreds of part-time Pentecostal pastors, not from spokespersons at central offices. Further, the media may shape Pentecostal public positions in ways uncomfortable to Pentecostal leaders; as Sidney Tarrow points out, the media do at least as much to control the construction of meaning as states or social actors.[65]

One trend that may continue for a time and merits watching has evolved in Chile. There Pentecostals have tended to flow into one of two major streams. Their political activism has tended to cast leaders in political brokerage roles, with pastors working with members of the political elite to obtain legal protection and privileges. Some pastors become partners in the high political networks. Others adopt a more prophetic stance, one critical of the ethical failures of governments and parties. Leaders of this tendency include persons whom Guillermo Cook describes as "erudite" Pentecostals, leaders who have ventured outside their churches for more advanced study in theology and social sciences.

Theological Roots

Attempting to understand Pentecostal politics or any other expression of the religion invariably leads to basic questions. What, after all, makes Pentecostals act as they do? Activities such as being slain in the spirit, healing, speaking in tongues, and denouncing Catholics and older Protestant groups as dead bodies have led superficial observers to consider Pentecostals marginal and esoteric. Not only are long-term Pentecostals down-to-earth, but they fit in well with mainstream twentieth-century philosophy and theology. Having traced these connections, one is less likely to dismiss Pentecostalism as groundless or unworthy of serious analysis.

As the histories of Latin American Protestant groups—historical, evangelical, and Pentecostal—differ, so do their beliefs or, rather, what they choose to emphasize within Christianity. "Beliefs" may be more appropriate than "theology," which implies systematic reflection by academically trained intellectuals aimed at describing the content of the faith.

The attempt to identify core beliefs here is preliminary, because few Pentecostals in Latin America are trained in theology and Pentecostal churches differ among themselves in what they emphasize. Pentecostal scholars such as Douglas Peterson emphasize speaking in tongues as a central belief, and Pentecostals in many places take speaking in tongues as the measure of whether a person has received the Holy Spirit. But there are important churches in Latin America that do not emphasize speaking in tongues. Kenneth Gill, associate director of the Billy Graham Center Library and a disciple of the Pentecostal scholar Walter Hollenweger, says that, so diverse are Pentecostals worldwide, he has spent more than twenty years trying to elaborate a comprehensive Pentecostal theology and has been unable to do so.[66]

However, reflection on Pentecostals in Latin America reveals central practices and beliefs that set Pentecostals there apart from most Catholics and from other Protestants. Pentecostals center their lives on *experience* of the Holy Spirit. This is an event radiating throughout one's body and evident to others, better described as individual than as subjective or illusory experience. It is a vividly felt contact with God. Unlike Catholic or historical Protestants, for whom experience is a secondary consideration, or evangelicals, for whom a decision for Christ is often a discrete, noncontinuous event, Pentecostals' experience of God is a primary and ongoing aspect of their religion. The structures of their worship are designed to enhance these experiences on a routine basis through expressive, intense, and per-formance-oriented liturgies. *La tomada del Espíritu* (seizure by the Spirit) noted years ago by Willems is typical of the kinds of experience that are at the core of Pentecostal practice.[67]

Pentecostals emphasize the gifts of the Holy Spirit, as described by Luke. They are confident that these gifts are present within the church and can be relied on. Wilson agrees: "Stated theologically, Pentecostal groups carry the doctrine of im-manence accepted by all Christian believers beyond the usually accepted bound-aries, since the grace, gifts, and power attributed to the church are believed to be accessible, at least on occasion, to every believer."[68]

To provide readers with a sense of what matters to Pentecostals I outline a the-ological basis for Latin American Pentecostalism. Remarkably, this sketch shows not a theology that is traditional, imported, cryptopsychological, or uncommon but one based on experience that is eminently contemporary, Latin American, Christian, and ordinary. This is not the place to elucidate a full theology of expe-rience,[69] but several observations about experience as emphasized by Pentecostals are in order.

A turn to experience has marked a variety of contemporary theologies. Experience is all-important because the contemporary age is characterized as one of experiences. As Jean Mouroux suggests, even when moderns turn to Christianity they ask, "What worthwhile experiences can you give me?" Contemporary theologians drawn to experience as a philosophical basis for their theologizing include giants of the Vatican II era such as Karl Rahner, Edward Schillebeeckx, and Bernard Lonergan.

In the United States and England major figures of contemporary philosophy such as Charles Sanders Peirce, William James, Josiah Royce, George Santayana, and Alfred North Whitehead argued over the structure of experience. Donald L. Gelpi, a Catholic theologian at Berkeley's Graduate Theological Union, has made a noteworthy attempt to employ the technical achievements of Peirce in tracing the outlines of a realist theology.[70]

Gelpi warns readers that "experience" is a "weasel word," there being no con-sensus among theologians about its meaning.[71] Nor do Pentecostals agree on its meaning. Contemporary theology, in the view of many theologians interviewed, is roughly in the same stage it was in the eleventh century, possessing brilliant and partial insights but lacking a coherent synthesis. Pentecostalism, in my view, will play a prominent role in the next millennium's Christian vision.

In Latin America Pentecostalism shares its emphasis on experience with other theologies and religions. Liberation theology is marked by an emphasis on praxis (knowledge derived from doing), especially as elaborated by major figures such as Gustavo Gutiérrez, Juan Luis Segundo, and Clovodis Boff.[72] Gutiérrez, the fa-ther of liberation theology, believes that a spirituality appropriate to Latin America is being created to replace the "spirituality of evasion" that has long char-acterized Latin Americans, and "every great spirituality begins with the attainment of a certain level of experience."[73] Traditional popular Catholicism and indigenous religion are based on experience as well.

Most important here is understanding the Christian character of Pentecostal grounding in experience.[74] One of the blanket criticisms of Pentecostalism is that it is little other than feeling, a precarious foundation for religion in that it opens the way for aberrations, faddism, and chaos. On this basis the Brazilian bishops in 1994 declined to endorse the Catholic charismatic renewal.[75]

Further, establishing religion on a foundation of emotion misplaces religion's central emphasis, calling attention to the experience rather than to the being encountered, God. Christian teachers have for centuries instructed their disciples that the feelings experienced in making contact with God are often secondary, distracting, and utterly unimportant. Disciples had to strive to live by pure faith, without directly seeing God in this life.

However, Christian experience, in a modern view, is not so much affective experience as its personal integration. Experience thus is first making contact with God and then maintaining communion with God. Contemporary theologians have recognized the function of affectivity. Mouroux believes that spiritual affectivity ("taking pleasure in the Lord" is the way many Pentecostals speak of it) heals and transforms through joy.[76] Contemporary theologians also focus not on experiences that are mystical (in the sense of extraordinary) but ones that occur within the ordinary and unforced religious life experiences of average persons.

That these experiences are commonplace in general populations was shown by Linda B. Bourque, Kurt Back, William C. McCready, and Andrew M. Greeley some years ago.[77] McCready and Greeley conclude: "There are a lot of mystics around, more than any one ever thought existed. They are neither prejudiced nor maladjusted nor narcoticized. They claim to have contact with the ultimate, and it does not seem to hurt them. On the contrary, it seems to have helped."[78]

Theologically, being grounded in experience has important consequences. In a profound sense, no institution or person mediates in a Pentecostal person's conversion to God.[79] No formal rite (not even baptism) is required, and the role of the pastor is limited. Testimony and fervor demonstrate the Pentecostal's faith. The Pentecostal movement does not require more than this testimony for acceptance as a convert and a participant in services. Neither any given level of preparation nor knowledge of Scripture is required at this entry level. Thus Pentecostalism is an open field for personal liberty.

Statistics are therefore often unreliable. Initial entry (not full membership) is based on self-identification. Men and women give testimony about their religious experience, attend regularly for a while, and are caught up in the whirlwind of active worship. Catholics and historical Protestants may sample Pentecostal life and be counted by churches as congregants (a lesser status of membership). Full membership in Pentecostal churches, however, is often denied neophytes and occasional attenders. Core membership is typically demanding and exclusive. Everett Wilson says: "Pentecostals have always tended to be elitist. They make converts prove themselves. Pentecostal pastors and core members are more concerned with the rectitude of their communities than adding numbers. Pentecostals regularly discipline members, especially if they do not measure up."[80]

As a result of intense religious experience persons aim their efforts at bringing their lives into conformity with the norms expected of a person living in contact and communion with God. These persons typically have a heightened sense of hope. This description fits what Wilson says of Latin American Pentecostals: "At [Pentecostalism's] roots lies the assertion that Christian faith, biblically and historically understood, no matter how orthodox or pietistic, must be *existential* [based on experience]. Though typically buoyant and enthusiastic, Pentecostals are basically skeptical of human intentions, efforts, and institutions. However, their movement views human brokenness not with despair, but with hope."[81]

Because of this strongly spiritual emphasis, some observers have seen Pentecostalism as the natural home for Latin Americans looking for a spiritual emphasis and not finding it in the post–Vatican II, thisworldly Catholic church.[82] This may be too facile, as Wilson points out: "Even while Pentecostals give a prominent place to glossolalia (speaking in tongues), the miraculous, and the prophetic, they are not characteristically mystical or ascetic."[83] In characterizations of Pentecostals as sects they are mistakenly depicted as otherworldly and uninterested in the progress of this world. Wilson insists: "They are clearly more concerned with God's immanence than his transcendence."[84] Virtually every Pentecostal I have interviewed over more than ten years has emphasized the pragmatic character of Pentecostalism, in contrast to the prevailing stereotypes.[85]

A negative consequence of Pentecostalism as a religion that emphasizes experience is a lack of unity. Wilson describes Pentecostalism as "a sprawling, decentralized movement that lacks unity of polity and doctrine."[86] The histories of older Pentecostal establishments in Chile, Brazil, and Central America show this fissiparousness. Serious sociological and theological questions about stability and about sustaining growth arise. Pentecostalism has no stated religious logic (theology) to validate it. It does not stress literacy, and this hampers its organizing for denominational cohesion. Its temporary efflorescence of voluntary religiosity[87] makes for an uncertain future. The question also arises of Pentecostalism's ascetic and moral standards' being so high (tithing, frequent church attendance, and abstinence from alcohol) that the majority of Latin Americans will never cotton to it.

Yet Pentecostalism has proved itself immensely adaptive and pragmatic. Pentecostals apparently sense an underlying unity, one built on core beliefs. The creation of yet another church or transfer of members to another denomination is not the rending of the body of Christ (the classical definition of schism) but a change of pastors or more likely, a change to a community that endorses and affirms a person better than the last one.

Conclusion

To provide exploratory and explanatory views of Pentecostalism in the chapters that follow, themes that need special treatment are taken up first. These include interchurch relations and the complexities of women's roles in Latin American religion, Catholic and Pentecostal. Pentecostalism is then examined within national contexts in five countries, with large Pentecostal populations—Chile, Brazil, Guatemala, El Salvador, and Puerto Rico. If Puerto Rico is a surprise leader, with at least one-third of its population Pentecostal, the surprise will not be for long, since Puerto Rican Pentecostals are changing the face of Protestantism on the U.S. mainland as well. The inclusion of Venezuela opens the religious world of the urban migrant and of Pentecostal minorities in Latin American society and politics.

Latin American Pentecostals move between poles of perfectionism and pragmatism. Practitioners are called to a high degree of sacrifice: 10 percent of income, no alcohol or tobacco, marital fidelity. Even more, Pentecostals are called apart from the world. For men this can mean giving up weekends with soccer and beer, no small sacrifice in lower- and middle-class life.[88] But religious experience leads them to pragmatism—to valuing survival in nations opening toward democracy. The political and religious environment has opened, offering Pentecostals new opportunities. Catholics and other non-Pentecostals watch as Pentecostals impressively fill a new niche in Latin America.

NOTES

1. *Newsweek* 108 (September 1, 1986), pp. 63–64.

2. A number of scholars accept William Menzies's description: "The Pentecostal movement is that group of sects within the Christian church which is characterized by the belief that the occurrence mentioned in Acts 2 on the day of Pentecost not only signaled the birth of the church, but describes an experience available to believers in all ages." *Anointed to Serve* (Springfield, Mo.: Gospel Publishing House, 1971), p. 90.

3. David B. Barrett, in a statistical survey for *International Bulletin of Missionary Research* 19, 1 (January 1995), pp. 24–25, combines Pentecostals and charismatics and estimates their number as 463,741,000 in mid-1995.

4. Harvey Cox, *Fire from Heaven: The Rise of Pentecostal Spirituality and the Reshaping of Religion in the Twenty-first Century* (Reading, Mass.: Addison-Wesley, 1995).

5. In addition to Cox's, especially useful views on Pentecostalism have been provided by Robert Mapes Anderson, *Vision of the Disinherited: The Making of American Pentecostalism* (New York: Oxford University Press, 1979); Walter J. Hollenweger, *The Pentecostals: The Charismatic Movement in the Churches* (Minneapolis: Augsburg, 1972); Grant Wacker, "Pentecostalism," in Charles H. Lippy and Peter W. Williams, eds., *Encyclopedia of*

American Religious Experience: Studies of Traditions and Movements (New York: Scribner, 1988), vol. 2, pp. 933–945; H. Vinson Synan, "Pentecostalism: Varieties and Contributions," in *One in Christ*, pp. 97–109; Stanley M. Burgess and Gary B. McGee, eds., *Dictionary of Pentecostal and Charismatic Movements* (Grand Rapids, Mich.: Zondervan, 1988); and *Pneuma* and other publications of the Society for Pentecostal Studies. Pioneering views of Pentecostal theology are offered by Donald W. Dayton, *Theological Roots of Pentecostalism* (Metuchen, N.J.: Scarecrow, 1987), and Matthew S. Clark, Henry I. Lederle, et al., *What Is Distinctive About Pentecostal Theology?* (Pretoria: University of South Africa, 1983). Speaking in tongues, a central phenomenon for many Pentecostals, is discussed by Cyril G. Williams, *Tongues of the Spirit: A Study of Pentecostal Glossolalia and Related Phenomena* (Cardiff: University of Wales Press, 1981). For bibliography, see Charles Edwin Jones, *Guide to the Study of the Pentecostal Movement*, 2 vols. (Metuchen, N.J.: Scarecrow, 1983).

6. For a Latin American survey, see Jorge Soneira, "Los estudios sociológicos sobre el Pentecostalismo en América Latina," *Sociedad y Religión* 8 (March 1991), pp. 60–67.

7. Emilio Willems, "Protestantism and Cultural Change in Brazil and Chile," in William V. D'Antonio and Frederick B. Pike, eds., *Religion, Revolution, and Reform* (New York: Praeger, 1964), pp. 93–108.

8. Subtitled *Culture Change and the Rise of Protestantism in Brazil and Chile* (Nashville, Tenn.: Vanderbilt University Press, 1967).

9. The fieldwork was carried out in 1959–1960, before the first Frei government in Chile and the military coup in Brazil.

10. *Time* 80, 56 (November 2, 1962). *America*, the Jesuit weekly, described "the Pentecostal breakthrough" in its January 31, 1970, issue.

11. Subtitled *A Study of the Pentecostal Movement in Chile* (London: Lutterworth, 1970).

12. Jean-Pierre Bastian, *Historia del Protestantismo en América Latina* (Mexico City: Ediciones Casa Unida de Publicaciones, 1990), p. 232.

13. See Cox, *Fire from Heaven*, pp. 182–183.

14. Samuel Escobar, "The Promise and Precariousness of Latin American Protestantism," in Daniel R. Miller, ed., *Coming of Age: Protestantism in Latin America* (Lanham, Md.: University Press of America, 1994), p. 11.

15. Cox, *Fire from Heaven*, pp. 161–184.

16. Subtitled *Baptism by Fire and Spirit* (Rutherford, N.J.: Fairleigh Dickinson University Press, 1976).

17. Flora, *Pentecostalism in Colombia*, p. 227.

18. Stephen D. Glazier, ed., *Perspectives on Pentecostalism: Case Studies from the Caribbean and Latin America* (Lanham, Md.: University Press of America, 1980).

19. *Practical Anthropology* 5 (1958), pp. 101–123.

20. David Stoll, *Is Latin America Turning Protestant? The Politics of Evangelical Growth* (Berkeley: University of California Press, 1990); David Martin, *Tongues of Fire: The Explosion of Protestantism in Latin America* (Oxford and Cambridge, Mass.: Blackwell, 1990). See also Miller, *Coming of Age*, and Virginia Garrard-Burnett and David Stoll, eds., *Rethinking Protestantism in Latin America* (Philadelphia: Temple University Press, 1993). For a critique of the treatment of Pentecostalism as part of fundamentalism, see Daniel Levine, "Protestants and Catholics in Latin America: Family Portrait," manuscript, Fundamentalism Project, University of Chicago, November 1991. For a differing view, see Russell P. Spittler, "Are Pentecostals and Charismatics Fundamentalists? A Review of

American Uses of These Categories," in Karla Poewe, ed., *Charismatic Christianity as a Global Culture* (Columbia, S.C.: University of South Carolina Press, 1994), pp. 103–116. For bibliographies, see Martin, *Tongues of Fire;* Stoll, *Is Latin American Turning Protestant?* Cecil M. Roebeck Jr., "Select Bibliography on Latin American Pentecostalism," *Pneuma: The Journal of the Society for Pentecostal Studies* 13, 1 1991), pp. 193–197. The most comprehensive source for works in Spanish or Portuguese, though dated, is *Bibliografía teológica comentada del area latinoamericana* (Buenos Aires: Instituto Superior Evangélico de Estudios Teológicos, periodically).

21. The hazards of this field of inquiry have been expressed by David Martin: "The whole field is fraught with propaganda, and the investigator is bound to be caught in a cross-fire whatever position he takes up." *Tongues of Fire,* p. 292. The complexities are not just conceptual but historical, as the editors of the *Dictionary of Pentecostal and Charismatic Movements* point out: "When points of delineation [between Pentecostal and charismatic] are decided upon and connected, the resulting line is invariably crooked, perhaps broken, and sometimes split into various branches." Burgess and McGee *Dictionary,* p. 1.

22. See comments by Pentecostal scholars: Douglas Petersen, "The Formation of Popular National Autonomous Pentecostal Churches in Central America," in *Conference Papers on the Theme "To the Ends of the Earth"* (Gaithersburg, Md.: Society for Pentecostal Studies, 1994), p. 13, and Everett A. Wilson, "Who Speaks for Latin American Pentecostals?" *Pneuma: The Journal of the Society for Pentecostal Studies* 16, 1 (1994), pp. 143–150.

23. Among other works, see Elizabeth Brusco, "The Household Basis of Evangelical Religion and the Reformation of Machismo in Colombia," Ph.D. diss., City University of New York, 1986; Cecília Mariz, *Coping with Poverty: Pentecostals and Christian Base Communities in Brazil* (Philadelphia: Temple University Press, 1994); Leslie Gill, "Religious Mobility and Many Words of God in La Paz, Bolivia," in Garrard-Burnett and Stoll, *Rethinking Protestantism,* pp. 180–198; Paul Freston, "Brother Votes for Brother: The New Politics of Protestantism in Brazil," in Garrard-Burnett and Stoll, *Rethinking Protestantism,* pp. 66–110; Rowan Ireland, *Kingdoms Come: Religion and Politics in Brazil* (Pittsburgh: University of Pittsburgh Press, 1991); and John Burdick, *Looking for God in Brazil: The Progressive Catholic Church in Urban Brazil's Religious Arena* (Berkeley: University of California Press, 1993).

24. Wilson, "Who Speaks for Latin American Pentecostals?" p. 144.

25. Philip Berryman, "The Coming of Age of Evangelical Protestantism," *NACLA Report on the Americas* 27, 6 (May/June 1994), p. 9.

26. Percentages given for growth are not the same as current percentages of Pentecostals within the national Protestant populations. Paul Freston estimates that Pentecostals represent no more than 60–65 percent of the current Protestant population in Brazil. Freston, "Brother Votes for Brother," p. 72.

27. Petersen, "The Formation of Popular National Autonomous Pentecostal Churches," p. 2.

28. Ibid.

29. David Stoll, "Is There a Protestant Reformation in Latin America?" *Christian Century* 107 (January 17, 1990), p. 46.

30. See discussion in Sepúlveda and Cleary in this volume and Everett A. Wilson, "The Dynamics of Latin American Pentecostalism," in Miller, *Coming of Age,* p. 97.

31. Petersen, "The Formation of Popular National Autonomous Pentecostal Churches," p. 3.

32. For the sake of cohesive argument, I am abstracting from the non-Protestant aspects of Pentecostalism. Walter Hollenweger has argued that Pentecostalism has as many Catholic as Protestant roots. Everett Wilson ("Dynamics," p. 93) notes that Latin American Pentecostalism "displays many resemblances to Roman Catholic practices."

33. See, for example, Charles Edwin Jones, "Holiness Movement," in Burgess and McGee, *Dictionary,* pp. 404–409, including an invaluable bibliography.

34. Not all of the Holiness precursors moved "forward" into the Pentecostal movement. Albert B. Simpson, founder of the Christian and Missionary Alliance, held his group apart, partly because he believed that not all should speak in tongues. The Church of the Nazarene also looked unfavorably on the practice.

35. Latin American Pentecostals did not acknowledge many of these debts, instead taking pride in their indigenous or criollo Pentecostalism.

36. See, for example, Leonard I. Sweet, ed., *The Evangelical Tradition in America* (Macon, Ga.: Mercer University Press, 1984), with especially illuminating chapters by Joel Carpenter and Grant Wacker; Donald W. Dayton and Robert K. Johnston, eds., *The Variety of American Evangelicalism* (Knoxville, Tenn.: University of Tennessee Press, 1991). See also Pentecostal views of evangelicals in "National Association of Evangelicals" and "Evangelicalism" in Burgess and McGee, *Dictionary.*

37. Marlise Simons, "Latin America's New Gospel," *New York Times Magazine,* November 7, 1982, pp. 45–47+; Enrique Domínguez and Deborah Huntington, "The Salvation Brokers," *NACLA Report on the Americas* 18, 1 (January/February 1984), pp. 2–36.

38. Pentecostals also dissociated themselves from evangelicals in part because Pentecostals were strongly pacifist. In the United States, changes have taken place on both sides. See, for example, the history of the National Association of Evangelicals as described by Cecil M. Roebeck Jr., in Burgess and McGee, *Dictionary,* pp. 634–636.

39. See, for example, Emilio A. Nuñez and William D. Taylor, *Crisis in Latin America: An Evangelical Perspective* (Chicago: Moody Press, 1989), p. 156.

40. For the sake of clarity of exposition I am focusing on major Pentecostal churches such as the Iglesia Metodista Nacional, the Iglesia Evangélica Pentecostal, the Assemblies of God, and the Church of God (Cleveland, Tenn.).

41. Interviews with Kenneth Gill at the Billy Graham Center, and Robert Coote at the Overseas Mission Study Center, June 19, 1995.

42. See Stanley M. Burgess and Gary B. McGee, "The Pentecostal and Charismatic Movements," in their *Dictionary,* pp. 1–6. For somewhat different use see Poewe, *Charismatic Christianity as Global Culture.*

43. Burgess and McGee, *Dictionary,* is an extraordinarily useful guide. See also Anderson, *Vision.*

44. Interviews with Dennis Smith, general coordinator, Centro Evangélico Latinoamericano de Estudios Pastorales, Guatemala City, June 1991 and February 1992.

45. Bishop Roger Aubry of Reyes, Bolivia, Father Franz Damen, also of Bolivia, and José Luis Idígoras of Peru are notable exceptions. See Escobar, "The Promise," pp. 25–29.

46. *Conclusiones, Conferencia General del Episcopado Latino-Americano, Rio de Janeiro, July 25–August 4, 1955* (Vatican City: Tipografia Poliglotta Vaticana, 1956), pp. 41–42.

47. Ibid., p. 41.

48. John Paul II, "Opening Address," in Alfred T. Hennelly, ed., *Santo Domingo and Beyond* (Maryknoll, N.Y.: Orbis Books, 1993), p. 48.

49. See, for example, Howard J. Wiarda and Harvey F. Kline, "The Context of Latin American Politics," in Howard J. Wiarda and Harvey F. Kline, eds., *Latin American Politics and Development,* 3rd ed. (Boulder: Westview Press, 1990), pp. 15 ff.; Glenn Dealy, *The Public Man: An Interpretation of Latin American and Other Catholic Countries* (Amherst: University of Massachusetts Press, 1977).

50. For a contrasting view of Latin American culture see Levine, "Protestants and Catholics."

51. See especially his "Sectas," in Ignacio Ellacuría and Jon Sobrino, eds., *Mysterium liberationis: Conceptos fundamentales de la teología de la liberación,* vol. 2 (San Salvador: Universidad Centroamericana Editores, 1991), pp. 423–445. See also "Las sectas, ¿Avalancha o desafío?" *Cuarto Intermedio,* no. 3 (May 1987), and *La cuestión de la "sectas"* (La Paz: Secretariado Nacional de Ecumenismo, 1990).

52. Damen, "Sectas," pp. 423–445.

53. Damen, "Las sectas, ¿Avalancha?," pp. 61–62; see also J. Cordova, *Conferencias fundamentalistas en El Alto* (La Paz: n.p., 1990), pp. 64–71.

54. Escobar, "The Promise," p. 50.

55. See, for example, for an early statement, Fraternidad Teológica Latinoamericana, "Declaración de Jaracaboa," in Pablo Alberto Deiros, ed., *Los evangélicos y el poder político en América Latina* (Grand Rapids, Mich.: Eerdmans, 1986), pp. 345–361. See also the account of a noteworthy meeting in 1991 by Elsa Romanenghi de Powell, "Participación de los evangélicos en la política latinoamericana: Una crónica," *Boletín Teológico* 23, 44 (December 1991), pp. 233–248.

56. Victor Arroyo and Tito Paredes, "Evangelicals and the 'Fujimori Phenomenon,'" *Transformation* 9, 3 (July–September 1992), p. 15.

57. Arroyo and Paredes, "Evangelicals," p. 16.

58. René Padilla, "Latin American Evangelicals Enter the Public Square," *Transformation* 9, 3 (July–September 1992), p. 7.

59. A careful presentation of North American politics is provided by A. James Reichley, "Pietist Politics," in Norman J. Cohen, ed., *The Fundamentalist Phenomenon: A View from Within, a Response from Without* (Grand Rapids, Mich.: Eerdmans, 1990), pp. 73–98.

60. See, for example, James C. Dekker, "North American Protestant Theology: Impact on Central America," *Mennonite Quarterly Review* 58 (August suppl.), pp. 378–393.

61. Romans 13.1. In the *Dios llega al hombre* ([New York: Sociedad Bíblica Americana, 1970], p. 357) version, "Todos deben someterse a las autoridades del gobierno."

62. For a comparison with Pentecostals in the United States, see Jerry W. Shepperd, "Sociology of Pentecostalism," in Burgess and McGee, *Dictionary,* pp. 794–799.

63. See also Juan Sepúlveda, "The Pentecostal Movement in Latin America," in Guillermo Cook, ed., *New Face of the Church in Latin America* (Maryknoll, N.Y.: Orbis Books, 1994), p. 73.

64. See, for example, the studies by Centro de Estudios Públicos reported in the Cleary and Sepúlveda chapter in this volume.

65. Sidney Tarrow, *Power in Movement: Social Movements, Collective Action, and Politics* (New York: Cambridge University Press, 1994), p. 119.

66. Interview with Kenneth Gill, Wheaton, Ill., June 22, 1994.

67. Willems, *Followers of the New Faith.*

68. Donald Dayton discusses the effect of stressing Luke's rather than Paul's views of Christianity in *Theological Roots,* pp. 23 ff. Everett A. Wilson, "The Dynamics of Latin American Pentecostalism," in Daniel R. Miller, ed., *Coming of Age: Protestantism in Contemporary Latin America* (Lanham, Maryland: University Press of America, 1994), p. 94.

69. See, for example, Donald L. Gelpi, *The Turn to Experience in Contemporary Theology* (New York: Paulist, 1994).

70. Gelpi offers an introduction to the technical issues involved in the different constructs of experience in *The Turn to Experience.*

71. Gelpi, *The Turn to Experience,* esp. pp. 1–3.

72. On Latin American theology and practice see Edward L. Cleary, *Crisis and Change: The Church in Latin America Today* (Maryknoll, N.Y.: Orbis Books, 1985), p. 64 and passim. On European theology see José María González Ruiz, "Ortodoxia/ortopraxis," in Casiano Floristán and Juan José Tamayo, eds., *Conceptos fundamentales del Cristianismo* (Madrid: Editorial Trotta, 1993), pp. 923–937. For the concept of praxis as used by Latin American social scientists, see Edward L. Cleary and German Garrido-Pinto, "Applied Social Science, Teaching, and Political Action," *Human Organization* 36, 3 (Fall 1977), p. 270. On orthopraxis as a starting point, see Robert L. Kinast, "Orthopraxis: Starting Point for Theology," *Proceedings of the Catholic Theological Society of America* 38 (1983), pp. 29–44.

73. Gustavo Gutiérrez, *We Drink from Our Own Wells: The Spiritual Journey of a People* (Maryknoll, N.Y.: Orbis Books, 1984), p. 52.

74. For an empathetic view of Pentecostal experience by an outsider, see Carmen Galilea W., *El Pentecostal: Testimonio y experiencia de Dios* (Santiago, Chile: Centro de Investigaciones Sociales–Centro Bellarmino, 1990).

75. *Latinamerica Press,* June 16, 1994, p. 6.

76. Jean Mouroux, *The Christian Experience: An Introduction to a Theology* (New York: Sheed and Ward, 1954), p. 272.

77. Linda B. Bourque, "Social Correlates of Transcendental Experience," *Sociological Analysis* 20 (Fall 1969), pp. 151–163; Linda B. Bourque and Kurt Back, "Values in Transcendental Experiences," *Social Forces* 47 (September 1970), pp. 34–38; Kurt Back, "Language, Society, and Subjective Experience," *Sociometry* 34 (1971), pp. 1–21; William C. McCready and Andrew M. Greeley, *The Ultimate Values of the American Population* (Beverly Hills, Calif.: Sage, 1976), esp. pp. 129–157.

78. McCready and Greeley, *Ultimate Values,* p. 156.

79. Galilea (*El Pentecostal,* p. 86) notes: "It is only the living, personal experience of the believer that determines that the believer can count on possessing the power of the gifts of the Holy Spirit, which sometimes can be expressed as charismatic gifts."

80. Personal communication, March 30, 1995.

81. Wilson, "Dynamics," p. 93, emphasis mine.

82. Timothy E. Evans, "Religious Conversion in Guatemala," Ph.D. diss., University of Pittsburgh, 1990, pp. 270–318.

83. Wilson, "Dynamics."

84. Ibid. Gelpi adds an insight for explaining the paradox of Pentecostal pragmatism: "Every version of pragmatism builds on a construct of experience." Gelpi, *The Turn to Experience*, p. 1.

85. Interviews in the United States, Guatemala, Puerto Rico, the Dominican Republic, Brazil, and Chile, 1981–present.

86. Wilson, "Dynamics," p. 93.

87. Phrase borrowed from Martin, *Tongues of Fire*, p. 294.

88. See Arturo Fontaine Talavera and Harald Beyer, "Retrato del movimiento evangélico a la luz de las encuestas de opinión pública," *Estudios Públicos* 44 (Spring 1991), pp. 63–124. They conclude with the hypothesis that Pentecostalism represents the feminization of Chilean culture.

2

Pentecostals, Politics, and Public Space in Latin America

MICHAEL DODSON

Present-day Latin America presents an intriguing panorama to the student of religion and politics. In the first place, the region's most venerable political structures are undergoing profound change. Latin America has long been noted for its pronounced statism and political authoritarianism. However, all across the region a transition to democratic government is currently under way. This transition is manifested in contested elections, a proliferation of political parties, and a general pattern of military withdrawal from the political arena. It is also marked by a growing trend toward the privatization of many state functions. It is true that some scholars view these developments with skepticism and have raised serious questions about the depth and durability of the current wave of democratization.[1] Nevertheless, despite this undercurrent of caution, there seems to be a consensus that for the time being political authority in Latin America derives more from the ballot than from the bullet.

A shift of similar magnitude is occurring in Latin American religion. Whereas Latin America was pervasively Roman Catholic for four and one-half centuries, not merely in religious terms but culturally, today it is the fertile ground of dynamic Protestant expansion. The historical Protestant churches labored for a century to penetrate the Catholic monopoly with only limited success. In scarcely two generations Pentecostalism, which in several senses of the word is a more popular brand of Protestantism than the historical variant, has spread exuberantly throughout the region. At present Pentecostalism appears to be replacing Roman Catholicism as the religion of the common people.[2]

How will the simultaneous democratization of Latin American politics and "Pentecostalization" of Latin American religion affect each other? This question is already being posed.[3] In raising it, some writers have stressed the social consequences that may flow from the rapid spread of evangelical churches; others have stressed Protestantism's political effects, particularly in stimulating and providing support for democratic values and practices.[4] At the same time, other writers are skeptical that religion and politics can interact in a mutually beneficial way. They see in the predominantly Pentecostal character of Latin American Protestantism today an apolitical, otherworldly religion that is, on its own terms, entirely apathetic toward politics. According to this point of view, although Pentecostal religion may facilitate authoritarian politics through passivity or by lending itself to the manipulations of the "Christian right," it does not foster democratic values or encourage the sense of civic commitment that is necessary to democratic politics.[5]

These conflicting interpretations of Pentecostalism and politics are not new. Indeed, this debate was first framed by two pioneering researchers, Emilio Willems and Christian Lalive d'Epinay. As early as the 1960s they recognized the degree to which Pentecostalism had become an established, popular religion in Latin America. For example, from his studies of Brazil and Chile, completed in 1960, Willems concluded that "the major Pentecostal sects have a larger constituency than all the historical Protestant churches together."[6] Willems studied both the historical Protestant churches (focusing especially on Methodists, Presbyterians, and Baptists) and Pentecostals, offering systematic comparisons between the two types of churches on a range of issues. Lalive d'Epinay focused on the Pentecostal experience in Chile. The two writers agreed that Pentecostalism is a religion of the poor, that it offers both psychological security and the minimal material security necessary to cope with a hostile environment, that it affords emotional release more than it challenges the intellect, that it encourages ceaseless proselytizing on the part of its members, and that it rejects the temporal realm in favor of cultivating the spiritual life. But whereas Willems saw signs to suggest that Pentecostalism might help promote modernization and democratization, Lalive d'Epinay argued forcefully that the evidence pointed to the opposite conclusion.

Lalive d'Epinay stressed the degree to which pastors dominated Pentecostal churches, defining the terms of membership, the nature of worship, and the relation of the church to the larger society.[7] He argued that in this respect Pentecostal churches exhibited an episcopal model of church organization rather than a congregational model. In fact, he compared the Pentecostal mode of organization to the hacienda system, with its hierarchy, paternalism, and subordination. In this comparison he sought to capture what he saw as the deeply paradoxical nature of Pentecostalism. On one hand, Pentecostalism represented a radical break with the existing society, its values and class structure. On the other hand, it reproduced one of the most traditional and conservative features of the old social order by organizing its members in a "quasi-military hierarchy."[8] Under the sway of an authoritarian leadership, Pentecostal churches withdrew their members radically from society, thereby depriving them of any opportunity to influence or alter it, especially in political terms. Lalive d'Epinay himself put it this way: "While

Pentecostalism disalienates the individual to begin with, since it allows him to overcome his uprooting and isolation by offering him entry into an organized, protective group, it then in turn alienates itself and 're-alienates' its members, since it looks upon itself as alien to the 'world' and effectively makes its members strangers to society."[9] On the basis of this analysis, he argued that Pentecostalism would not be a positive force for change as Latin America pursued modernization. He concluded that it would be "a force for order rather than an element of progress, a defender of the status quo and not a promoter of change."[10]

Conceding that Pentecostalism was less congenial to political involvement than historical Protestantism, especially in the North American context, Willems nevertheless thought he detected ways in which Pentecostalism might be a positive factor for social and even political change. He did not necessarily expect that influence to be exercised through the direct integration of Pentecostals into the political arena. Rather, he envisioned an indirect influence through the shaping of the political culture of the region and the personal values of the people. Willems noted the fundamental egalitarianism inherent in Pentecostal theology. Every convert is understood to have received the Holy Spirit, thereby becoming a full and equal member of a spiritual community. Furthermore, each convert shares in the mandate to evangelize others not yet in the faith; he or she becomes a prophet. As Willems observed, "Vested in religious symbolism, it [prophetism] constitutes a mode of social control which may be exercised by any member of a congregation over anybody else, including the pastor. It minimizes the social distance between the common members and the pastor, between laity and clergy. It is an institutionalized way of keeping authority within the group in a state of continuous flux."[11] In short, Willems viewed the Pentecostal churches as having a congregational mode of organization that facilitated egalitarian relationships.

Pursuing this theme of egalitarianism, Willems argued that the poor in Chile and Brazil chose Pentecostalism as a "symbolic protest against the traditional social order."[12] Indeed, he went on to call Pentecostalism "a symbolic subversion of the traditional social order."[13] The poor, he argued, were choosing "an egalitarian denomination in which the individual, particularly the layman, is in full control of church affairs."[14] Active participation was expected and enthusiastically embraced despite the fact that it imposed demanding responsibilities on each member. Willems concluded that Pentecostalism, as a conscious rejection of the old hierarchical and authoritarian mode of organization in religion and an eager embrace of equality and participation, had the potential to instill a more democratic ethos into new generations of Latin Americans.

In the time since Willems and Lalive d'Epinay wrote, Pentecostalism has continued its aggressive growth throughout Latin America. It has begun to make inroads in countries such as Peru, where it had almost no presence when Willems was conducting his research. In countries such as Guatemala, its growth was explosive during the 1970s and 1980s, leading some writers to see it as a natural religious corollary to political authoritarianism and repression much as Lalive d'Epinay had suggested.[15] Less noted was the dramatic growth of Pentecostalism in Nicaragua during a period when the country was experiencing a popular left-wing revolution.[16] Though disparate in political direction, however, Guatemala and Nicaragua shared a widespread social dislocation caused by economic modernization and protracted, violent political conflict. Indeed, throughout Latin America this has been the context in which Pentecostalism has been studied over the past two decades.

Today, however, the context is changing. If present trends hold, in the years ahead Pentecostalism will function in a milieu that is considerably different from that of Willems and Lalive d'Epinay's time. Not only politics but society itself may be more democratic in Latin America's future. Moreover, Pentecostalism will have sunk even deeper roots into Latin American soil. Future studies are likely to show with ever greater clarity how much diversity actually exists among Pentecostal churches.

In anticipation of that future, this seems a good time to ask the old questions again in relation to the newly evolving societal context. As practiced in Latin America, is Pentecostalism uniformly apolitical? Does it encourage passivity, quiescence, or lack of interest in politics and government? Insofar as lack of interest in politics is evident in Pentecostal behavior, can this be explained by theology, or does it derive more from an ethic of social conduct that is imposed within congregations regardless of theological understandings? To the extent that Pentecostalism is in fact political, does it have anything to contribute to the building of a more democratic society or polity? Scholars have scarcely begun to explore empirically the ways in which Pentecostalism might contribute to the formation or strengthening of an active civil society. Could Pentecostalism serve to energize the poorest classes to take a more active role in civil society in those Latin American countries where a viable civil society already exists? Where a viable civil society has yet to be constructed, can Pentecostalism play a meaningful part in its formation? Questions such as these have a special urgency in a time of democratic transition. No definitive, empirically based answer can be given here, but some interesting possibilities can be explored.

Reframing the Question of Pentecostalism and Politics

The present trend toward democratization in Latin America has had an interesting effect on scholarship. Concern with revolution has waned as revolutionary movements and regimes have exhausted their energies and lost their attraction. Marxist analysis has declined in relevance correspondingly. Pronounced religious revivalism has turned some scholars back to Weber and other "nonmarxist" sociologists of religion. Meanwhile, political scientists have shown increasing interest in electoral behavior, political parties, and the ways in which forms of political organization (e.g., the type of electoral system, whether the system is parliamentary or presidential) affect the building and maintenance of democratic government.[17] In light of these shifts, a theorist who has been adduced infrequently with regard to Latin America, Alexis de Tocqueville, may be helpful in exploring the possible interrelation of Pentecostalism and politics in this time of transition.

When Tocqueville wrote about American democracy in the 1830s, he took some pains to highlight the importance of religion in the development of democracy. He traced American democracy to Puritan roots and, in effect, sharply contrasted religion's political role in North and in South America. Whereas Roman Catholicism had reinforced social inequality in Latin America, Puritanism had encouraged in North America a "social state" marked by equality of condition and social mobility. This latter social order was, in turn, highly conducive to democracy in government. Tocqueville ended a lengthy discussion of North American colonial history with these forceful words: "I have already said enough to put Anglo-American civilization in its true light. It is the product . . . of two perfectly distinct elements which elsewhere have often been at war with one another but which in America it was somehow possible to incorporate into each other, forming a marvelous combination. I mean the spirit of religion and the spirit of freedom."[18] In fact, Tocqueville was so impressed with Protestantism's positive role as to conclude that in America "freedom sees religion as the companion of its struggles and triumphs."[19]

Is there a prospect that in Latin America today freedom can see religion as the "companion of its struggles and triumphs"—that democracy can advance with religion's support? During the 1960s and 1970s those who participated in the Catholic church's *comunidades eclesiales de base* (Christian base communities—CEBs) certainly took this view, albeit in a politically more repressive context than the present.[20] The development of CEBs at the grass roots, together with the work of creating a theology of liberation, was aimed directly at fostering greater freedom, including political freedom, in Latin America.[21] However, as a resource in the struggle for political freedom the base-community experiment faltered, in no small measure because of the resistance of hierarchical authorities within the church. In recent years the CEB as a form of "new social movement" has been overtaken by events; the numbers of CEBs have dwindled, and they have adopted a less overtly political orientation. But what about the Pentecostal churches? Is there any point in asking whether they can be an ally to freedom? I will argue that there is, but first a bit more must be said about Tocqueville's analysis of the contributing factors in American democracy in order to see what relevance that analysis may have for Latin America.

Tocqueville insisted repeatedly that the distinguishing characteristic of American democracy (and therefore of the coming democratic age) was "equality of condition."[22] When he compared America with Europe, what stood out in Tocqueville's mind was the absence of any form of aristocracy in the former. He considered that the political forms adopted in America, including administrative decentralization, a free press, and a multiplicity of civil associations, reinforced the effects of equality of condition. Americans had developed a political culture of which the love of equality was the most pronounced feature. Potentially, Tocqueville thought, this love of equality could conflict with and undermine Americans' attachment to liberty. Should that occur, he argued, despotism might arise from democratic soil.

The culprit in this pessimistic scenario—the danger to be found in the love of equality—was something Tocqueville called "individualism." For Tocqueville, individualism was a sentiment, a "habit of the heart" that led men and women to withdraw from the society of their fellows, to consider that they owed nothing to others and were owed nothing by others. It threatened to create a kind of social anomie in which people existed in proximity to one another but without social bonds of any kind.[23] By discouraging cooperation and participation in common endeavors, individualism opened the way to one of two undesirable extremes— anarchy or despotism. In other words, apathy toward collective action was the greatest danger produced by equality of condition. What impressed Tocqueville about America and made the country a model to be emulated by others was the efficiency with which Americans had learned to avoid this danger.

Tocqueville went on to argue that "Americans have combated by free institutions the tendency of equality to keep men asunder, and they have subdued it."[24] He described the "immense assemblage of associations" that had been generated in America, demonstrating what he saw as the "necessary connection" between equality of condition and the "principle of association."[25] He also saw a healthy reciprocity between explicitly political associations and civil associations, each serving to reinforce and invigorate the other. In short, Tocqueville described an America in which a vigorous civil society combined with free political institutions to preserve equality of condition while avoiding the dangers of individualism.

Perhaps more than at any other time in the region's history, Tocqueville's analysis speaks directly to the conditions of Latin America today. Some countries are undergoing redemocratization after lengthy interludes of militarism; others are embracing democratic politics for the first time. In the former, for example, Chile and Argentina, civil society survived the ravages of military rule but in a somewhat truncated form and had to be "reconstructed."[26] In the latter, for example, El Salvador, Haiti, and Paraguay, to a large degree civil society has yet to be created. In each type of country the grip of aristocracy is weakening in both urban and rural society.

I do not say that inherited and customary inequality have disappeared, only that they are less and less binding. The certainties of the old system of social inequality (exhibited most tellingly in the patron-client networks that Latin Americanists have studied for years) are being replaced for more and more poor Latin Americans by the uncertainty of something similar to Tocqueville's "equality of condition." When Willems and Lalive d'Epinay wrote about Pentecostalism, Latin America's population was 40–50 percent rural. What Tocqueville called the "chain of aristocracy" still bound half the population in a prescribed order of inequality. Today the population is nearly 75 percent urban.[27] Formerly "rooted" men and women have been uprooted by the millions by political conflict, economic modernization, and the militant free-market policies of the present moment. Their situation cannot be compared directly with that of 1835 America, where persons had begun to "lose their class identity for each other." Nevertheless, in a crucial sense relentless urbanization, coupled with strict, market-oriented economic policies, has broken the chain of aristocracy and "sever[ed] every link of it."[28] In this new context, Pentecostalism may have the potential to generate a different kind of impact from the one commonly attributed to it.

Disputing the Pessimists

Optimism about Pentecostalism's potential for positive contributions to civil and political society in Latin America is relatively rare. For example, one seldom sees the enthusiasm for its democratic potential expressed by Amy Sherman, who has argued that Pentecostalism could pave the way for Latin American democracy by promoting the values of toleration and participation. In her view, Pentecostalism is inimical to "big government" and offers "biblical support for such free-market propositions as private property, economic initiative, and man's creative capacity."[29] Although one might quarrel with some or all of these assertions, the point is that Sherman's reading of Pentecostalism's democratic affinities is fairly unusual. Her analysis draws heavily on David Martin's argument that Pentecostalism may serve to undergird democracy even if it is not explicitly oriented to politics, but Martin's analysis is less overtly ideological and partisan. As did Willems, he stresses the participatory and egalitarian nature of Pentecostal congregations, which he considers "sociologically consonant with democratic polities and . . . part of the popular base on which such polities might rest" but not themselves basically political.[30]

In contrast to Martin's rather tepid optimism, there is a great deal of pessimism to be found on the part of other writers. Among the most vigorous arguments against the democratic potential of Pentecostalism are those of Jean-Pierre Bastian. Bastian contrasts historical Protestantism and Pentecostalism. The former articulated a form of "radical liberalism" that challenged the prevailing political culture of Latin America in the nineteenth and early twentieth centuries. The latter is "top-down and authoritarian" and represents "a relay point for the vertical social control of a society blocked in its evolution toward a liberal and democratic modernity."[31] In Bastian's view, much of the success of Pentecostalism can be attributed to state patronage, and the religious movement itself has adopted the corporatist strategies and organizational forms characteristic of the traditional Catholic culture of Latin America.[32]

Judging from the uncompromising nature of his conclusions, one might guess that Bastian would find little utility in the application of a Tocquevillean analysis to the study of religion and politics in Latin America today. Yet he himself offers some data that might support just such an analysis. For example, he cites studies

of Mexico, Brazil, and Ecuador that show rural people using Pentecostal movements to challenge power structures that dominate and exploit them.[33] Bastian
counters the thrust of these studies by emphasizing what he sees as the extreme
paternalism, even authoritarianism, of intrachurch governance and leadership
among Pentecostal churches. He describes the Pentecostal pastor as a "cacique," a
"caudillo" who is "the absolute master" of the religious enterprise.[34] In making
this case, of course, Bastian is reprising the argument of Lalive d'Epinay. However,
he extrapolates from the experience of a number of very large Pentecostal denominations that may not be at all typical of the vast majority of Pentecostal
churches throughout Latin America. One could argue that the majority of
Pentecostal churches in Latin America are relatively small and much less centralized and authoritarian than Bastian contends. At the very least, this is an issue that
calls for further research.[35]

In the meantime, let us consider the evidence that can be gleaned from the
more typical Pentecostal church. By its very nature Pentecostalism is an extremely
fragmented religious movement. Charisma and the free interpretation of signs
and wonders are centrifugal forces that pull constantly against efforts to impose
doctrinal orthodoxy or monolithic pastoral authority. Most Pentecostal churches
are "small groups with a high degree of interpersonal relations that are local in
orientation and dedicated to the 'work of the lord' in their immediate neighborhoods and adjacent areas."[36] Pastor and congregation alike will be from the neighborhood where the church is located, the church will have little institutional
structure, and it will have a surprisingly democratic mode of organization.
Within the church, relationships are more horizontal than vertical, and women
play a prominent role in all aspects of church life except the pastorate itself. The
lives of all members of the church are centered on the religious community,
which places strong demands on their time, energy, and resources.[37] Such intense
involvement certainly could deflect Pentecostals' attention from the daily concerns and routines of politics, but it could also teach them a lesson that
Tocqueville thought crucial in a democratic age: that they "become powerless if
they do not learn to help one another."[38] Where better to learn such a lesson than
in the "moral association" known as the Pentecostal church?

Pentecostals are "born-again" Christians, and the significance of being born
again bears emphasizing. It means, in effect, taking on a new identity, becoming
a new person who lives in a new way. The underlying theology that guides this
new life can be sharply dualistic, dividing life's experiences into good and evil,
holy and diabolical. When faith is understood in this way, daily life is experienced
as a constant struggle to resist the temptations of the old life. To be effective in
this struggle believers adopt strict standards of personal behavior, and this has
important individual and social repercussions. Among other things, it can lead to
sobriety, faithfulness in marriage, the assumption of greater responsibility within
the family, and increased reliability in the workplace. This dualistic theology is a

far cry from the "social gospel" of liberal Protestantism, but it clearly has association-building qualities if it can strengthen families, purify neighborhoods, and sustain religious communities.

Pentecostal theology is usually premillennial and apocalyptic. Converts firmly believe in Christ's return "accompanied by the rapture of the saints."[39] Until then their lives unfold in the midst of a struggle between two cosmic forces, God and the devil. God's struggle with the devil for control of human lives is manifested in signs and wonders, which can range from transcendent, all-encompassing events such as war, waves of political repression, or earthquakes to the much more particular level of one individual's hunger, illness, or personal tragedy. The gifts of the Spirit are used to cope with such calamities. In Pentecostal worship these gifts are demonstrated in the power to lay on hands and encourage healing or to speak in tongues. As we have seen, these powers are not monopolized by the pastor, although he must certainly possess them. The power to lay on hands and speak in tongues lies at the core of Pentecostalism, and one is struck by how egalitarian, participatory, and indeed communal this power is. Participation is essential because personal experience is more central to worship than knowledge or training. Members are qualified to participate on the basis of their own suffering and openness to God's healing grace. Symbolically, by laying on hands and speaking in tongues they mediate grace to one another. This produces what one writer calls the "permanent spontaneity" of Pentecostal worship, a facet that would seem to militate against excesses of authoritarianism on the part of the pastor.[40] As Juan Sepúlveda observes, in Pentecostalism "the traditional division between the 'qualified agents' who convey a legitimate religious speech, and the ones who only participate as consumers of such speech, disappears."[41]

To summarize, although Pentecostal theology may have the immediate effect of drawing a convert's attention away from political affairs and social involvements, it is not inherently hostile to the concerns and values of civil society or of politics. Access to the gifts of the Holy Spirit is empowering, and it is actively shared. Laying on of hands and the search for healing are communal or, in Tocqueville's terms, associational activities. As they are practiced over time, there is no reason to think they would not be extended to concerns of the body as well as the soul. They could easily grow into a concern for education, health care, insuring against future calamity, and other similar social concerns.

Pentecostals in Civil and Political Society

The fact is that Pentecostals are already active in civil society in Latin America. Everett Wilson's study of the Liceo Cristiano, an extensive system of private schools established in El Salvador by the Centro Evangelístico, a Pentecostal congregation, demonstrates vividly the extent to which Pentecostals have begun to fill the public space with social works, even in countries with a weakly developed civil society.[42] The scope of the Liceo is impressive; it enrolls 24,000 students on thirty-four campuses nationwide. What began as a strictly educational enterprise gradually expanded to include the provision of "rudimentary medical and dental services and supplementary nutritional and welfare services for the students and their families."[43] Wilson's study makes two further points related to the present argument. First, the Liceo experience is being duplicated in many other Latin American countries, where Pentecostals are busy creating the social infrastructures that are needed to sustain community building among the poor. Second, although international church bodies play an important role in this endeavor, the driving influence and control are usually local. The entire experience can teach Pentecostals about "the close tie that unites private to general interest." In this way, "local freedom . . . leads a great number of citizens to value the affection of their neighbors and of their kindred, [and it] brings men together and forces them to help one another in spite of the propensities that sever them."[44]

Let us recall that Tocqueville's concern about democratic societies was that individualism would encourage apathy. However, the apparent indifference of Pentecostals to public affairs may not be the apathy that so alarmed Tocqueville, at least not in the long run. Those who join Pentecostal churches have had negligible influence in the political arena to begin with. If democratization continues, they may have greater influence in the future, and experience can teach them the limits and potential of that influence. Clearly, those who can generate viable systems of education working from the grass roots are capable of exerting a broader influence in society.

In the meantime, there is a role to play in strengthening civil society. For most poor Latin Americans, membership in a Pentecostal church is likely to be their first experience of actual social equality. Active participation in the church is also apt to be a new experience and their first exposure to associational life. Finally, the new powers acquired through conversion and participation are exercised in an association that is "civic" in Tocqueville's sense of the word; members associate and cooperate to meet common needs. Poor people in Latin America may be far more likely to learn the "principle of association" this way than through participating in elections, joining political parties, bringing suits in the courts, or engaging in the activities of conventional, secular interest groups. Moreover, learning the principle of association in this way encourages what Tocqueville called "administrative decentralization," which fosters civic-spiritedness at the local level because so many practical, immediate issues are decided there.[45]

Having emphasized Pentecostalism's potential relevance to civil society, we should not ignore the fact that Pentecostals have not turned their backs on politics itself everywhere and at all times in Latin America. Guatemala's experience is already well known. Two evangelicals (both of them men with a strong Pentecostal orientation) have served as president of the country, one of them having been popularly elected. The former military leader and born-again Christian

José Efraín Ríos Montt is currently head of the Guatemalan congress. Guatemala has generally been considered an exception in Latin America, but it is not really such an aberration. As Pentecostal churches become more rooted and secure, one factor motivating them toward a greater interest in politics may be a desire to rectify generations of discriminatory treatment by the state in favor of Roman Catholicism. In the name of fair play and for the sake of protecting evangelical interests, they may assume a more active role in the political arena. Alberto Fujumori's aggressive courting of the evangelical vote in Peru during the 1990 presidential campaign and his strong support from that sector in the balloting illustrate the potential receptivity of Pentecostals and other evangelical Protestants on this issue.[46]

Speaking more generally, it is clear that Pentecostals are now taking more interest in elections in various Latin American countries. They have even run for office, with some success, in Brazil, El Salvador, Guatemala, and Peru, among other countries.[47] New evangelical parties have been created recently in El Salvador and Nicaragua, and this too is a trend that may well spread.[48] Moreover, Pentecostals clearly have opinions on political issues and are willing to express them. One interesting result of polling is that their attitudes are not uniformly conservative or reactionary. Roberto Zub's discussion of the 1990 elections in Nicaragua is instructive. Whereas some leftist observers had speculated that 90–95 percent of Protestants voted for candidates of the conservative United Nicaraguan Opposition (UNO) coalition, analysis of the data suggested otherwise. Sixty-eight percent of the members of the Foursquare Gospel Church voted for UNO, but it should be noted that this church's membership is more middle-class and business-oriented than that of other Pentecostal churches and UNO was explicitly a probusiness party. Sixty percent of Assemblies of God members voted for UNO, but almost 20 percent voted for the revolutionary party, the Fronte Sandinista de Liberación Nacional (Sandinista National Liberation Front—FSLN). Only 38.5 percent of the members of the Church of God voted UNO, and nearly a quarter voted Sandinista.[49] These data hardly fit the stereotype of a uniformly reactionary religion.

Although data from Nicaragua may not be generalizable to the rest of Latin America, Zub's results certainly suggest the need for further investigation of the degree to which and the circumstances under which Pentecostals and other evangelicals may embrace politics. Compared with other groups in civil society, Pentecostals in Nicaragua were more interested in entering the political arena. When asked if an evangelical party could be organized in Nicaragua, two-thirds of Church of God members and more than 85 percent of Assemblies of God members said yes. Asked who among a range of existing or potential political actors could most effectively solve the country's economic problems, the single most common answer given by Pentecostals was "an evangelical government."[50] Very few Pentecostals pointed to existing political parties as competent to deal with the nation's economic difficulties, thereby confirming the expected skepticism regarding traditional political parties. But neither did they point to "private enterprise" as the answer. Some answered "God" but in percentages well below their appeal to an evangelical government. Such findings certainly challenge the stereotype of Pentecostals as passive, indifferent, or even hostile toward politics.

When Zub's findings are juxtaposed with those of Kenneth Coleman and his colleagues at the University of North Carolina, who examined extensive survey data gathered in El Salvador in 1989 by the late Martin Baró, S. J., what emerges is the profile of a more aware and discriminating Pentecostal citizen than has been supposed. Father Baro's surveys were conducted in the late stages of a protracted internal war. The results indicate that Protestants were almost as sensitive to the existence of social injustice in Salvadoran society as Catholic or religiously unaffiliated respondents.[51] As Coleman suggests, a perception of injustice is the necessary first step toward demanding government action.[52] Salvadoran Protestants of all types strongly supported a political solution to the war—negotiations with the rebel forces of the Frente Farabundo Martí de Liberación Nacional (Farabundo Martí National Liberation Front—FMLN). In large numbers (nearly 70 percent) they favored making political concessions to the guerrillas such as the purification of the armed forces in order to root out violators of human rights.

Finally, Baro's data strongly challenge the common assumption that Pentecostals uncritically accept the legitimacy or efficacy of the powers that be or show a marked preference for the most conservative political parties and movements. For example, the 1989 elections in El Salvador were won decisively by the Alianza Republicana Nacional (National Republican Alliance—ARENA) party, the most conservative party in the race. However, evangelicals voted for ARENA at a significantly lower rate than Roman Catholics and expressed much more skepticism as to the likelihood that ARENA would reduce human rights violations in the country. As Coleman put it:

> This finding suggests the opposite of the "common knowledge" about religio-political alliances in Central America. . . . [In El Salvador] poor Protestants doubted the integrity of electoral processes and the possibility of reform, while more affluent Catholics were generally willing to take a chance on the possibility that U.S. pressure for electoral reform might produce meaningful outcomes. Whatever the political implications of Protestantism in El Salvador, they do not entail a close association with the governing rightist party or with the electoral processes that brought ARENA to power.[53]

With Pentecostals supporting and even participating in the Workers' party in Brazil, on the one hand, and showing a strongly critical attitude toward conservative parties or governments in Nicaragua and El Salvador, on the other, one is driven to conclude that Latin American Pentecostalism may be much more complex and open to politics than we once thought.

Conclusion

The age-old problem in Latin America, as Tina Rosenberg points out, is that so many of its people have been "inhabitants" rather than "citizens."[54] Far from exercising any of the power of the state or any influence in the society, they have merely been subject to the exercise of power and influence of others and have never thought of the state as in any way belonging to them. When persons such as these join Pentecostal churches, it is hardly surprising that they display indifference toward government and politics; they were already alienated from them. Lalive d'Epinay set the tone for one scholarly view of these converts by describing them as "re-alienated." Numerous writers from Lalive d'Epinay to Bastian have therefore seen Pentecostalism as simply confirming poor Latin Americans in their status as inhabitants rather than citizens.

Writers from Willems to Martin have, however, offered a more optimistic assessment. In highlighting the "congregational" aspect of Pentecostal experience, they point to ways in which Pentecostalism might favor the development of a citizenry among the poor in Latin America. For the sake of democracy, one can hope that their optimism is justified. After all, Pentecostalism is filling up a great deal of the social space in Latin America today, especially within the ranks of the poor. Therefore, its capacity to foster or mediate civic behavior or lack thereof will be important for both civil and political society. Among the tens of millions of Latin Americans who are merely inhabitants of their countries today, many are or will become Pentecostals. As their countries proceed with the transition to formal political democracy, how many of these millions of Pentecostals will also find that church membership facilitates their personal transition from inhabitant to citizen? What I have argued in this essay, more in the spirit of Willems than in that of Lalive d'Epinay, is that the high degree of participation Pentecostal membership encourages is a necessary attribute of civil society. The increased sense of personal efficacy that conversion and membership bring can help to overcome the alienation that is so threatening in a state of increasing equality of condition. The finding of one's voice in the context of an association has the potential to take members of Pentecostal churches beyond the cultivation of the spiritual life alone. It can, although there is no guarantee that it will, lead to participation in the wider activities of civil society—fostering education, creating structures to find or deliver health care, seeking legal protection for their churches and religious activities, and so on. To the extent that this happens, Pentecostalism will become a companion to freedom in a democratizing Latin America.

NOTES

1. Among the many useful articles to appear on this topic in recent years, the following bear mentioning in connection with the present discussion: Jan Knippers Black, "Elections and Other Trivial Pursuits: Latin America and the New World Order," *Third World*

Quarterly 14, 3 (1993), pp. 545–554, on the distance that can exist between the holding of elections and the establishment of democratic institutions; Tina Rosenberg, "Beyond Elections," *Foreign Policy* 84 (Fall 1991), pp. 72–91, on the essential distinction between "inhabitants" and "citizens"; and Philippe C. Schmitter, "Dangers and Dilemmas of Democracy," *Journal of Democracy* 5, 2 (April 1994), pp. 57–74, on the many dilemmas that confront those who would construct democratic polities.

2. Numerous scholars have described Pentecostal growth in Latin America. Two who can be cited here because their work will be discussed further in this chapter are David Martin, *Tongues of Fire: The Explosion of Protestantism in Latin America* (Oxford and Cambridge, Mass.: Basil Blackwell, 1990), and David Stoll, *Is Latin America Turning Protestant? The Politics of Evangelical Growth* (Berkeley: University of California Press, 1990).

3. The emerging literature examines evangelical Protestantism in its many variations, but interest focuses increasingly on Pentecostalism. Particularly when one is discussing evangelicalism at the popular level, Pentecostalism is typically what is involved.

4. On the first point, the best-known recent work is Martin, *Tongues of Fire*. See also Carmelo Alvarez, ed., *Pentecostalismo y liberación: Una experiencia latinoamericana* (San José, Costa Rica: Editorial Departmento Ecuménico de Investigaciones, 1992), esp. pp. 89–100. On the second issue, in addition to Martin, see Amy L. Sherman, "The Public Role of Evangelicals in Latin America: Implications for the Consolidation of Democracy," paper presented at the International Studies Association convention, Atlanta, Ga., March 31, 1992.

5. For particularly vigorous arguments in this vein see Sara Diamond, *Spiritual Warfare: The Politics of the Christian Right* (Boston: South End Press, 1989); Enrique Domínguez and Deborah Huntington, "The Salvation Brokers: Conservative Evangelicals in Central America," *NACLA Report on the Americas* 18, 1 (January/February 1984), pp. 2–36; Jaime Valverde, *Las sectas en Costa Rica: Pentecostalismo y conflicto social* (San José, Costa Rica: Editorial Departmento Ecuménico de Investigaciones, 1990); and Heinrich Schafer, *Protestantismo y crisis social en América Central* (San José, Costa Rica: Editorial Departmento Ecuménico de Investigaciones, 1992), esp. pp. 215–233.

6. Emilio Willems, *Followers of the New Faith: Culture Change and the Rise of Protestantism in Brazil and Chile* (Nashville, Tenn.: Vanderbilt University Press, 1967), p. 134.

7. Christian Lalive d'Epinay, *Haven of the Masses: A Study of the Pentecostal Movement in Chile* (New York: Friendship Press, 1969), p. 122.

8. Ibid., p. 131.

9. Ibid., p. 130.

10. Ibid., p. 145.

11. Willems, *Followers of the New Faith*, p. 139.

12. Ibid., p. 156.

13. Ibid., p. 249.

14. Ibid., p. 156.

15. In addition to Stoll, *Is Latin America Turning Protestant?* and Domínguez and Huntington, "The Salvation Brokers," see also Linda Green, "Shifting Affiliations: Mayan Widows and *Evangélicos* in Guatemala," in Virginia Garrard-Burnett and David Stoll, eds., *Rethinking Protestantism in Latin America* (Philadelphia: Temple University Press, 1993),

pp. 159–179, and David Stoll, *Between Two Armies in the Ixil Towns of Guatemala* (New York: Columbia University Press, 1993), esp. pp. 167–195.

16. Abelino Martínez, *Las sectas en Nicaragua: Oferta y demanda de salvación* (San José, Costa Rica: Editorial Departmento Ecuménico de Investigaciones, 1989).

17. A stimulating example of the sort of article that has appeared recently is Juan Linz, Arturo Valenzuela, and Pilar Domingo, "The Failure of Presidential Democracy," *Journal of Latin American Studies* 27, 3 (1995), pp. 740–763.

18. Alexis de Tocqueville, *Democracy in America,* vol. 1, trans. George Lawrence, ed. J. P. Mayer (New York: Harper and Row, 1969), pp. 46–47.

19. Ibid.

20. Superb accounts of the CEBs can be found in Phillip Berryman, *The Religious Roots of Rebellion: Christians in Central American Revolutions* (Maryknoll, N.Y.: Orbis Books, 1984), and Scott Mainwaring and Alexander Wilde, eds., *The Progressive Church in Latin America* (Notre Dame, Ind.: University of Notre Dame Press, 1989).

21. Nicaragua is a particularly vivid case in point. See John M. Kirk, *Politics and the Catholic Church in Nicaragua* (Gainesville: University of Florida Press, 1992), and Michael Dodson and Laura Nuzzi O'Shaughnessy, *Nicaragua's Other Revolution* (Chapel Hill: University of North Carolina Press, 1990).

22. In addition to vol. 1, pp. 50–57, see also *Democracy in America,* vol. 2, ed. Phillips Bradley (New York: Vintage Books, 1990), pp. 94–97.

23. Tocqueville, *Democracy in America,* vol. 2, pp. 98–99.

24. Ibid., p. 103.

25. Ibid., p. 107.

26. Manuel Antonio Garreton, "Popular Mobilization and the Military Regime in Chile: The Complexities of the Invisible Transition," in Susan Eckstein, ed., *Power and Popular Protest: Latin American Social Movements* (Berkeley: University of California Press, 1989), pp. 259–277.

27. Michael J. Kryzanek, *Latin America: Change and Challenge* (New York: Harper-Collins, 1995), p. 27.

28. Tocqueville, *Democracy in America,* vol. 2, p. 99.

29. Sherman, "The Public Role of Evangelicals," p. 18.

30. Martin, *Tongues of Fire,* p. 22.

31. Jean-Pierre Bastian, "The Metamorphosis of Latin American Protestant Groups: A Sociohistorical Perspective," *Latin American Research Review* 28, 2 (1993), p. 56.

32. Jean-Pierre Bastian, "Religión popular protestante y comportamiento político en América Central: Clientela religiosa e estado patrón, Guatemala y Nicaragua," *Cristianismo y Sociedad* 24, 88 (1986), p. 42.

33. Bastian, "The Metamorphosis," pp. 46–47.

34. Ibid., p. 48.

35. In his *Las sectas en Nicaragua,* cited above, Abelino Martínez makes clear that the great majority of Pentecostal churches in Nicaragua are small congregations with a low level of "institutionalization." Just how typical is this type of Pentecostal church across the breadth of Latin America?

36. Luis Samandú, "El Pentecostalismo en Nicaragua y sus raíces religiosas populares," *Pasos* 17 (May/June 1988), p. 2.

37. Luis Samandú, ed., *Protestantismos y procesos sociales en Centroamérica* (San José, Costa Rica: Editorial Universitaria Centroamericana, 1990), p. 245.

38. Tocqueville, *Democracy in America,* vol. 2, p. 109.

39. Martínez, *Las sectas en Nicaragua,* p. 29.

40. Adonis Nino Chavarría, "Breve historia del movimiento pentecostal en Nicaragua," in Alvarez, *Pentecostalismo y liberación,* p. 55.

41. Juan Sepúlveda, "Pentecostalism as Popular Religiosity," *International Review of Missions* 78, 309 (January 1989), p. 87.

42. Everett A. Wilson, "Latin American Pentecostalism: Challenging the Stereotypes of Pentecostal Passivity," *Transformation* 11, 1 (January–March 1994), p. 19.

43. Ibid. Wilson goes on to show how these rudimentary services evolved into formation of the Clínica Médica Cristiana and a sophisticated school lunch program.

44. Tocqueville, *Democracy in America,* vol. 2, p. 104.

45. Matthew Mancini, *Alexis de Tocqueville* (New York: Twayne, 1994), p. 40.

46. Phillip Berryman, "The Coming of Age of Evangelical Protestantism," *NACLA Report on the Americas* 27, 6 (May/June 1994), p. 10.

47. Ibid.

48. Roberto Zub, "The Growth of Protestantism: From Religion to Politics," *Envío* (December 1992), pp. 19–30. The initial efforts of evangelical parties in El Salvador and Nicaragua, in contrast to those in Guatemala, have not been very successful. But one of the parties in El Salvador, the Movimiento de Unidad, ran a Pentecostal candidate for president of the country in the 1994 elections. It is surely too soon to tell whether these parties will be able to build effective electoral bases.

49. Ibid., p. 24.

50. Ibid., p. 27.

51. Coleman indicates that, although Baro did not attempt to differentiate Pentecostal respondents from other Protestants, it can be assumed that the vast majority of non-Catholic unaffiliated respondents in the survey were Pentecostals.

52. Edwin Eloy Aguilar, José Miguel Sandoval, Timothy J. Steigenga, and Kenneth M. Coleman, "Protestantism in El Salvador: Conventional Wisdom Versus Survey Evidence," *Latin American Research Review* 28, 2 (1993), p. 130.

53. Ibid., pp. 134–135.

54. Rosenberg, "Beyond Elections," pp. 29–30.

3

Pentecostalism and Women in Brazil

CECÍLIA LORETO MARIZ AND
MARÍA DAS DORES CAMPOS MACHADO

$\mathcal{M}$ax Weber observes that "the religion of the underprivileged classes is characterized by a tendency to allot equality to women," pointing out that salvation religion appeals to those classes and to women because it glorifies virtues close to their interests.[1] Yet, women seem to constitute the majority in all Christian churches, not just in most religions of the poor.[2] The greater proportion of women in Latin American Pentecostal churches does not, therefore, come as a surprise.

Pentecostalism does have a special appeal for the underprivileged. Writing of Brazil, Peter Fry and Gary Howe consider it a "cult of affliction" because it attracts mostly the poor, the sick, the unemployed, alcoholics, blacks, and women, who, in general, tend to face more material and emotional hardships.[3] Pentecostalism's promise of solutions for everyday problems may be another strong appeal to the lower classes and to women.[4] But, since the female churchgoing majority is not an exclusively Pentecostal phenomenon, our question is not why there are more women than men in Pentecostal churches but what Pentecostalism offers these women.

We begin by briefly reviewing the broad assertions in the literature concerning the benefits that women receive from Pentecostal conversion. These assertions tend to focus on new roles for both women and men and the ways in which these changes benefit women. Then, drawing on our field research in Brazil, we describe the changes experienced by female Pentecostals in their basic conceptions of themselves as individuals and as believers. We argue that although female Pentecostal believers cannot be considered "feminists"—especially in the sense of mainstream North American feminism—the conversion experience does lead to

41

a revaluing of the self in relation to God and others that increases women's autonomy and undermines traditional machismo.

"Domesticated" Men, Public Women, and Family Values

There are basically two interpretations of the role of Pentecostalism in the life of the oppressed. The first is that these churches offer marginalized people symbolic power that compensates for their lack of material power.[5] According to this view, religion, like magic, in fact reinforces the inferior social position of those groups. Pentecostalism thus constitutes an alienation. Another interpretation is that, although not always capable of modifying the social position of these groups, Pentecostal religion is of some benefit to them, constituting a short-range defense mechanism for the oppressed. This view points out the benefits that women and the poor receive and emphasizes Pentecostalism's ability to reduce oppression.

This second interpretation has been the dominant one in the most recent studies of Pentecostal women in Latin American societies, such as those of Elizabeth Brusco, Cornelia Flora, María das Dores Machado, Hanneke Slootweg, David Smilde and Monica Tarducci.[6] In general, these studies claim that the values of Pentecostalism supersede the machismo prevalent in those societies. Furthermore, they call attention to the fact that, although Pentecostalism reinforces many patriarchal values, it helps women defend their interests.[7] Specifically, these researchers examine the different ways in which Pentecostalism can help female believers in their everyday lives. Most of them agree that Pentecostal churches, in addition to offering a support network for women, help increase women's self-confidence and bring their men back to home life.

Moreover, Pentecostalism appears to redefine the relationship between gender and public versus private spaces. All the studies are unanimous in identifying new values for men's behavior and considering the "domestication" of men to be the most important gain for Pentecostal women in Latin American societies. According to this line of interpretation, Pentecostalism helps women by creating a new model for men to follow. The renewing qualities of this Pentecostal model for men are greater and more perceptible in Latin societies where machismo is stronger.

Salvatore Cucchiari underlines the differences between the notion of Latin masculinity and the image of God in Pentecostalism. For him Pentecostalism portrays God as having qualities that, according to a *machista* view of the world, would be considered feminine. He suggests that the new conception of God may affect the traditional relationship between the genders.[8] The domestication of men occurs through the restriction of "male behavior detrimental to women, such as alcoholism or the irresponsible fathering of children," and through Pentecostal emphasis on family life and the household.[9] Thus, Pentecostal preoccupation with the family seems advantageous for women.[10]

This domestication of men occurs concomitantly with women's increased participation in the public sphere. In Brazil we observed that the consequences of the transformation vary with social class. Machado suggests that the transformation will be greater for lower-class women.[11] These women may become deeply involved in evangelizing, preaching in the streets, in prisons, and in other public places. One of our interviewees, a member of the Pentecostal Igreja Universal do Reino de Deus (Universal Church of the Kingdom of God), L. R., thirty-five, married, and mother of a nine-year-old daughter, says that on weekends when her husband works she travels to cities near Rio de Janeiro to bring them "the word of God." Moreover, for lower-class women facing financial difficulties, Pentecostalism not only reinforces the family structure by encouraging men to spend less on drinking but also serves a strategic function in the struggle for survival of these poor women and their families.[12]

In addition to changes in men's and women's roles, Pentecostalism offers women comfort for their general family concerns. The literature shows that relationship problems play an important part in accounts of conversions. In fact, women seem to reinterpret and redefine any difficulties they face as family problems.[13] In our interviews with Brazilian Pentecostal women,[14] the main subjects mentioned by respondents were their families, particularly husbands who were unfaithful and/or alcohol abusers. One of our interviewees, now a member of the Igreja Universal do Reino de Deus, reports that before her conversion she had put a macumba (Brazilian black magic) spell on her husband to force him to leave. She explains: "I put a seven-month spell on my husband that I had to renew within seven months. . . . This cost me a lot of money. . . . That's where my whole salary went." In addressing the family Pentecostalism is, in fact, closely concerned with the major everyday problems (usually related to the family) of women.

Although this emphasis on the family is a common characteristic of all religions, some writers consider the almost exclusive Pentecostal preoccupation with family and private life a symptom of political alienation and a hindrance to social transformation.[15] In contrast, David Martin views this stronger emphasis on domestic life as a cultural innovation that fosters social change because it breaks with Hispanic (or Luso-Hispanic) militarism and machismo. Martin asserts that the notions that changes in people's private lives cannot affect social structure and that culture is primarily dependent on social structure are themselves reflections of machismo.[16]

Pentecostalism's "New Woman" and "New Man"

Rather than focus on the advantages of Pentecostalism for women, we will examine the way in which women redefine their gender roles on the basis of a concept of the individual that gives rise to the idea of a "new woman" or a "new man." The break with older concepts of the individual and individual liberty does not necessarily mean a transformation of the explicit values regarding the family, sexual codes, or the social functions of men and women. Although Pentecostal discourse does not question so-called patriarchal values, it does involve innovations in family relationships that threaten the machismo of Latin societies.

Pentecostalism is a process of individualization for both men and women. Believers see themselves as individuals free from the oppression of evil and consequently responsible for their own welfare as well as that of loved ones. In attributing greater autonomy and responsibility to the individual, Pentecostalism reaffirms the concept of the modern individual who creates his or her own destiny through choices and reflection. Despite being miraculous, Pentecostal deliverance from evil helps to create a rational individual.[17] Thus, in its emphasis on individual choice for freedom, Pentecostalism to a certain degree implies a rationalization of the conscience.[18]

Pentecostal individualism stresses individual freedom in relation to natural passions and instincts but not to social or moral codes. Because it considers strict obedience to moral codes not as a source of oppression but rather as proof of the liberation of the individual, Pentecostalism limits individualism by articulating it with holistic principles. The redeemed believer's interests must coincide with the plan of God, and therefore the idea of opposing feminine and masculine interests (typical of much of mainstream North American feminism) makes no sense in Pentecostal terms. Our aim in this chapter is therefore not to try to determine whether Pentecostalism caters to or satisfies particular male or female interests. Rather, we examine the discourse of Brazilian Pentecostal women to identify their conceptions of the individual and of freedom and attempt to understand the appeal of this discourse to women.

God Is More Important Than the Family

A predominant value held by the women we interviewed was their sense of duty regarding the care of family members, especially their husbands, children, and grandchildren. Although their joining the church did not challenge or change their traditional role, most of these women claimed that God was the most important issue in their lives; the family took second place. An example of this type of discourse can be found in our interview with M. J., fifty-four, a government worker who lives in a favela (shantytown) in Niteroi, a medium-sized city near Rio de Janeiro. M. J. suffered considerably when, as often happens to middle-aged women, her husband left her for another woman:

> I struggled to keep the family together; I didn't want the separation. Even today I love him, except that now God is number one. He [the husband] is just another person. . . . I thank my God with all my heart because through this event, I recovered the heart I'd given my husband. Today I've changed in relation to him. It's not that I

don't love him but that I love him the way I should have thirty years ago. . . . I see him as just another person.

Despite its emphasis on the family, the church helped M. J. to view herself as an autonomous individual. After she joined the Pentecostal church, she came to accept the idea of divorce. "I didn't agree with the separation, but today I agree because of the fact that I began to read the Holy Bible, and there I saw a passage that says that if a woman doesn't love a man she can surely separate. . . . Nobody belongs to anyone, it's written in the Bible."

Through church some women redefine their duties in relation to their children. D. S., sixty-three, a maid who lives with her adult children and grandchildren, said that one of her daughters had criticized her for joining the church. "My daughter thought that after I joined the church I'd changed and that I didn't like anyone anymore. She even said: 'What kind of a church lets a mother not care about her daughter or about anything anymore?'" D. S. explained that her behavior at home and attitude in relation to her daughters had in fact changed. Although she was still concerned about them and the grandchildren, praying for them all the time, she did not do all her housework as she had before because she did not have the same amount of time. Besides working, she attended church every day. "Before I used to do [the housework]. I would cook, I'd clean up the house, but then I tried to get away from all that. I also hold a job, and I don't have time." The church helped this woman to free herself from the obligation of taking care of her adult children. Because they put into their families all the meaning for their own lives, many women continue to have little time or money for themselves. D. S.'s autonomy with regard to her children indicates that she had acquired a new conception of the individual. "We all have problems with our children, because a pastor's son isn't necessarily born a pastor too, and a believer's son isn't born a believer." Individuals do not inherit religion; they choose it.

By placing a duty on women that goes beyond their families and households, the church gives them goals outside the home. Their main duty is now the work of God, and this may account for the generally negative initial reaction of husbands and children. There are many reports of husbands' hostile reactions to their wives' conversion. For example, N. P., a black maid from a favela in Rio de Janeiro, reported that her husband performed macumba rituals to keep her from attending church. Like many others interviewed, she was proud of having confronted her spouse's resistance to her religious choice and even having eventually converted him. Conversion undoubtedly gives women a certain emotional independence from their families. We thus witnessed what others call an "institutional contradiction" between the religious community and the family—namely, the church contesting the dominant family model.[19]

Pentecostal pastors try to discourage women from carrying their independence too far with regard to their spouses and homes. One respondent told us that she became so involved in missionary work that she took her youngest children and moved close to the area of the mission, leaving her house and older children behind. When her pastor found out, he ordered her to return home, saying, "In order for the woman to do the work of the Lord, she must be united with her family." Many women mentioned that their pastors reminded them not to forget their duties as wives and mothers. M. S., a thirty-six-year-old seamstress, commented on her pastor's concern with "women who, because they became believers, don't want their husbands anymore." According to M. S., her pastor said, "You are wives, and you must fulfill your duties as wives." Another interviewee commented that "in the family cult (*corrente da familia*) we hear that the women should treat their husbands with tenderness and faith . . . and must be able to forgive and have patience; forgiveness is fundamental." Female believers cannot forget to respect and care for their husbands and children. L. R. also stressed that women must believe in their husbands: "After Jesus came into my heart, I became more responsible and came to love my husband more. I take care of him with more affection and love. I think I learned to become a good housewife, you know? I started listening to him more. When he asks me to do something, I do it."

In order to avoid more tension in the family, Pentecostal women learn that it is their duty to follow their husbands even if they are not a believer. M. J., the poor Pentecostal quoted earlier, said, "I don't drink, but if my husband asks me to accompany him to a bar, I go because he likes his beer. . . . I drink my fruit juice." Likewise, M. N., from the middle class, explained "You have to have a balance. For example, if your husband goes to a dinner at work, as a Christian woman you also go to the dinner. . . . You don't have to drink or dance, but you go to honor your husband." G. A., a middle-class woman from the Igreja Nova Vida (New Life church), adopted a similar attitude in attending Catholic mass with her husband; she believed that she should go with him even though she did not share his religious beliefs. Going along with the husband was often a matter of tolerance rather than submission. Sometimes women saw it as a strategy aimed at bringing their spouses to visit their own churches, where perhaps their hearts would be touched. The dearest hope of a Pentecostal woman is to convert her husband and her entire family.

Men as Victims Rather Than Oppressors

Slootweg believes that if the husband does not convert, marital conflict intensifies,[20] but most women we interviewed said that their husbands' opposition decreased over time even when they did not convert. Although this type of assertion may be interpreted as part of a concocted discourse whose aim is ultimately to justify conversion, it is possible to suppose that there is, in fact, a decline in family conflict at some point after the woman's conversion to Pentecostalism. Machado suggests that most husbands cease to oppose their wives' religiosity when they discover that, most of the time, they appear more obedient.[21] As

Pentecostal women learn to ease the tension of marital arguments, conflict may, in fact, decrease.[22] For example, the conversion of N. R., twenty-five, provoked an extremely violent reaction from her husband, who even threatened her with a knife to make her leave the Igreja Universal do Reino de Deus. Her reaction was to stop attending church temporarily, instead listening to the pastor's sermons on the radio. After some time, she was able to attend church again while her husband was away at work. Our respondents confirmed that Pentecostals tend to react calmly to aggression, partly to avoid hostility and partly to attract family members to church.

The church teaches women that the best strategy for attracting people to church is to be tolerant toward them, respect their wishes, and avoid being too insistent about inviting them to join. D. S., whose problems with her daughter we have mentioned earlier, reported, "After entering the true church, I stopped talking, because in the church we learn to accept people the way they are, and to convert someone we need to know how to talk about God without being insistent. . . . If a person doesn't want to go, if she/he has a hard heart, nobody can do anything." Once again, Pentecostal emphasis on individual will reflects a new conception of the individual. Thus conversion changes not only believers' attitudes toward themselves but also their attitudes toward others. Pentecostal tolerance in response to aggression is also based on a new conception of the individual relationship with good and evil.

After conversion, women "discover" that if their husbands get drunk or mistreat them they are not acting of their own free will; rather, the devil has taken possession of them. People are seen as easy prey for the devil, who makes them act aggressively, selfishly, and destructively. Pentecostals adopt a tolerant attitude toward a person whose behavior is wrong and negative because, as D. O., a college student, age twenty-six, from the Assembly of God church put it, "He doesn't do wrong because he wants to, he's being used. . . . These people are being used, and they're unhappy." Consequently, all oppressors are seen as being oppressed by the devil and as victims for whom one should pray. The women see their aggressive husbands as victims, too, and therefore tend to adopt a more tolerant attitude toward them and try to handle marital conflicts more calmly. By symbolically inverting the relation of power and oppression, the women often do not consider the interests of their spouses as opposing theirs; consequently, they interpret marital conflicts not as conflicts of interest but rather as the result of one of the parties' being possessed by evil and therefore not guilty of their misdeeds. Because they are alienated from their own free will, confronting them is meaningless; they need to be liberated from the devil.

Most of the Pentecostal conversion accounts (of both men and women) that we have analyzed describe a redefinition of what is evil and how it relates to individuals. Converts come to believe that all the bad things in the world (sin, conflict, illness) have only one source, the devil, and they see only one solution, God. Thus they cannot blame others for their problems or expect them to solve those problems. Only God can give and help. This conception of evil reinforces individual autonomy, tolerance toward others, and self-criticism.

Both the sick and the sinner, the depressed and the aggressor are possessed by the devil. Therefore, whatever the problem, first of all they must be delivered. In their conversion testimony, most Pentecostals refer first to their personal *libertação* (deliverance). The women interviewed, for instance, spoke of their own deliverance from things that ranged from Afro-Brazilian Spiritualist practices and beliefs to depression, irritability, and illness. They adopted a self-critical attitude, acknowledging they had had evil with them, but because they had not known it they did not feel guilt. The word "repentance" rarely appears in their conversion accounts.

After deliverance, individuals become conscious of the power of God's word. Knowing the Truth, they now have the responsibility for their own happiness in this world and their salvation in the next. Converts also pray for and try to save those near them; female believers often refer to God's biblical promise to save the faithful's households as well. Many women embrace Pentecostalism with this hope. An earlier study about men who had quit drinking because of Pentecostalism pointed out that, in most cases, the conversion of those men's wives or mothers had preceded their own.[23]

The responsibility that women believers take upon themselves regarding the spiritual well-being of their families seems to be greater than that of men believers because women mediate between God and their families. The woman not only brings her relatives into the church but also helps them in the process of deliverance. Bishop Edir Macedo, the head of the Igreja Universal do Reino de Deus, offers examples of men who were freed from evil through the deliverance of their mothers.[24] Machado observes the important role that women play in the process of deliverance of other members of their families, particularly their husbands and children, in this church. In her interpretation, the fact that almost all cases of demon possession involve women does not mean that the latter are more vulnerable to evil than men; rather, it indicates that the forces of evil that act on their spouses and children also manifest themselves in women in the deliverance sessions. In other words, women serve as channels of liberation for other family members.[25] In addition to praying for and proselytizing them, through deliverance sessions women can also bring their family members to God.

Because they feel spiritually stronger and recognize the fragility of nonbelievers, Pentecostal women do not hold their spouses and loved ones responsible for their families' difficulties. Pentecostal women's sense of responsibility extends to material concerns as well. They do not view men as the sole breadwinners; they too feel responsible for the material achievement of their families. Denominations that embrace a "gospel of prosperity" encourage women not only to help their husbands financially but also to try independently to achieve more. When the husband is a nonbeliever, the woman, as a believer, is held even more responsible than her spouse for the couple's prosperity. In contrast to the Marianist Catholic tradition, whereby the indicator of female spiritual superiority is women's ability to suffer and to endure pain, in Pentecostalism, especially where influenced by the "theology of prosperity," this female superiority must make women more active and more capable of material achievement than non-believing men. Even in those churches in which prosperity is less emphasized, as in the case of the Assembly of God, women assume a greater sense of responsibility for material concerns. For example, C. P., from a favela in Rio de Janeiro, decided to build a house for her family in spite of her spouse's initial opposition to the project. Pentecostalism helps women to be more assertive and confident in their ability to act accordingly.

Pentecostal groups also attribute greater moral and ethical responsibility to women when they allow them to occupy official positions of leadership. Although in most Brazilian Pentecostal churches women cannot be pastors (one exception is the Igreja Universal do Reino de Deus, which has ordained women pastors since 1993), many of them allow women to preside at services. In the traditional Assembly of God church as well as in other smaller churches, such as the Igreja Evangelica Senhor de Tempo Fim (Evangelical Church of the Eternal Lord), these women, known as "missionaries", preach, heal, and perform nearly all of the functions of pastors. Missionary women also serve as intermediaries between the pastor and church members. In addition, women play very strong extraofficial leadership roles as pastors' wives and prophets. Some of our interviewees, for instance, mentioned their conversations with the pastor's wife, particularly about sexuality and family life.

More Duties, Not More Rights

After conversion, men and women do not seek more rights; instead they accept more restrictions and add duties to their lives. In Brazil, Protestant churches have been characterized by strict practices and repression of the body and all the festivities of Brazilian culture.[26] Traditional Pentecostalism has continually reaffirmed these puritan values. The literature on Pentecostalism and gender has interpreted the puritan restriction of masculine behavior as a victory for women and an extension of their rights. The official discourse does not encourage converts to fight for either their individual rights or the rights of their category or gender. The extension of feminine rights is, therefore, an unintentional consequence of an increase in male duties.

Feminist researchers such as Gouveia[27] have interpreted this female self-limitation as a sign of Pentecostal women's alienation. The Pentecostal emphasis on individuals' duties rather than on their rights, however, distinguishes its conception of individual freedom from that of most North and South American feminism. Since no one is oppressed by anyone but the devil, to be free is to be able to disobey the devil's will. Asceticism proves that one is free.

The restrictions that Pentecostal women impose on themselves reflect a new concept of liberty. N. R., a member of the Assembly of God, explained how her idea of freedom had changed. She said that she had been very reluctant to become a believer and join the Assembly of God because of its restrictions on leisure and dress: "I though I was going to be in prison, but I was wrong. It's freedom. . . . I can go to the beach now, but I don't. I'm not going to miss church to go to the beach." According to this conception, what freedom means is not the absence of restrictions but resisting temptation and remaining faithful to the values and responsibilities one has assumed. The freedom that Pentecostals seek is not from social or religious laws but from the human selfishness and desires identified as devilish. One is free when one is able to give up bad habits. Pentecostal liberation is a personal transformation, explained M. B. After the baptism in the Holy Spirit "the person changes, even though there are things that you had never managed to give up before."

In general, women who become Pentecostal already had an austere lifestyle prior to conversion. Many, especially the married, drank little or no alcohol, and their sexual activity was restricted to their spouses or partners. Conversion does not represent as great a break with a past lifestyle for women as for men. In fact it seems to reaffirm the dominant feminine lifestyle rather than to transform it. A great number of Pentecostal churches, however, preach the abandonment of "vanities" such as earrings, makeup, haircuts, and pants and shorts for these women who had so little else to restrict in their lives. Most of the Pentecostal women we interviewed talked about this issue of dress and feminine beauty.

Some women approved of this strict code regarding dress and makeup and explained that their choice of a church had been positively influenced by that code. For example, M. S., a low-income seamstress, reported that her church's code was very strict: "I thought I wouldn't get used to it. You couldn't wear short or long pants or cut your hair or anything like that. I thought the doctrine was right. . . . I believe that if you're a Christian you have to be different." She also explained that her church was against going to the beach: "The question is not the beach but the clothes you wear there." The austere dress code was also appealing to R. P. and Z. J., both poor women from the Assembly of God. They were impressed by the believers' modest apparel and attracted to the church precisely because of this style. Some Pentecostals argue that the discreet, nonprovocative clothes protect poor women from sexual harassment, as seems also to happen among Afro-American Pentecostals.[28]

The strictness of doctrine in fact serves as a dividing line between different Pentecostal denominations and is one of the factors responsible for individual decisions to join or leave a given church. The ascetic code of conduct that preaches against alcohol, cigarettes, and participating in Carnival is widespread throughout the Pentecostal churches. Nevertheless, there are many churches with less stringent dress codes that attract women who reject the traditional Pentecostal sobriety. Middle-class and Neo-Pentecostal churches such as the Igreja Universal do Reino de Deus are generally more flexible. Some women explained that they had avoided joining denominations with very strict dress codes (for instance, forbidding the wearing of pants and sleeveless clothes). Most of these women were middle-class like M. N., who told us that in her church women did not need to change their way of dressing. She also explained that this had helped her husband to accept her conversion, because he had been worried about seeing her with her hair tied in a bun and wearing a long dress as traditional Brazilian believers did. M. N. also said that she went to the beach quite often and had no problem with wearing a bikini there.

Our data confirm the conclusion of Ahaunna Scott's study on Appalachian Pentecostals that career and the consequent social mobility allow women to contest the rigid dress code.[29] In most middle-class churches, restrictions regarding dress are minimal or nonexistent. For example, D. U., a twenty-six-year-old member of the Assembly of God church, was the child of a specialized manual worker with little education but had managed to become a student at a state university. There she felt peer pressure regarding her way of dressing. She told us that in her church other young people like herself debated the prohibition of bikinis and long pants, arguing that it was not in the Bible. Nevertheless, she concluded that these rules were right because "the world is looking to believers" and they had to be an example to others.

Despite these variations, Pentecostal women all stress their personal transformation. They see the solution to all their problems in their own transformation and not in the transformation of those around them—who will have to help themselves by undergoing their own personal transformation. The new individual that each must be is not the passive suffering individual of the traditional feminine role but an individual responsible for her own happiness and material achievement.

Conclusion

Pentecostalism involves individualist assumptions and values, but its individualism differs from much of liberal feminism. Through conversion, men and women alike learn to see themselves as autonomous beings responsible for their own achievement. Pentecostalism therefore alters people's conceptions of individualism and individual freedom, and this implies a transformation of the family and of gender relations. Although these new models represent an improvement in the position of women, especially in societies where machismo predominates, they fail to address the rights considered fundamental by many North and South American feminists. Pentecostalism does not embrace the kind of individualism that is at the core of the feminist project.

Pentecostalism is individualistic inasmuch as it emphasizes a personal choice of faith and the possibility of changing the course of one's life. This change depends solely on one's relationship to God. The individual's choice is the key to all personal or social transformation. This belief breaks with the traditional and patriarchal worldview while increasing individual responsibility and establishing equality between genders.

At the same time, Pentecostalism's assumption that the free individual is always committed to God's law limits the individualism it fosters in granting autonomy to believers. Pentecostalism seems to adopt an intermediate position between traditional machismo and feminism, which is seen as threatening the continuity of the family that is the raison d'être of many oppressed women. It is for this reason that Pentecostalism seems to be so appealing to women, who, upon conversion, acquire greater autonomy in relation to their husbands and families while avoiding direct confrontation. In entering the church, women are in fact seeking greater independence, but their intention is only their salvation and the salvation of their husbands and their households. According to the Pentecostal view, individuals cannot hold their own happiness as the main goal of their lives; God must be placed above all. Because of their commitment to God, Pentecostals do not adopt a modern individualism, just as they do not submissively conform to a traditional view of society.

Thus Pentecostal women no longer see men as masters they must obey. Nor, however, do they view them as oppressors they must rebel against. Rather, men are seen as victims of evil as they once were themselves, and therefore women feel responsible for their husbands and try to help them. The belief in demonic possession in everyday life relieves men of responsibility for their acts and in a certain way also legitimates women's autonomy. Deliverance from the devil—or, rather, the exorcism practiced in Pentecostal churches—contributes to the process of individualization for both men and women. Pentecostalism is able to resolve marital conflict because it redefines the relationship between the individual and evil.

Rejecting a fatalistic view of life, the Pentecostal woman no longer sees herself in the traditional role of victim and servant of her husband and family, nor does she become a rebel who fights against masculine oppression and tries to free herself from it. The Pentecostal woman, on the contrary, views herself as stronger than the masculine oppressor, who is a sinner. Because of her strength, she feels responsible for the salvation of her husband and family, as well as for their material prosperity. With their distinctive concepts of freedom and of evil, Pentecostal women do not demand sexual liberty or the right to drink alcohol, and they deny those rights to men. For the Pentecostal, the liberated individual is one who can resist temptation, not a transgressor of moral and divine laws.

NOTES

1. Max Weber, *The Sociology of Religion* (Boston: Beacon Press, 1972), p. 104.

2. For instance, in Brazil women are in the majority in the Spiritualist religions, both Kardecist and Afro-Brazilian, as well as in the Catholic church, where women outnumber men in the charismatic-renewal movements, in the base communities, and at Sunday masses.

3. Peter Fry and Gary Howe, "Duas respostas à aflição: Umbanda e Pentecostalismo," *Debate e Crítica* 6 (1975), pp. 75–94.

4. In Western history, magic is also often associated with the most oppressed social classes. See, for example, Weber, *The Sociology of Religion.*

5. F. C. Rolim, *Pentecostais no Brasil* (Petrópolis: Vozes, 1985); Christian Lalive d'Epinay, *O refugio das massas* (São Paulo: Paz e Terra, 1970).

6. Elizabeth Brusco, "The Reformation of Machismo: Asceticism and Masculinity Among Colombian Evangelicals," in Virginia Garrard-Burnett and David Stoll, eds., *Rethinking Protestantism in Latin America* (Philadelphia: Temple University Press, 1994), pp. 143–158; Cornelia Butler Flora, *Pentecostalism in Colombia: Baptism by Fire and Spirit* (Rutherford, N.J.: Fairleigh Dickinson University Press, 1976); María das Dores Machado, "Charismatics and Pentecostals: A Comparison of Religiousness and Intra-family Relations within the Brazilian Middle Class," paper written for the 22nd International Conference on Religion and Society, Budapest, Hungary, July 1993, and "Adesão religiosa e seus efeitos na esfera privada: Um estudo comparativo dos Carismáticos e Pentecostais de Rio de Janeiro," Ph.D. diss., Instituto Universitario Pesquisa, Rio de Janeiro, 1994; Hanneke Slootweg, "Mujeres pentecostales chilenas," in Bárbara Boudewijnse, Frans Kamsteeg, and Andre Droogers, eds., *Algo más que opio: Una lectura del Pentecostalismo Latinoamericano y Caribeño* (San José, Costa Rica: Editorial Departamento Ecuménico de Investigaciones, 1991); David A. Smilde, "Gender Relations and Social Change in Latin American Evangelicalism," in Daniel Miller, ed., *Coming of Age: Pentecostalism in Contemporary Latin America* (Lanham, Md. University Press of America, 1994); Monica Tarducci, "Pentecostalismo y relaciones de género: Una revisión," in A. Frigerio, ed., *Nuevos movimientos religiosos,* vol. 1 (Buenos Aires: Centro Editorial de América Latina, 1993).

7. Eliane Gouveia's study is an exception. Gouveia was the first to examine the situation of women in Pentecostal churches in Brazil. Comparing women from the Congregação Cristã do Brasil and Brasil para o Cristo, she concludes that both churches are patriarchal and androcentric but the former, because it is a sect rather than a church and less open to the wider society, is the more oppressive of women. In drawing this conclusion she assumes that these women were better off before conversion (outside the church) than they are now. Eliane Gouveia, "O silêncio que debe ser ouvido: Mulheres pentecostais em São Paulo," Master's thesis, Universidade Pontificia Católica de São Paulo, 1987.

8. Salvatore Cucchiari, "Between Shame and Sanctification," *American Ethnologist* 14, 4 (1990), pp. 607–707.

9. Tarducci, "Pentecostalismo y relaciones de género."

10. John Burdick, *Looking for God in Brazil: The Progressive Catholic Church in Brazil* (Berkeley: University of California Press, 1993); Machado, "Adesão religiosa."

11. Machado, "Adesão religiosa."

12. Cecília Mariz, *Coping with Poverty: Pentecostal Churches and Christian Base Communities in Brazil* (Philadelphia: Temple University Press, 1994).

13. The emphasis on family is not exclusive to Pentecostalism. On the contrary, family is a central theme for all religions, especially in contemporary society, in which religion increasingly deals with private life.

14. The empirical data we refer to in this chapter were mostly collected for two ongoing research projects carried out in Rio de Janeiro state: Cecília Mariz and María das Dores

Campos Machado, "Identidade, sincretismo e transito religioso: Uma comparação entre carismáticos e Pentecostais," supported by Conselho Nacional de Pesquisa and the Brazilian Research Council, 1994, and Machado, "Adesão religiosa."

15. For example, Lalive d'Epinay, *O refugio das masses;* Rolim, *Pentecostais no Brasil.*

16. David Martin, *Tongues of Fire: The Explosion of Protestantism in Latin America* (Oxford and Cambridge, Mass. Basil Blackwell, 1990), p. 181.

17. Cecília Mariz, "O mal e o demônio no discurso pentecostal," paper presented at the Seminar on Evil, Instituto Sociologico Estudos Religiosos, Rio de Janeiro, 1994.

18. Pentecostalism may therefore be an example of what Weber calls "rationalizing charisma" and what Berger claims to be a modernizing consequence of a movement with antimodernizing intentions. Peter Berger, *A Fair Glory* (New York: Free Press, 1992).

19. R. Stephen Warner, "Work in Progress Toward a New Paradigm for the Sociological Study of Religion in the United States," *American Journal of Sociology* 98, 5 (1993), pp. 1044–1093.

20. Slootweg, "Mujeres pentecostales chilenas."

21. Machado, "Adesão religiosa."

22. Burdick, *Looking for God in Brazil.*

23. See also Cecília Mariz, "Alcoholismo, gênero e Pentecostalismo," *Religião e Sociedade* 16, 3 (1994), pp. 80–93.

24. Edir Macedo, *Orixàs, caboclos e guias* (Rio de Janeiro: Universal Produções, 1990).

25. Machado, "Adesão religiosa."

26. See, for example, R. Alves, *Protestantismo e repressão* (São Paulo: Ática, 1982); P. Velasques Filho, "Sim a Deus e não a vida: Conversão e disciplina no Protestantismo brasileiro," in A. G. Mendonça and P. Velasques Filho, eds., *Introducão ao Protestantismo no Brasil* (São Paulo: Edições Loyola, 1990).

27. Gouveia, "O silêncio que debe ser ouvido."

28. C. Gilkes, "Together and in Harness: Women's Tradition in the Sanctified Church," *Signs: Journal of Women in Culture and Society* 10 (1985), pp. 678–699.

29. Ahuanna Scott, "They Don't Have to Live by Old Traditions: Saintly Men, Sinner Women, and an Appalachian Pentecostal Revival," *American Ethnologist* 21, 2 (1994), pp. 227–244.

❧ 4 ❧

Private Power or Public Power: Pentecostalism, Base Communities, and Gender*

CAROL ANN DROGUS

*A*s the number of Latin American Pentecostals has grown, so have expectations and fears about their potential power. Most research has focused on how Pentecostals use their power in the public realm of politics and economics. Less attention has focused on their impact on power in the private realm of gender attitudes and roles.[1] This imbalance may reflect the common perception, noted elsewhere in this volume by Hannah Stewart-Gambino and Everett Wilson, of Pentecostalism's deep conservatism with respect to women's roles. This stereotype leads to the attendant assumption that Pentecostalism could not be a source of change or emancipation for women. Yet there are good reasons to examine the topic of women and Pentecostalism further.

First, most Pentecostal converts are women.[2] Thus, any study of the Pentecostal public sphere, political attitudes, and behavior is likely to be incomplete unless it considers the possible effects of gender. Moreover, for Latin American women—particularly poor women, who make up the majority of Pentecostals—private-sphere power may be at least as important materially and personally as public power. Second, Pentecostal conversion may be more likely to change private-sphere attitudes and behaviors than public ones. Religion and family, perhaps because both are associated with the private sphere, are intimately related in most contemporary religions, including Pentecostalism.[3] Thus,

*An earlier draft of this chapter appeared as *Religious Change and Women's Status in Latin America: A Comparison of Catholic Base Communities and Pentecostal Churches,* Kellogg Institute for International Studies Working Paper 205 (1994).

religion's impact on gender relations may well be greater than on political beliefs. Third, although religion—especially a gender-conservative religious ideology such as Pentecostalism—has long been considered "the major cultural reinforcer of modern industrial patriarchy," growing evidence suggests that it cannot be so easily dismissed.[4] Religions are not monolithic belief systems but multifaceted sets of often contradictory or conflicting symbols open to a range of interpretations. Even when official doctrine and organization discriminate against them, disempowered individuals can reconceptualize dominant ideologies to produce individual and collective values and strategies for survival and empowerment. Religions with quite conservative gender attitudes contain elements that women can and do utilize to combat subordination.[5]

This chapter examines the ways in which Pentecostalism may affect women's gender attitudes and roles. It asks whether Pentecostalism fosters women's empowerment in either the public or the private sphere. It also contrasts Pentecostals' experiences with those of women in Catholic Christian base communities (*comunidades eclesiales de base*—CEBs), often considered the Pentecostals' opposites and competitors for the souls of the poor. The contrast is instructive, because it shows that although neither religious group sets out explicitly to change gender roles or attitudes, both actually do so, albeit in strikingly different ways. Few testable hypotheses about religion and gender have been advanced. Moreover, the evidence here comes not from a single systematic comparison but from studies of Pentecostals and CEBs throughout the region, some of which only tangentially address gender issues.[6] As a result, the conclusions must be tentative. The analysis does, however, yield suggestive contrasts that can inform both theory and future empirical research.

Traditional Gender Systems and Pentecostal Mechanisms of Cultural Change

Before exploring how Pentecostalism might change individual worldviews and, particularly, attitudes toward gender, a brief summary of traditional gender ideologies will be useful. Such ideologies are never static, and gender roles and attitudes in the region are in considerable flux. The following therefore describes an ideal-type rather than an average contemporary experience.

Traditional Latin American gender ideology is highly patriarchal, legitimating male power over females generally and especially within families. It has traditionally divided the world into two spheres: the house (private) and the street (public).[7] Men dominate both spheres. Ideally, men alone move in the public sphere of the street. Within the house, they have ultimate authority.

In the extreme version of this patriarchal ideology, submissive women are confined to the house, where their virtue can be safeguarded. Yet the home is also woman's sphere of power or, at least, influence. In her "proper sphere" she may exercise considerable discretion and even authority, especially vis-à-vis her children. Women are often also considered the spiritual focus of the family, even if the authoritarian father is its legal lord. Many scholars claim that Catholic theology and popular religion have reinforced the concept of *marianismo*, an ideal of femininity modeled on the Virgin Mary, which identifies women's "natural" roles—virgin, wife, and mother—as wholly private.[8] *Marianismo* denies women access to public power, even within the church. In compensation, women are offered a circumscribed, although often personally fulfilling, sphere of spiritual authority and action in the home.

This ideology produces a gendered division of labor in which men are responsible for wage earning and all public activities while women are responsible for family reproduction: cooking, cleaning, and child and health care. As a result, men's and women's self-interests and prestige spheres differ.[9] Typically, female prestige depends upon the home and its care; it may be humble so long as it is clean, the children's clothes ragged so long as they are pressed. In a distorted version of patriarchal ideology often caricatured as *machismo*, men, in contrast, are expected to be tenuously attached to the home, their prestige dependent upon "manly" activities including drinking, gambling, and extramarital affairs. If a man chooses to remain within the family, patriarchal ideology dictates that he be its head; in the distorted patriarchy of *machismo*, however, men may prove their manliness by abandoning family responsibilities, undermining women's ability to fulfill their prescribed roles.

The ideal of a separation of spheres has always been unattainable for most social classes, including those most attracted to Pentecostal groups and CEBs, the rural and urban poor. In contemporary Latin America, moreover, the ideal is constantly eroding as women enter the paid labor force, gain education, and become visible in politics. Yet *marianismo* and a patriarchal model persist as ideology. This ideal and women's continuing underrepresentation in the public sphere constitute the background against which changes in gender attitudes and roles must initially be viewed.

Pentecostalism sets out to reinforce patriarchal gender norms, not to undermine them. Nonetheless, it may offer new ideas and roles that women can utilize to reinterpret gender norms and may even ultimately destabilize the prevailing hegemonic gender ideology.[10] Religion can contribute to changing gender attitudes and roles in two ways. First, new doctrine or symbols that challenge prevailing cultural norms may alter converts' worldviews. Second, new organizational or participatory structures may draw women into leadership roles.

Religious Ideas and Gender

Edward Cleary has pointed to Pentecostals' pragmatic bent, and this is perhaps nowhere more apparent than in the extraordinary degree of attention the churches give to family issues. They offer women very practical advice on how to be better wives and mothers through special classes, campaigns, and publications. Pentecostal churches in Guatemala, for example, offer a women's magazine "designed 'to help women fulfill their God-given feminine destinies.'"[11] These churches devote so much of their time, preaching, and resources to the family, in fact, that Elizabeth Brusco describes them as having a "feminine ethos."[12] This ethos may attract women converts, who perceive Pentecostals as addressing issues that fall to women in the traditional gender-based division of labor.[13]

It is thus not only the stereotype but also the real intent of most Pentecostal groups to promote conservative gender relations and morality. Anna Adams notes in this volume that some Pentecostals even enforce a strict segregation of the sexes at religious services or require women to follow strict dress codes, presumably in part to ensure their sexual purity. Control over women's sexuality is essential to patriarchal authority. Similarly, Pentecostals stress motherhood as women's appropriate "God-given" role, and most support a patriarchal family structure.[14] Colombian Pentecostals, among others, cite Scripture in arguing that men should have authority over women.[15] One Brazilian Pentecostal quotes from the New Testament: "When the woman doesn't want to submit to the order of the husband, that's the start of a fight, right? But if the woman is a true Christian, she is going to want to obey. For the Apostle Paul said: Women must obey their husbands. Like it or not, she has to obey."[16] Within the Pentecostal family, the husband is officially the ultimate authority, and the wife is expected to be submissive.

Even if Pentecostals do intend to promote conservative gender values, however, it does not follow that all of Pentecostalism naturally reinforces patriarchy. The religious message is not entirely clear-cut: Pentecostal churches also leave an opening for defining women's domestic roles in a more egalitarian way. Colombian Pentecostal churches illustrate this ambiguity: Although most defend ultimate patriarchal authority, church educational materials also encourage more egalitarian relations within marriage.[17] In addition, the religious community in some senses becomes the final arbiter for Pentecostal couples. Men are the nominal household heads, but both men and women must submit to the will of God, usually as interpreted by the church. The pastor and the church community can exercise considerable influence over domestic behavior, particularly through public prophetic denunciation. Women, then, can turn to a higher authority in the church in case of domestic disputes. The overarching authority of the church potentially equalizes male and female relationships.

Pentecostalism's scriptural notion of equality before Christ more directly contradicts female subordination. Pentecostals accept the "priesthood of all believers": Men and women may be called to preach and may do so with equal authority. As Cornelia Butler Flora suggests, this implies a public role for women in spreading the faith.[18] The belief in women's equal religious potential provides grounds for enhanced status in both church and family.[19] It also allows them to claim religious inspiration and justification for challenging male authority. Elaine J. Lawless has shown, for example, that North American women Pentecostal preachers exploit the "tension between the God-given inferiority of women submissive to men and the belief in equality before God" to pursue independent, nontraditional paths.[20]

Finally, Pentecostalism may implicitly subvert some popular assumptions of machismo and *marianismo*. Popular *marianismo* holds that women's greater religiosity and men's inherent waywardness lead to gender-specific paths to salvation. As Evelyn Stevens explains, women "know that male sinfulness dooms the entire sex to a prolonged stay in purgatory after death, and even the most diligent prayerfulness of loving female relatives can succeed in sparing them only a few millennia of torture."[21] Women, with their greater moral ability, may be saved by their own piety, but religious salvation is seemingly marginal to male life, a by-product of the piety of female relatives. In contrast, as Salvatore Cucchiari points out with respect to Sicilian Pentecostals, their "unisex criteria for redemption"—conversion and baptism in the Holy Spirit—undermine traditional gender assumptions.[22] A single salvational code applies to all, and women "can compete with men and women alike in regard to the central prestige value of the community—sanctification—and achieve a validated success in that competition."[23]

Although Pentecostalism's explicit gender code sets out to reinforce traditional, patriarchal values, its family norms are ambiguous in ways that could give women greater equality. Its implicit acceptance of the religious equality of men and women could also tend to equalize gender relations. Moreover, we must keep in mind that Pentecostal groups differ in their conservatism on gender norms. Anna Adams points out that Pentecostals distinguish among themselves according to the degree of strictness of women's segregation, dress codes, and so on. Cecília Mariz and María das Dores Campos Machado note the same tendency in Brazil, adding that individuals may choose a church partly for its strictness, with middle-class Pentecostal women preferring less rigorous standards than the poor. Thus the blanket stereotype of Pentecostals' gender conservatism needs to be modified to allow for its ambiguities within groups as well as differences across them.

New Forms of Religious Participation for Women

Pentecostalism also offers women unaccustomed opportunities for official and unofficial leadership and new roles in the religious community. Leadership roles within women's groups are especially common, perhaps as a result of women's predominance within many Pentecostal churches. Colombian Pentecostal churches, for example, encourage the formation of mothers' or women's clubs.[24] Women are also usually the leaders and primary participants in *cultos a domicilio*, worship services held in individual homes.[25] Many of these groups' activities—social welfare, prayer, church maintenance and cleaning—simply replicate women's domestic roles. They may nonetheless be a source of status within the church. Moreover, such groups may give women new skills, such as public speaking or fund-raising, and enhance their sense of efficacy in bringing about change.[26]

Yet single-sex groups can never offer women status on terms of equality with men. That requires opportunities for leadership in the church as a whole. And, indeed, Pentecostal groups have historically presented women nontraditional opportunities as teachers and preachers that "allow a greater status for women in the same fields of activity which grant status to men."[27] Their tradition of female evangelism includes the woman who brought Pentecostalism to Mexico.[28] Another woman, Aimee Semple McPherson, founded a major Pentecostal church, the Foursquare Gospel. Women pastors and even lay teachers gain both authority in a nontraditional role and skills useful in other public roles. Because their religious vocation legitimates—and for pastors may even necessitate—travel alone, for example, women with little experience beyond a neighborhood or village may learn how to function independently in a wider realm.[29]

Women's access to such roles, however, continues to be significant but restricted. Men dominate in activities that require interpretation of the Word, and these are usually the official roles. Preaching, for example, may require only conversion and charisma, and so in some instances a woman can preach. In most churches she is considered incapable of scriptural authority, however, so she cannot be appointed a pastor. A growing number of Pentecostal churches seem to accept women pastors but still informally proscribe women's leadership above a certain level.[30] Women also lack access to administrative positions based on working one's way through the ranks, as some key ranks are closed to them.[31] These restrictions reinforce patriarchal male dominance of religion. They also mean that religion does not open new career or income opportunities for Pentecostal women.[32]

The Pentecostal emphasis on spiritual experience, however, opens up important although unofficial leadership roles for women. Even when women are excluded from official status as preachers, they can perform an important religious and ritual role by speaking in tongues, testifying, and other "Spirit-inspired" activities. Pentecostal women can attain leadership and status by becoming faith healers, for example.[33] In these "Spirit-dominated" activities women and men are truly equal in their religious potential. Women may even generally be esteemed as more "in touch" with the spiritual side of religion.[34]

Pentecostalism thus holds a potential for women to engage in nontraditional roles that confer status on both men and women equally, to take some leadership positions, and to participate actively in extradomestic activities. The legitimating context of religion may provide a bridge to expanding roles by offering leadership opportunities and skills, as well as a potential justification for greater equality for women in the form of new beliefs about women's worth and roles as Christians. Yet Pentecostalism's overall gender ideology or code is certainly ambiguous: women are equal only in circumscribed areas, and opportunities for equality are embedded in a framework that accepts and reinforces male superiority. This very ambiguity, however, may make Pentecostalism "an effective crucible" for gender-role redefinition. The next section explores the ways in which women respond to this mixture of opportunity and traditionalism.

Public Power, Private Power, and Pentecostal Women

Women can reconceptualize gender roles in a number of ways, each of which may contribute to enhancing their independence and power. Studies of Pentecostalism in Latin American have generally emphasized its impact on the exercise of public-sphere power, but for poor women private power relations may have more immediate relevance. Thus we need to address two questions about Pentecostalism's impact on women: First, do women expand the definition of what roles are considered appropriate for them, demanding greater power in the traditionally male public sphere? Second, do they demand higher status within the private-sphere roles traditionally ascribed to them?

In looking at the extent to which women assume nontraditional roles, it may be useful to start with religious roles. Pentecostalism, as we have seen, certainly offers women new roles, including leadership roles, but to what extent do women take advantage of these opportunities?

Women are crucial to the maintenance and expansion of Pentecostal churches. They are active in the single-sex organizations and many devote considerable time to these groups, which may even take on "the lion's share of responsibility for the church."[35] In Colombia, women are also the key recruiters. For this reason, Pentecostal churches can be described as largely family- and neighborhood-based.[36] Women's groups sometimes even produce vibrant new churches. In Quetzaltenango, Guatemala, for example, a 2,000-member Neo-Pentecostal church originated in a Presbyterian women's prayer circle that broke with the parent church to form its own organization.[37]

Despite their critical role in maintaining, expanding, and founding Pentecostal churches, women do not seem to respond in large numbers to leadership opportunities outside of women-only groups. Some women act as pastors in the Foursquare Gospel churches in Colombia, usually serving jointly with their husbands.[38] Women are less prominent at the local level, however, than the policy and perceptions of the national Foursquare Gospel church leaders would suggest.[39] This church, at least, apparently offers more leadership roles to women than they actually utilize. Except for a few individual examples mentioned elsewhere in the literature, Pentecostal women generally do not seem to preach.[40]

Women's leadership is probably most often unofficial, as in the example of faith healers cited previously. Regina Novães notes that leadership of the Assembly of God community she studied in northeastern Brazil was divided between an official, male deacon and a woman who had no official role but was the recognized spiritual co-leader of the congregation and much sought out for counsel and as-sistance.[41] Although there is no evidence of a significant expansion of women's official religious leadership, there may be greater expansion of unofficial roles.

Information about whether Pentecostal women attempt to expand their roles in the nonreligious public sphere is sparse. Anecdotal and impressionistic evi-dence suggests that many Pentecostal women are employed outside the home.[42] However, given the social class of converts, paid employment is an unreliable in-dicator of embrace of nontraditional roles, since the conquest of the "right" to work outside the home is meaningless to poor women, such as most Pentecostals, whose poverty forces them to work and who must compete in a very unequal job market for undesirable, low-paying jobs. Mariz and Machado argue, however, that Pentecostalism's "theology of prosperity" may at least encourage women to gain a sense of economic responsibility, especially if the male household head is a non-believer. Pentecostal women may have a religious motive for taking on more eco-nomic responsibility and may gain more control over economic resources as a re-sult.

We also know relatively little about whether Pentecostal women take on new roles in traditionally male areas such as politics. No systematic evidence of polit-ical activism by Pentecostal women has emerged, although at least one major Pentecostal woman politician, Brazil's Benedita da Silva, has been elected to pub-lic office by a left-of-center party.[43] Evidence also suggests that women from Catholic and various Protestant denominations in Colombia have about the same level of political interest, suggesting that Pentecostalism at least does not further exclude them from this realm.[44]

In contrast to the scant evidence of Pentecostal women's attempting to expand their religious, economic, or political roles, one clear theme emerges from the nu-merous portraits of Pentecostal life: Women do seek to improve their position within the domestic sphere. Researchers have often noted a particular long-term strategy that Pentecostal women adopt for stabilizing their households: They at-tempt to capture a larger share of male income for the sustenance of the family.[45] Goldin and Metz found that Guatemalan women Pentecostals generally focused in their conversion stories on the problems created by male family members' drinking.[46] Women converts frequently hope to convert their husbands as well in order to change their behavior.[47]

Alternatively, women may join Pentecostal churches seeking a godly spouse with Pentecostalism's endorsed qualities of sobriety, frugality, and sexual fidelity. One young Chilean Pentecostal woman states:

> All the men in my neighborhood are good for nothing. Growing up, I had a boyfriend, and he was the same as the others. All he wanted was to play around (*pololear*,) drink, and watch soccer. So I dumped him. The problem around here is, where do you go to find a man who takes life seriously? . . . A friend told me about the church here in town. . . . I met a wonderful man. He never drinks, never smokes, he is polite, and he has a good job.[48]

Gaining control of income spent on alcohol and in the male prestige sphere generally—through selection or conversion of a spouse—can be of considerable importance for working-class women. It may also give women more de facto authority and equality in family decisionmaking, in part because it harmonizes men's and women's expectations. Emilio Willems noted long ago that the asceticism and moral code expected of Pentecostal converts is actually quite consonant with the traditional behaviors and values assigned to women in Latin America. Male converts are essentially called upon to adopt female moral norms.[49] They must become more ascetic in their consumption patterns, renouncing spending on drink or women and bringing their spending into line with female preferences for spending on family consumption.[50]

Successful conversion of husbands can thus give Pentecostal women a particular advantage in gaining control of household resources. Pentecostal communities and ministers can also exert considerable pressure on members' moral behavior and frequently do so in a way that brings men's behavior into line with women's expectations.[51] Women often benefit when families submit their disputes to church authorities who endorse a "female" moral code. Even in the controversial area of birth control, when Colombian Protestant couples turn to church counseling services, counselors usually support the woman's desire for birth control over the man's objections.[52]

By reinforcing women's moral code and extending it to men, Pentecostal churches may open the way for attitudinal and behavioral changes that empower women, truly equalizing domestic roles. Brusco argues that conversion empowers Colombian women in their family relations.[53] Colombian Protestant families generally communicate more, and "women, particularly, benefit from this increase in status through inclusion."[54] Van den Eykel concludes that these familial patterns reinforce church teachings that make the man more responsible to the family and that this in turn facilitates communication and confidence between spouses. Although John Burdick is more cautious in interpreting women's acceptance of Pentecostalism's patriarchal worldview as empowering, most researchers see it as such.[55]

Moreover, Pentecostal support for a patriarchal family does not imply total female submission. Women are not expected to submit to mistreatment. David Dixon describes the case of an abused wife who was taken in and protected by a small neighborhood church in a Chilean *población* (shantytown).[56] In theory, at least, women might also use a husband's ungodliness as a reason for divorce, as M. J., a woman interviewed by Mariz and Machado, apparently said. Similarly, Mariz and Machado note that Brazilian Pentecostal women often use the requirements of their religious calling to free themselves from oppressive obligations to their spouses or grown children.

Pentecostal women also reveal surprisingly egalitarian attitudes toward domestic roles. A survey comparing two Colombian Protestant denominations that promote substantial religious roles for women (Presbyterians and Foursquare Gospel) with denominations that do not revealed that the women from those two denominations exhibited more autonomy and greater rejection of traditional gender stereotyping of family roles.[57] For example, only 7 percent of Presbyterian and Foursquare Gospel women said that women should be obedient to their husbands, in contrast to 36 percent of women from other denominations. Only 4 percent believed that home duties were exclusively the wife's in contrast to 27 percent of other religious women.[58] The rejection of traditional gender assumptions by all the respondents is itself notable, but the women from more inclusive churches still stand out. Pentecostalism may thus join North American Mormonism as a strongly patriarchal religion that nonetheless tends toward equality in adherents' actual domestic roles.[59]

Pentecostalism is in many respects compatible with traditional hegemonic gender ideologies: It supports patriarchal family structures, the idea of God-given domestic roles for women, and the notion that only men may hold certain official religious roles. It promotes little expansion of women's traditional roles. What is more interesting, however, is that Pentecostal women do reconceptualize *men's* and, to a lesser extent, women's domestic roles.[60] At the same time, the new roles it opens to women in the religious sphere, the actual equalization of domestic roles it seems to foster, and the emphasis on religious equality are all potentially destabilizing to hegemonic ideologies of machismo and *marianismo*. Thus, we must distinguish carefully between what Pentecostalism sets out to do (reinforce male dominance) and what it actually does (equalize some male-female relationships). The opening that Pentecostalism provides for the empowerment of women is narrow, but it is an opening. Understanding of its significance may be facilitated by a comparison with the impact on gender relations of CEBs.

Public and Private Power in CEBs

Christian base communities are difficult to characterize because of their diversity, but it is helpful to recall that they developed in the wake of Vatican II and the birth of liberation theology. These two developments gave CEBs their distinctive characteristics: an emphasis on lay participation and formation, location among the poorer rural and urban classes, and for some groups—those in Brazil described in the research cited here—a liberationist orientation, including an emphasis on consciousness raising, social justice, and activism. Because both CEBs and Pentecostals seem to find their greatest adherence among the poor, the two are often painted as rivals. Given their difference in emphasis (Pentecostals on personal salvation, CEBs on social justice) they are also often portrayed as opposites.

Like the Pentecostals, CEBs did not set out to recruit women, nor did they, at least initially, view themselves as a vehicle for women's emancipation. Given women's predominance among the Catholic laity, however, it is not surprising that they have also proven to be the primary constituency of the CEBs. In terms of numbers, CEBs, like Pentecostals, are women's religious organizations. What contributions, then, through ideas and organization, might CEBs make to empowering their women members?

Attitudes and Organizational Opportunities

In contrast to Pentecostalism's "feminine ethos," The CEBs' social-justice ethos tends to marginalize familial issues. CEBs have no equivalent of Pentecostal women's magazines or courses on mothering. Liberationist priests rarely mention domestic issues in their sermons, focusing instead on "large political and social issues" of interest in the class-based analysis of liberation theology.[61] Private issues such as drugs, alcoholism, and unemployment naturally arise as CEB members discuss their lives in concrete terms. They generally interpret such problems not as moral or personal issues but in the context of the shared problems of working-class families—a context that tends to politicize them, focusing attention on social action rather than on family or personal change.[62]

Although CEBs do not actively promote patriarchal gender ideology, they often reinforce it. In addition to simply neglecting family, liberationists initially subordinated gender to class as a source of oppression. When they began to consider how women, specifically, might fight oppression, they often stressed the "special roles" and "talents" springing from biological motherhood. As Sonia Alvarez notes, such "essentialist" interpretations of women's roles "do not question the socially constrictive, exclusive identification of women with maternity and the family."[63] CEB discourse on the family is still in flux, however, and at least some pastoral agents now actively promote greater equality of domestic roles.[64]

Although their message on private-sphere roles and relations is mixed and subdued at best, CEBs do foster the idea of greater female participation in the *public* sphere. They promote a "unisex" concept of the "conscientized Catholic." Base-community members who have participated in consciousness raising are expected to act for social justice in the public sphere. This undifferentiated appeal to believers to take up the social struggle, when it is made to a predominantly female laity, both requires and legitimates new social roles, particularly in politics.[65] It supports the idea that men and women should participate side by side in the same movements for land, justice, and so on.

CEBs thus often open new roles to women by promoting social movements through which they may participate in the public, political sphere. In addition, they open many of the same religious opportunities as Pentecostalism. CEBs promote single-sex groups such as mothers' clubs. Lay women can also lead mixed groups; male and female laity can conduct Sunday celebrations in the absence of a priest and may be part of a ministerial team that can perform baptisms or marriages. Thus, like Pentecostal women, CEB members can play a significant role in worship, but along with many of their Protestant sisters they may not be ordained.

The symbolic and organizational opportunities for Pentecostal and CEB women are in some ways similar: An acceptance of some women's roles as "natural" combines with a new unisex standard that fosters equality, and women are offered new religious leadership roles. The key difference seems to be that Pentecostals do more to promote equality in the private and religious spheres while CEBs demand women's public-sphere participation as well as providing some opportunities to act on that demand. Perhaps as a consequence, CEB women seem more successful in pressing for public power than in pursuing private equality.

Public Power and Private Costs

CEB participants interviewed in São Paulo, Brazil, appear more likely to expand their definition of appropriate roles to include those in the public sphere than Pentecostals. The difference should not be overstated, because CEB members differ in the extent to which they adopt new roles and attitudes. Even in religion, however, the evidence suggests that CEB members may respond more enthusiastically than Pentecostals to the available opportunities to expand and reconceptualize roles, gaining new forms of power.

Like their Pentecostal counterparts, women in CEBs play a critical role in religious life. In addition to being instrumental in founding the groups, mothers' clubs—virtually identical in function to Pentecostal ones—often run CEBs on a day-to-day basis. Indeed, many people comment that "if the Mothers' Club closes its doors, the CEB will close."[66] CEB women are also heavily involved in religious activities in sex-integrated groups. Women often predominate in community councils, liturgy committees, and the important ministries. They generally lead the Sunday worship services. Many serve as community representatives to the diocese, although women's participation appears to drop dramatically below that level in both Brazil and Colombia.[67]

Some women CEB leaders have recognized the limits on their roles and begun to push for a greater voice in the church. Many respondents complained that although they did most of the work they were denied access to decisionmaking roles above the community level. This sentiment appears to be widespread among women leaders throughout the archdiocese of São Paulo.[68] Since 1990, several women in one diocese of the city have experienced significant rifts with the bishop over what they perceive to be a disregard for their views and their work with women's groups.[69]

CEBs appear to give women leaders, at least, a sense of empowerment in the religious sphere, perhaps as a result of their new opportunities for participation and status. They also appear to facilitate women's assumption of nonreligious, public roles.[70] Their impact has probably been negligible in the economic sphere, however. Just as for Pentecostal women, although many CEB women work outside the home, this is probably less an indication of emancipation than of necessity. Only four of thirty Brazilian CEB members interviewed had decided to work largely for their own fulfillment.[71]

In contrast, CEBs have had an impact on women's political roles. Most important, they have contributed to the emergence of women leaders involved in social movements and partisan politics.[72] Forty percent of the women interviewed— twelve of thirty—have become politically active in an ongoing way. All the women claim that the CEBs have legitimated political discussion for them. The interviewees nearly unanimously claimed that they had had no interest in politics before joining the CEB. Women commonly said they had simply voted the way their husbands told them to. They claimed to have developed both interest in and knowledge of politics.[73]

For many, the CEB was a revelatory experience, giving them practical skills and opening up a realm of possibilities for participation in the public arena that they had never even imagined. Taking on new roles, however, does not necessarily lead women to reassess their domestic roles. Some women simply justify incursions into politics as the moral or religious actions of mothers who of necessity are forced into the distasteful world of politics, thus neutralizing any challenge to their gender ideology. Even women leaders generally continue to accept their domestic roles as primary and to use the essentialist language of mothers' "special roles" to justify their actions.[74]

At the same time, however, activist women also seem to be in a process of rethinking the balance between domestic and public roles. Many CEB women leaders believe in women's equality and right to participate. They reject a submissive attitude toward men as dehumanizing. They may even criticize the church because, as one woman said, "There's that idea, you must be submissive to the man, that was put in women's heads. . . . But it can't be that way. Because we have to be free, too; we have to be something."[75] The phenomenon of women's gaining greater confidence, authority, and an increasing conviction of their *right* to participate in religious and social life on equal terms seems to occur among women leaders in countries as diverse as Brazil, Mexico, Chile, and Peru.[76] Their husbands' roles and their husbands' perceptions of women's roles, however, often remain unchanged. When husbands are active, a tendency toward equality of domestic roles seems to follow.[77] The many husbands not active in the CEBs, however, have no motivation to reconceptualize their own gender roles or accept and support their wives' equality.

In contrast to most Pentecostal women, then, a significant minority of active women CEB members both expand their public roles and begin to believe in equality for women within and outside the home. However, CEB leaders' new roles often produce domestic conflict rather than harmony and equality. Ironically, then, although some women achieve greater status and authority in both religious and political realms through the CEBs, they do not generally do so in their domestic lives.

Religion, Gender, and Power: Implications for Research

Cecília Mariz broadly summarizes the contrast between the CEBs and Pentecostal churches: Pentecostals bring men into the private sphere, while CEBs politicize women and bring them into the public sphere.[78] Both religions seem to offer women opportunities for equality, authority, and power but in different ways. Whereas Pentecostals may gain authority, status, and stability at home, many CEB women sacrifice domestic peace for more power in public—especially political—roles.

Comparison of Pentecostals and CEBs suggests several general conclusions about religion and women's power. First, in both cases one must distinguish between the manifest intention and latent effect of religion. Pentecostals actively promote an ideal that identifies women "naturally" and exclusively with the home and exalts the patriarchal family. CEBs less aggressively promote patriarchy but at least implicitly reinforce the notion of women's "natural" roles and domestic talents. Neither religion fundamentally questions a patriarchal order, yet each produces ideas and offers opportunities that women can and do take advantage of to gain greater power.

Second, Latin American women's experiences support the idea that ambiguity on gender ideology may be precisely what makes religion an "effective crucible" for change.[79] Mariz and Machado argue that Pentecostalism treads a middle ground between gender traditionalism and mainstream North American feminism; CEBs do as well, and this may be what makes both groups viable sources of at least incremental change. Both groups legitimate greater autonomy and individuation for women via their unisex standards, the CEBs calling for conscious Christian activism and the Pentecostals for subservience to God rather than family and religious evangelism. But neither requires women to reject their familial attachments, and by and large they do not. Perhaps no movement that directly challenges or subverts gender ideology could succeed as well, particularly among poor women, for whom financial independence and an abandonment of domestic roles are neither feasible nor desirable options. It is not clear yet, however, whether such changes will, as Salvatore Cucchiari predicts, ultimately "destabilize" the prevailing hegemonic gender ideology.[80]

Third, a comparison of the two groups suggests the importance of looking at both men and women when considering religion's impact on women's empowerment. The Pentecostal strategy of women's empowerment in the home depends heavily on the successful conversion of male partners. The CEB experience, in which women's expansion of public power produces familial discord unless husbands are also active participants, reveals another aspect of the fragility of empowerment that depends on changing women's attitudes or roles without changing men's as well. One suspects that further research on Pentecostals will reveal similar conflicts where women's expansion of their religious roles is opposed by nonbelieving spouses. It will be interesting to see whether Pentecostal women respond to these conflicts in much the same way as women in the CEBs.

Finally, the contrast between women's experiences and expansion of power in Pentecostal groups and CEBs suggests that just how a religion opens the possibility of gender equality may be crucially important to how women gain power. Both groups have some notion of religious equality between the sexes. As we have seen, however, Pentecostalism is more likely (at least until recently) to stress domestic equality and generally deemphasizes public activism for both men and women. CEBs, in contrast, have tended to ignore family issues and posit a unisex standard for Christian activism. This difference in emphasis appears to parallel the different ways in which women reconceptualize their roles, with Pentecostal women rethinking private life and CEB women rethinking the possibilities of public life.

Evidence regarding Pentecostalism's impact on women's lives remains scarce, however, and given the religion's growth and the large numbers of women attracted to it, the topic deserves continued attention. In particular, Pentecostalism's impact on women's status and well-being in the family deserves further analysis. An implicit debate has emerged over whether Pentecostalism's domestication of men truly enhances women's power in the home or whether Pentecostal women purchase greater male responsibility in the family through submission.[81] More systematic attention should be paid to the specific ways in which Pentecostalism bolsters women's equality and status and the possible limitations on those changes.

In addition, in view of the diverse responses of Catholic women to the opportunities presented by CEBs, future studies of Pentecostal women would do well to ask whether there are not greater differences among them than have so far been suggested. The portrait of Pentecostal women that has emerged is much less differentiated than what we know of women in the CEBs. Yet Pentecostalism certainly offers women opportunities to reinterpret their roles in nontraditional ways. Lawless shows that North American Pentecostal women preachers utilize their religious calling to forge independent, nontraditional roles.[82] Dixon's and Mariz and Machado's examples of Pentecostal women's challenging, separating from, or divorcing "ungodly" spouses suggest the potential of Pentecostalism for defining new limits of independence and submissiveness. Where are the women who take advantage of the opportunity to do so?

If nontraditional Pentecostal women exist, then a whole new line of research must be opened to find the variables that account for intragroup differences in response. Possibilities suggested by the CEBs include personal history, religious imagination, and perhaps socioeconomic factors.[83] As Mariz and Machado note, social class is almost certainly an important explanatory variable, and attention must also be paid to differences in local leadership and group structure.[84] If Pentecostals are more uniform than CEB members, this may suggest that conversion religions produce more uniformity of belief than those that, like CEBs, are basically continuous with existing identities and belief systems.[85] Alternatively, analysis might focus on factors that might affect women's ability to challenge gender roles. For example, some evidence suggests that CEB members are more financially secure than Pentecostals and freer from problems such as alcoholism that undermine family stability.[86] Perhaps only women in secure financial and family situations can take advantage of opportunities to expand their roles, while others benefit most directly from greater control in the household.

Future research on Pentecostalism and gender must also address the direction of causality at work in these religious groups. Most research has suggested, at least implicitly, that religion influences the way people think about gender roles. It is also possible, however, that women join religious groups precisely because these confirm their preexisting beliefs about gender roles. Mariz and Machado's report of women's choosing a church partly in terms of the strictness of its gender code suggests the latter. Religious groups may still play an important role in consolidating and acting on these beliefs. Women in the CEBs, for example, sometimes claim that the church provided their first viable opportunity for political involvement. Nonetheless, causality remains an important theoretical issue.

Inevitably, as Pentecostalism is compared with traditional and CEB Catholicism, the question of which is "better" for women will be raised. Pentecostalism's contribution to women's domestic power may seem conservative compared with CEBs' "progressive" inclusion of women in the public sphere. Yet domestic equality may provide a strong basis for conquering new roles, while CEB women's public leadership now seems to be promoting a rethinking of equality in general. It may be that each is performing a necessary function, changing a particular bit of hegemonic gender ideology in such a way that women's empowerment in both realms can gradually be expanded for women of all religious denominations. Moreover, the two can be seen as similar in providing women greater motivation and legitimation for autonomy, individuation, and action outside their domestic roles without directly challenging those roles. This can be considered a feminist project, if not one in the mainstream of liberal feminism.

Latin American Pentecostalism and CEBs are provocative evidence that even ostensibly patriarchal religions do not always or only oppress women. They almost always contain at least some elements that women can seize and use for their own empowerment. The evidence to date suggests that Pentecostal women have been particularly successful in gaining power within the private realm. As their belief in their personal equality grows, they may yet expand their exercise of public power as well. Cornelia Butler Flora observed twenty years ago that Pentecostalism gave women the skills and confidence to work publicly for social change but denied the legitimacy of either men's or women's doing so.[87] Whether Pentecostal women now capitalize on their gains to move into the public sphere as their sisters in the CEBs have done may depend largely on whether their religion provides them a motive and justification for doing so.

NOTES

1. On Pentecostalism and women in Latin America, see John Burdick, "Gossip and Secrecy: Women's Articulation of Domestic Conflict in Three Religions of Urban Brazil," *Sociological Analysis* 51, 2 (1990), pp. 153–170; Elizabeth Brusco, "The Reformation of Machismo: Asceticism and Masculinity Among Colombian Evangelicals," in Virginia Garrard-Burnett and David Stoll, eds., *Rethinking Protestantism in Latin America* (Philadelphia: Temple University Press, 1993); Leslie Gill, " 'Like a Veil to Cover Them': Women and the Pentecostal Movement in La Paz," *American Ethnologist* 17, 4 (1990), pp. 708–721; and Myrna Van den Eykel, "A Comparative Study of the Political and Social Activism of New Religious Groups in Colombia," Ph.D. diss., George Washington University, 1986. The earliest comparative work is Cornelia Butler Flora, "Pentecostal Women in Colombia: Religious Change and the Status of Working-Class Women," *Journal of Interamerican Studies and World Affairs* 17, 4 (1975), pp. 411–424.

2. Elizabeth Brusco, "The Household Basis of Evangelical Religion and the Reformation of Machismo in Colombia," Ph.D. diss., City University of New York, 1986; Cecília L. Mariz, "Religion and Coping with Poverty in Brazil," Ph.D. diss., Boston University, 1989; Gill, " 'Like a Veil.' "

3. Tim B. Heaton and Marie Cornwall, "Religious Group Variation in the Socio-economic Status and Family Behavior of Women," *Journal for the Scientific Study of Religion* 28, 3 (1989), p. 285.

4. Sheila Briggs, "Women and Religion," in Beth B. Hess and Myra Marx Ferree, eds. *Analyzing Gender: A Handbook of Social Science Research* (Beverly Hills, Calif.: Sage, 1987), p. 408. Several works address this aspect of change tangentially. On women in Christian base communities, see Carol Ann Drogus, "Religion, Gender, and Political Culture: Attitudes and Participation in Brazilian Basic Christian Communities," Ph.D. diss., University of Wisconsin–Madison, 1991; John Burdick, "Gossip and Secrecy." On Protestant women, see Burdick, "Gossip and Secrecy"; Brusco, "The Household Basis"; Van den Eykel, "A Comparative Study."

5. See, for example, Elaine J. Lawless, *God's Peculiar People: Women's Voices and Folk Tradition in a Pentecostal Church* (Lexington: University of Kentucky Press, 1988). See also Lawless, *Handmaidens of the Lord: Pentecostal Women Preachers and Traditional Religion* (Philadelphia: University of Pennsylvania Press, 1988).

6. The section on CEBs relies heavily on my own study of women in São Paulo, one of only a few to look explicitly and systematically at gender issues. This may bias the interpretation of CEBs, because São Paulo's CEBs are unusually liberationist and probably more likely than other such groups to encourage women's political activism. CEBs closer to traditional Catholic models are less likely to be a source of *new* ideas or roles for women. Since I focus on religious change and its impact on changing gender roles, the choice of Brazilian CEBs, precisely because they do depart from traditional Catholic models, seems warranted. I do include information from studies of CEBs in other countries to achieve a more balanced portrait.

7. Brusco, "The Household Basis," p. 149.

8. Evelyn P. Stevens, "*Marianismo*: The Other Face of Machismo in Latin America," in Ann Pescatello, ed., *Female and Male in Latin America* (Pittsburgh: University of Pittsburgh Press, 1973); Maxine Molyneux, "Mobilization Without Emancipation? Women's Interests, the State, and Revolution in Nicaragua," *Feminist Studies* 11, 2 (1985),

pp. 227–254; and Shulamit Goldsmit and Ernest Sweeney, "The Church and Latin American Women in Their Struggle for Equality and Justice," *Thought* 63, 249 (1988), pp. 176–188. By "traditional Catholicism" I mean both preconciliar and popular Catholicism, that is, the official doctrine and instruction of the Catholic church prior to the reforms of the Second Vatican Council (1962–1965) and the unofficial folk religion practiced by the urban and rural poor.

9. Brusco, "The Household Basis."

10. Salvatore Cucchiari, "Between Shame and Sanctification: Patriarchy and Its Transformation in Sicilian Pentecostalism," *American Ethnologist* 17, 4 (1990), p. 688.

11. David Martin, *Tongues of Fire: The Explosion of Protestantism in Latin America* (Oxford and Cambridge, Mass.: Basil Blackwell, 1990), p. 220.

12. She suggests that this emphasis may result from women's early involvement in directing the Pentecostal churches. Brusco, "The Household Basis."

13. Brusco, "The Household Basis," p. 218.

14. Flora, "Pentecostal Women," p. 415.

15. Van den Eykel, "A Comparative Study," p. 328.

16. Burdick, "Gossip and Secrecy," p. 163.

17. Van den Eykel, "A Comparative Study," pp. 327–328.

18. Flora, "Pentecostal Women," p. 416.

19. Van den Eykel, "A Comparative Study," p. 337; Flora, "Pentecostal Women," p. 92.

20. Lawless, *Handmaidens of the Lord,* pp. 145–146.

21. Stevens, "*Marianismo:* The Other Face," p. 95.

22. Cucchiari, "Between Shame and Sanctification," p. 703.

23. Ibid.

24. Brusco, "The Household Basis," p. 216.

25. Brusco, "The Household Basis," p. 212.

26. Flora, "Pentecostal Women," p. 424.

27. Ibid, p. 418.

28. Martin, *Tongues of Fire,* p. 166.

29. Flora, "Pentecostal Women," p. 418.

30. *Latinamerica Press* 25, 4 (1993), p. 2. As Mariz and Machado note in this volume, the Igreja Universal do Reino de Deus began ordaining women pastors in 1993.

31. Frederick J. Conway, "Pentecostalism in Haiti: Healing and Hierarchy," in Stephen D. Glazier, ed., *Perspectives on Pentecostalism: Case Studies from the Caribbean and Latin America* (Washington, D.C.: University Press of America, 1980), pp. 21–22; Regina Novaes, *Os escolhidos de Deus: Pentecostais, trabalhadores e cidadania* (São Paulo: Marco Zero, 1985), p. 58, n. 17.

32. Mariz, "Religion and Coping," p. 148.

33. Conway, "Pentecostalism in Haiti," pp. 21–22.

34. Cucchiari, "Between Shame and Sanctification," p. 703. Cucchiari's study is based on a Sicilian case, but most studies of Latin American Pentecostals also describe women's participation in spirit experiences.

35. Brusco, "The Household Basis," p. 216; Rowan Ireland, *Kingdoms Come: Religion and Politics in Brazil* (Pittsburgh: University of Pittsburgh Press, 1991).

36. Brusco, "The Household Basis," p. 212.

37. Gabriele Kohpahl, "Facing the World with Spiritual Life: Neo-Pentecostalism in Guatemala," Master's thesis, University of California–Los Angeles, 1989.

38. Van den Eykel, "A Comparative Study," p. 331.

39. Ibid., p. 232.

40. See Novaes, *Os escolhidos de Deus,* on leadership and Brusco, "The Household Basis," and Ireland, *Kingdoms Come,* on women active in gender-segregated groups. A network of Latin American women theologians and pastors now claims four hundred members, but it is unclear how many of these may be Pentecostals. *Latinamerica Press* 25, 4 (December 6, 1993), p. 2.

41. Novaes, *Os escolhidos de Deus,* p. 77.

42. Mariz, "Religion and Coping"; David E. Dixon, "Popular Culture, Popular Identity, and the Rise of Latin American Protestantism: Voices from Santiago *Poblacional,*" Paper presented to the 17th International Congress of the Latin American Studies Association, Los Angeles, Calif., September 23–27, 1992.

43. June E. Hahner, *Emancipating the Female Sex: The Struggle for Women's Rights in Brazil, 1850–1940* (Durham, N.C.: Duke University Press, 1990), p. 203.

44. Specifically, there is little difference between women from Protestant denominations that support women's participation and women from Catholic and Protestant groups that do not. See Van den Eykel, "A Comparative Study."

45. This argument is clearly and fully explicated in Brusco, "The Household Basis." Other research reaching the same conclusion includes Burdick, "Gossip and Secrecy"; Liliana R. Goldin and Brent Metz, "An Expression of Cultural Change: Invisible Converts to Protestantism Among Highland Guatemala Mayas," *Ethnology* 30 (1991), pp. 325–338.

46. Goldin and Metz, "An Expression of Cultural Change," p. 328.

47. Burdick, "Gossip and Secrecy," p. 164.

48. Dixon, "Popular Culture, Popular Identity," pp. 20–21.

49. Emilio Willems, *Followers of the New Faith: Culture Change and the Rise of Protestantism in Brazil and Chile* (Nashville, Tenn.: Vanderbilt University Press, 1967).

50. Brusco, "The Household Basis," 200.

51. Novaes, *Os escolhidos de Deus;* Brusco, "The Household Basis"; Burdick, "Gossip and Secrecy."

52. Van den Eykel, "A Comparative Study," pp. 326–327.

53. Brusco, "The Household Basis." Perhaps the earliest study to strike this note, however, is Willems, *Followers of the New Faith.*

54. Van den Eykel, "A Comparative Study," p. 337.

55. Willems, *Followers of the New Faith;* Brusco, "The Household Basis" and "The Reformation of Machismo"; Van den Eykel, "A Comparative Study"; Gill, "Like a Veil." For non–Latin American examples that support this claim, see Cucchiari, "Between Shame and Sanctification", Charles W. Peek, George D. Lowe, and L. Susan Williams, "Gender and God's Word: Another Look at Religious Fundamentalism and Sexism," *Social Forces* 69, 4 (1991), pp. 1205–1222.

56. Dixon, "Popular Culture, Popular Identity," p. 26.

57. Only the Foursquare Gospel is Pentecostal, but Van den Eykel does not suggest any evidence of a difference between the two groups. Van den Eykel, "A Comparative Study."

58. Van den Eykel, "A Comparative Study," pp. 340–341.

59. Merlin B. Brinkerhoff and Marlene M. MacKie, "Religious Denominations' Impact upon Gender Attitudes: Some Methodological Implications," *Review of Religious Research* 25, 4 (1984), pp. 365–378.

60. Flora also notes that the reconceptualization of men's roles under Pentecostalism is clearer and more dramatic than that of women's. Flora, "Pentecostal Women," pp. 414–415.

61. Burdick, "Gossip and Secrecy," p. 160.

62. Mariz, "Religion and Coping."

63. Sonia Alvarez, "Women's Participation in the Brazilian 'People's Church': A Critical Appraisal," *Feminist Studies* 16, 2 (1990), p. 388. Male liberation theologians have begun to include women in the list of oppressed and to discuss sexism, but the essentially marxist basis of their analysis remains unchanged. In an effort to recognize women's rights within the church, however, Leonardo Boff argued that there is no decisive argument against the ordination of women. See Paul Sigmund, *Liberation Theology at the Crossroads: Democracy or Revolution?* (New York: Oxford University Press, 1990), p. 84.

64. Madeleine Adriance, "Daughters of Judith: Feminist Consciousness in Rural Base Communities in Brazil," paper presented at the annual meeting of the Society for the Scientific Study of Religion, Raleigh, N.C., October 29–31, 1993.

65. Carol Ann Drogus, "Reconstructing the Feminine: Women in São Paulo's CEBs," *Archives de Sciences Sociales des Religions* 71 (1990), pp. 63–74.

66. Carol Ann Drogus, *We Are Women Making History: Political Participation in São Paulo's CEBs,* University of Wisconsin–Milwaukee Center for Latin America Discussion Paper 81 (1988).

67. Van den Eykel, "A Comparative Study," p. 317; Drogus, "Religion, Gender, and Political Culture."

68. This interpretation is based on unpublished transcripts of interviews conducted by Rede Mulher in 1984 and 1985. I am grateful for access to this material.

69. Carol Ann Drogus, "Popular Movements and the Limits of Political Mobilization at the Grassroots in Brazil," in Hannah Stewart-Gambino and Edward Cleary, eds., *Conflict and Competition: The Latin American Church in a Changing Environment* (Boulder: Lynne Rienner, 1992), p. 82.

70. Mariz, "Religion and Coping," pp. 195–196.

71. Drogus, "Religion, Gender, and Political Culture."

72. On political attitudes and activity specifically, see Drogus, "Religion, Gender, and Political Culture," chap. 7.

73. Ibid.

74. Drogus, "Reconstructing the Feminine."

75. Interview, São Paulo, August 4–8, 1986.

76. Catherine Ferguson, "The Poor in Politics: Social Change and Basic Church Communities in Santiago, Lima, and Mexico City," Ph.D. diss., University of Denver, 1990.

77. Adriance, "Daughters of Judith," p. 15.

78. Mariz, "Religion and Coping," p. 196.

79. Cucchiari, "Between Shame and Sanctification," p. 693.

80. Ibid., p. 688.

81. The sides of the debate are represented by Brusco, Willems, and Van den Eykel, on the one hand, and Burdick, on the other.

82. Lawless, *Handmaidens of the Lord.*

83. Drogus, "Religion, Gender, and Political Culture."

84. Daniel Levine has argued that in CEBs, differences can be accounted for by the attitudes of local pastoral workers and connections to larger church structures. Daniel H. Levine, *Popular Voices in Latin American Catholicism* (Princeton: Princeton University Press, 1992). Similarly, Pentecostal groups seem to be strongly shaped by local pastoral leaders, and there is some evidence that whether or not they are connected to a larger

church organization affects their theology, political attitudes, and so on. Ireland, *Kingdoms Come.*

85. Other hypotheses relating to the religious groups rather than the characteristics of members should also be investigated. Ireland, for example, suggests that different types of Pentecostal groups—established churches versus breakaway sects—have quite different potentials for political rebelliousness. Ireland, *Kingdoms Come.* Another hypothesis suggested by the available evidence is that the degree of women's predominance is a key. See Francis B. O'Connor, *Like Bread, Their Voices Rise: Global Women Challenge the Church* (Notre Dame, Ind.: Ave Maria, 1993). Although both Pentecostals and CEBs are predominantly female, the Pentecostals generally appear to be more gender-balanced, and this difference may explain Pentecostal women's reluctance to challenge gender stereotypes.

86. Mariz, "Religion and Coping."

87. Flora, "Pentecostal Women," p. 424.

❀ **5** ❀

Interchurch Relations: Exclusion, Ecumenism, and the Poor

GUILLERMO COOK

$\mathcal{A}$re Pentecostals ecumenical? Only a few years ago this question would have been considered pointless, and many students of Pentecostalism may still so consider it. Most Latin American Pentecostals are suspicious of the term "ecumenical." At the same time, the extent of their relationships with other Christians and, in some cases, non-Christians is remarkable.

As other chapters in this volume make clear, Pentecostalism is not a uniform phenomenon. Like any other human experience, religion is affected by historical and cultural factors and by social class and personal history. The Troeltschian and Weberian models of religious organization help one discern the movement of Pentecostal groups from sects to established churches. Young Pentecostal churches are impelled by a zeal to convert everyone, including fellow Protestant Christians (not to mention Roman Catholics), to the experience of Baptism in the Holy Spirit. Although there is a tendency toward exclusivism, sectarian movements can be breeding grounds for radical social experiments that in time may open them up to the world at large. Pentecostals are no exception. The experiments in interchurch relations that I shall document here, although certainly more characteristic of a later, more organized and "intellectual" phase of the movement (at least as far as the leadership of the movement is concerned), have their roots in Pentecostal theology and experience.

Pentecostal churches and denominations have participated for years in intra-Protestant ecumenical activities. Pentecostals were the backbone of nationwide programs such as Evangelism-in-Depth, which brought together thousands of evangelical Christians in ten Latin American countries from the late 1950s to the early 1970s. Pentecostals have been the key players in citywide evangelistic crusades with prominent preachers. They are indispensable participants in American

Bible Society distribution programs and increasingly occupy important positions on the local boards of this ecumenical agency.

Even when they have not headed them, Pentecostals have worked closely with conservative social action agencies in several Latin American nations. More recently, they have been the key leaders in COMIBAM, a notable missionary movement from Latin America to the larger world. These activities, however, have been largely overlooked by ecumenists and students of Protestantism, who have failed to perceive their significance.[1] The focus of most research has been, up until recently, on the negative features of Pentecostalism.

The phenomenal growth of the Pentecostal churches in Latin America has been the object of study by sociologists and of concern on the part of the Catholic and historical Protestant churches. Everett Wilson comments that "social scientists . . . are apparently more willing than religious observers to recognize the indigenous and reconstructive character of Pentecostalism. Ironically, the very features anthropologists tend to commend require the emphasis on subjective experience, freedom of action, and view of reality that non-Pentecostal evangelicals [and "ecumenicals," I might add] are likely to reject!"[2] Another observer comments that although "the phenomenon is a growing concern to the Roman Catholic Church—long dominant in the region—and among 'mainline' or 'historic' Protestant churches . . . its relevance to the ecumenical movement has not yet been fully explored."[3]

That ecumenical implications of the Pentecostal experience have not been entirely overlooked by the ecumenical movement and even from that of a few Pentecostals was demonstrated by the 1988 World Council of Churches (WCC)–Latin American Pentecostal Consultation in Salvador, Brazil. Since that consultation, ecumenical reflection and dialogue have increased not only through the auspices of agencies such as the WCC and the Consejo Latinamericano de Iglesias (Latin American Council of Churches—CLAI) but also with encouragement from evangelical entities such as World Vision.

One cannot blame Pentecostals for their hesitancy to enter upon this process. Aside from their well-known free-church suspicion of "superchurches" and their believers'-church concern for maintaining the boundary between commitment to Gospel fundamentals, and lack of it,[4] Pentecostals are intensely aware that non-Pentecostals of all stripes have often built walls around themselves that have effectively excluded Pentecostals.

Elitist Prejudice and Pentecostal Exclusion

Over the years, imperfect understanding of the Pentecostal movement in Latin America and around the world has led to stereotypes that have contributed to Pentecostal isolation. Many observers have tended to think of Pentecostalism both as a religion of the alienated and as alienating in itself. Statements such as the following, obtained through extensive interviews by Gordon Spykman and the Calvin Center with grass-roots Pentecostals in Central America, have seemed to support this perspective: "Brothers, this life is of little value, and it gives us nothing. But since we know Christ Jesus, we must build him a church so that we can place our burdens, our lives in His hands. I am poor, but we are rich in the Lord. God is preparing us for that place for which he will rapture us to be with Him forever."[5] In other words, Pentecostals have seemed too preoccupied with the next world to be concerned about relationships in this one. However, the same research has documented the active involvement of countless grass-roots Pentecostals in movements of resistance and social change, together with Catholics, Protestants, and professed atheists.[6]

Christian Lalive d'Epinay's WCC-commissioned study of Chilean Pentecostalism concluded that Pentecostal communities were "havens of the masses," thus implying a kind of otherworldly escapism. David Martin, a sociologist, employs the image of a "new cell taking over from scarred and broken tissue,"[7] within which familial, communal, and ecclesial ties are renewed, women are protected "from the ravages of male desertion and violence," new disciplines are implanted, and priorities are reordered. "Within the enclosed haven of faith a fraternity can be instituted under firm leadership, which provides for release, for mutuality and warmth, and for the practice of new roles."[8] This incipient mutuality has the potential for widening relationships with other sisters and brothers.

From their earliest beginnings, Pentecostals have been dismissed by the mainline denominations as sects, implying a lack of ecclesial validity. During the 1980s it was fashionable to link Pentecostals, directly or indirectly, with a conservative United States political agenda. David Stoll has argued that this form of condescension, coming from radical groups involved with the poor, overlooked the creativity of popular religious movements in adapting foreign religious elements to their own use.[9] Martin defends the historical validity of sectarian movements, such as the Anabaptists, the Methodists, the Quakers, and the Swedenborgians, which have often have been the seedbeds of radical change.[10]

Pentecostals' sectarianism, then, may be a necessary function of their search for identity. As they grow in numbers and maturity, Martin suggests, Pentecostals will become more secure and perhaps more aware of their social responsibilities.[11] And social involvement is one of the chief routes to ecumenical awareness. Indeed, ecumenism is already apparent, broadly speaking (though the term may never be used) at the two extremes of the movement—among the highest leadership, ecclesiastical leaders and theologians, and at the very grass roots of religious life, where it is multifaceted, experiential, and even interfaith. Ecumenical contacts are less in evidence at the intermediate levels of Pentecostal life—the local denominational hierarchy and the upwardly mobile and prosperity-conscious Pentecostal laity. But, as with everything else in Latin America, even this is subject to change. Seen from another perspective, the incipient Pentecostal ecumenism is a function of several interacting factors: poverty and systemic violence, Pentecostal growth, popular religiosity, professional contacts, and overtures from mainline churches.

Pentecostal Unity in the Spirit

Before moving on to more sociological dimensions of Pentecostal ecumenism, it is important to emphasize that the church's pneumatic (Spirit-centered) theology is centered on a firm belief in the unity of all true believers in Jesus Christ through the action of the Spirit of Jesus. The scriptural passages that speak of that unity are, for Pentecostals, indispensable.[12] Christian unity, for Pentecostals, is a theological fact based upon the unity of the Trinity, the present and future hope that drives them, both a factor in and a requirement for the growth of the church, and—for an increasing number of perceptive leaders—an imperative in the contemporary era of the divine kairós.[13] This unity works in two directions. Pentecostals have much to contribute, including an intense experience of community and a new emphasis on the universal priesthood of the believer,[14] but they are challenged to show humility and repentance as well:

> The Lord himself has slapped us in the face because of our earlier exclusivism and spiritual pride. He has taught us that His Kingdom is not enclosed within the walls of temples where we speak in tongues and prophecy. . . . As Ezekiel 37 states and Jesus said in John 3, the Spirit blows from the four winds, and we don't know from whence He comes and where He is going. For too long we have thought of ourselves as the salt among "corrupt" churches. Although it is true that in our beginnings we were a renewing force in the midst of a flickering and rationalistic Christianity, now is the time to place ourselves, with our strengths and spirituality, at the service of the Oikoumene—not, however, as superior teachers but as brothers and sisters and fellow servants.[15]

Evangelicals and ecumenicals alike agree that "what Pentecostals are offering to the ecumenical movement is a *spirituality* of ecumenism—a universal rediscovery of the Spirit for all Christian denominations." It is "an emphasis on the experience of the Holy Spirit and of God's presence and work wherever the Spirit wishes."[16]

Erudite Pentecostals and Ecumenical Awareness

Since the earliest days of the International Missionary Council, Pentecostal leaders such as Donald Gee of England (at the Edinburgh Conference in 1910) and David duPlessis of South Africa (at the Willingen Conference in 1952) extended tentative hands of fellowship to the ecumenical movement. At the New Delhi WCC Assembly, two Chilean Pentecostal groups were admitted to membership:

the Iglesia Pentecostal de Chile and the Misión Iglesia Pentecostal. There was not, however, widespread sympathy for these initiatives.[17] DuPlessis went on to initiate Pentecostal contacts with the Vatican. This top-level dialogue had no noticeable impact, however, upon interchurch relations in Latin America.

Over the past quarter-century, a growing number of Pentecostal leaders in Europe, United States, and Latin America have ventured outside of their own Bible colleges and theological institutes to undertake more advanced studies in theology, missiology, and the social sciences. Already the effects of this can be seen in the cautiously positive attitude of some denominational leaders toward interchurch contacts and theological dialogue. In Latin America a handful of Pentecostal churches have joined the ecumenical movement at either the international or the local level.[18]

The move from a sectarian self-identity toward an ecumenical perspective, argues Cheryl Bridges Johns, a past president of the Society for Pentecostal Studies and a participant in the Catholic-Pentecostal dialogue, is a function of the maturation of the Pentecostal movement. Her analysis has relevance for an understanding of ecumenical relations in Latin America. Pentecostalism, she judges, is moving out of a turbulent adolescence into adulthood. In its infancy at the beginning of the century, the movement represented a radical subculture that was pacifist, ordained women for the ministry, and brought blacks and whites together for worship long before any of this was acceptable in the historical churches. Early Pentecostals understood that they had a dual prophetic role: to denounce the religious status quo and to announce the norms of the new divine order that were being worked out within their separated groups. But they were denounced, derided, and marginalized as sects by the mainstream churches. This rejection, says Johns, however hurtful, did contribute to enhancing a Pentecostal ecumenical awareness. Rejection only served to cement family relations "in the Spirit" inside the movement. At the same time, Pentecostals opened themselves up to the world in evangelism and acts of social compassion. All of this was preparation for the eventual extension of family boundaries.[19]

Another generation of Pentecostals, acutely aware of their marginalization, felt the need to relate to other Christians and to be accepted by them. Gradually, Pentecostals gained grudging though never full acceptance from their mainstream brothers and sisters. Even as speaking in tongues and other controversial gifts became less and less divisive—and through the charismatic-renewal movement, even acceptable—Pentecostals found that they remained social outsiders. A collective sense of shame caused Pentecostals to ape the manners of their religious "betters," even to the point of joining them in doctrinal controversies such as modernism versus fundamentalism that were not inherently part of the Pentecostal ethos. The price for acceptance was accommodation to the status quo. Pentecostals, says Bridges, were co-opted by the system.

But even while the Pentecostal movement seemed to be desperately searching for acceptance, a new generation of Pentecostal leaders had begun to call it to account. The road less traveled, the only way out for Pentecostalism, Bridges concludes, was to accept its sectarian status and turn it into an instrument for integration and transformation.[20]

Changing Self-Awareness in Latin America

This new self-awareness has begun to affect some Latin American Pentecostal intellectuals. "In the 1960s some churches began a critical process which includes openness and participation with other churches."[21] Two ecumenical gatherings, the First and Second Latin American Evangelical Conferences (in 1961 and 1965)[22] produced the Unión Evangélica en América Latina (Evangelical Union in Latin America—UNELAM). This new movement "showed an openness to the Pentecostal churches with an invitation to participate actively in the ecumenical movement. Some churches accepted the challenge."[23] At the third such conference a committee was appointed to convene the founding assembly of the CLAI in Oaxtepec, Mexico, in 1978. In this meeting leaders played a decisive role:

> Many Pentecostal churches were not only open to participate, but willing to vote in favor of this new conciliar experience. Many historic churches left with doubts about the future of CLAI, but the Pentecostals who initiated the process in Oaxtepec [returned] to ratify the new council in Huampaní [Peru], in 1982. . . . Pentecostals who stayed in CLAI were convinced of the importance of this historic step in the search for unity in our continent. Working with them has constituted a unique experience of a positive attitude toward the ecumenical cause.[24]

It is important to point out, however, that the leaders who joined the CLAI were representatives of only one of three streams in the Latin American Pentecostal movement. Immigrant churches with European roots such as the Congregação Cristã do Brazil (of Italian Waldensian extraction) and missionary churches such as the Assemblies of God and the Full Gospel Church of God (which came from the United States and still depend to some degree on North America initiatives) have been largely suspicious of the ecumenical movement and even more hostile to the Roman Catholic church.

The Pentecostal churches that have been more open to the ecumenical movement are the national churches with deep roots in Latin American soil. Chief among them are the Pentecostal Church of Chile, which joined the WCC in 1961; the Evangelical Union of Venezuela, which was founded in 1956 by a group of dissident Assemblies of God pastors united by a desire to leave sectarian attitudes behind; the Church of God in Argentina, whose president, Dr. Gabriel Vaccaro, held high positions in both the WCC and the CLAI; and the Christian Church of Cuba. Each of these pioneer churches has established fraternal ties with ecumenical churches in Latin America and the United States.[25]

Yet probably more significant than the official ecumenical ties of a handful of Pentecostal groups are the informal ways in which independent Pentecostal congregations are beginning to relate to other Christians and to learn from them. As one Catholic observer notes:

> While evangelical churches occasionally work together on large campaigns, especially around visiting evangelists, they tend to see one another as rivals on a day-to-day basis. One of the more interesting examples of such collaboration I have encountered is in-service courses given to pastors, in which those trained in more liberal traditions often help independent Pentecostal pastors come to a more sophisticated understanding of the scripture and a more self-critical approach to their own ministry.[26]

Charismatic Renewal

The charismatic-renewal movement, which erupted in U.S. mainline Protestant and Catholic churches during the 1970s, produced an incipient ecumenism in the years immediately following in places such as Argentina, Brazil, Ecuador, and Costa Rica. Christians from Pentecostal, evangelical, mainline Protestant, and Roman Catholic churches worshiped freely together for a few years[27] before extraneous forces from each theological stream nipped this spontaneous ecumenical movement in the bud. Conservative Pentecostals sought to impose a fundamentalist and authoritarian interpretation of the renewal, evangelicals were eager to convert Catholics, mainline Protestants snubbed the movement for its lack of social concern, and the Vatican placed it under stricter hierarchical control.

Fundamentalist groups from the United States stepped into the vacuum and denatured the original message of the renewal. What was once a small movement concerned with a holistic communication of the Gospel—including to some degree the good news for the poor—became the "prosperity gospel."[28] This is the phenomenon that the Catholic and mainline Protestant churches have labeled, with some cause, "the sects," unfortunately applying the same label to a much broader range of Pentecostals.

Middle-class charismatics in Latin America practice a pragmatic ecumenism at the political level. Political parties are being formed in a number of countries that bring together Protestants and Catholics around a common conservative political agenda. Whether these initiatives will prove significant remains to be seen. Everett Wilson is probably correct when he insists that right-wing movements are not representative of the majority of Pentecostals.[29]

Thus, various forces—among them scholarly dialogue at the leadership level of church unity movements and middle-class Pentecostal political awareness—have worked to increase the ecumenical awareness of conservative Pentecostals.

Probably the most decisive factor, however, has been Latin America's appalling sociocultural malaise. This crisis is compounded of unequal distribution of land, capital losses to wealthy nations, huge masses of displaced people, an unpayable foreign debt, hundreds of thousands of street children, corrupt politicians, festering shantytowns, drug cartels, spiraling violence, and deadly epidemics. This is the social context of the "Protestant explosion" in Latin America. Extreme poverty and Pentecostalism, both growing, now overlap. Mass movement that it is, Pentecostalism shares the plight of the rest of the masses in Latin America.

Ecumenism and the Poor

A younger generation of Latin American Pentecostals is letting its voice be heard in international forums.[30] In 1985, the Church of God (Cleveland, Tenn.) convened a Pentecostal Consultation of Liberation Theology in Río Piedras, Puerto Rico. It was my privilege to attend, along with forty-five church leaders from northern Latin America. The conference, which preceded a worldwide congress on the Holy Spirit, was an open-minded one. From various perspectives, the speakers—all but myself Pentecostals—discussed the pros and cons of liberation theology for their church and mission.[31]

The social awareness of a significant number of the new-generation leaders was evident. Two presenters were perhaps typical of the distinct approaches to ecumenism that can be found in Pentecostalism. One was appreciative of the ecumenical movement although firmly Pentecostal and evangelical; the other is now the general secretary of COMIBAM, a Latin American missionary movement to the Third World that involves conservative Protestants from a broad range of evangelical churches.

The national churches that are most open to ecumenical relationships are those that are most aware of the plight of the poor and the structural dimensions of sin. Their proximity to the worsening plight of the impoverished masses moves growing numbers of Pentecostal churches to sometimes quite radical responses. One such response was that of the Unión Evangélica Pentecostal Venezolana (UEPV), which in 1987, published a pastoral letter to fellow Christians in an attempt to clarify a misunderstanding regarding its nature and mission: "We shall not deny that we are a 'believers' church' and a church of the poor. Our churches are made up of peasants, indigenous peoples, workers, students, and unemployed. This is the reality of our church. It is also the reality of the immense majority of Venezuelans."[32] The letter went on to outline the main characteristics of the UEPV: that it has opted for the poor, that it practices ecumenism, that it is not tied to any political party, and that it is, above all, Pentecostal. It points to the church's ties with other churches and ecumenical service agencies and concludes:

> We do not deny our identity with these actions. But we do affirm that we are not sectarian. Sects are hermetically closed and dogmatic groups that believe that they pos-

sess the absolute truth and are closed to dialogue. We believe in the ecumenical spirit that calls us to Christian fellowship, to interconfessional dialogue, and that impels us to accept each another as members of the same body—the Universal Church. . . . We shall continue to affirm our openness to dialogue . . . while maintaining our Pentecostal peculiarities.[33]

Ecumenism and Systemic Change

People who live in violent societies have a remarkable capacity for adaptation. New awareness and defense mechanisms appear that often have the effect of drawing diverse peoples together against a common threat. Such has been the case in Latin America, where ultraconservative Protestants and "progressives" have set aside their theological and ideological differences for a common, usually conservative, cause. When the identity of "the enemy" changes or new challenges appear, a new self-awareness requires new strategies. In Chile, for example, after the return to formal democracy, the leaders (mostly Pentecostal) of two ideologically competing interchurch councils agreed to work together to coordinate their approach to social and political involvement and chose a respected evangelical Anglican archbishop to lead them.

In several Central American countries, guerrilla and military violence has left thousands of peasants and indigenous people dead or injured. Perhaps the only positive side effect of this situation has been the breakdown, at the grass roots, of divisions between Christians, Protestants and Catholic. In the words of one spokesperson,

> What God is doing amidst his people really escapes our theological comprehension . . . especially among the base of the Christian Community. . . . This eagerness for liberty, this enthusiasm for building a new society, this revolution, is evangelizing the church. This may seem like heresy, but today it is the truth. Never before have we seen how evangelical Christians and Catholics can meet together in a village of the highlands to celebrate their faith, because there are no longer ministers nor priests in this zone.[34]

In the midst of hopelessness, the Christian faith without barriers has brought hope to the peasants of Guatemala, El Salvador, Honduras, and Nicaragua. At the height of the violence, many of them met secretly in ecumenical base communities in such numbers that it exceeded "the limits and technical capabilities" of the support groups. "A people which . . . had been silent and bent over . . . [has] overcome this situation to rise up proudly amidst the pain, with hope." Observers called it "a miracle . . . of God."[35]

The reality that this reflects is that of the Christian base communities (*comunidades eclesiales de base*—CEBs). In the 1980s a kind of Protestant base community began to appear in Central America in the context of popular insurrection and violent governmental repression. Protestants—whether Pentecostals, evangelicals, or members of historical churches—tend to be very conservative in this region, but despite—or because of—this ecumenical CEBs have appeared in modest numbers, particularly in Guatemala.[36] Members of the ecumenical base communities that I have been able to observe, Catholic or Protestant, contribute valuable elements from their respective traditions. Pentecostals bring their fervor, evangelicals their emphasis on the written Word, and Catholics a stress on critical reflection in a rich liturgical context.

Congregation and Base Communities

Although CEBs and Pentecostals have often been counterposed by students of comparative religious phenomena, the truth is that both movements inhabit the same symbolic world of the poor and dispossessed.[37] There has always been a measure of sometimes radical social involvement among grass-roots Pentecostals in Latin America. For example, Pentecostals joined the leftist Ligas Campesinas (Peasant Leagues) in their struggle for better working conditions in the cane fields of northeastern Brazil.[38] Another case in point is that of Benedita Souza da Silva. At age fifty-plus she is both a powerful leader in the Workers' party and a respected Pentecostal lay woman. One of thirteen children born to a laundress and a car washer who was also a macumba priest, Benedita had worked since she was ten as a street vendor, a market porter, a house cleaner, a nurse's aide, and a school janitor. She had married at sixteen and borne five children in five years, of whom only two had survived infancy. At twenty-six she had converted to evangelical Protestantism and joined an Assembly of God congregation. Her role models were Archbishop Helder Cámara and her grandmother, María Rosa, a former slave. In her own words, "For years, a Brazilian politician has always been rich, white, and male. Now we have a new profile: a black woman from a poor background."[39]

Although her profile is unusually high, da Silva's experience represents the upsurge of the poor and marginalized (blacks, Amerindians, women) clamoring for a place in the sun and determined to do something about it.

In an eye-opening comparative study of Pentecostals and CEBs, the Brazilian sociologist Cecília Mariz points out that most scholarly studies assume that over the long term the CEBs "will exert a leftward influence in Brazilian political life and that Pentecostalism, by its encouragement of private piety and docility, will indirectly support the forces of conservatism." This is not, however, what her field research in the shantytowns of Recife has revealed.[40] Both movements have found that there are limits to their capacities to put their official ideologies into practice:

> Despite their different assumptions and intentions, it seems that the attempt of the adherents of these two movements to unify their faith with their lives has strikingly similar results. When Pentecostals try to restrict their lives to spiritual matters and

[CEB] members try to transform all spiritual questions into everyday problems, they experience the limits of the applicability of their ideal values and conceptions.[41]

Pentecostals, Mariz observes, "are not able to live only a spiritual life, but find themselves involved in politics as well." The CEBs face similar limitations; their spiritual needs require satisfaction alongside "the fight for social justice and equality."[42]

Because they are organized in similar ways and their members have many experiences in common, the two groups in effect encourage behaviors that are surprisingly similar. Consequently, attempting to live by the precepts of these movements generates behavior that does not entirely reflect the values expressed in their official systems of discourse.[43] Both movements foster self-esteem, provide national support networks, "develop leadership skills, promote literacy, and encourage a sober and ascetic life-style." When these "experiences, dispositions, and abilities" are brought together, they "can facilitate social mobility and . . . enable the members to promote or defend their interests in the arena."[44]

Does this similarity of social contexts, spiritual needs, and overall impact—despite dissimilar ideologies—imply that Pentecostals and CEB members relate to each other as fellow Christians or as fellow marginalized members of oppressive societies? The answer to this question may become clearer in the following section. Meanwhile, in this interaction the grass-roots Pentecostal congregations seem to be winning over large numbers of CEB members to their congregations when barely a decade ago the current seemed to be flowing slowly in the opposite direction. The Centro Ecumênico de Documentação e Informação (Ecumenical Documentation and Information Center—CEDI), a well-known Brazilian ecumenical research center and think tank, has this to say:

Intellectuals, ecclesiastical authorities, and pastoral agents are every day more amazed at the conversion of leaders of social movements and activists in grass-roots pastoral formation to groups belonging to autonomous [i.e., "national"] Pentecostalism. Even more surprising is the change that takes place in the lives of converts: eroded family and neighborhood relationships are restored, violence is rejected, and conduct is guided by acceptable norms.[45]

What is the reason for this amazing change of allegiance? I shall suggest three: cultural alienation, institutionalization, and disillusionment with the established churches.

Cultural alienation. Base-community leaders may be relying too much on sociological analysis and overlooking the existential and spiritual needs of the poor. In some cases, the movement seems to be viewed as elitist. The historian Peter Winn comments that the different approaches to literacy of the Pentecostals and the CEBs may be a factor in the drift of the latter to the former: "The [CEBs], with their stress on Bible reading and the analysis of the written word, emphasized a literacy that many poor Brazilians did not possess."[46] One illiterate woman who moved from a base community in a Rio shantytown to a Pentecostal church explained it this way: "I used to be a Catholic. But when these Bible circles came, all they did was read, read, read. There was no more prayer. I felt they only liked those who could read."[47] This criticism is revealing, because the Brazilian CEB coordinators had once used literacy as a keystone of their consciousness-raising methodology,[48] somehow overlooking the fact that the people belonged to an oral culture.

Institutionalization. José Comblin, a Belgian liberation theologian and ardent CEB apologist, suggests that the CEBs have turned in upon themselves too much and need to learn from Pentecostals about how to share their faith with the unchurched. The CEBs of northeastern Brazil

> show little interest in adding new members; they are self-contained, a world unto themselves. There is no dialogue with the masses; their programs reflect their own self-interests rather than the real needs of the people. . . . In contrast, what allows for the very strong missionary spirit of the Pentecostals is precisely their freedom of action. No group has exclusive claim its own turf. Every community must work to win a following.[49]

Disillusionment with the established churches. Another clue to the growth of Pentecostalism at the expense of the base communities in Brazil is found in the following statement from a leading Brazilian daily:

> The decline of the so-called historical churches . . . and the growth of the Pentecostal sects can be seen as the consequence of the disillusion of urban Brazilians, who do not find in the former a source of spiritual compensation for the bitterness of their daily lives. Disillusionment largely explains why five churches of the "new denominations" appear in Rio de Janeiro every week. This is a religious phenomenon of great consequence, if one pays attention to the recently converted mother who remarked: "We seize on whatever religion is closest to us.". . . The more dehumanizing life becomes in urban spaces, it would seem, the less space there is for acceptance of historical religions. . . . The poorer the population of Rio becomes, the less Catholic it is.[50]

Seizing on whatever religion is closest expresses a kind of eclectic ecumenism that is unstructured and unplanned.

Needs of the Poor: Eclectic Ecumenism

The pastor of a grass-roots Pentecostal congregation sums up the general attitude of the very poor toward religious differentiation as follows: "I pick up everything that comes my way [on the radio]: mass, spiritist service, everything."[51] As early as 1980, the Brazilian marxist sociologist Carlos Rodrígues Brandão carried out extensive research among CEB members, Pentecostals, and spiritists in a typical small town in the interior of São Paulo state. One of his most startling conclusions was that "confessional distinctions tend to blur the closer one gets to the grass roots":

> On certain sacred days Brazilian peasants will take candles to the priest for a blessing—one of the few times they step into the parish church, because this is a function that only a priest is deemed powerful enough to perform. . . . The same peasants may listen to Pentecostal broadcasts and attend the tent meetings of a grass-roots Pentecostal healer in order to resolve a physical problem that the "saints" were either unwilling or unable to address. Or they may just as readily seek the services of a local spiritist *macumbeiro* whose magic has been found to be powerful in specific instances.[52]

But is this ecumenism or something closer to syncretism? The point is that grass-roots Pentecostals, pastors among them, are part of this mobile mass of people. This eclecticism is seemingly less a matter of a syncretism of beliefs than a natural folk response to the supernatural. Peasants and the very poor in the large urban centers of Latin America seem willing to resort to any being or force that might have the power to resolve their problems. In the words of one folk practitioner, "As long as it is religious and it is for our good, it is all the same thing."[53] This eclecticism may be another explanation for the tremendous growth of Pentecostalism in Brazil for the mobility within the "popular" Pentecostal movement—a mobility that in time may bring Pentecostals to greater awareness of the world around them.

Pentecostalism and Amerindian Religiosity

Pentecostals have had considerable growth among the Amerindian populations of Central America and the Andean region. This is perhaps because their churches are similar to the native village structure, which combines a sharing community with authoritarian or patriarchal leadership. The close relationship of native pastors to their congregations guarantees that church activities are embedded in a culturally appropriate authoritarian system that does not necessarily break entirely with village life. A student of one Mayan Protestant denomination asserts that

> deliberation and dialogue within the community are factors of great importance in the culture of the Mayas. The individual has traditionally defined his or her identity in terms of the community, principally the family and the village. Decisions are not made individually, but rather in the framework of these social relationships, to which they are responsible. So too, the Mayan [Protestants are] a community in which in-

dividual Christians are bound together. . . . They also find in and through the community material solidarity in a variety of ways. . . .

Through their membership in this new community the Mayan [Protestants] are interconnected with the community of the whole church beyond the circumstances of their village. Within the village they distance themselves from others who, for example, practice the traditional indigenous religion. But this distancing is not so strong that the responsibility to the village community would be completely shattered. . . . The social practice and the theology of the Mayan [Protestants] are shaped by the membership to both the inner circle of the church and the outer circle of the indigenous community.[54]

Although Pentecostalism has been criticized as a divisive and individualistic "ideology of sin and salvation," the same critics grudgingly recognize that it is filling a "social vacuum created by the destruction of families and communities." A study of Mayan widows and evangelicals reveals that "rather than a turning away from Mayan values, these evangelical affiliations, in spite of their fire-and-brimstone discourse, provide Mayan women and their families with a mechanism to recapture control over their lives."[55]

In the ancient Maya heartland, "sin and salvation," "fire and brimstone," and Pentecostal ecstasies may be responding to the millennial mystique of Maya religion, which is still very much alive among highland peoples. In the words of a prominent Pentecostal leader, "We Pentecostals are very suspicious of anything that smells of the ancient cult. We consider it paganism; but we would like to think that Pentecostals are closest to the ancient Maya religiosity of any Protestant movement."[56] Although Pentecostal leaders are usually wary of allowing their members to work with other Protestants, Catholics, and Maya religionists on common projects, there is evidence that some Amerindian Protestants and Pentecostals maintain a sub-rosa relationship with the religious symbols of their forefathers. Indeed, from confidential conversations and reports from Maya Protestants and from my own observations, I know that some Protestant pastors participate secretly in Maya religious ceremonies. Maya religiosity is deeply embedded in the soul of every highland peasant in Guatemala and is at the heart of the family value system.[57]

Women are particularly active as agents of change and cohesion. They "are trying to regain a sense of community, sharing, group undertakings in a respectful and dignified way, so emblematic of Mayan culture."[58] However, the women in the Linda Green's study tend to move back and forth between the various religious groups; this suggests that they gain only partial satisfaction from any one of them: "The fluidity with which the women cross religious boundaries points to the pragmatic approach they have adopted as they struggle to meet exigencies." Choices are made not on doctrinal grounds but "from available options, trying to recapture piecemeal elements of community" that have been destroyed in the violence and genocide.[59] "We have to ask how ordinary people choose between the religious discourses available to them, bend these to their own purposes, and wend their way in and out of particular groups."[60]

Orality, Literacy, and Ecumenism

The fluid attitude of peasant and traditional ethnic cultures toward the available religious resources seems to be a characteristic of most oral cultures. Pentecostals move between their fundamental oral culture and the literate and dogmatic culture of mainline Pentecostalism. "The process of institutionalization is gradually moving 'mainline' Pentecostals away from the popular sector of society, and may be slowing their numerical growth." Meanwhile, "the dissident sector of Pentecostalism ["store-front" Pentecostalism] is growing because they find in their own popular religion the supernatural protection, community identity, and the experience of power over the sacral world that mainline Pentecostals are leaving behind."[61]

Borrowing categories from students of oral cultures, in particular Walter J. Ong, a Roman Catholic,[62] Quentin Schultze, a Protestant communications specialist, develops a kind of model for understanding Pentecostals. Some of his insights may help us locate and elucidate Pentecostal ecumenism at its various social levels. "Oral culture is an organism, whereas more literate culture is an organization." Literacy impels "conversionist" religions "to rationalize and bureaucratize faith" on the basis of documents that determine the range of acceptable belief and practice. "Literacy also enables religions to establish organizations that maintain the documents."[63] It is these same organizations, as we have seen, that determine the extent of a church's relationships with other churches and expect their members to follow them. It is at this level that the very limited elite or erudite ecumenism is found. By contrast, "magico-religious" faiths are "singularly eclectic in that shrines and cults move easily from place to place." In other words, without objectifying the faith through the written or printed word, these faiths are enormously fluid and localized. As a result, they are also "more universalistic" and less "particularistic." They simply lack the cultural mechanism for establishing nuanced dogma regarding belief and practice.[64]

Ong and Schultze suggest seven salient features of oral cultures: "powerful immediacy, presentness, playfulness, performance, parabolic morality, conventionality, and commonality."[65] Three of these features are especially relevant to the subject at hand:

Immediacy and presentness. Pentecostals experience the faith not principally as a set of objective doctrines or abstract theological tenets, but as a living, dynamic work of the Holy Spirit in their everyday lives."[66] Since there is no place in oral religiosity "for the major questions and concerns of the modern West and Enlightenment worldviews,"[67] it follows that decisions regarding human relationships are not determined primarily by theoretical considerations such as proof

texts, purity of doctrine, religious affiliation, ecclesiastical polity, or conciliar pro-
nouncements but by more immediate factors.

Commonality.   Perhaps the most obvious and significant characteristic of an oral
culture is the high level of shared life." The Latin root of the word "communication" signifies "to make common." Commonality is a matter of common experience as well as proximity. Schultze observes that although various students of
Pentecostalism point to one or another positive effect of the movement, few seem
to see "the direct relationship between orality and the resurrection of community
in the region." One of Pentecostalism's major contributions to Latin America "is
a widespread resuscitation of social bonds through spiritual language. . . . Using
the language of the people, free of ecclesiastical intermediaries and status differences, Pentecostalism linguistically helps to empower its adherents to build community."[68] The sociology of religion offers a helpful insight at this point. In non-
structured religions, "the religious subject is the group and one's individuality can
find expression only in the group," but structured religions tend to personalize religious relationships. They offer solace to every person because they are primarily oriented toward individuals.[69]

Immediacy, presentness, and commonality—in short, communication—is
what relationships between Christians and between them and the world are all
about. Pentecostals are either in fact or potentially ecumenical because their culture and religion are primarily oral. The more they move toward the literate pole,
the more sectarian they tend to be, until they break out into the world of the literate elite, where formal ecumenism can take place in certain contexts. The majority of Pentecostals, however, remain suspicious of formal ecumenism.

Why is this? Again, the sociology of religion may offer us insight. Popular or
oral religiosity does not automatically make for open relationships. The source of
the religious experience is also very important. "There is an 'ecstatic' source of religion (which is at the same time ethically 'closed') and another 'dynamic' religious source which is ethically 'open.'"[70] I interpret this to mean, in the context
of this study, that the historical circumstances behind the beginnings of the various Pentecostal churches—whether "ecstatic" withdrawal or "dynamic" response—may have something to do with the way in which they manage their relationships to other churches and to the world at large.

Conclusion

Pentecostals in Latin America are not inherently sectarian, because unity is germane to their pneumatic theology. They are inherently ecumenical because of
their rootedness in oral culture, which is highly relational. Although many of
them are suspicious of anything ecumenical, Pentecostals demonstrate varying
degrees of formal and informal ecumenism. The most significant and for religious leaders most disquieting manifestations of ecumenism are to be found
among the very poor and in the midst of revitalized traditional cultures. This is

a function of cultural identity and daily existence rather than of structure, liturgy, and dogma. In sum, Pentecostals in Latin America are as ecumenical—and as eclectic—as their origins, culture, context, and doctrine either allow or encourage them to be.

NOTES

1. I develop this further in Guillermo Cook, ed., *New Face of the Church in Latin America: Between Tradition and Change* (Maryknoll, N.Y.: Orbis Books, 1994).

2. Everett Wilson, "Latin American Pentecostals: Their Potential for Ecumenical Dialogue," *Pneuma: The Journal of the Society for Pentecostal Studies* 9, 1 (1987), p. 87.

3. Miriam Reidy, "Latin American Pentecostalism: Sleeping Giant," *One World* (May 1988), p. 6.

4. I endorse Donald Dayton's insistence that Pentecostalism is far more than a North American religious phenomenon. It has its roots in many traditions, including German Pietism, English Methodism, and the Swedish free-church movement. Donald Dayton, "Algunas reflexiones sobre el Pentecostalismo latinoamericano y sus implicaciones ecuménicas," *Cuadernos de Teología* 11, 2 (1991), p. 7.

5. Gordon Spykman et al., *Let My People Live: Faith and Struggle in Central America* (Grand Rapids, Mich.: Eerdmans, 1988), p. 78.

6. Ibid., pp. 216, 221, 222.

7. David Martin, *Tongues of Fire: The Explosion of Protestantism in Latin America* (Oxford and Cambridge, Mass.: Basil Blackwell, 1990).

8. Ibid., pp. 284 ff.

9. David Stoll, *Is Latin America Turning Protestant? The Politics of Evangelical Growth* (Berkeley: University of California Press, 1990).

10. Martin, *Tongues of Fire*, pp. 235, 237. Donald Dayton agrees: "It is not useful to think of Pentecostalism primarily as a sect." Whereas one can understand the motives behind such labeling coming from a Roman Catholic church that is losing its grip on the masses, "one cannot understand why some Latin American Protestants use the same kind of analysis." Mainline Protestantist denominations in Latin America began as sects. "It is easy to forget," says Dayton, "that Methodists were seen (by Presbyterians for example) in the nineteenth century in the same way that Pentecostals are now looked down upon by Methodists." Dayton, "Algunas reflexiones sobre el Pentecostalismo latinoamericano," p. 8. One might add that the majority of the historical churches that entered Latin America, mostly via the United States (e.g., Scottish Presbyterians, English Congregationalists and Methodists, Baptists, and even Pietist Lutherans), originated in persecuted sectarian movements. See Guillermo Cook, *The Expectation of the Poor: Latin American Base Ecclesial Communities in Protestant Perspective* (Maryknoll, N.Y.: Orbis Books, 1985).

11. Ibid., p. 229.

12. César Soriano, "La misión del Pentecostalismo latinoamericano en la construcción de la esperanza," paper presented at the Latin American Pentecostal Conference, Buenos Aires, Argentina, April 19–22, 1989.

13. Miguel A. Petrella, "La misión del Pentecostalismo latinoamericano en la construcción de la esperanza," paper presented at the Latin American Pentecostal Conference, Buenos Aires, Argentina, April 19–22, 1989.

14. Gabriel Vaccaro, *Aportes del Pentecostalismo al movimiento ecuménico* (Quito: Consejo Latinoamericano de Iglesias [CLAI], 1991), pp. 13–20.

15. Ibid.

16. P. A. Hardiment, "Confessing the Apostolic Faith from the Perspective of the Pentecostal Churches," *One in Christ* 23, 1–2, (1987), p. 67; Karl-Wilhelm Westmeir, "Themes in Pentecostal Expansion in Latin America," *International Bulletin for Missionary Research* 17, 4 (April 1993), p. 133.

17. John Thomas Nichol, *The Pentecostals* (Plainfield, N.J., Logos, 1966), pp. 219, 220.

18. A major venue for ecumenical dialogue in the United States is the Society for Pentecostal Studies (SPS), which brings together scholars from mainline Pentecostal, ecumenical Protestant, and charismatic Roman Catholic institutions. For example, the SPS's official organ, *Pneuma,* has published nuanced articles in which Pentecostal authors interact both appreciatively and critically with the Catholic base ecclesial communities.

19. Cheryl Bridges Johns, "The Adolescence of Pentecostalism: Searching for a Legitimate Sectarian Identity," *Pneuma: The Journal of the Society for Pentecostal Studies* 16, 2 (1994), passim.

20. Ibid.

21. Carmelo Alvarez, "Latin American Pentecostals: Ecumenical and Evangelical," *Pneuma: The Journal of the Society for Pentecostal Studies* 9, 1 (1987) p. 92.

22. Up until the 1970s, *evangélico* was equivalent to *Protestante* in Latin America. Although Catholics and ecumenicals use it as an adjective to signify attitudes and actions that harmonize with Gospel principles and ideals, conservative Protestants now use it as a self-designation in the North American sense.

23. Ibid.

24. Alvarez, "Latin American Pentecostals," p. 92.

25. Ibid., pp. 93, 94.

26. Philip Berryman, "Evangelicals and Catholics in Mega-Cities," manuscript. This has also been my experience. As I write, I have been teaching a course on ecclesiology at a Pentecostal institute some of whose students have also taken courses at Catholic and Protestant ecumenical institutions.

27. Guillermo Cook, "Book Summary: *Os deuses do povo* (The Gods of the People), by Carlos Rodriguez Brandão," *Missiology: An International Review* 18, 2 (April 1982), passim.

28. Guillermo Cook, "The Church, the World, and Progress in Latin America in Light of the Eschatological Kingdom," in Harold D. Hunter and Peter D. Hocken, eds., *All Together in One Place: Theological Papers from the Brighton Conference on World Evangelization* (Sheffield: Sheffield Academic Press, 1993), pp. 202–203.

29. Wilson, "Latin American Pentecostals," p. 86.

30. See, for example, Juan Sepúlveda, "Pentecostalism and Liberation Theology," and Luis Segreda, "Evangelization and the Holy Spirit in an Urban and Multicultural Society," in Hunter and Hocken, *All Together in One Place,* pp. 51–64, 134–149.

31. Fidencio Burgeño, "Consultation on Pentecostalism and Liberation Theology," in *CELEP, a Decade in the Service of Jesus Christ: Documents on the Life and Mission of the Church* (San José, Costa Rica: Centro Evangélico Latinoamericano de Estudios Pastorales, 1985), pp. 150–155.

32. UEPV, "La carta de Valencia: Carta pastoral de la Unión Evangélica Pentecostal Venezolana," manuscript, 1987.

33. Ibid.

34. Jonathan L. Fried and Marvin Gettleman, eds., "Religion and Revolution: A Protestant Voice," in *Guatemala in Rebellion: Unfinished History* (New York: Grove Press, 1983), pp. 230–231.

35. Ibid., p. 231.

36. For a more detailed treatment of this phenomenon, see Guillermo Cook, "The Genesis and Practice of Protestant Base Communities in Latin America," in Cook, *New Face,* pp. 150–155.

37. Carlos Rodrígues Brandão, a Brazilian social scientist, has found that grass-roots Pentecostals partake of the same community solidarity as the Catholic base communities. This is an integral part of their world. Brandão, *Os deuses do povo* (Rio de Janeiro: Editora Brasilense, 1980), pp. 54–56; see also Cook, *The Expectation of the Poor,* p. 228.

38. Francisco Cartaxo Rolim, *O que é pentecostalismo?* (São Paulo: Editors Brasilense, 1987), pp. 51–70.

39. *New York Times,* November 17, 1992.

40. Cecília Mariz, "Religion and Poverty in Brazil: A Comparison of Catholic and Pentecostal Communities," *Sociological Analysis* 53, special issue (1992), p. 63.

41. Ibid.

42. Ibid., p. 64.

43. Ibid., p. 64.

44. Ibid., p. 69.

45. CEDI, "Protestantismo autônomo, uma inversão sedutora?" in *Aconteceu no mundo evangélico,* special supplement 548 (1990), pp. 5, 11.

46. Peter Winn, *Americas: The Changing Face of Latin America and the Caribbean* (New York: Pantheon Books, 1992), p. 383.

47. Ibid.

48. The basic-education movement, pioneered by an intellectual, idealistic, and radical young Catholic Action elite in the 1960s, was one of the sources of the Brazilian CEBs. It gradually developed from a literacy program into a movement that had a growing stake in changing the basic socioeconomic structures of Brazil. Its leadership debated the relative merits of a nondirective versus a directive methodology and eventually chose the latter. See Cook, *The Expectation of the Poor,* esp. pp. 267–268.

49. Cook, *New Face.*

50. *O Estado,* 1993; cf. *Veja,* (1991), pp. 32–38.

51. Brandão, *Os deuses do povo,* pp. 125–127.

52. Ibid.

53. Ibid., p. 127.

54. Heinrich Shafer, *Church Identity Between Repression and Liberation: The Presbyterian Church in Guatemala.* (Studies from the World Alliance of Reformed Churches, no. 20, 1991), pp. 89, 90. I substitute "Protestant" for "Presbyterian" to indicate that the same phenomenon exists throughout Maya Protestantism, including Pentecostalism churches.

55. Linda Green, "Shifting Affiliations: Mayan Widows and *Evangélicos* in Guatemala," in Virginia Garrard-Burnett and David Stoll, eds., *Rethinking Protestantism in Latin America* (Philadelphia: Temple University Press, 1993), p. 175.

56. Interview by telephone, July 1994, with Church of God missionary, Rev. Richard Waldrop, in Guatemala.

57. Mario Fernando Higueros Fuentes, "Imagenes parentales y familiares en la formación religiosa: Análisis de un país centroamericano," Master's thesis, Facultad de Teología, Universidad Pontificia de Salamanca, 1986.

58. Green, "Shifting Affiliations," p. 175.

59. Ibid.

60. David Stoll, "Introduction," in Garrard-Burnett and Stoll, *Rethinking Protestantism,* p. 6.

61. Cook, "Book Summary," p. 254; cf. Brandão, *Os deuses do povo,* pp. 109–111, 139–141.

62. Walter Ong, *The Presence of the Word: Some Prolegomena for Cultural and Religious History* (New Haven: Yale University Press, 1967), and *Orality and Literacy: The Technologizing of the Word* (London: Methuen, 1982).

63. Quentin J. Schultze, "Orality and Power in Latin American Pentecostalism," in Daniel R. Miller, ed. *Coming of Age: Protestantism in Latin America* (Lanham, Md.: University Press of America, 1994), p. 73.

64. Ibid.

65. Ibid., p. 73.

66. Ibid., p. 75.

67. Ibid., p. 77.

68. Ibid., 81, 82; cf. Martin, *Tongues of Fire,* pp. 83, 171, 175, 180.

69. J. Gómez Caffarena, "Religión," in Casiano Floristán and Juan José Tamayo, eds., *Conceptos fundamentales de Pastoral* (Madrid: Ediciones Cristiandad, 1983), p. 864.

70. Gómez Caffarena, "Religión," p. 864. Gómez borrows this concept from Henri Bergson, *Las dos fuentes de la moral y de la religión* (Buenos Aires, n.p., n.d.).

❄ 6 ❄

Chilean Pentecostalism:
Coming of Age

EDWARD L. CLEARY AND JUAN SEPÚLVEDA

The clash between Chilean Pentecostals and North American missionaries on September 12, 1909, was so violent that police restrained followers, and Chile's premier newspaper, *El Mercurio*, commented on the events. Chilean Pentecostals went on to become, as Walter Hollenweger says, the first self-sufficient church in the Third World.[1]

Pentecostalism now occupies an established place in Chilean society. It has been growing and changing for almost ninety years, long enough to mark one of the main paths of perhaps the twentieth century's greatest religious movement through Latin America. Hence Chile has special import for social scientists and students of religious and mission studies. The churches that make up this movement demonstrate amazing vitality. Even now they are attracting converts at a very high rate. They also show, however, the problems, often unacknowledged, that one associates with maturing organizations. The reasons for Pentecostalism's appeal and its problems will be explored below. After examining its dramatic beginnings and the context for its initial growth, we will review some classical sociological studies of Pentecostalism and then trace its development through turbulent years of change and repression up to the current democratic period.

Pentecostalism's Introduction and Growth

Chile's Protestant history begins in the 1800s with the immigration of small English or German ethnic groups, Anglican, Lutheran, Methodist, and other, bringing with them pastors who tended to limit their efforts to their own flocks. A few Baptists and Methodists pushed for conversion of others.

The religious conflicts of Europe during the 1600s had left a legacy of church-state union in both Catholic and Protestant countries. Elaborate legal barriers and tacit understandings marked off separate parts of the world to exclude religious change. Catholicism was forbidden to return to Scandinavia, and Protestantism limited itself to immigrant Protestant groups in Latin America. Burial, marriage, and owning of property by outsiders were controlled. In Sweden even in this century the Catholic church was prohibited from owning property or organizing public worship. By contrast, Chile began early in this century to offer a context of welcome to other religions. According to the great chronicler of church-state relations in Latin America J. Lloyd Mecham, "Separation of church and state was a cherished political ideal of advanced thinkers in Chile."[2] The Chilean historian Luis Galdames characterized Chileans of this period as ready for the separation of church and state because of "simple tolerance and religious indifference."[3] The separation was accomplished with the constitution of 1925, whereby liberty of conscience and freedom of worship were guaranteed. The Catholic church remained the dominant religious influence and received favorable treatment by the state, but in Mecham's judgment "the tolerance of Chileans and the constitutional guarantees of freedom of religion have been favorable to the Evangelical movement."[4]

In various ways Chile's tolerance and religious indifference were special. In contrast to many Latin American countries, Chile had no intense anticlericalism that might demand constitutional reforms or oppose the Catholic church. A notable percentage of Chileans have long been indifferent to religion. Galdames noted in 1911 that about one-fourth of the people did not consider themselves "sincere" Catholics.[5] "As for increased religious indifference, this was evidenced by the astonishing scarcity of men at Mass and the general laxity in the observance of fasting and confession,"[6] Mecham judged. According to Kenneth Scott Latourette, "In the 1950s a careful survey indicated that in all of Chile only 3.5 percent of the men and 9.5 percent of the women went to mass on Sunday."[7] Mecham reports a higher percentage: 13 percent women and 7 percent men for Sunday mass attendance.[8] (This great disparity between women and men is also an issue for Pentecostals.)

Chile's "spiritual anemia"[9] was also evidenced by a scarcity of Chilean clergy, which made certain geographical areas especially vulnerable. John Considine reported that the rural areas were only thinly supplied if at all.[10] The country offered an opportunity for other religions, one that Protestant mission leaders came to call *campos blancos,* fields waiting for harvesters. A major figure of Chilean Catholicism, the Jesuit Father Alberto Hurtado,[11] inquired in the 1940s if Chile was a Catholic country. On what evidence he could muster he responded that Chile in many senses had ceased being a Catholic country and was more appropriately considered a missionary territory.[12] This evaluation, shared by others, was part of the motivation for the revitalization of core groups within the church.[13]

Pentecostalism arose from events within Chile rather than being introduced from abroad. Similar foundational events were, however, occurring elsewhere in Pentecostalism. As David Martin, the renowned English sociologist of religion, notes, "A whole series of sparks [were] struck at roughly the same time [as in Chile] in Los Angeles, Armenia, Wales, Korea, and South Africa."[14] Martin goes on to point out that in Chile the spark was struck within Methodism but the explosion took place through Pentecostalism.[15]

Perhaps no one was better suited than Willis C. Hoover to help to bring about the birth of Chilean Pentecostalism. His medical training and his Midwestern populism had provided him with a mind that was open, searching, vigorous, and trusting of common impulses. Born in Freeport, Illinois, and a physician by 1884, he assumed the rectorship of a Methodist high school in northern Chile in 1889. His theological studies came later. Unlike most Methodist missionaries of the time, Hoover threw himself into work among lower-class Chileans. The impact of other Methodist pastors was limited to converts from the more educated sectors of society because of the rationalist-modernizing character of their preaching. By 1902 Hoover was in Valparaíso as pastor of the largest Chilean Methodist Episcopal church. Valparaíso, as Chile's principal seaport, had a privileged and wealthy class, but Hoover's greatest appeal was not to them but to immigrants from the countryside seeking work in the city. He built upon popular religious experience and was willing to try virtually any known evangelistic method. He opened branch chapels, conducted house-to-house visitations, and taught adult classes. As had the Methodist circuit riders, he used his converts to bring in other converts. He pressed ahead as the caudillo, with sureness and energy.

When, despite all this converts still amounted to only a trickle, Hoover searched the missionary repertoire of the early twentieth century. Minnie F. Abrams, a classmate of Mrs. Hoover at the Chicago Training School for Home and Foreign Missions, sent the Hoovers her book *The Baptism of the Holy Ghost and Fire,* which described the Pentecostal experience in India in 1905. After inquiries about the Pentecostal phenomenon in various parts of the world, Hoover, as superintendent of the Methodist Central District and pastor of its largest parish, began to encourage the pursuit of similar experiences. From the 1909 Methodist Chile Conference on, Chilean Pentecostalism took form, and it went on to change the face of Protestantism in Chile.

Depending on the point of view of the storyteller or historian, the events of 1909 have been described with various shadings. In a recent retelling by Arturo Fontaine and Harald Beyer, Nellie Laidlaw ("a woman of dubious reputation") becomes a principal figure for her prophecies in tumultuous services.[16] According to Hoover himself, "Laughter, weeping, shouting, singing, strange tongues, visions, ecstatic trances during which the person fell to the ground and had the impression of being transported to another place . . . This was accompanied by various experiences . . . which were generally of great benefit to those who had them, generally changing these people."[17]

Hoover and the participants in the services experienced rejection and censure from the Methodist Chile Conference, and Hoover decided to submit to the discipline of the church. In the course of his trial within the Methodist Chile

Conference the next year, his teachings were declared "anti-Methodist, contrary to the Scriptures, and irrational."[18]

After the 1910 conference, the majority of the two Valparaíso congregations and the Santiago congregation decided to abandon the Methodist Episcopal church to establish the National Methodist church. On May 1 of that year Hoover left the Methodist Episcopal church to take charge of the new church at the invitation of Chileans.

Chilean Pentecostalism attracted large groups of followers not at first in Santiago or Valparaíso, where it was founded, but in the provinces (nine of Chile's twenty-seven) south of Concepción and north of Puerto Montt. At the time of the early expansion of Pentecostalism, in the 1910s and 1920s, this area was much like a frontier. Both the Catholic church's lack of pastoral care and the fragility of frontier society may have played a part in Pentecostalism's putting down roots there.

Beginning in the 1940s, Pentecostalism grew rapidly in the so-called countryside of the Central Valley region and in the lower-class sections of Santiago and Valparaíso.[19] In many places the Catholic church either gave the peasants little systematic attention or was identified as "allied with the landowners *at the expense of the peasants.*"[20] Recognizing its vulnerability in the countryside, the Catholic church began to take countermeasures.[21]

Christian Lalive d'Epinay's research, including reflections on previous studies in Chile, shows, according to David Martin, that "Pentecostals were those who had some individual niche in the interstices of society, however precarious that niche might be."[22] In Chile Pentecostals were regarded by the upper classes as *el bajo pueblo.*[23] Those who tried Pentecostalism and stayed with it were small artisans, semiskilled workers willing to travel where work was needed, and others in the lower classes. Whereas literacy was a key factor in older forms of Protestantism—adherents being expected to read the Bible for themselves—Pentecostalism emphasized orality.[24] Many Chileans in the early twentieth century were illiterate and found the emphasis on oral and highly participatory religious services, incorporating their own spoken testimonies, attractive.

The main thrust of Protestantism in Chile was becoming Pentecostal. Between 1932 and 1934 La Iglesia Metodista Pentecostal, the original Chilean Pentecostal church, underwent a painful split.[25] Hoover and other pastors organized La Iglesia Evangélica Pentecostal. The two churches rank first and second among Pentecostal churches in Chile and account for about half of the Protestants in the country.[26]

The Hoover-led churches and others that broke off from them became Chilean institutions to such an extent that some descendants of the early Pentecostals call themselves criollo Pentecostals.[27] They contrast themselves to latecomers from worldwide Pentecostal churches such as the Assemblies of God.[28] Some criollo Pentecostals originally looked upon more recent arrivals as mission products with heavy North American ideological baggage, but by now virtually all Pentecostal churches are Chilean in leadership, membership, and finances.[29] Estimates place Pentecostals at about 90 percent of Protestants in Chile.[30]

Pentecostalism in the 1960s

By 1960 an estimated 10.8 percent of the Chilean population were Protestant, the largest percentage in all of Latin America.[31] Poblete and Galilea took it for granted years later that "among the countries of Latin America conquered by Catholic Spain, Chile has been traditionally considered the country with the largest number of Protestants."[32] Both the estimates of Protestants in Chile (too high) and in other countries (too low) should have been questioned, but Chile's reputation in Protestant circles, especially the novelty of Pentecostalism, attracted the attention of the pioneering scholars Emilio Willems and Christian Lalive d'Epinay.[33] Willems was at Vanderbilt University and Lalive d'Epinay, a young Swiss sociologist, enjoyed sponsorship by the World Council of Churches. Chilean social science was just beginning to be organized in universities and institutes, and therefore Chileans were unable to respond to these studies professionally and critically at that time. As Jeffrey Puryear points out, "Research was occasionally carried out in Chilean universities before 1955, but it was not part of their institutional goal."[34] Then, too, an adequate response from within Pentecostalism was hampered by the lack of academically trained members. Lalive d'Epinay and Willems therefore received attention and deference that their work did not merit. Lalive d'Epinay's work in particular became for many outside observers a "safe-haven" paradigm for explaining Pentecostalism.

Willems attempted a work of extraordinary scope, for the times, covering Pentecostals not only in Spanish-speaking Chile but in Portuguese-speaking Brazil. His conclusions are consistent with the spirit of modernization theories in seeing Pentecostalism as fostering a work ethic. Employers often prefer to hire Pentecostals because they are punctual and disciplined; Pentecostalism and the capitalist wage system reinforce one another.[35] They help persons moving from traditional rural patterns to adapt to urban life. Pentecostalism helps persons and families rise above anomie and socioeconomic pressures toward the integration of personal and family life. Reaching out to convert others empowered newcomers, turning them into active participants. Although enthusiasm for Willems's ideas of "lower-class culture" has waned,[36] one can profitably read his work for his closeness to what was happening to individuals.[37]

In part because Lalive d'Epinay's work was published in Spanish and was supported by the World Council of Churches, it received attention from Chileans "as the best-established" theory of Chilean Pentecostalism.[38] It was impressive, especially for Chileans, in its apparent thoroughness: review of documents, multiple interviews, participant observation, and questionnaires administered to Pentecostal pastors and two control groups. It was, however, seriously flawed in omitting the opinions of the persons in the pews.

Lalive d'Epinay created an imaginative view of Chilean Pentecostalism that gained considerable attention. He pictured Pentecostalism as re-creating for those transposed from countryside to city the traditional structure of the hacienda. The Pentecostal pastor became the *patrón,* keeping the faithful out of politics and rendering them conservative and passive in relation to authority. Moral renewal took precedence over economic advance and did not necessarily lead to increased capital accumulation. This religion had little effect on social mobility or on the attitudes and values thought necessary for economic development. It was, in Lalive d'Epinay's terms, "alienating" but expressive in its own way of social discontent.

For Lalive d'Epinay the political product of this religion was passivity; he described Pentecostals as being on "sociopolitical strike"—of reconstructing a moribund society. What many remember of his work is his image of Pentecostalism as a "refuge for the masses," facilitating an escape from the world.

Cauldron of Pentecostal Change, 1960 to the Present

More careful studies by Chileans are helping to create a better picture of Pentecostalism. Juan Sepúlveda,[39] Renato Poblete,[40] Carmen Galilea,[41] Cristián Parker,[42] Humberto Lagos and Arturo Chacón,[43] Juan Guillermo Prado[44], Katherine Gilfeather,[45] and others[46] have begun this work of systematic interpretation.

To trace the contribution of Chilean Pentecostal scholars one must return to the geographical areas that Lalive d'Epinay investigated. The groups among which Pentecostalism spread its roots suffered from profound social exclusion. They lacked effective channels for participation in organized life and had scant access to the services and benefits provided by the state, such as education and health. They observed the "democratization" and "modernization" of Chile from the sidelines. In a sense, for the adults of this sector the choice was between refuge in a cantina and refuge in a Pentecostal community. Further, becoming Pentecostal brought another mark of social exclusion: belonging to a religious minority in a society that was numerically and culturally Catholic. Hence, Pentecostals grew up with the feeling of being second-class citizens.

This situation began to change, however, in the early 1960s. Chile was being transformed into a social laboratory for confrontation between advocates of reform and proponents of revolution.[47] The Christian Democratic party, representing the reform alternative, took power in 1964. It needed to build a strong base among the lower classes to counterbalance the hegemony of the left, communist or socialist, in the labor movement. Also, the government's model of economic development, based on increasing industrial capacity to reduce imports, required a much enlarged internal market. Thus began an impressive work of state-sponsored social engineering aimed at integrating those on the margins (where Pentecostals lived) with those in the center of society.

Armed with agrarian reform legislation, the state moved vigorously toward labor organizing in the agrarian sector.[48] With the legal creation of neighborhood associations and other types of organizations such as women's centers,[49] it began a process of co-option aimed at taking over the grass-roots movement. This movement had arisen from land invasions supported by the left, and the issue to which these organizations especially devoted themselves was the provision of housing, a crucial aspect of the lives of the excluded. Suddenly the environment in which Pentecostalism was operating was inundated with social and communitarian organizations. A climate of rising expectations for social change pervaded this world, and the larger religious world was affected by this climate. A reinvigorated pastoral policy of the Catholic church, arising from the enthusiasm of the recently concluded Vatican Council, was created for this political context of "social promotion." Programs designed to involve Protestant and Pentecostal churches came from outside the country with the help of the Church World Service (National Council of Churches of the United States).[50]

These processes constituted an enormous challenge for Pentecostal preachers and for the relations between the churches and society. With or without the support of pastors and denominational leaders, many lay members and some pastors joined the new social organizations or unions, especially in rural areas. Many Pentecostals assumed leadership positions in these organizations. In rural and semirural settings where population groupings were small and organizational resources scarce, many churches and their pastors began to act as interlocutors for the municipalities in the implementation of communitarian programs. Other churches preferred to create their own service programs, typically combining voluntary work of members with resources provided through foreign aid. These programs included preventive medicine, food supplementation, literacy, and emergency aid for victims of frequent floods or less frequent earthquakes.

This process affected the Pentecostal world. The degree of social involvement of the local church fundamentally depended on its local leadership. Its pastor's understanding of the Gospel and his reaction to the changes that the country was experiencing determined the type of orientation that he gave his congregation. In a few cases, by contrast, the central leadership of a denomination took a favorable stance toward the social involvement of its members, as occurred especially among Pentecostal churches that had been more involved in the ecumenical movement.[51]

In the last years of the Frei government (1964–1970), the sociopolitical climate became more conflictive and polarized. The lack of cooperation of the economic elite made it impossible for the government to carry out its social programs, especially the provision of more housing. The frustration of expectations drove the popular movement, originally mobilized to support government policies, toward the leftist opposition. Salvador Allende headed the forces of the left (Unidad Popular) that represented the revolutionary alternative to reform. This became *la vía chilena al socialismo (the Chilean road to socialism)*.

The election of Salvador Allende, a socialist, as president in 1970 became an important test of the "safe-haven" theory. Renato Poblete, a Jesuit sociologist, reported his observations to Harvey Cox, a theologian friend at Harvard: (1) Pentecostals had voted in large numbers, (2) Pentecostal leaders had generally opposed Allende and supported the Christian Democrats, and (3) ordinary members of Pentecostal churches had voted for Allende.[52]

At the sociopolitical level, the years of Allende's Unidad Popular (1970–1973) were characterized by a heightening of expectations of social participation and a deepening of political cleavages. Politics became all-absorbing and divisive for many persons and their families. Pentecostals were faced with the choice of either full commitment to the political conflict or observer status. Whereas individuals were able to choose the first, the churches in general, as might be expected, chose the second, distancing themselves from the conflict. In this context a number of leaflets were distributed in the churches by foreign conservative Protestant organizations (alluding to the experience of Christians "behind the Iron Curtain").[53] The effort did not succeed in involving the Pentecostal churches in an open campaign against the Unidad Popular regime. Thus, Pentecostal churches and individuals were not buried in safe havens; they became involved in social movements and politics when they judged that benefits were to be gained from it.

The impending military takeover in 1973 and the numerical prominence of Pentecostal churches again forced public choice on the churches. On the one hand, the divisive and belligerent character that politics had acquired drove the local congregations in the direction of separating themselves from the conflict. On the other hand, the profundity of the national crisis moved the leadership of important Pentecostal churches, including the largest, the Iglesia Metodista Pentecostal, to involve themselves for the first time in ecumenical initiatives to increase mutual understanding and reconciliation among political sectors, especially to avoid civil war.

On the Sunday previous to the coup, prominent Pentecostal leaders gathered in front of the governmental palace, along with Cardinal Raúl Silva Henríquez, Lutheran Bishop Helmuth Frenz, and representatives of other Protestant churches, Orthodox churches, and the Jewish community, to pray for peace in Chile. It was apparent from this event that the political future of Chile would no longer be something "apart" for the Pentecostal leadership.[54]

The coup and the subsequent sixteen and one-half years of military rule produced another, drastic change in Chile. This aspect of Chilean history is being well documented,[55] and here we take up two issues relating to the religious field. First, the government's systematically repressing and outlawing political parties and social organizations and the social consequences of the difficult economic adjustment begun by the military indirectly produced in the general populace a shift toward the churches. Especially in the popular sectors, the churches, inasmuch as they were the only places that were authorized for meetings, were filled with persons seeking protection, spiritual support, exchange of information, and the like. At the grass-roots level, the increased drift of the population toward the churches enhanced the perception that the recess from party politics improved the conditions for gaining converts.

Secondly, the historical and social weight of the Catholic church, summed up in the thought of its bishops (most of them inspired by Vatican II), turned it into the principal defender of human rights. This produced the first great crisis in relations between the Catholic church and the state since Chile's achievement of national independence. It was this withdrawal of moral support by the Catholic church that caused the government to turn to the country's second religious force. If this search found a ready partner in an important segment of the Protestant (not exclusively Pentecostal) leadership, this was not principally because of any alleged political affinity but rather for reasons relating to religious power.

In the request for support on the part of the military regime there was an implicit recognition of the social and political importance of the Protestant world in Chilean society ("for the first time in history," some Protestant leaders keep repeating in amazement).[56] The manifestation of this recognition came in the presence of Gen. Augusto Pinochet during the inauguration of a "Protestant Cathedral" (in reality, the mother church of the Iglesia Metodista Pentecostal) two days after 2,500 Protestant pastors and lay persons had publicly expressed their unconditional support for the military government.[57] This symbolic recognition of the importance of Protestants in Chilean society encouraged hope that the military government would introduce legislation leading to full religious equality. This hope was the principal motive for Protestant support of the regime.

The appearance of broad popular Protestant support for the military regime (in reality the support of a select group of leaders and not an official representation of their congregations) was created through wide media coverage, especially the live television broadcast of the "Protestant Te Deum," an annual event first held in September 1975. Leaders of this sector of Protestantism, when asked, always asserted that the motivation for this was nonpolitical, but they made no great effort to counter the widely held political interpretation of it as support for the regime.[58]

The first critical voices from the other Protestant world took up the question of churches' being used politically by the regime and also the presumption of the so-called Consejo de Pastores in acting as if it represented all Protestants. Gradually these critical voices gained strength. The Confraternidad Cristiana de Iglesias, established in 1982, assumed an increasingly prophetic stance, denouncing the repression and injustices of the military regime.

As this critical posture was gaining greater attention in the 1980s, it was also making evident the profound division in the Chilean Protestant world. Each side claimed that the other was unauthorized to speak for the church. In the past, internal differences (doctrinal or theological) were glossed over as typical of a religious minority seeking its space in society. Superficially this division could be depicted as just another expression of classical theological debates (fundamentalists versus liberals) or ideologies (conservatives versus progressives) or as a reflection of the turbulent situation in the country.

Distinct models of historical evolution and organizational development in the Protestant, preponderantly Pentecostal, world emerged. One sector represented, consciously or not, a type of institutional development similar to the historical model of the Catholic church, treating the state or political society as its partner. From this model, a sort of neo-Christendom, are taken symbols such as the "cathedral," the "Te Deum," and the participation of political figures in important religious ceremonies. The other sector, in contrast, has seen a type of institutional evolution that, recognizing the tradition of independence of the state, consciously or unconsciously conceives the church as part of civil society.

Growth: Class, Clergy, and Women

Chilean Pentecostal churches have experienced sustained growth since the 1930s. A slight deceleration occurred in the 1960s, but steady growth resumed in the 1970s and 1980s (Table 6.1). Neither the 1982 census nor that of 1992 is fully comparable with earlier censuses. The 1982 census takers did not ask about religious affiliation, and the 1992 census takers inquired about religion only of persons fourteen or older.

Much has been written about the causes of growth of the Pentecostal movement.[59] Most attention has been given to the massive changes in society that have made Pentecostal growth possible, but understanding must be also sought in the characteristics of the Pentecostal churches. The churches were not mere shelters

TABLE 6.1   Protestants in the Chilean Population, 1920–1992

	Population	Protestants	Percent
1920	3,785,000	54,800	1.44
1930	4,365,000	63,400	1.45
1940	5,065,000	118,400	2.34
1952	6,295,000	225,500	4.06
1960	7,374,000	425,700	5.58
1970	8,884,000	549,900	6.18
1982	11,329,000	1,132,900[a]	10.00
1992	9,660,367	1,278,644[b]	13.20

[a]Estimated by Juan Sepúlveda.
[b]Respondents 14 years and older only.

Source: National Census, various years.

in turmoil. Rather, they possessed dynamic ways of reaching out and educating, lively and participative ways of worshiping, preachers with unreconstructed humble backgrounds, and the capacity to translate the Christian message into everyday language that was descriptive and personal rather than doctrinal or rationalistic.

Carmen Galilea of the Centro Bellarmino, who has spent years observing Pentecostals, suggests that they

> emphasize personal piety. This is the fruit of religious experience, of giving testimony, and of missionary outreach. They believe in justification by faith but the certitude of faith is found in baptism in the Holy Spirit. . . . Their meetings are distinguished by great cordiality, liberty of expression, informality, and spontaneity. Within the group individuals can freely communicate their feelings, joys, and worries. They are a community of faith but a community in which familiarity and human warmth are present.[60]

Galilea notes that, in marked contrast to Catholic practice, ordinary, nonordained Pentecostals are impelled to make converts.[61] Pentecostal churches are also reaching out to other countries, sending them Chilean missionaries at a modest rate.[62]

Growth based more on individual religious experience and initiative than on doctrine has also produced a distinctive diffused organizational pattern. Some churches are large and centrally organized, with thousands of members; others have been founded by a single pastor or an ambitious lay person. As Galilea has observed all over Santiago, "These small communities are born of the conviction that believers can and ought to proclaim their faith wherever they will."[63]

Beyond personal appeal, the greater or lesser receptivity to Pentecostalism of ordinary people has also been affected by problems, conflicts, and tensions resulting from social strains. Thus Pentecostal growth has been facilitated in periods when large sectors of the population have experienced heightened social exclusion. The reality of social exclusion and the turbulent economic situation brought a constant threat of failure for many and generated a search for ways of coping. In this context Pentecostalism had special appeal, offering a plan for life.

The only period of deceleration occurred in the 1960s, which were noted for public schemes to promote national integration, increased urban and rural organization, and optimistic plans for social change. Despite the failure of these idealistic schemes, the government plans nonetheless had great capacity for raising expectations and generating hope. Pentecostalism grew more slowly then because of lesser receptivity on the part of ordinary people. Conversion to Pentecostalism returned to its previous rate of growth after 1973 with the political decline and acute economic adjustments that occurred under military rule.

The social and cultural space of Pentecostalism in Chilean society is especially that of the dependent underclasses. Indeed, lower-social-class origins has been the mainstay of observations about Pentecostalism in Latin America and elsewhere.[64]

But in Chile, the picture has been changing. In a survey conducted in 1990 by the Centro de Estudios Públicos (CEP), 48.3 percent of Pentecostals[65] identified themselves as middle-class, 48.0 percent as lower-class, and 3.7 percent as upper-class. A degree of confirmation of this self-designation is offered by educational attainment, given the high correlation between education and income, especially in developing countries. Secondary education has frequently been associated with entry into the middle class. Forty-one percent of Pentecostals in the CEP study had completed nine to twelve years of schooling and 9 percent had completed thirteen years or more.[66]

This marked change in social status raises a number of questions to be addressed below. Two other characteristics are key to understanding Chilean Pentecostalism: the special character of its clergy and the position of women within the communities.

Chilean Pentecostal pastors are noteworthy for maintaining their humble origins and for their ability to communicate aspects of Christianity to persons from the lowest sectors of society. On-the-job training and apprenticeship have been favored over lengthy professional preparation. Hoover himself went through a similar process.

C. Peter Wagner, a leading figure in the church-growth school, attempted to a penetrate the puzzle of Pentecostal clergy in 1971: "Somehow the Latin American Pentecostals have developed more culturally meaningful patterns of church life than many other Protestant denominations. . . . One of the most interesting laboratories . . . is Chilean Pentecostalism [in which] ministers are trained in streets rather than in seminaries."[67] According to Wagner, "virtually none of the great leaders of the Chilean Pentecostal churches has spent any time in a seminary or Bible institute." From this he turned to Lalive d'Epinay's detailed description of the intricate process of preparation of ministers through stages of street preaching, Sunday-school teaching, preaching in church, and then becoming pastor.[68] Approval for advancement took results (gaining converts, for example) into account. Reaching the pastorate required twenty years' work for some candidates. Almost 60 percent of pastors in the 1970s were over fifty years old, reflecting the long period of working at the grass roots. Hoff notes that this practice continues, with few being ordained before forty years of age.[69] As a result, Jean-Baptiste August Kessler Jr., noted, "It is astonishing to note the care and reverence the people show toward their pastor."[70]

Contemporary training continues along the lines described by Wagner, but increasingly pastors avail themselves of biblical-theological education, generally through extension programs offered by interdenominational seminaries such as the Comunidad Teológica Evangélica or biblical institutes established by Pentecostal churches or missionaries.[71] Access to pastoral ministry through academic theological education is still the exception.[72]

The Pentecostal clergy stands in marked contrast to the Catholic and other Protestant clergy, which until rather recently tended to come from the middle and upper social strata and had to undergo lengthy academic training in isolation from ordinary people. These students and lesser numbers of seminarians from the lower classes thereby acquired a primarily literate culture that tended to separate them from the lives of common people.

The Chilean Catholic clergy on the leading edge of reform throughout Chile's modern history has tended to come from the upper-middle and upper classes, recruited among the Jesuit, Sacred Heart, and Holy Cross religious communities and among diocesan students. When priests found their way to working with lower-class groups in the cities and the countryside, many remarked on the adjustments needed in cultural and pastoral outlooks.[73] Many students now making their way to Catholic seminaries come from the lower classes. Seminaries and religious communities have adjusted their programs to include some experience of life at the bottom. Few priest or ministers of the historical Protestant churches, however, are rooted in the lives of parishioners to the same degree as Pentecostal pastors.[74]

Age differences are also notable, with Chile's Catholic clergy often entering full-time ministry at twenty-five or twenty-six years of age, long before many Pentecostal pastors. Considerable deference is accorded experienced and effective older Pentecostal pastors by working-class Chileans. The older age of Pentecostal clergy may mean greater willingness on their part to look for compromise during inevitable conflicts. Many of the implications of class and age for Pentecostal growth have yet to be examined systematically.

From a purely statistical viewpoint, the CEP survey mentioned above shows that among "observant Protestants" women form a large majority, by a proportion of 2.3:1.[75] Repeated observations of many Pentecostal congregations confirm this figure. Women also play a far more active role than men in the life of the congregation, acting as evangelizers and educators, engaging in pastoral work through visits to the infirm at home and in hospitals, helping other needy people, and engaging in many activities to sustain worship and community life.

In most churches even the most active participation of women rarely provides them access to directive positions, much less to ordained ministry.[76] But Pentecostalism offers women not only the opportunity to express their private religious devotion but also a way to develop a publicly recognized and honored apostolate. Thus Pentecostalism offers lower-class women access to public space, an access typically denied them by the machismo of popular culture.

In the case of married women whose husbands do not share their beliefs, women's determination to exercise their religious faith operates, although not consciously, as a struggle for space for personal advancement and expression. In cases where wives and husbands share a faith and belong to a Pentecostal community, the participation of both partners equally (in terms of the right to participate) in common life within the congregation redounds within family life as an advance in the democratization of relations. In both cases religious militancy has as one of its effects a significant increase in dignity and self-esteem for women, without this necessarily being accompanied by feminist discourse.

The Contemporary Situation: Stunning Revelations

The CEP survey referred to previously received unusually wide attention for a work on religion. A lengthy TV presentation emphasized the considerable inroads that Pentecostalism had made in numbers and social-class penetration, but Pentecostal scholars and pastors were shocked to learn that less than half of were found to be "observant." Only 48 percent of those who identified themselves as evangelicals (the great majority being Pentecostal) attended church at least once a week; while 13.7 percent attended church once or twice a month, almost 38 percent very seldom or never attended. The study also revealed that the annual rate of increase of the population identifying itself as Protestant was steadily rising. Fontaine and Beyer estimated the rate of growth as 2.5 percent between 1920 and 1940; 3.2 percent between 1940 and 1970; and 4.2 percent between 1970 and 1990.

In terms of organizational recruitment, attendance, and membership, the data show high attraction (4.8 percent annual growth), a high percentage of recent converts (26 percent having joined in the past ten years), a high proportion not observant (52 percent do not attend church weekly), and a high standard of membership criteria (militant or observant).[77]

Pentecostalism in Chile still has a high growth rate, of some 4 percent yearly growth. Pentecostalism is like a great harvester that takes in many new converts but also leaves a large residue of nonpracticing Pentecostals. What happens to ex-Pentecostals? Systematic study of the question is lacking. The problem may never have been seen so clearly as in the results of the CEP study. For Pentecostals, a Pentecostal is by definition "observant," even militant; they point to frequent sermons critical of those who attend only on Sunday. In these terms, the Pentecostal/Protestant portion of the Chilean population is 7 percent, not the 13–16 percent shown by the national census or the CEP study.[78] Pentecostal pastors carried this concern to an annual meeting, the second Encuentro Nacional de Diálogo Pentecostal at Buin in December, 1992, but hints of it had been apparent earlier. The great chonicler of Christianity in the nineteenth and twentieth centuries, Kenneth Scott Latourette, on one of his field trips in 1956 heard from Protestant missionaries in Santiago of "a large erosion of membership . . . especially the Pentecostals."

Pentecostalism, as a perfectionist religion, is extremely demanding, and many converts fail to measure up. What has alienated the dropouts? Is it the professional advancement of second- or later-generation Pentecostals?[79] Or is it that young persons feel that the churches do not grant them enough space to be young in Chilean society? The change in the social composition of Pentecostals and the passage of time have revealed serious weaknesses.[80] Thirty years ago Willems noted that "proud as the Pentecostals leaders may be of their lack of formal theological training, they still live in a society where formal recognition of professional skill is highly valued."[81] A recent study shows the high value that contemporary Pentecostal Sunday-school teachers place on university education.[82] Paul B. Hoff, president of the Pentecostal Bible Institute in Santiago, points to class background and lack of education as issues: "Lay pastors are seldom able to provide biblical teaching. This problem is intensified because the pastor's knowledge of the Bible is limited to what they hear from the older men, who themselves have had no systematic teaching. . . . The preacher utters whatever comes to mind."[83] Thus, says Hoff: "While middle-class Chileans often admire the zeal, faith, and sincerity of the Pentecostals, they are repelled by lack of preparation of their preachers. . . . Parents complain that their college-age children are bored with the sermons and leave the church."[84]

Older approaches are not working well for some sectors. Hoff quotes the president of a Pentecostal group in Vitacura, an affluent sector of Santiago, as saying that few persons are won over by street preaching: "It is not uncommon to see Pentecostals preaching to empty street corners. Yet they continue to rely on this method and seem incapable of adapting to new circumstances."[85] Galilea in her study of Pentecostal preachers notes both their insecurity about what methods to use with the middle classes and fear about the outcome of preaching to them.[86]

Bernice Martin, in a salient follow-up study to David Martin's *Tongues of Fire*, found important clues to Pentecostal adaptation to middle-class life in Chile and elsewhere.[87] Key to understanding Pentecostal behavior has been the self-discipline that gives shape to economic and social lives. Pentecostal discipline has a strong *contra mundum* bent (against alcohol, tobacco, dancing, and soccer and the associated socializing), but, unlike that of Catholic monks, Pentecostal discipline is pragmatic rather than dogmatic. With increasing middle-class status, some Pentecostals are adapting to a more worldly life. Martin concludes that Pentecostals have the capacity to retain a moral and spiritual core while selectively adapting to the pleasures of consumerism.

Another finding of the CEP study came as a shock to some pastors: Many observant Protestants did not conform in their moral positions to those advocated by their pastors. Fontaine and Beyer were surprised to find that the positions of Protestants on moral themes were closer to the opinions of Catholic bishops than to those of the Catholic laity.[88] Between 63 percent (in a 1990 survey) and 52 percent (in a 1991 survey) of observant Protestants opposed a divorce law; between 82 percent (in 1990) and 68 per cent (in 1991) were against abortion in all cases, and 54 percent were opposed to sexual relations before marriage. Pentecostal commentators felt, however, that the percentages were lower than might have been expected, that large numbers of Protestants expressed morally liberal positions, and that the picture would have been even more surprising if the CEP survey had included persons from the very large pool of Protestants who did not attend church weekly. Clearly, the Pentecostal pastors were confronting a picture of followers fitting into a pluralistic society and acting independently.

Another challenge facing the Pentecostal movement in Chile is the division and atomization of the Pentecostal movement. There are probably 1,500 Pentecostal denominations in a country of 14 million persons.[89] Isolated from each other, they are not strong enough to respond to many challenges. For some Pentecostal leaders unity, understood as cooperation, interchange, coordination of efforts, has become an urgent need.

Conversion and Society

Pentecostalism has had an impact on the individual and family lives of members. Conversion is almost invariably described by members as a change in their way of seeing and experiencing life. Lalive d'Epinay captured this in an interview with a convert:

> I was fifteen. Then I felt something happening in me; I felt repentance and began to weep and to ask Him to forgive my sin and transform my life. And I heard a voice— but not a voice of anyone near me—which spoke to me and said: "Your sins are forgiven you." And at the moment my life changed completely, to such a extent that when I left the church, I felt that everything had changed, that the streets and trees and houses were different. It was a very poor district, with some houses in ruins and unmade streets. But for me, everything was new and transformed.[90]

The basic conversion experience brings with it changes in lifestyle for the converted and indirectly has an impact on society as well. Among the examples often cited by Pentecostal and other observers the most obvious is the control of alcoholism and other destructive behaviors. There is abundant anecdotal evidence pointing to a notable decrease in alcoholism and similar addictions, but systematic studies are lacking.

Pentecostal conversion has also been an important factor in relieving dysfunctionality in poor families. Chilean observers have often characterized poor families and others from almost all sectors of Chilean society as "consensual families," wherein couples live together by agreement without the benefit of legal marriage.[91] In this context Pentecostalism has been seen as a significant element of stabilization and regularization of the couple and the family. More stable commitment has also helped to reduce abuse of women[92] and presumably family violence as well.

Relations with the Catholic Church

A warming of relations between Catholics and Protestants took place especially in the days after Vatican II (1962–1965). Gatherings, study days, communal prayer, and public worship were encouraged among Catholics, historical Protestants, and ecumenical Pentecostals. Out of these efforts grew the Fraternidad Ecuménica in 1973. This group continues its largely spiritual activities. Other church groups forged courageous links to offer assistance to many persons during the military regime (1973–1990).[93]

A notable cooling of relations between Catholics and many Pentecostal churches has taken place since the mid–1980s. The sociologist Katherine Gilfeather and others have attributed this to "sectarian proselytism."[94] An impasse in interchurch relations exists at the institutional level, but a larger field exists that resembles the variety of human groupings in Santiago's Parque Florestal in late afternoon. At one extreme are groups reaching out to others: the Centro Ecuménico Diego de Medellín,[95] the Instituto Pedro de Córdoba,[96] the smaller Pentecostal churches that joined the ecumenically minded World Council of Churches (the first Pentecostal groups anywhere to do so),[97] the Fundación de Ayuda Social de las Iglesias Cristianas,[98] and the National Catholic Commission on Ecumenism under Francisco Sampedro Nieto.[99] At the other extreme are the Pentecostal churches that do not cooperate even with other Protestant groups, much less with Catholics. In between, a great many Catholics and Pentecostals pass one another by, without conflict, adjusting to differences in gait.

Young clerics and seminarians form an important resource for future relations. Among the young clergy, Cristián Parker found many Catholic priests well disposed to seek dialogue and cooperation with Pentecostals.[100] But a wide gulf in educational achievement separates the Catholic and the Pentecostal clergy.

Gilfeather reports on a possible bridge for this gap—a project that could offer Pentecostal pastors the intellectual basis for ecumenism. She emphasizes the Comunidad Teológica Evangélica as an institute that students from some ninety Pentecostal churches have attended. The curriculum is designed to foster a more inclusive Christian body than the Pentecostal model. Presumably this would open the door for dialogue with other Christians who are Catholic. However, exposure to a broader, more inclusive theology has had the effect of opening Pentecostal students to other Protestants; 68 percent rejected the idea of dialogue with Catholics.[101] Gilfeather's study shows the long path that ecumenism has to travel.

Conclusion: Contemporary Politics

Pentecostal churches have an established place within Chilean society. Over a period of almost ninety years they have gradually transformed Chile from a traditionally Catholic country to one that is also Pentecostal. The churches are also experiencing problems of aging movements, with many dropouts and a lack of moral conformity.

Chile has turned from military government to an unusually complex democracy.[102] With the return of political parties, the role of the Catholic church, once the voice of opposition during repression, has been reduced. Space is available for Pentecostal churches to speak on moral and social issues.

Given Pinochet's recognition of Pentecostals and the ostentatious support for him of many Pentecostal leaders, Chileans gained the impression that Pentecostals were conservatives.[103] By contrast, Pentecostals showed their political independence in the CEP survey: Most observant Pentecostals had a negative opinion of Pinochet and a positive opinion of Patricio Aylwin, identified themselves as independent, and favored direct election of local officials, and less than 15 percent identified themselves as sympathetic to the right.[104]

The presence of Pentecostals in politics has implications for Latin America that can be explored only briefly. Chile may offer models for other countries of two streams within Pentecostal leadership. Some pastors choose brokerage with the government, working with elite members and increasingly becoming part of the elite. Others prefer to maintain a distance between themselves and elite members, allowing them to evaluate the elite's fulfillment of their political and social responsibilities. The prophetic quality sometimes associated with Pentecostalism is thus maintained. However, experience rather than doctrine is the basis of Pentecostal theological tendencies,[105] and this has inclined Pentecostalism in Chile more toward pragmatism than toward prophecy.

In terms of internal voice Pentecostals have great strength. Who one is as a person and how one relates to others in the church community is based on the Pentecostal experience of God, allowing those who have received it a special status—a right to speak and to be heard within the community. External voice is another matter. Chilean Pentecostals are finding a voice in the public sphere. They began by responding to the questions of power holders and newspaper and television reporters about their positions on abortion, divorce, premarital sex, and the like, and have gone on to take the initiative in expressing their ethical views.

But a more involved issue remains: Will Chilean Pentecostals seek power? Talking about a moral issue is seldom sufficient in a parliamentary democracy. Having power would mean that Pentecostals could decide what issues ought to come up for public debate and legislation. The skepticism of Pentecostals about human intentions, efforts, and institutions[106] works against the seeking of power. The experience of political success draws Chilean Pentecostals forward.

Chile's Pentecostals have been latecomers to direct involvement in politics, behind the Protestant and Pentecostal plunge into politics in Venezuela, Brazil, Peru, Guatemala, and Argentina, in part because of Chile's long military tutelage. In 1992 a clear change was noted. A handful of Pentecostals began standing for national parliamentary elections. Local politics experienced what *Las Ultimas Noticias* (May 17, 1992) called "a true explosion." Pentecostals stood for election as mayors or local council members.

The march of events following the electoral defeat of the military government also appears to confirm tendencies evident before the fall of Pinochet. The sector that supported Pinochet continues to have the greater public visibility. The same practices (the Te Deum, the invitations to political authorities) are continued with the same enthusiasm but now in favor of the new democratic authorities. The change in the political scene has produced a softening in the prophetic sector.

Many Pentecostals are leaving behind their self-image as "pilgrims." They want to feel fully at home, recognized as full citizens, in Chilean society. This common aspiration has impelled the leaders of Pentecostal sectors to seek mutual understanding within the Pentecostal community and a healing of the wounds of the past.[107]

NOTES

1. Walter Hollenweger, "Methodism's Past in Pentecostalism's Present: A Case Study of Cultural Clash in Chile," *Methodist History* 20 (July 1982), p. 169.

2. J. Lloyd Mecham, *Church and State in Latin America: A History of Politico-Ecclesiastical Relations,* rev. ed. (Chapel Hill, N.C.: University of North Carolina Press, 1966), p. 217.

3. Luis Galdames, *Historia de Chile: La evolución constitucional 1810–1925,* vol. 1, *1810–1833* (Santiago, 1926), p. 493, cited by Mecham, *Church and State* pp. 217–218.

4. Mecham, *Church and State,* p. 222.

5. Galdames, *Historia de Chile* p. 493, quoted by Mecham, *Church and State,* p. 218.

6. Mecham, *Church and State,* p. 218.

7. Kenneth Scott Latourette, *Christianity in a Revolutionary Age: A History of Christianity in the 19th and 20th Centuries,* vol. 5 (Grand Rapids, Mich.: Zondervan, 1969), p. 213.

8. Mecham, *Church and State,* p. 222.

9. Latourette, *Christianity in a Revolutionary Age,* pp. 212–213.

10. John Considine, *New Horizons in Latin America* (New York: Dodd, Mead, 1958), pp. 328, 331.

11. Hurtado, who died in 1952, is revered as a modern saint. His work is analyzed in Alejandro Magnet, *El Padre Hurtado* (Santiago: Editorial Pacífico, 1957, 3rd ed., revised), and in Octavio Marfán, Alberto Hurtado: Cristo estaba en él (Santiago: Editorial Patris, 1993).

12. Alberto Hurtado, *¿Es Chile un país católico?* (Santiago: Editorial Splendor, 1941).

13. Brian Smith's unsurpassed study of the Catholic church in Chile records the context and processes of renewal. See his *The Church and Politics in Chile: Challenges to Modern Catholicism* (Princeton: Princeton University Press, 1982).

14. David Martin, *Tongues of Fire: The Explosion of Protestantism in Latin America* (Oxford and Cambridge, Mass.: Basil Blackwell, 1990) p. 76.

15. Martin, *Tongues of Fire,* p. 76.

16. Arturo Fontaine Talavera and Harald Beyer, "Retrato del movimiento evangélico a la luz de las encuestas de opinión pública," *Estudios Públicos* 44 (Spring 1991), p. 67.

17. Willis C. Hoover, *Historia del avivamiento pentecostal en Chile* (Santiago: Imprenta Excelsior, 1948 [1931]), p. 14.

18. Hoover, *Historia del avivamiento pentecostal,* p. 62.

19. Census data for 1992 show continuing religious disparities by region. See Cristián Parker, "Radiografía a la religión de los chilenos," *Mensaje* 428 (May 1994), pp. 178–181. Frank W. Young of the Cornell University Rural Sociology Department has conducted a census analysis of patterns of growth of Pentecostalism in Chile compared with those of the Reformation. See his "Evangelicals in Chile: Reproducing the Reformation Distribution," *Rural Sociology* 60, 3 (Fall 1995), pp. 481–492.

20. Hannah Stewart-Gambino, *The Church and Politics in the Chilean Countryside* (Boulder: Westview Press, 1992), p. 71.

21. Ibid.

22. Martin, *Tongues of Fire,* p. 79.

23. See Gabriel Salazar, "The History of Popular Culture in Chile: Different Paths," in Kenneth Aman and Cristián Parker, eds., *Popular Culture in Chile: Resistance and Survival* (Boulder: Westview Press, 1991), pp. 13–39.

24. Quentin J. Schultze has treated the orality of Pentecostalism as an essential element in his "Orality and Power in Latin American Pentecostalism," in Daniel R. Miller, ed., *Coming of Age: Protestantism in Contemporary Latin America* (Lanham, Md.: University Press of America, 1994), pp. 65–88.

25. Charles Jones, "Willis Collins Hoover," in Stanley M. Burgess and Gary B. McGee, eds., *Dictionary of Pentecostal and Charismatic Movements* (Grand Rapids, Mich.: Zondervan, 1988), p. 445. A refinement on Jones's dating is needed: In 1932 the two church groups had been virtually formed, the two sides of conflict being clear. In 1933 the pastors who supported Hoover were expelled from the Iglesia Metodista Pentecostal, but in January 1934 the conference was celebrated with both parties present, and the two were formally separated thereafter. The legal disputes continued for some time.

26. From the Iglesia Metodista Pentecostal further subdivisions resulted in the Iglesia Unida Metodista Pentecostal (60,000 estimated members), the Iglesia Pentecostal de Chile (30,000 estimated members), the Misión Pentecostal Apostólica (30,000 estimated members), and many other churches. From the Iglesia Evangélica Pentecostal came the Iglesia Pentecostal Apostólica, the Iglesia de Dios Pentecostal, the Iglesia Evangélica de Dios Pentecostal, and others.

27. See Juan Sepúlveda, "Pentecostalism and Liberation Theology," in Harold D. Hunter and Peter D. Hocken, eds., *All Together in One Place: Theological Papers from the Brighton Conference on World Evangelization* (Sheffield: Sheffield Academic Press, 1993), pp. 53–56.

28. Paul Hoff estimates that these mission churches "include no more than 35,000 people." "Chile's Pentecostals Face Problems Due to Isolation," *Evangelical Missions Quarterly* 27, 3 (July 1991), p. 244.

29. The criollo Pentecostal churches also contrast with the Catholic church in Chile, more than half of whose priests in the 1960s were foreign. See *PMV Special Note 15* [Brussels: Pro Mundi Vita Institute, n.d.], p. 3.

30. Juan Guillermo Prado, *El Mercurio,* November 2, 1980; Hoff, "Chile's Pentecostals," p. 244; Patrick Johnstone, *Operation World,* 5th ed. (Grand Rapids, Mich.: Zondervan, 1993), pp. 160–161.

31. W. Stanley Rycroft and Myrtle M. Clemmer, *A Factual Study of Latin America* (New York: Commission on Ecumenical Relations and Mission, United Presbyterian Church, USA, 1963), p. 234, reported by Mecham, *Church and State,* p. 222.

32. Renato Poblete and Carmen Galilea, *Movimiento pentecostal e iglesia católica en medios populares* (Santiago: Centro Bellarmino, 1984), p. 3.

33. Christian Lalive d'Epinay, *Haven of the Masses: A Study of the Pentecostal Movement in Chile* (London: Lutterworth, 1969); Emilio Willems, *Followers of the New Faith: Culture Change and the Rise of Protestantism in Brazil and Chile* (Nashville, Tenn.: Vanderbilt University Press, 1967).

34. Jeffrey Puryear, *Thinking Politics: Intellectuals and Democracy in Chile, 1973–1988* (Baltimore: John Hopkins University Press, 1994), p. 13.

35. However, both Willems and Lalive d'Epinay rejected the kind of relationship that Max Weber saw between Pentecostalism and the growth of large-scale capitalist activity. As Martin (*Tongues of Fire*, p. 229) says, "That . . . is not the contemporary issue, since Pentecostals are not within striking distance of the social position that would make such a connection possible."

36. In their survey of work on Chilean Pentecostalism, Poblete and Galilea do not mention Willems. See *Movimiento pentecostal*, pp. 7–23.

37. See excerpts from Willems in H. McKennie Goodpasture, ed., *Cross and Sword: An Eyewitness History of Christianity in Latin America* (Maryknoll, N.Y.: Orbis Books, 1989), pp. 234–238.

38. Fontaine and Beyer, "Retrato," p. 70.

39. Besides contributions to *Religión y Sociedad*, Sepúlveda's publications include "Pentecostalism as Popular Religiosity," *International Review of Missions* 309 (January 1989), pp. 80–88; "Pentecostal Theology in the Context of the Struggle for Life," in Dow Kirkpatrick, ed., *Faith Born in the Struggle for Life* (Grand Rapids, Mich.: Eerdmans, 1988), pp. 298–318; "Pentecostalism and Liberation Theology," in Hunter and Hocken, *All Together in One Place*, pp. 50–64; "Reflections on the Pentecostal Contribution to the Mission of the Church," *Journal of Pentecostal Theology* 1 (1992), pp. 93–108.

40. See esp. Poblete and Galilea, *Movimiento pentecostal;* Renato Poblete, Carmen Galilea, and Patricia van Dorp, *Imagen de la iglesia y religiosidad de los chilenos* (Santiago: Centro Bellarmino–Centro de Investigaciones Sociales, 1979). Poblete became more acutely aware of Pentecostalism while a student at Fordham University. With Joseph Fitzpatrick as mentor, Poblete explored the world of Puerto Rican Pentecostalism in *Sectarismo portorriqueño* (New York: Centro Intercultural de Documentación, 1969).

41. Besides works cited elsewhere, see *El Pentecostal: Testimonio y experiencia de Dios* (Santiago: Centro Bellarmino, 1990); *El predicador pentecostal* (Santiago: Centro Bellarmino–Centro de Investigaciones Sociales, 1990); and *Lugares de culto en Gran Santiago* (Santiago: Centro Bellarmino, 1989).

42. See, in addition to "Radiografía," "Christianity and Popular Movements," in Aman and Parker, *Popular Culture*, pp. 41–65.

43. See esp. Humberto Lagos S., *Sectas en Chile: ¿Opresión o liberación?* (Santiago: PRESOR, 1985); Humberto Lagos S. and Arturo Chacón Herrera, *Los evangélicos en Chile: Una lectura sociológica* (Concepción: Ediciones Literatura Reunida, 1987); Humberto Lagos S., *La función de la minorías religiosas: Las transacciones del Protestantismo chileno en el período 1973–1981 del gobierno militar* (Louvain la Neuve: n.p., 1982)

44. Juan Guillermo Prado, *Seminarios e institutos teologícos evangélicos* (Santiago: Centro Bellarmino–Centro de Investigaciones Sociales, 1992); *Las sectas juveniles* (Santiago: Talleres Offset La Nación, 1984).

45. See esp. Katherine Gilfeather O'Brien, *El rol de ecumenismo protestante como posible solución al impasse en las relaciones entre la iglesia católica y la comunidad pentecostal* (Santiago: Centro Bellarmino–Centro de Investigaciones Sociales, 1992).

46. Hans Tenneke, *El movimiento pentecostal en la sociedad chilena* (Iquique: Editor Centro de Investigación de la Realidad (CIREN), 1985); Andrés Droogers (see below); Matthew S. Bothner (see below); Servicio Evangélico para el Desarrollo (SEPADE), *En tierra extraña: Itinerario del pueblo pentecostal chileno* (Santiago: Amerinda, 1988); Manuel Canales, Samuel Palma, and Hugo Villela, *En tierra extraña 2: Para una sociología de la religiosidad popular protestante* (Santiago: Amerinda-SEPADE, 1991). The Comisión Nacional de Ecumenismo de la Conferencia Episcopal de Chile and the Arzobispado de Santiago have also published various works, including Francisco Sampedro, ed., *Pentecostalismo, Sectas y Pastoral* (Santiago: Comisión Nacional de Ecumenismo de la Conferencia Episcopal de Chile, 1989).

47. See, for example, William V. D'Antonio and Frederick B. Pike, *Religion, Revolution, and Reform: New Forces for Change in Latin America* (New York: Praeger, 1964).

48. In contrast to 1964 (the year of Eduardo Frei Montalva's election as president), when of a total of 335,537 agricultural day laborers only 1,647 (.004 percent) belonged to labor unions, in 1972, of a total of 335,343,207,910 (62 percent) were unionized. See Manuel Castells, "Reforma agraria, lucha de clases y poder popular en el campo chileno," Centro de Investigaciones en Desarrollo Urbano, Santiago, mimeo, p. 9.

49. Until the middle of the 1960s the popular movement was concentrated in the labor movement. By 1972 it had expanded, to an estimated 800,000 members in a vast network of territorial organizations up and down the country, a number larger than the membership of all the rural and urban unions combined. See Manuel Castells, "El movimiento de pobladores y lucha de clases en Chile," *Revista Latinoamericana de Estudios Urbanos Regionales* (EURE), vol. 3 (Santiago: CUDU, 1973), pp. 9–35.

50. On Ayuda Cristiana Evangélica, see Lalive d'Epinay, *Haven of the Masses*, pp. 179–186.

51. The first two Pentecostal churches in the world to join the ecumenically oriented World Council of Churches were Iglesia Pentecostal de Chile and Misión Iglesia Pentecostal. The motive for their joining is believed to have been more a matter of service than of theological discussion.

52. Cox, *Fire from Heaven*, p. 170.

53. Copies of the book *Torturado por Cristo*, by Richard Wurmbrand, and various issues of the magazine *La Voz de los Mártires* began arriving without charge and in large quantities at the houses of Protestant pastors and church leaders.

54. After the military coup some pastors, Protestant as well as Catholic, interpreted the military intervention as a response from God to the prayer meeting. For this reason, some students of church-state relations, especially Humberto Lagos, have seen in this event a religious version of the appeals for military intervention by Allende's opposition. In our opinion, the most prominent leadership of this prayer meeting and similar initiatives acted sincerely to seek an accord (such as a plebiscite, which had the support of Allende) that would have avoided a bloody solution.

55. Lengthy accounts are provided by Pamela Constable and Arturo Valenzuela, *A Nation of Enemies: Chile Under Pinochet* (New York: Norton, 1991), and Mary Helen Spooner, *Soldiers in a Narrow Land: The Pinochet Regime in Chile* (Berkeley: University of

California Press, 1994). See also reservations about the Spooner volume expressed by David Gallagher in *The Times Literary Supplement,* September 9, 1994, p. 26.

56. According to a booklet describing the presidential reception, "The Chilean Protestant church is pleased because for the first time in the history of its one hundred years of existence, the head of state formally received its directors, pastors, and leaders, valuing the spiritual force constituted by 15 percent of the Chilean population." "Introducción al acto en el Salón Plenario del Edificio Diego Portales, 13 diciembre, 1974," in Pedro Puente Oliva, ed., *Posición evangélica* (Santiago: n.p., 1975), p. 45.

57. The principal paragraph of the document of support read as follows: "The military pronouncement of the armed forces in the historic process of our country was the response of God to the prayers of all believers who see in marxism Satanic forces of darkness in their highest expression." Puentes, *Posición evangélica,* p. 43.

58. Paradoxically, the same government that "for the first time" recognized the importance of Protestants and favored true religious equality also for the first time intervened directly in the internal affairs of Protestant churches, openly favoring sectors that lent it unconditional support.

59. Commentaries on this theme are provided by Juan Sepúlveda, "El crecimiento pentecostal en América Latina," in Carmelo Alvarez, ed., *Pentecostalismo y liberación* (San José, Costa Rica: Editoral Departamento Ecuménico de Investigaciones, 1992), pp. 77–88 and André Droogers, "Visiones paradójicas sobre una religión paradójica: Modelos explicativos del crecimiento pentecostal en Brasil y Chile," in Bárbara Boudewijnse, André Droogers, and Frans Kamsteeg, eds., *Algo más que opio: Una lectura antropológica del pentecostalismo latinoamericano y caribeño* (San José, Costa Rica: Editorial Departamento Ecuménico de Investigaciones, 1991), pp. 17–42.

60. Carmen Galilea, *Católicos carismáticos y Protestantes pentecostales: Análisis comparativo de sus viviencias religiosas* (Santiago: Centro Bellarmino–Centro de Investigaciones Sociales, 1992), pp. 8–9; see also summary, pp. 57–58.

61. See also Catholic Bishop Roger Aubrey's similar analysis in his *La misión siguiendo a Jesús por los caminos de América Latina* (Buenos Aires: Ediciones Guadalupe, 1990).

62. Gilfeather, *El rol,* p. 9; see also Johnstone, *Operation World,* p. 161.

63. Galilea, *Católicos carismáticos,* p. 8.

64. In the United States Pentecostals are still ranked low on income and educational attainment. See, for example, Barry A. Kosmin and Seymour P. Lachman, *One Nation Under God: Religion in Contemporary American Society* (New York: Crown, 1993), pp. 256–263.

65. Defined by the survey as "observant," attending church at least once a week.

66. Fontaine and Beyer, "Retrato," pp. 88, 86.

67. *Christianity Today,* August 6, 1971, pp. 5–8.

68. Christian Lalive d'Epinay, "The Training of Pastors and Theological Education," *International Review of Mission* 57 (April 1967), pp. 185–192.

69. Hoff, "Chile's Pentecostals," p. 246.

70. Kessler quotes David Brackenridge in his *A Study of the Older Protestant Missions and Churches in Peru and Chile* (Goes, Netherlands: Oosterbaan and le Cointre, 1967), p. 318.

71. See Prado, *Seminarios;* Hoff, "Chile's Pentecostals," esp. p. 249.

72. As Prado shows in his *Seminarios,* only a few Pentecostal churches have their own seminaries or biblical institutes.

73. See Aldunate's reflection in "Carpintero Segundo," in Aníbal Pastor et al., *De Lonquén a Los Andes: 20 años de la iglesia chilena* (Santiago: Rehue, 1993), pp. 111–129.

74. Hoff ("Chile's Pentecostals," pp. 246–247) sees poverty and lack of education of preachers also as grave weaknesses, alienating the increased membership from the middle classes.

75. Fontaine and Beyer, "Retrato," p. 84.

76. With the exception of a few congregations, Pentecostalism has inherited the masculine exclusivity of ordination. Nonetheless, because the differentiation between clergy and laity in Pentecostalism is much less accentuated than in traditional Christianity, the lack of access to ordination is rarely felt by Pentecostal women as an impediment to their apostolate. In strictly religious terms, the spirituality of women is highly appreciated. Elderly women often enjoy considerable spiritual authority, exceeding that of some pastors.

77. Fontaine and Beyer, "Retrato."

78. The national census of 1992 showed Protestants as 13.2 percent of the national population aged fourteen years or older (*El Mercurio,* September 3, 1993); Fontaine and Beyer ("Retrato," p. 91) reported 16 percent. See also estimates in Hoff, "Chile's Pentecostals," p. 244.

79. Arturo Chacón comments in a similar vein in *La Nación,* March 15, 1995.

80. Besides Hoff (below), see also Johnstone's summary of the issues in *Operation World,* p. 161.

81. Emilio Willems, "Validation of Authority in Pentecostal Sects of Chile and Brazil," *Journal of Scientific Study of Religion* 6 (Fall 1967), p. 258.

82. Matthew S. Bothner, "El soplo del Espíritu: Perspectivas sobre el movimiento pentecostal en Chile," *Estudios Públicos* 55 (Winter 1994), tables 19 and 20, p. 295.

83. Hoff, "Chile's Pentecostals," p. 246.

84. Ibid.

85. Hoff, "Chile's Pentecostals," p. 248.

86. Galilea, *El predicador,* pp. 41–43.

87. Bernice Martin, "New Mutations of the Pentecostal Ethic Among Latin American Pentecostals," *Religion* 25 (1995), pp. 101–117.

88. In a complementary study, in progress, of the Catholic church and politics in Chile and Peru, Brian H. Smith and Michael Fleet pursue this aspect at greater length.

89. Gilfeather, *El rol,* p. 22.

90. Lalive d'Epinay, *Haven of the Masses,* p. 48.

91. Some scholars, especially the anthropologist Sonia Montecinos in a prizewinning work *Madres y huachos: Alegorías del mestizaje chileno,* 2d ed. (Santiago: Cuarto Propio—CEDAM, 1993), attribute this tendency to the legacy of the encounter between the Spanish *conquistadores,* whose legal wives remained in Spain, and indigenous women. See Cynthia Rimsky, "La identidad de los chilenos," *Evangelio y Sociedad* 15 (1992), pp. 2–6.

92. See Slootweg, "Mujeres pentecostales chilenas," in Boudewijnse, Droogers, and Kamsteeg, eds., *Algo más que opio,* pp. 77–93.

93. See, for example, Patricio Orellana and Elizabeth Quay Hutchison, *El movimiento de derechos humanos en Chile, 1973–1990* (Santiago: Centro de Estudios Políticos Latinoamericanos Simón Bolívar, 1991).

94. Gilfeather, *El rol.*

95. See esp. *Pastoral Popular* and publications of Ediciones Rehue.

96. See esp. the publications of its director, Cristián Parker.

97. For details see J. L. Sandidge, "World Council of Churches," in Burgess and McGee, *Dictionary,* p. 902.

98. On the origins of the Fundación, see Orellana and Hutchison, *El movimiento,* pp. 143–198.

99. See esp. *Pentecostalismo, sectas y pastoral* (Santiago: Conferencia Episcopal de Chile/Comisión Nacional de Ecumenismo, 1989).

100. Interview with Cristián Parker by Hannah Stewart-Gambino, June 1995.

101. Gilfeather, *El rol,* esp. p. 64.

102. The system has been called binomial majoritarianism. Chile's constitution, produced by the previous military government, imposes representation in congress from the right without full voter participation.

103. Fontaine and Beyer, "Retrato," esp. pp. 104–105.

104. Chilean life has been strongly organized around political parties. The independent position of many Pentecostals has been interpreted as lack of interest in politics or unpredictability. See, for example, Fontaine and Beyer, "Retrato," pp. 102–112.

105. On experience as the theological basis of Pentecostalism, see Cleary in this volume.

106. Everett A. Wilson, "The Dynamics of Latin American Pentecostalism," in Miller, *Coming of Age,* p. 93.

107. Since March 1991 a group called the Comité de Coordinación Evangélica has been meeting with some regularity. The group includes leaders of the Confraternidad Cristiana de Iglesias, the Consejo de Pastores, and other churches that remained neutral during the period of greatest division under the military regime, such as the Anglicans and the Baptists. In the beginning this group considered itself the Protestant response to President Patricio Aylwin's call for national reconciliation during the public presentation of the final report of the Truth and Reconciliation Commission.

❀ 7 ❀

Pentecostalism, Conversions, and Politics in Brazil

ROWAN IRELAND

*I*n numerical terms there is no hyperbole in the notion of an explosion of Protestantism in Brazil. In what is nominally the country with the world's largest Catholic population, some 20 million out of a population of 150 million are Protestant.[1] The vast majority of those Protestants—*crentes* (believers), as they are generally called in Brazil—are Pentecostals. Protestantism in Brazil has exploded numerically as, especially in the past thirty years, millions of Brazilians, in urban and rural areas in every major region of the country and up as well as down in the class structure, have converted to a wide range of Pentecostal churches. The Assemblies of God have remained the largest single group, with a still expanding membership estimated at 8 million in 1990. The Congregação Cristã was estimated at upwards of 2 million and Brasil para o Cristo at 1 million at the same time. These numbers in the older Pentecostal churches were augmented by membership in a second generation of churches branching out of the original groupings during the 1950s and 1960s, many of them numbering in the hundreds of thousands. And by the 1980s there was phenomenal growth in a "third wave" of churches, represented by Bishop Edir Macedo's Igreja Universal do Reino de Deus. This church, which has now established temples in New York, had over 600,000 members in 1990 in seven hundred temples spread throughout Brazil; its message was diffused through fourteen radio stations, a press, and a television station in São Paulo.[2]

Behind the explosion of numbers in recent decades is a longer history of institutional development and consolidation first at the local and eventually at the national level.[3] In the early years of the twentieth century, small Pentecostal congregations were established by Swedish missionaries in Belém, in the north of Brazil, and by an Italian in São Paulo. After the initial Euro-American input (the two Swedes and the Italian had briefly been associated with Pentecostals at the

123

Chicago mission of William H. Durham), the slow expansion from the 1920s onward was indigenous. But though in this sense rooted from the beginning in the
local, the members of small congregations, meeting in private houses or tiny
shanty temples, felt and were made to feel that they were a marginalized minority group.

This remained the case at least up to the 1960s, but by the 1970s and 1980s
Pentecostalism was well established even at the national level. In 1977 I attended
a special service in the large central regional temple of the Assemblies of God in
Abreu e Lima, close to Recife in northeastern Brazil. A congregation of six hundred celebrated the trimphant consolidation of the Assemblies in the region and
throughout Brazil. The service marked the end of a week of study in which pastors, evangelists, deacons, and senior members of congregations from all over the
region had taken part. The church-triumphant theme dominated the exhortations that night. The pastor of the regional church took the theme of his address
from a hymn, sung by the choir, about the founding of the Assembly in Belém in
1919. He pointed to his mother, seated with dignitaries of the church and the
town, as the link with the beginning. He recounted the story of the church's
growth in the region. Groans of anguish accompanied his stories and images of
the trials of early days—*crentes* dismissed from jobs because they owned up to
being *crentes,* politicians listening to priests and preventing the establishment of
temples. But then he referred to the times to be greeted with alleluias—over
12,000 members of the Assembly, baptized and with certificates that can now be
used to get jobs, temples where the Catholics now have nothing.[4]

By the 1980s Brazilian Pentecostals not only constituted the major, visible, organized religious group in thousands of Brazilian localities but had clearly arrived
at the level of the national institutional matrix. Paul Freston has given us an account of the formation of an extremely influential coalition of mainly Pentecostal
Protestant politicians in the congressional Constituent Assembly that produced
the present Brazilian constitution in 1988. Behind it he shows us a council of
leading Pentecostal pastors who were responsible for mobilizing the votes of
Pentecostals in support of *crente* politicians. The same group may have played a
decisive role in the presidential elections of 1989, when they swung Protestant
support behind successful candidate Fernando Collor against the Workers' party's
Luís Iñácio da Silva.

The Protestant explosion in Brazil is not, then, merely numerical; it involves a
rapid institutional inclusion of organized Pentecostalism at all levels of Brazilian
society. But the question remains, What is the social, cultural, and political impact of the explosion? More pointedly, Is the Pentecostal explosion the epicenter
of transformations of Brazilian society as deep as the Protestant explosion in
Europe in the sixteenth and seventeenth centuries?[5] Or, as a marxist-inspired
stereotyping of Pentecostalism among the "popular classes" used to have it, does
the explosion, in its individual and institutional aspects, merely reinforce alienation, diverting the most oppressed classes from political engagement and rein-

forcing the hegemony of the rich and powerful?[6] Are Pentecostals so otherworldly in their concerns as to stand aside from the social engagements in which gender and race relations in civil society are being transformed?[7]

These are grand questions, and I cannot hope to address them fully in this chapter. But I can indicate where case-study data and argument are taking us on subissues that must be addressed on the way to answering these questions. First, there is the issue of the range of *crente* political dispositions and behaviors. Nested in this issue are questions about the uniform characteristics of *crentes* as citizens and about the likelihood that Pentecostal leaders of the kind described by Freston will succeed in mobilizing *crentes* in political campaigns. Second, there is the issue of the way or ways in which Pentecostalism informs biography such that when *crentes* go out from their congregations and return to home and neighborhood their dispositions as citizens have been significantly shaped.

The Range of Crente *Political Dispositions and Behaviors*

Many observers of Pentecostals in Latin America have challenged the stereotype of the uniformly politically conservative evangelical Protestant. Phillip Berryman is only the latest challenger when he chides the left for neglecting possible allies among evangelicals in the struggle against doctrinaire neoliberalism.[8] The challenges have been diverse, with a range of concessions to stereotype. Some, like Berryman when he points to participation by evangelicals in Brazil's Workers' party, have mounted the challenge on the basis of observed behavior in the formal political arena and local community associations.[9] At least some Pentecostals in some circumstances, it seems from these studies, act out of Pentecostal moral vision to become citizens adept not only at critique of their political economies but at political action for change. Others have argued that the Pentecostal challenge to the political-economic status quo might come not so much from immediate, overt political behavior as over time, from the nurturing of a Pentecostal counterculture and the practices of a distinctive Pentecostal way of life.[10] In David Martin's richly developed argument, meant to apply throughout Latin America, Pentecostals may vote conservatively or appear to endorse the status quo by remaining apolitical or refusing to adopt causes espoused by the left, but in their world apart they acquire the values, expectations, motivations, and disciplines that make them latent carriers of liberal-democratic transformation.

On this dimension of difference among challengers I have tended to the latter perspective, though I have not been surprised by the reports of Pentecostals as actors in radical politics, at least on the local scene. John Burdick has taken me to task for failing to note that Brazilian Pentecostals participate in movements for radical and gender justice as well as being, in some localities, stalwarts in Latin America's largest and most vital party of the left, the Brazilian Workers' party.[11] The involvements that he found among the Pentecostals he studied in the state of Rio de Janeiro do not surprise me, but the Pentecostals I studied in a semirural town on the periphery of Greater Recife (most intensively in the years 1977–1988) did not act in the same way as Burdick's. The difference, I believe, is not a difference between Pentecostals or even between observers but one of time and place: In semirural towns of the Northeast at the time, there were neither parties nor movements for radical change for Pentecostals to join.

In early 1993, a brief return to Campo Alegre (the name I give to the town where I had done my earlier fieldwork) confirmed this belief. Campo Alegre had become the center of its own municipality, the third municipal elections had just concluded, the Workers' party had fielded candidates for council, and, though Pentecostals had been far from a solid bloc, a few had been prominent in support of Workers' party candidates. Of particular interest to me was that my friend Severino, through whom I have been exploring the complexities of Pentecostal political orientations since 1977, had, by all accounts, skillfully mobilized support for a Catholic neighbor whose candidacy had been endorsed by the Worker's party. Severino's own account of his involvement will be examined below. For the moment it is enough to note that the mere fact of Severino's small involvement in radical politics suggests to me that the difference between observers who posit long-term latent radicalism and those who report actual involvement of Pentecostals in radical or party politics does not involve a serious difference about the possibility and actuality of Pentecostals as critical citizens.

But there are important differences about the extent of variety in the politics of Brazilian Pentecostals and differences too about how Pentecostal belief and/or practice works and is worked on to affect quality of citizenship. Emilio Willems, in comparison with most more recent observers, minimizes variety in the politics of Brazilian Pentecostals.[12] All Pentecostals, in the religious communities that they construct, symbolically subvert the traditional social order. Political challenge spills over as an unintended consequence from Pentecostal religious life. In their religious beliefs and practices, the poor come to see themselves as having a status altogether different from and higher than that awarded them in the secular society or in the Catholic church. They learn how to organize themselves without traditional hierarchy and acquire both the skills and the confidence to demand a more egalitarian order in society at large. Echoing a powerful sociological account of the social origins of revolution, Willems seems to imply that Pentecostals become critical citizens through their experience of status incongruence: From the incongruence between their status and experience in their religious world, on the one hand, and in the social, political, and economic relations of everyday life, on the other, arises a critical consciousness and the aspiration to achieve congruence. Insofar as there is variety among Pentecostals as Brazilian citizens it will arise from different strategies drawn from a Pentecostal repertoire as to how congruence might be achieved. But, in possibly different ways, all Pentecostals will have a potential to contribute to the development of a less authoritarian, more democratic Brazil.

John Burdick acknowledges variety in Pentecostal citizenship in the form of concessions to the old stereotype of Pentecostal conservatism and quiescence.[13]

He finds, nonetheless, a central Pentecostal logic that, political circumstances permitting, will facilitate Pentecostal participation in social movements and lead individual members of conservative-leaning collectivities such as the Assemblies of God toward involvement in radical-left party politics. Yes, the ordinary Pentecostals of Duque de Caxias, focused on the Kingdom that is not of this world and acutely aware of corruption, will usually not bother to cast votes; they shy away from the morally dubious wheeling and dealing of local politics; they seem disposed to accept poverty, valuing the simple, trusting virtues of the poor exalted in the Gospels; they value God-ordained order and legitimate authority and abhor the confusion, violence, and disorder that normally accompanies radical struggle in the workplace or residential area in Brazil. But they do not renounce the world entirely, regarding themselves as obliged to strive for "improvement" and "cleanliness" in the world; accepting poverty, they feel called to fight against unjust and degrading immiseration; their "sacralization of poverty carries with it a compelling denial of legitimacy of the rich and powerful."[14]

Here, then, in the religious logic of Pentecostalism, in what Clifford Geertz would recognize as a distinctive Pentecostal religious culture, is room for "the development of a highly critical social consciousness" and for the social-movement and party-political action Burdick describes. But these developments from religious culture through critical social consciousness to radical political involvement will be conditional on opportunity, in Burdick's view. Pentecostals, moved to critical consciousness by religious culture, will often stay out of radical politics because Catholic activists marginalize them or because traditional patron-client politics blocks out alternative politics. Conversely, under conditions of opportunity, Pentecostals will tend to act radically and effectively, unrestrained by the clerical caution or the emphasis on organic social harmony that reins in Catholic lay activists. I think Burdick is arguing that, despite all the tensions and inconsistencies of Pentecostal religious culture, the impulse toward critical citizenship will be experienced by all Pentecostals, or at least by all Pentecostals of the Assemblies of God that constitute the largest single Pentecostal church in Brazil.

My own studies of members of the Assembly of God in Campo Alegre lead me to disagree. Attempting a Geertzian exploration of Pentecostal religious constructions of past and future, I found not one but at least two Pentecostal logics that nurtured quite divergent political dispositions. One of these, the religious culture of the sect *crente,* as I called it, was very close to the single logic so well reconstructed by Burdick, though, as already noted, through the 1980s I found no instance of the sustained radical action in movements or party politics of the kind that Burdick found. The other, the religious culture of the church *crente,* moves and motivates members of the Assembly of God to eschew political involvement and to endorse conservative, even authoritarian agendas, if only as a consequence of lack of interest in developing a critique of a rejected secular order.

The Pentecostals I called church *crentes* are much less disposed than sect *crentes* like Severino to consider any public dimension in the private troubles of everyday life.[15] These troubles are trials in which the individual *crente* is required to re-

main faithful to the terms of salvation won for us by Jesus Christ against the powers of darkness. That fidelity is found and guaranteed in maximum immersion in
the life of the temple and risked by political engagement—thought likely to be
fruitless anyway—in the world beyond it. God's time and space in the temple
must be protected by leaders of the church, who may enter into alliances with legitimate power to do so. The organized church for the church *crente* becomes the
unit of citizenship, negotiating the structures of unequal wealth, power, and ex-
pertise for the prosperity of the church. In this way, time and space won for God
may be maximized and, through that victory, the individual's chances of sustained fidelity to the terms of salvation increased. The individual church *crente*,
then, is not concerned to exercise critical citizenship, however sharply aware of
corruption, sin, and injustice in the world at large. The church *crente*, from deep
religious motivation, abdicates citizenship. In turn, church pastors in the Campo
Alegre region, exercising a sort of collective citizenship for the victory of their
church, have negotiated and made alliances with local elites, and those alliances,
in effect, help preserve the political-economic status quo.

The sect *crente* abdicates citizenship to no one and is disposed, in the living of
a religious culture, to critical citizenship. Among the Bible stories through which
Pentecostals depict the world, sect *crentes* emphasize those that demonstrate a
public dimension to private troubles and the responsibility of the individual to
determine and challenge those who are responsible for gross injustice in the
world. The sect *crente*, while acknowledging the need for withdrawal from the
world and caution in worldly involvement, seeks engagement in the world to fulfill the responsibilities of faith rather than withdrawal from it within the confines
of the temple. It is this religiously motivated engagement and sense of responsibility to challenge injustice that dispose the sect *crente* to critical citizenship.[16]

I will elaborate the argument about how different ways of being Pentecostal affect citizenship below. But there is yet another type of Brazilian Pentecostal citizen to add to the abdicating and critical types discussed so far. This is the pragmatic citizen, my term for a type that was foreshadowed for me by some members
of the leadership of the Assemblies of God in the Northeast of Brazil but has become much clearer as a distinct type in Paul Freston's discussion of the "third
wave" of Pentecostalism in Brazil. For Freston, the "third wave" is represented
mainly by the Igreja Universal do Reino de Deus, as noted above.

In Freston's account, the new church embodies a religious culture markedly
different from the first wave of small local marginalized sects and the second wave
of established churches of the kind that the Assemblies of God now constitute.
The Igreja Universal do Reino de Deus calls for and receives converts to therapeutic healing and individual success in this life. In contrast to older Pentecostal
groups, Freston claims, the new church "offers a moralized version of the yuppie
gambling ethic, an overnight flight to rapid enrichment."[17] This is the message
announced in mass gatherings that have filled the Maracanão stadium in Rio de
Janeiro and spread through radio and television stations owned by the church. At

its upper levels, executive-style leaders play hard at electoral politics: "the Universal Church shows a frankly pragmatic relation to politics, characteristic of a business empire expanding on many fronts."[18]

This noncritical pragmatic citizenship is clearly very different from both the abdicated and the critical Pentecostal citizenship described earlier, but like them it seems to emerge from yet another distinctive Pentecostal religious culture and a particular way of living that culture.

Ways of Being Pentecostal in Brazil

Until this point, the small response to the grand question about the implications of the Protestant explosion for deep social and political transformation in Brazil has been to argue that only one of at least three types of Pentecostal religious culture found in Brazil disposes Pentecostals as citizens to be agents of deep transformation. In this section I shall elaborate that argument as I reflect on the different meanings that conversion has had in the lives of Pentecostals. Again, it seems to me, only one of several modes of Pentecostal conversion is at all likely to dispose some Pentecostals to become critical citizens, whether in civil society . or in the arenas of state politics.

My reflections start with and were provoked by Severino, who has been my star case of the sect *crente* in Campo Alegre. Because of his thoughtfulness, his conversational eloquence, and his prestige among all *crentes* in Campo Alegre, I have relied on him as a sort of guide to the whole range of themes and variations in Pentecostal cultures and types of citizenship to be found among members of the Assembly of God in the town. Until my most recent interviews with him, in December 1992 and January 1993, I had regarded Severino as having worked out a coherent religious culture, drawing, with deliberation, from a known repertoire of Pentecostal myth, belief, and practice. I thought of Severino as living out of that religious culture, as those of us who have been influenced by Geertz are wont to think of the way religion works in everyday life. His critical citizenship emerged from a Pentecostalism that I believed I, and he too, could distinguish from the Pentecostalism of those coreligionists who had abdicated their citizenship. Variety among Pentecostals, on a scale from abdicated citizenship to Severino's critical citizenship, could be explained in terms of quite different Pentecostal logics or religious cultures.

But reflection on my more recent interviews has led me to question whether I had not relied too exclusively on clearly and permanently different religious cultures to explain different types of citizenship. Those interviews, from which extracts are presented below, led me to the following conclusions:

1. Severino does indeed continue to articulate a distinctive Pentecostal logic or Pentecostal religious culture that accounts for the critical citizenship displayed in his participation in the 1992 electoral campaign.

2. Over time, however, Severino's religious culture develops: He draws on the wider Pentecostal or wider still evangelical Christian repertoire as he reflects upon and reinterprets the myths, beliefs, and religious orientations that inform his citizenship.
3. It is inconsistent with Severino's own discourse and incompatible with my knowledge of his biography to speak of his critical citizenship's arising simply from his living out of a fixed religious culture, acquired once and for all at the time of conversion.
4. The quality of Severino's citizenship is to be accounted for not only by his religious culture but by the developmental quality of that culture. In the context of what I had previously learned about Severino, the recent interviews suggest to me that Severino might be a case of continuing spiritual conversion, a kind of conversion that several rather diverse Christian theologians may help us appreciate.
5. The differences in quality of citizenship between Severino and church *crentes* may be explained not only in terms of different Pentecostal religious cultures but also in terms of different modes of conversion to Pentecostalism. These different modes of conversion mediate how Pentecostal convictions, shared across the different religious cultures, are expressed in everyday life.

In this paper I wish to elaborate points 4 and 5, but some further details about Severino and his situation, not evident in the interview extracts, must first be recorded. Severino, now approaching sixty years of age, became a *crente* as a young teenager. He was the son of a poor itinerant sharecropper and rural laborer, and his account of his conversion suggests that it had to do with freeing himself from many aspects of his father's condition. Against the will of his father, young Severino attended night school to learn to read and write. Turning away from his father's folk Catholicism, he started attending the meetings that his Pentecostal teacher conducted after classes. His conversion, marked first by baptism of water and later by the experience of baptism in the Spirit, he describes as a slow process of "reading, reading, reading and thinking, thinking, thinking," a process that continues.[19]

Severino's conversion story is very different from most of those I heard from members of the Assembly of God in Campo Alegre. Most members of the Assembly focus their whole religious biography around the story of a once and completed conversion; that is how religious biography is told even in contexts other than public testimonies, where we might expect highly stylized accounts. In the usual telling, after a life of dissipation or feeling lost and directionless there is an arrival. Conversion is an arrival at the truth, at the rules for good living, at a right relationship with God. It is a turning away from the world and a settling down into the world that is a part of the church, where the corrupting social engagements of the material world can be excluded as far as possible. In Severino's telling of his religious biography, the one conversion figures less prominently, and, using imagery curiously similar to that favored in the primers and hymns of the Catholic base communities, he describes that conversion as a setting out on a journey. The conversion has provided orientations and training for the journey, but the reading and thinking must go on. Conversion has committed him to analyzing a changing world, to talking about his changing responsibilities in the world, to working out what God would want him to do for the good of his changing neighborhood. In this sense, Severino's conversion is a continuing one.

That does not mean that he does not share much of the simple, conservative theology of his coreligionists. He reminds me of this, firmly, in the 1993 interview. I asked questions that I hoped would prompt him to talk about any religious motivations in his foray into electoral politics in the 1992 municipal elections. Severino's first responses indicated that he saw no connection. As a *crente* his responsibility in the community was "to preach, to counsel, to show that the Gospel is true, that it is salvation for all who believe." "I asked him, Is there any relationship between preaching and the sort of action you have taken in the material world?" "No, no," he replied, "these are completely different things."

But he agreed that he was completely different from other *crentes*, who would never engage politically on the left as he had done because they believed that, as *crentes*, they should keep out of politics: "Let's put it this way. Many [*crentes*] don't want to enter into political matters because they think there's no need, that it's not worthwhile. But people who live here can't get by without political involvement; I think the group can't get by without political involvement because, though not all politicians are good and true, there is a sort of politician that we need."

Here Severino appears the mildest of political radicals. But he was beginning to indicate a significant *religious* difference—a difference with consequences for his politics—from those many other *crentes*. He agreed with those others that it was not so good for a *crente* to become a politician and that preaching the truth was prior and sufficient. But, unlike them, he felt a responsibility as a *crente* to know the material needs of his neighbors, to know who could best help in the political struggle to satisfy those needs, and, at least, to help that person.

The key to knowing and discerning, for Severino, was *convivência*, living and sharing experience and talking about experience. Through *convivência* with all his neighbors, not just with fellow *crentes*, the *crente* learns about needs, about what sort of political action is necessary, about legitimate alliances, about what to accept and reject in the world. When I asked him whether his own political involvement was at odds with his need to withdraw from the material world, he noted, first, that we (fellow workers and neighbors) had to work together:

> I arrive at the conclusion that I'm not going to display myself as a *crente* out there in
> the world doing everything. But at the same time I can't stop living with them or
> lending them my support. We can't have a *crente* completely in the world—I'm not

going to go along with it completely, drinking and playing around, defrauding people. But I have to live with them. I have to act politically to succeed on the two sides:
managing my journey and at the same time defending any person as he deserves to
be defended.

This theme of *convivência* as the basis for knowing and discerning right conduct is, I have come to realize, at the heart of Severino's religiosity. Those things
that *crentes* must do first and foremost, seeking salvation and preaching the
Gospel, require *convivência*. Severino, in the years that I have known him, has
never spoken of his conversion as an arrival at the fully articulated rules for salvation or the complete message to be preached. It appears much more of a setting out with a responsibility to weigh what the rules mean in given situations
and what constitutes witness and effective communication of the faith in everyday life. Salvation and evangelization, for Severino, are slow processes, requiring
constant analysis of the world, sharing life with one's neighbors and talking with
them. Here, in a way of holding and living the revelations of his first conversion,
is the basis for Severino's religious differences from those coreligionists I have
called the church *crentes,* and in those religious differences are the seeds of divergent types of citizenship.

In the first part of the interview, then, we see Severino affirming Pentecostal
constants: the separation of religion and politics, the primacy of evangelization
and the seeking of individual salvation in the life of a *crente,* a respect for established authority in church, state, and civil society. But in the rest of the interview
we see him reflecting on his responsibilities in his community, puzzling about his
social identity as he applies broad principles of New Testament morality to a
complex, changing society. As he reflects, puzzles, and analyzes, his discourse is
very similar to that of Catholic base community (CEB) leaders I have been inter-
viewing in São Paulo and very dissimilar to that of the church *crentes.* And
Severino, in the quality of his citizenship, is much closer to CEB Catholics than
to that large group of his coreligionists.

But those Pentecostal constants are never far away. If the voice of the faith-
informed citizen sounds base-community Catholic, the voice of the man of faith
remains identifiably Assembly of God Pentecostal. Knowing that Severino is neither carelessly eclectic nor prone to compartmentalize his life into discrete areas
of activity, I have been led to consider that he shares a mode of living out of religious faith and myth with the base-community Catholics despite his differences
from them on articles of faith and religious myth. It is this mode of living faith
that I call continuing conversion. Cecília Mariz, reflecting on similarities and differences among Pentecostals and base-community Catholics in Recife, has antic-
ipated this line of thought. She notes the tendency toward political conservatism
that is deeply rooted in the constants of Pentecostal religious culture, and she
compares this with the critical citizenship that is nurtured in the religious culture
of the base communities.[20] But she finds similar experiences of and emphases on
a particular sort of conversion in both groups and suggests that this sort of con-

version stimulates critical citizenship because it involves "a questioning of the world as taken for granted . . . and experiencing the limits of a conventional commonsense view of life and becoming critical of it." In the case of the Pentecostals,

> the requirement of converting counteracts a fatalistic outlook on life by encouraging people to disagree with and rebel against reality as conventionally defined. It disposes people to believe that their lives can be changed. Even Pentecostalism, with its otherworldliness and its respect for constituted authority, fosters a critical, nonfatalistic outlook on life that can work against the movement's official posture of avoiding involvement in "worldly" affairs.[21]

Social scientists tend to operate with a notion of conversion that is too simple and undifferentiated to allow appreciation and further investigation of this point. We tend to think of conversion as an event, a precise turning to a clearly defined set of beliefs and/or practices and/or commitments shared with a group of fellow devotees. Conversion is a problematic discontinuity demarcated by distinctive continuous states on either side of the conversion happening—the solid-state before and the even more solid-state after. The discontinuity, the conversion itself, demands explanation in terms of some psychological disposition or set of social circumstances. The consequences of conversion in terms of quality of social participation and citizenship may be inclusive: By virtue of conversion the convert is incorporated as an endorsing, noncritical participant into the dominant economic and political projects of the society. Alternatively, they may be exclusive: The convert, protected by high walls of practice and symbol, is excluded by choice and/or rule from active, critical participation.

This allows for two types of conversion that I think are to be found among Pentecostals in Brazil. These are once and complete conversions that involve self-exclusion from full social engagement, as found among the church *crentes* of Campo Alegre, and those once and complete conversions that involve the decidedly uncritical inclusion found among members of the Igreja Universal do Reino de Deus described by Paul Freston. But neither of these types will do in the case of Severino. The need for another type emerges as we ask two questions that address the central puzzle presented by the 1993 interview. How does Severino's retention of basic Pentecostal beliefs and orientations, which he shares with his coreligionists the church *crentes,* figure in his sect-*crente* religious culture? How do the shared beliefs and orientations that among church *crentes* are conducive to abdicated citizenship become, in Severino at least, compatible with if not conducive to critical citizenship? The answer, I now think, lies in the dynamic mode in which Severino holds all his beliefs and orientations. Believing that the Kingdom is not of this world, Severino *also* feels called on to continue discerning good and evil in the world and to build on the good. Retaining the simple and clear morality to which he turned at conversion, Severino is *also* drawn to go on working out what that morality requires of him in a changing world. The responsibility to turn away from the world of his father was not completed at the time of his teenage conversion; he must keep turning. Fidelity to the initial conversion requires continuing conversion, and, in Severino's case, that continuing conversion demands that he include himself critically in the wider society.[22]

This third type of continuing, socially engaging conversion that Severino has helped me define does not make him unique among Pentecostals, but it does help us understand one way in which Pentecostal religious culture works in the lives of many Pentecostals to dispose them to radical citizenship. I suggest, though I cannot prove it, that Severino exemplifies and illuminates the type of conversion that Mariz found motivating Pentecostals in Recife toward the radical citizenship of the CEB Catholics. Severino, I claim, is a Pentecostal akin to the radical Pentecostal citizens who speak in John Burdick's publications, and I would suggest that Burdick's cases of Dalila and Murão, who have advanced further into radical politics than Severino in different circumstances, speak the language of continuing, socially engaged converts when they discern the Pentecostal devil in the social system and seek to create the conditions for evangelization in the political struggle against immiseration.

Conclusions

I conclude this analysis with a pairing of three types of conversion and three types of political citizenship found among Brazilian Pentecostals. The critical citizen of some recent studies of Brazilian Pentecostals is likely to live Pentecostal religious culture as a continuing conversion that is a turning toward social engagement. The pragmatic political operator of third-wave Pentecostalism has experienced a once and complete conversion that includes him or her in would-be upwardly mobile postmodern Brazil. The abdicated citizen I found in the church *crentes* of Campo Alegre is that sort of citizen as a consequence of living the religious culture acquired at conversion as a once and complete guide for salvation within the haven of the church.

Further research is likely to indicate that this typology is altogether too neat and incomplete. But it does help us see where we are with research to hand in addressing the grand question about the historical impact of the Protestant-Pentecostal explosion. We do not know yet whether there are long-term unintended effects of millions of Brazilians' becoming "followers of the new faith," as Willems called them. But the exercise in typology attempted here suggests some conclusions about the likelihood of Pentecostals' being protagonists in movements for intended social change either in the formal political arena or, more widely, in civil society.

Our typology suggests, first of all, that even as more and more Brazilians become Pentecostal *crentes,* there is ever less likelihood of a mobilization of Pentecostals for the transformation of Brazil's social, political, or economic institutions. This is so not only because of the disillusionment and fragmentation that followed the attempted mobilizations in the congressional elections of 1986 and the presidential election of 1989[23] but for reasons suggested by our typology. As three generations of Pentecostalism have developed and different streams have emerged in one or another Pentecostal church, Brazilian Pentecostals have become more variable in their propensity to be mobilized for anything other than purely religious ends. At the same time, Pentecostal religiosity has become so variegated that there is no clear affinity between some one Pentecostal religious culture and any identifiable social, political, or economic project.

Second, the typology suggests that a large number of Pentecostals of the first- and second-wave churches who are critical of Brazilian social, political, and economic injustices will express that critique only within the temple and in a private, inner life. The point is well taken that there may be long-term, unintended consequences for the wider society of critical practice in the religious sphere. In the meantime, those *crentes* who live out the religious culture acquired or confirmed at conversion as a complete and sufficient guide for salvation and evangelization and who exclude *convivência* as a requirement of faith will abdicate not only political citizenship narrowly conceived but social agency as well.

Third, pragmatic Pentecostal citizens may well be active social agents but not for a Brazil constructed out of critical religious vision. If Freston has characterized them adequately, these third-wave Pentecostals seem to espouse a sort of Christianity that includes them in the world on the world's terms. The North American evangelical Christian Jim Wallis has described a sort of contemporary born-again religiosity that seems very similar: "The Gospel message has been molded to suit an increasingly narcissistic culture. Conversion is proclaimed as the road to self-realisation. Whether through evangelical piety or liberal therapy, the role of religion is presented as a way to help us uncover our human potential—our potential for personal, social, and business success, that is."[24] A new Brazil, arguably, is not made by those who are followers of this new faith.

Finally, however, the typology reminds us of Brazilian *crentes* whose faith and mode of conversion call them like prophets to discern and challenge a broad band of injustice and corruption in the world. John Burdick has shown us how broad that band may be and how astutely and tenaciously that better world of Pentecostal moral vision may be pursued. The Pentecostals of Duque de Caxias, like Severino, live a faith that calls them to engage deeply in the very world that the forces of darkness rule—a faith that, as they tell it, calls on them to help bring the Kingdom of God into contemporary Brazilian reality. Perhaps it is in the negotiation of such tensions that citizens with the capacity to be agents of deep historical change are born. And perhaps Burdick is right in thinking that there are more Pentecostals of this kind of faith than I once thought there were. The evidence is not yet in.

NOTES

1. This commonly accepted estimate is found in Paul Freston, "Brother Votes for Brother: The New Politics of Pentecostalism in Brazil," in Virginia Garrard-Burnett and

David Stoll, eds., *Rethinking Protestantism in Latin America* (Philadelphia: Temple University Press, 1993), p. 67.

2. The 1990 estimates are reported in *Latinamerica Press,* September 20, 1990, and the source cited there is the National Council of Christian Churches. For details of the growth of the various Pentecostal groups up to the 1980s see Francisco Cartaxo Rolim, "Igrejas pentecostais," *Revista Eclesiástica Brasileira* 42 (March 1982), pp. 29–59. The growth of the Igreja Universal do Reino de Deus is documented in *Veja,* April 25, 1990, and in Freston, "Brother Votes for Brother."

3. This story, up to the 1970s, has been well told by Francisco C. Rolim, "Igrejas pentecostais," pp. 29–59. Freston, "Brother Votes for Brother," is the major source for the story of institutional growth and consolidation at the national level through the 1980s and into the 1990s.

4. Fuller descriptions of this and other services of the Assembly of God in the region may be read in Rowan Ireland, *Kingdoms Come: Religion and Politics in Brazil* (Pittsburgh: University of Pittsburgh Press, 1991), chap. 4.

5. David Martin has posed just this question in his magisterial review of the literature on Pentecostalism in Latin America. See David Martin, *Tongues of Fire: The Explosion of Protestantism in Latin America* (Oxford and Cambridge, Mass.: Basil Blackwell, 1990).

6. A sophisticated form of this argument, with some impressive supporting evidence was once presented by Francisco Rolim. See Francisco Cartaxo Rolim, *Religião e clases populares* (Petrópolis: Vozes, 1980). I have tried to summarise Rolim's argument of that time in *Kingdoms Come.*

7. John Burdick, as we shall see, has considered the stereotype of Pentecostal alienation and otherworldly orientation contained in this question and found it wanting.

8. Phillip Berryman, "The Coming of Age of Evangelical Protestantism," *NACLA Report on the Americas* 27, 6 (May/June 1994), pp. 6–10.

9. See Regina C. Novaes, *Os escolhidos de Deus: Pentecostais, trabalhadores e cidadania* (São Paulo: Marco Zero, 1985); John Burdick, "Struggling Against the Devil: Pentecostalism and Social Movements in Urban Brazil," in Garrard-Burnett and Stoll, *Rethinking Protestantism,* pp. 20–44; Cecília Loreto Mariz, "Religion and Poverty in Brazil: A Comparison of Catholic and Pentecostal Communities," *Sociological Analysis* 53, S (Supplement 1992), pp. S563–S570.

10. See Emilio Willems, *Followers of the New Faith: Culture Change and the Rise of Protestantism in Brazil and Chile* (Nashville, Tenn.: Vanderbilt University Press, 1967); Martin, *Tongues of Fire;* Ireland, *Kingdoms Come,* chaps. 3 and 4.

11. John Burdick, "The Progressive Catholic Church in Latin America: Giving Voice or Listening to Voices," *Latin American Research Review* 29 (Spring 1994), pp. 184–196.

12. Willems, *Followers of the New Faith.*

13. Burdick, "The Progressive Catholic Church."

14. Ibid., p. 30.

15. For a fuller discussion of differences between church and sect *crentes,* see Ireland, *Kingdoms Come,* pp. 93–102; and "The *Crentes* of Campo Alegre and the Religious Construction of Brazilian Politics," in Garrard-Burnett and Stoll, *Rethinking Protestantism,* pp. 45–65.

16. See Ireland, *Kingdoms Come,* chap. 4, for a more detailed account of a distinctive sect-*crente* religious culture. As we shall see, further fieldwork in Campo Alegre has led me

to supplement this account of difference in quality of citizenship arising out of variation in religious culture with an account of different ways of living a largely shared religious culture. Variation in what I call type of conversion also affects quality of citizenship.

17. Freston, "Brother Votes for Brother," p. 70.

18. Ibid., p. 71.

19. Severino's conversion story is related in greater detail in Ireland, *Kingdoms Come*, pp. 61–67.

20. Mariz, "Religion and Poverty," pp. 64–65.

21. Ibid., p. 65.

22. In another version of this chapter ("Pentecostalism, Conversions, and Politics in Brazil," *Religion* 25 [1995], pp. 135–145) written for the journal *Religion*, I show how this continuing socially inclusive type of conversion is informed not only by the case of Severino but also by the writing of two Christian theologians, Jim Wallis and Bernard Lonergan.

23. See Freston, "Brother Votes for Brother," for a full account of these developments.

24. Jim Wallis, *The Call to Conversion* (Tring, Herts.: Lion Publishing, 1981), p. 28.

❁ **8** ❁

Guatemalan Pentecostals: Something of Their Own

EVERETT WILSON

Guatemala has become the focus of special attention for observers of Latin American religion. A remarkable religious efflorescence, Protestant, Catholic, and indigenous, has been taking place in the country. Some observers have held the anxiety arising from prolonged violence and social dislocation responsible for these religious stirrings.[1] This simplistic view has given way to more probing questions about foreign influence, sectarian preferences, cultural traditions, and pragmatic choices in conversions. I shall examine these questions here with reference to Guatemala's Pentecostals, seeking a more comprehensive explanation that affords greater room for Guatemalan initiative and better reveals Pentecostals' motives, expectations, and institutional life.[2]

This chapter sheds light on the largest and most widespread of the new religious movements, the popular Pentecostals—their origins, their relationship to preceding Protestant efforts, their place in Guatemala's troubled history, and their actual or potential role in national life.[3]

These religious movements, mainly among indigenous Maya and marginal rural and urban ladinos, are viewed as the purposeful creation of Guatemalans. Living in perpetual crisis, through religious motivation and cohesion they have formed religious associations as a means of exerting control over their own lives. This religious initiative provides insight into the sentiments, options, and approaches of other Guatemalans living on the margins of society.[4]

The contemporary era in Guatemala and the emergence of an increasingly visible evangelical movement began with a failed effort at reform. The post–World War II political movement led by Juan José Arévalo (1945–1950) and Jacobo Arbenz (1950–1954) was overthrown by a U.S.-supported counterrevolution in 1954. Speaking for the emerging middle sectors, these leaders addressed their country's social ills and moved toward political modernity by adopting a new

constitution with reform measures that protected civil rights, supported organized labor, and promised land reform.[5] The movement's abrupt ending, with
reprisals against popular leaders and the political opposition, introduced a period
of repression and heightened tensions while the condition of the popular groups
continued to deteriorate.

The main resistance to the counterrevolution came in the 1960s from guerrillas, some of them dissident military officers. Focused on the primarily ladino
populations of the eastern departments where the leaders hoped to establish popular support, this resort to arms produced a brutal reaction and set the stage for
continuing conflict, including the appearance of paramilitary death squads.[6]
Thereafter, anticommunism, with continuing U.S. support, was used as a means
to resist demands for change.

Meanwhile, the persistence of traditional folk Catholicism among the Maya,
who made up half of the population, had prompted a campaign by Catholic
Action to advance post–Vatican II orthodoxy.[7] The objective was to correct unacceptable popular practices that were traditionally left in the hands of local indigenous communities, bringing them into line with approved teaching and ecclesiastical authority. At the same time that Catholic renewal was heightening
religious sentiments and challenging traditions, however, Protestantism began to
acquire visibility in 1957 with the celebration of the movement's seventy-fifth an-
niversary in Guatemala.[8]

Tensions increased further in the 1970s as progressive priests committed to liberation theology encouraged indigenous support for the Ejército Guatemalteco
de los Pobres (Guatemalan Army of the Poor—EGP). Following military defeats
in eastern Guatemala, rebel forces moved to the Maya departments of the north.
These combined ideological and military efforts elevated the struggle to the status of a crusade, leaving little room for neutrality in the Indian communities
where the violence was centered.[9] The apocalyptic nightmare that followed had
taken an estimated 100,000 lives by the mid-1980s.[10]

Against this backdrop of increasing government reprisals, a devastating earthquake stunned Guatemala on February 4, 1976, leaving 20,000 dead, 80,000 injured, and one person in eight homeless.[11] Recovery efforts brought new conflicts.
Considerable foreign aid poured into Guatemala, much of it provided or distributed by North American religious agencies. (Many agencies were described as
right-wing.) Previously unacknowledged evangelical Protestants became visible
participants in recovery efforts and in civic life. Critics complained vociferously
that a U.S.-promoted Protestant offensive in Guatemala was well under way.[12]

The military reign of terror that followed in the Quiché region and the disap-
pearance and assassination of scores of Catholic laypersons and priests made the
conflict appear essentially a war of religion. The seizure of power by Gen. José
Efraín Ríos Montt, a self-proclaimed evangelical and dictator from March 1982
to August 1983, further seemed to demonstrate that repressive forces and sectarian aspirations were conspiring to frustrate reform in the country.[13]

This profile of the evangelicals in Guatemala has been substantially revised as scholars have demonstrated that the situation was far more complicated than the facile conclusions of some journalists in the early 1980s. Moreover, it has become apparent that the North American religious right, despite its aggressive rhetoric, lacked the ability or the commitment to provide the support ascribed to it and, more important, did not exert significant influence over the grass-roots Guatemalan evangelicals.[14]

More important, the interpreters of these events simply ignored the efforts made by Guatemalans themselves to address their own problems. As a result, definitions, organizational models, and a presumption of religious motivation that have little to do with the Guatemalan experience have skewed interpretations of the evangelical churches. The groups that emerged with considerable strength in the 1980s had, in fact, begun to take shape much earlier.

Protestantism Takes Root

The conditions that have facilitated Protestantism's becoming a religious alternative in contemporary Guatemala are rooted in the nineteenth-century policies of Guatemalan president Justo Rufino Barrios (dominant from 1871 to 1885).[15] An advocate of the liberal thinking that prevailed in much of late-nineteenth-century Latin America, Barrios has been likened to Mexico's Porfirio Díaz in his zeal for economic development, maintaining rigid social control, offering inducements to expand new cash crops, attracting immigration, and improving transportation and communications, all the time denigrating the Indian population and treating the Catholic church with contempt. Catholic religious orders were expelled, education and marriage were made civil institutions, members of the hierarchy were exiled, extensive church properties were confiscated, and religious processions and clerical garb were proscribed. The caudillo's anticlerical policies, observed historian Hubert Herring forty years ago, "so crippled the Church in Guatemala that she has never recovered her influence."[16]

Although Barrios's policies continued throughout the dictatorships of his successors until 1945, he went beyond the anticlerical liberalism of Porfirio Díaz by introducing a rival form of Christianity. In 1882 Barrios invited the North American Presbyterian Board of Foreign Missions to enter the country, which, given the considerable popular resistance to a religious option, amounted to an official imposition of Protestantism.[17] It was the good fortune of Guatemalan evangelicals, however, to have a number of capable representatives, some of whom remained for decades and distinguished themselves by their study of Indian languages and culture. These missionaries influenced a small but strategic group of Guatemalans, founding schools and promoting health services in addition to more conventional evangelistic efforts that resulted in the founding of Protestant churches and the training of national pastors.[18]

Whereas much of the Presbyterian work was undertaken in areas of Indian concentration in the western departments, a second evangelical effort, that of the Central American Mission, of similar theological persuasion, further extended Protestant influence after 1899 primarily in the central and south-central departments.[19] By World War I a Nazarene Mission in the north, the Society of Friends in the east, and the Primitive Methodists in the west were also at work, with considerable support for educational and social service programs.[20]

By 1937, in a comprehensive review made of Protestant efforts, Kenneth G. Grubb reported an evangelical community of 40,000 people, about 1.7 percent of the national population, the product of a half-dozen North American missions.[21] "The fact that the main reforms introduced by Barrios have never been reversed is of paramount importance to evangelical workers," Grubb concluded, noting that "no less helpful has been the general sympathy with the objects of evangelical missions which influential members of Guatemalan society have not hesitated to show."[22] Although the Protestant community remained small, its members played a positive role in the country for a full century before a visible evangelical presence emerged in the early 1980s (Table 8.1).

The primary expression of Protestantism in Guatemala, however, is not one of the historical groups but the popular Pentecostals, often simply grouped together ambiguously with marginally Christian groups as "sects."[23] The failure of scholars to identify and treat the popular Pentecostals in reconstructing the development of Guatemalan Protestantism has distorted the explanations they have given

TABLE 8.1   Reported Communicants of the Guatemalan Historical Protestant Churches, 1937–1993

	1937	1956	1961	1969	1981	1993
Presbyterian	2,805	5,700	8,000	11,750	16,263	23,000
Central American Mission	6,596	6,609	6,397	11,928	38,480	67,700
Nazarene	1,500	1,800	2,123	2,500	11,350	24,014
Primitive Methodist	176	691	570	1,000	7,000	n.a.
Society of Friends	3,015	5,432	7,000	650	4,683	n.a.
Baptist	n.a.	1,703	1,513	2,500	7,178	16,500
Plymouth Brethren	n.a.	n.a.	n.a.	3,500	12,500	30,000
Adventist	296	2,835	2,950	6,389	17,207	4,000
Total	14,388	24,885	28,553	33,828	114,661	201,000

Sources: Kenneth G. Grubb, *Religion in Central America* (New York: World Dominion Press, 1937); *World Christian Handbook* (1956); Clyde W. Taylor and Wade T. Coggins, eds., *Protestant Missions in Latin America: A Statistical Survey* (Washington, D.C.: Evangelical Foreign Mission Association, 1961); William R. Read, Victor M. Monterroso, and Harmon A. Johnson, *Latin American Church Growth* (Grand Rapids, Mich.: Eerdmans, 1969); PROCADES, *Directorio del movimiento protestante en Guatemala* (1982); Patrick Johnstone, *Operation World*, 3d ed. (Grand Rapids, Mich.: Zondervan, 1993).

for evangelical growth. Moreover, by disregarding the nature, resources, and aspirations of these groups, studies have also neglected the insights that the growth of evangelicalism among these groups offers about the popular sectors that Pentecostals for the most part represent.

The Rise of the Pentecostals

Although the Pentecostals resemble the Protestant evangelical churches that have been at work in the country since 1882, these popular insurgents were largely ignored by the major missions and nationalized denominations. Only in 1935, when it became apparent that Pentecostals had their own concerns, were proselytistic, and disregarded the informal comity arrangements that had for half a century kept the established missions working cooperatively in their own assigned territories, did the historical groups, apparently in reaction to Pentecostal inroads, formally organize the Evangelical Alliance.[24] By 1950 the Pentecostals accounted for a significant proportion of Guatemala's evangelicals, an estimated 12 percent.[25]

The three largest of these groups, all of which are distributed throughout the national territory—the Iglesia de Dios del Evangelio Completo (Church of God), with churches in Guatemala since 1916, the Asambleas de Dios en Guatemala (Assemblies of God), the formalization in 1937 of efforts begun in the late 1920s, and the Iglesia del Príncipe de Paz (Church of the Prince of Peace), a 1953 spin-off from the Asambleas de Dios—report a combined membership approximately equal to the number of adherents of all other Guatemalan Protestant groups. If other Pentecostal churches and the various Neo-Pentecostal churches are added, this grouping in the aggregate accounts for two-thirds of all of Guatemalan evangelicals. In absolute numbers, at least 10 percent of Guatemalans, an estimated community in excess of 1 million, are identified as popular Pentecostals (Table 8.2).[26]

These Pentecostal groups in Guatemala are essentially different from other evangelicals in respect to their origins and their autonomy. Although the denominations that preceded them between 1882 and World War I formed under the direct influence of North American missionaries around the theology, polity (ecclesiastical organization), economic support, and paternalism of foreign-based missions, Guatemalan Pentecostals were left free to adapt, modify, and implement Protestant emphases at will, in large part because of the Pentecostals' emphasis on the spontaneity and diffusion of spiritual authority.

Treatments of these groups, at least until David Stoll called the assumption into question, have overlooked the fact that the foreign investment in personnel and programs could not possibly account for their growth and institutional development.[27] Although each of the three main Pentecostal organizations received at least indirect initial stimulus from outside the country, from the beginning their ties with foreign denominations have been tenuous, having developed after the

TABLE 8.2   Guatemalan Popular Pentecostals, 1994 Estimates

Denomination	Number of Churches	Membership
Asambleas de Dios	1,600	136,000
Iglesia de Dios del Evangelio Completo	1,300	125,000
Iglesia del Príncipe de Paz	900	75,000
Espíritu Santo	333	30,000
Iglesia de Dios de la Profecía	200	10,000
Iglesia de Dios Pentecostés	200	10,000
Monte Basán	100	10,000
Manantial de la Vida	50	5,000
Iglesia de Dios "Bethesda"	60	4,000
El Camino Bíblico	45	4,000
Iglesia Cuadrangular	40	3,000
Apostólica de la Fe en Cristo Jesús	25	3,000
Iglesia de Dios "Nueva Jerusalén"	25	2,000
Iglesia Mundo Extendido	25	2,000
Iglesia "Bíblia Abierta"	15	1,000
Iglesia de Dios Pentecostal	15	1,000
Iglesia "Palestina"	10	1,000
Total	4,943	422,000

Source: Various estimates, including a rather complete profile provided by the Guatemalan Pentecostal executive leader José Everildo Velásquez.

initial Guatemalan congregations had come into existence. They have received little financial underwriting, and one of the three, the Iglesia del Príncipe de Paz, founded by a charismatic Guatemalan leader, has thrived as a national movement without any foreign patronage.

Moreover, few of the North American Pentecostal personnel, unlike many of their colleagues from other missions, remained long enough to establish themselves in the new culture, to learn an indigenous language, to create a personal following, or to develop forms of financial or administrative dependency.[28] The several missionaries who remained for an extended time were apparently esteemed by their Guatemalan colleagues less for their administrative, technical, or theological contribution than for their identification with the common people in the rigors of hard work and a vision of establishing what the Guatemalans often referred to simply as "the work of the Lord" (*la obra*). Although these and other missionaries sometimes secured North American funds for capital projects, especially urban church buildings and schools, with few exceptions they themselves had little to offer besides their visionary example and moral support.

The Guatemalan popular Pentecostals, however, owe the historical Protestants (the Reformation churches and their derivatives) a debt for the introduction and acculturation of evangelical Protestantism. That debt, in addition to a favorable legal-political climate and, often, a positive institutional image, included linguistic and translation work, leadership formation, social (e.g., agricultural) projects, and various forms of education, all of which tended to give Guatemalan pastors and lay leaders (and their children) of humble social origins opportunities for personal and career development far beyond those otherwise available.

In time, however, after the historical Protestants had experienced insurgencies and organizational modifications that made them more acceptable to nationalistic sentiments, the Pentecostals took the process considerably farther—and acquired at least a few experienced leaders from the existing missions—in adapting Protestant beliefs and practices to Guatemalan culture. The results were autonomous organizations independent of foreign direction and underwriting and culturally compatible with the socially marginalized ladinos and Maya. Sharing the traditional culture of the common people whom they evangelized—the folk Catholicism of the rural and urban ladinos and the syncretic *costumbre* of the indigenous populations—even the first Guatemalan Pentecostals worked in a cultural climate with which their beliefs, methods, and objectives though apparently contradictory—were remarkably compatible.[29]

After modest growth for three decades, Pentecostal increases accelerated during the troubled decades that followed the overthrow of Jacobo Arbenz.[30] Whereas there were only token numbers of adherents of these groups among the republic's 25,000 evangelicals in the 1930s, in the 1950s the Pentecostals grew from 12 percent to 33 percent of the total.[31] By 1982, the centennial of the evangelical presence in Guatemala, Pentecostals made up half of all evangelicals and continued to grow more rapidly than the historical denominations.[32] By 1990, with the emergence of the Neo-Pentecostals, the two groupings together accounted for two-thirds of the total evangelical community of more than 2 million, 20 percent of the national population.[33]

Despite the humble origins of the vast majority of the Pentecostal converts, they are nevertheless organizationally self-sustaining and administratively independent. According to conservative estimates, in the aggregate the popular Pentecostals contribute at least US$10 million annually in support of their movement and have acquired real estate with a market value probably far in excess of US$50 million.[34]

Almost half of the popular Pentecostals are Maya, more than token numbers of whom have advanced to positions of regional or national leadership in one or another of the denominations.[35] Their memberships, among whom women hold leadership positions at the local level, have displayed uncommon initiative, discipline, and tenacity—qualities that have obvious implications for the civic life of a suffering, demoralized, and politically paralyzed society.

Neo-Pentecostals Become Prominent

Just as the popular Pentecostals were displacing the established historical denominations as the country's largest evangelical grouping in the late 1970s, a new variety of evangelical church, the Neo-Pentecostals, had begun to gain acceptance. Still relatively small at that time, by the end of the decade these groups had combined memberships that compared with those of the historical Protestant churches. Although all Neo-Pentecostal groups tend to be similarly contemporary in their styles, each has its own variation on the same themes. All emphasize empowerment in the form of prophetic authority expressed in emphases on miracles, healing, exorcism, and prophecy. These groups are generally centered in a dominant, central, urban church, such as Ríos Montt's Verbo (Church of the Word) congregation in Guatemala City's Zone 4. Some others, notably Elim, the first and largest such group, radiated throughout Guatemala just as had the popular Pentecostal churches.

Several of the Neo-Pentecostal groups, consisting initially of Pentecostalized elements of the historical denominations, began almost a generation before they were generally recognized in the 1980s. The Elim church started under the leadership of a former member of the Central American Mission, while the other large Neo-Pentecostal group, El Calvario, came into being as the Hispanic American Inland Mission in 1947 and turned Neo-Pentecostal in 1963, after which it began to grow rapidly (Table 8.3.)[36]

Some observers believe that the Neo-Pentecostals present a model of a Pentecostal church of the future, at least to the extent that the popular Pentecostals have yet to come to terms with the lifestyles and values of the middle groups while the Neo-Pentecostals already consist largely of persons from these social sectors. The latter have the professionally qualified members and greater material resources, as well as the experience, self-confidence, and connections, to address the issues of the larger society.

From the growth patterns it appears that the types of persons who might earlier have gravitated to the historical groups have become Neo-Pentecostals instead. It also appears that some Catholic charismatics have found their way into these churches. But, increasingly, Pentecostal leaders suspect that considerable numbers of their better-established recent converts and many upwardly mobile young people from Pentecostal families have made the switch, finding in these groups desirable companionship and extended social contacts as well as more relaxed standards of dress and conduct.

The Neo-Pentecostal churches, some of which are not noticeably distinct from the more socially established popular Pentecostal churches, according to some perceptions often consist of persons who are eager to apply the potential of their movement to the larger social and political tasks of the country.[37] Although to some observers features of these churches have seemed to be merely garish imitations of North American charismatic styles and right-wing politics, members of these groups, often activists with the means and the desire to engage in public life, have a strong sense of civic responsibility and support schools, social service programs, and, inevitably, political activities.[38] If Pentecostals and Neo-Pentecostals are not likely to vote as a bloc, they nevertheless share many concerns about the

TABLE 8.3   Guatemalan Neo-Pentecostals, 1994 Estimates

Church	Number of Congregations	Membership/Attendance
Elim Christian Mission	714	50,000
El Calvario	462	60,000
Verbo	25	15,000
Bethany (Quetzaltenango)	20	15,000
Word in Action	10	12,000
El Shadai	1	10,000
Christian Fraternity	1	10,000
Total	1,233	172,000

Source: Johnstone, *Operation World,* and estimates provided by José Everildo Velásquez.

future of their nation and, to some extent, a network of informal communication for contributing to the political process.

Churches That Work

From their beginnings the autonomous Pentecostal groups developed an infrastructure capable of continual expansion. *La obra*—the nurturing of a congregation and the evangelization of a community—became the primary occupation of many adherents, often with considerable vision and sacrifice. The results of their efforts, occurring under adverse circumstances with limited and poorly qualified personnel, developed into a durable ecclesiastical institution with a capacity for growth and increasing complexity. With few compensations other than a sense of mission and a network of appreciative companions, they built their churches as much through effective organization as through unrelenting effort. "The Full Gospel Church of God has grown from a small handful of persecuted Indian believers in the Western highlands of the country," noted an observer, "to one of the largest evangelical bodies on the national scene."[39]

These movements relied heavily on the local congregation. Almost entirely responsible for its own affairs even in the hierarchically organized Iglesia de Dios, an extended family or several families formed a nucleus in a designated location, a house or other available structure, or even met outdoors. These hosts became the patrons, though not necessarily the pastors, of the new congregation, their leadership and commitment often becoming the main reason for the effort's success. "Since the Iglesia de Dios is 'a church of the poor,'" observes Richard Waldrop, "there is spontaneity in the growth and organization of churches."[40]

Once established, however, the group attracted interested members of the community, some of whom typically attended for a long time without confessing the religious experience requisite to joining the church. As conversions were made, instruction and baptism by immersion were expected of the sincere believers, who were then required to conform to the group's demanding standards of conduct. Strong peer pressure, including discipline and sanctions, was applied to converts to fulfill the group's ideals. What statistical reports of Pentecostal growth fail to reveal about these popular groups, in addition to the extraordinary effort evangelists invested and the resistance they often encountered, are the demands that conversion made on proselytes. Often described as "legalistic" because of their rigorous codes of conduct, the churches required a convert to assume unusually high personal commitment and detachment from otherwise legitimate activities. An appraisal of the relative costs of conversion, from (sometimes) family ostracism to the requirement to pay a tithe (10 percent of one's income), would indicate that the Pentecostal convert's faith was more than nominal.[41]

Many converts do not continue to attend church regularly and drop out of Pentecostal congregations. That many do not remain faithful is borne out in the Pentecostals' annual reports, which, for given years, indicate as many "restored" members (indicating a previous lapse) as conversions.[42]

A large proportion of the congregations acquire their own church building (*templo*), often beginning with a gift of land from a member of the congregation or a sympathetic nonmember but requiring everyone's contribution of materials and labor for construction. The contrast between the members' usually humble homes and the often better-constructed churches is notable. Although membership demands are onerous, the groups' survival and growth demonstrates that members are generally conscientious in support of their church, in which they have a proprietary interest (in effect, as stockholders with voice and vote) as recognized by the association's official status as a corporation.

When the pastor is supported entirely by his congregation, he receives his salary (or designated offerings) at its pleasure. Support, in rural Guatemala often given in kind, can easily be withheld in the event that the leader loses the confidence of his flock. Many pastors, at least at the beginnings of a new church, moreover, are self-supporting, demonstrating the same commitment to the group's evangelistic objectives as the laypersons from whom they are sometimes distinguishable only by their moral leadership in the congregation.[43]

Most groups have one or more lay pastors (*obreros locales*) and several deacons and deaconesses (*diáconos* and *diaconeses*), lay men and women to whom is entrusted the oversight of the church. They have a strong voice in making church policies, receive recognition and moral support, and in the event of an extreme disagreement have the option of leaving the congregation to identify with another group of similar if not identical beliefs and practices without suffering disparagement in the larger evangelical community.

The Iglesia de Dios, along with other Pentecostal groups, early adopted a system of dependent missions or satellite churches (*campos blancos*) placed by an established congregation in the care of lay elders who nurtured them until they were self-sustaining. The elder in charge of each then became pastor and eventually completed the formal requirements for receiving ministerial recognition.[44] Ordination, in effect, was achieved through an apprenticeship based on years of satisfactory service and evidence of a vocation and often did not occur until completion of eight to ten years of uninterrupted, satisfactory service. As a consequence, sometimes notably effective pastors nonetheless carry on their work without receiving formal recognition.

The Asambleas de Dios, with larger proportions of its churches among the ladino populations in the eastern departments, has functioned similarly to the Iglesia de Dios, which more often took root among indigenous populations of the highlands. If the Iglesia de Dios congregations tended toward the consultative concept of governance traditional in the indigenous communities, ladino congregations among both groups tended to accept the strong-man (caudillo) form of leadership. In whichever format, however, a rough consensus is essential to the groups' survival.

The Guatemalan Asambleas de Dios adopted early a document developed in El Salvador, the *Reglamento local,* a manual of doctrine and practice outlining the group's principal doctrines, prescribed conduct, and responsibilities of the membership.[45] As a result, an important part of the Pentecostal tradition was accountability, in effect published bylaws enforced by sanctions against members who failed to honor their commitments. But probably more than simply a manual, the *Reglamento* represented a desire on the part of the adherents to regularize their often unstable existence by adopting a guarantee of reliability and reciprocity. The *Reglamento,* like the corresponding zone organization adopted by the Iglesia de Dios, not only maintained uniformity among constituents but created ties between congregations that relieved their isolation and provided a supportive network.

Guatemalan Habits of the Heart: The Appeals of Pentecostalism

Even with the mechanisms that enabled the emerging Pentecostals to extend and conserve their organizations, their membership and national influence remained small until the troubled times following the overthrow of the Arbenz government in 1954 tended to favor crisis conversion.[46] Against a backdrop of the ongoing deterioration of the rural agricultural sector and the unsettling cold war climate, developments made many sectors of Guatemalan society especially vulnerable to change. Armed insurgency, death squads, intensification of religious concerns, and a major earthquake all created a search for reassurance.[47]

Leaders of the historical Protestant groups, in view of the growth and increasing recognition of their movement, were inclined to attribute their success to the cumulative institutional efforts begun a century earlier. Whereas these churches had initially relied on foreign resources, personnel, and methods, Guatemalans had nationalized the movements early on.[48] Although the evangelicals had not yet begun to participate directly in political activities, the social impact of their educational efforts could be identified in Guatemalans of prominence who had attended Protestant academies, including presidents Juan Joseé Arévalo and Julio

César Méndez Montenegro.[49] When, on November 28, 1982, Ríos Montt appeared with the Argentine evangelist Luis Palau before a half-million or more evangelicals at the Protestant centennial celebration in 1982, the occasion produced unrestrained rhetoric from both evangelicals and their detractors, both of whose assessments, as time has demonstrated, considerably inflated and distorted the significance of the event.

Virginia Garrard-Burnett's analysis of this era clarifies the developments that have been made a matter of propaganda by interpreters at both ideological extremes.[50] With insight into both the nature of the evangelical movement and the conditions surrounding its emergence, she demonstrates that evangelical growth, rather than being primarily a result of the military exploitation of fundamentalist religion in the 1980s, had assumed substantial proportions earlier, following the overthrow of the Arbenz government.

She also corrects earlier misinterpretations of Ríos Montt as a pivotal figure in the rise of the evangelical groups, recognizing that his regime's policies—he was always first and foremost a military officer—were little influenced by his personal religious beliefs and had limited impact on the course of Guatemalan evangelicalism. She calls attention to the nationalistic, constructive impulses that lay behind the formation of the evangelical churches and sees a coincidence of evangelical growth with the deteriorating social conditions and heightened religious sensibilities brought on by crisis. Although Garrard-Burnett is apparently referring more to the Pentecostals than to the historical Protestant denominations, she concludes that in Guatemala "Protestantism is the religion of the disaffected, the helpless and the hopeless. For this reason if for no other, Protestantism continues to flourish."[51]

According to this portrayal, however, Guatemalan evangelicalism, rather than the result of either seductive foreign influence or a prolonged effort by some Guatemalans to reshape their country along the lines of Protestant individualism, is largely a by-product of a failed revolution that left the distressed sectors with little recourse. Large numbers of the poor and disaffected, according to this view, were panicked into the new religion rather than recruited, convinced, or converted. If the movement is born of despair and demoralization, however, what sustains and animates its members, who are often, apparently, vigorous, buoyant propagandists energetically proselytizing their relatives and friends and organizing substantial institutions?

The resignation attributed to Pentecostals because of their alleged premillennial doctrines is also too facile an explanation of these popular movements made up of men and women faced with overwhelming personal problems who are obviously investing a great deal in their churches and presumably getting something in return. Although statistics indicate that attendance in all evangelical churches improved after the earthquake of 1976, the Pentecostal groups grew even more rapidly despite their presumably having received no more external financial assistance or other forms of support. Furthermore, the conclusion that Guatemalans resorted to ideologically neutral evangelical churches to escape military suspicion, however likely, does not account for the conversions that were made outside the military zone and the ongoing institutional development that the Pentecostals achieved during times of relative security. The present analysis has attempted to show how Guatemalan Pentecostals, for themselves, their families, and their religious communities, faced their dismal condition with religiously motivated idealism and on their own initiative constructed an institution appropriate to the needs of the marginal sectors. Only by ignoring the Pentecostals' independence, initiative, and organizational tendencies can these groups be represented as passive and largely irrelevant to social changes occurring in the troubled country.

Although Pentecostal leaders, long unacceptable to the evangelical establishment, were conspicuously absent from leadership roles in the coordinated evangelistic programs and public events of the 1960s and 1970s, their memberships made up an increasing proportion of the country's Protestants.[52] Whereas the historical groups were growing rapidly, apparently through a trained clergy, well-directed programs, and incremental increases, the Pentecostals were growing even more rapidly by the exponential formation of new, usually small, congregations. The Asambleas de Dios en Guatemala reported increases from 32 churches and 1,553 adherents in 1951 to 500 churches and 84,000 adherents in 1972.[53] Since similar growth had occurred among the other Pentecostal organizations, the Pentecostal adherents should be factored out of the evangelical statistics to provide a clearer representation of the extent and composition of the evangelical movement (Table 8.4).

Thus, while the events of 1982 brought to world attention the rise of an evangelical movement, inconspicuously the Pentecostals had been becoming a majority of the country's evangelicals. However unintentionally, the efforts and aspirations of the socially marginal people who made up these grass-roots movements (and apparently doubled the attendance at the 1982 centennial celebration) had edged into visibility the more socially prominent historical Protestants.

The question remains why Guatemalans in such large numbers became evangelical and, at that, adherents not of the better-recognized and socially respected Protestant denominations and missions but of their own improvised, grass-roots, morally rigid associations based on Pentecostal emphases. The usual answers about foreign seduction, massive financial investment, panic, and overpowering evangelical programs are precluded by the demonstration that these evangelicals were not foreign operations, that their growth was closely related to the misery and anxieties of the popular groups, and that the evangelical groups growing most rapidly were closest to traditional outlooks and were required in conversion to undergo the least cultural change.

The answer emerging from the profile of these groups is that, despite the Pentecostals' view that at conversion they completely dissociate themselves from their former values, companions, and conduct to begin a new existence, their new

TABLE 8.4 Pentecostals as a Percentage of All Guatemalan Evangelicals, 1937–1993

	1937		1956		1961		1969		1982		1993	
	Number	%	Number	%	Number	%	Number	%	Number	%	Number	%
Historical Protestants	30,000	88	28,000	70	32,000	68	47,000	65	114,000	35	255,000	32
Popular Pentecostals	4,000	12	12,000	30	15,000	32	22,000	30	140,000	42	420,000	50
Neo-Pentecostals							3,000	5	76,000	23	150,000	18
Total Evangelicals	34,000	100	40,000	100	47,000	100	72,000	100	330,000	100	835,000	100

Sources: Grubb, Religion in Central America; World Christian Handbook; Taylor and Coggins, Protestant Missions in Latin America; Read, Monterroso, and Johnson, Latin American Church Growth; PROCADES, Directorio; Johnstone, Operation World.

beliefs, nevertheless, in many comfortable ways resemble the old. The fact that their movements grew much more rapidly throughout the country than did those of the other evangelicals suggests at least that their message and values were not incompatible with the values and aspirations of either ladino or indigenous Guatemalans.

On the contrary, their popular styles, tastes, and approaches were replete with the familiar, whether in the primitive democracy and mutual trust that their associations provided or in the folk music and accepted social conventions, such as standards of hospitality and relationships between the sexes, that they perpetuated. In the vacuum brought about by the absence of a religious consensus, Guatemalans became Pentecostals in substantial numbers not because they had to abandon their outlook on life but because their spiritual lives were rekindled (a common Pentecostal simile) in the context of their new associations. Whatever the other attractions of evangelical conversion, the familiarity of Pentecostal faith, not its foreignness, was a strong attraction for the Guatemalan poor and distressed.[54]

Already dislodged from the institutional structures that had previously oriented their lives, popular Pentecostals made relatively easy transitions to evangelical beliefs and practices, finding that their basic values and social structures were reinforced within the Pentecostal communities. Although mediated in a radically different manner, in an intimate congregational community with few sacraments and little hierarchy, the transcendent worldview that most Guatemalans accepted was restated in the beliefs of the Pentecostals and, moreover, in a cultural idiom that appeared more compatible than other options. Rather than abandoning most traditional values, Pentecostalism provided a means of preserving and implementing them even more consistently and fervently, forcing literal compliance, for example, in areas where often only token acceptance was the norm.

In effect, several hundred thousand marginal Guatemalans found in Pentecostalism something new and exhilarating, an experiential, personal faith that, beyond mere piety, gave them the confidence and motivation to confront their immediate anxieties and the quandaries of an uncertain future while at the same time preserving values and codes of conduct that were familiar and therefore reassuring.

Moreover, the appeals of Pentecostalism tended to compound as the movement grew. Despite the tendency of Pentecostals at times to offend their neighbors with their exclusiveness, their behavior may bring at least grudging respect from the community at large and, for the subject, a sense of personal dignity and value resulting from praiseworthy conduct.[55] Such personal reinforcement, easily lost in an insecure, increasingly impersonalized society, has become all the more important for large numbers of socially marginal people. Evangelical faith for many persons restored an indispensable sense of value lost in the process of social transition.

These rewards are not sufficient to preclude the lapse of many participants, but it cannot be overlooked that reported growth is presented as a net figure, the numbers of new members less persons who are no longer active, indicating a substantial retention as well as a continuing appeal to prospective converts.[56] The Pentecostal groups now extend over a second and third generation with remarkable commitment to their beliefs and practices while remaining (literally) young and vigorous, as new converts filter into their churches, often finding positions of leadership within a relatively brief two or three years.

Conclusion: Politics and Civic Culture

Although popular Pentecostalism has become a religious alternative for many socially marginal Guatemalans, the movement is still too small, inexperienced, and divided to display much political importance or independence.[57] The Pentecostals' contribution may lie primarily in the development of human capital, cultivating civic culture among popular groups. The skills needed to function in a voluntary organization, including effective communication, acceptance of responsibility, planning, discussion of issues and options, and the grooming and accountability of leadership, are immediately apparent among Pentecostals. An observer may enter a church to find an adolescent directing the meeting or attend a business session where a lively debate is taking place on how to spend the group's money. Given the abysmal literacy and educational levels of Guatemala, the development of such skills and experience acquires magnified importance, since, as the careers of the children of evangelical leaders demonstrate, they readily transfer to other areas of life.[58]

The concern, accordingly, is less with determining whether evangelicals as individual citizens will increasingly play a part in the republic's future—their life chances, in fact, are considerably enhanced—than with recognizing the underlying assumptions and the political overtones of their religious orientation. Critics from various quarters have blamed evangelicals for retreating from reality, for obstructionism, and for having lent their support to reactionary forces, although such criticism carries with it the dubious assumption that these groups, made up usually of the least advantaged elements in ephemeral voluntary associations, are somehow expected to play major roles in Guatemala's political process.

Events since the mid–1980s, including the election and subsequent ouster of a second evangelical president, Jorge Serrano, and the reentry of Ríos Montt into Guatemalan politics, demonstrate how little these personalities determined the evangelical course in Guatemala.[59] Despite the disappointment surrounding the short-lived Serrano presidency, however, these groups apparently are tempted to accept help from an otherwise unacceptable source. Moreover, the Pentecostals are notoriously independent, as in the refusal of the Asambleas de Dios, the largest evangelical group in the country, even to participate in Guatemala's

Evangelical Alliance. Political participation, accordingly, is likely to be personal, pragmatic, and tentative.[60]

NOTES

1. Attributing evangelical growth to specific causes is hazardous. Since other Latin American countries have experienced similar movements, "first evangelical presidents" and "largest proportional Protestant movements" are of dubious significance. It must be recognized that Guatemala's social profile includes some of the worst nutritional, health, housing, educational, and labor statistics in the hemisphere, undoubtedly intensified by ethnic discrimination, exploitative labor policies, lopsided economic development, weak civilian institutions, excessive foreign influence in domestic politics, dictatorship, and intransigent resistance to change. These conditions in themselves, however, are not sufficient reason for religious change, since Guatemalans are already a deeply religious people.

2. Reflective treatments of Guatemalan evangelicals include Edward L. Cleary, "Evangelicals and Competition in Guatemala," in Edward L. Cleary and Hannah Stewart-Gambino, eds., *Conflict and Competition: The Latin American Church in a Changing Environment* (Boulder: Lynne Rienner, 1992); Sheldon Annis, *God and Production in a Guatemalan Town* (Austin: University of Texas Press, 1987); Virginia Garrard-Burnett and David Stoll, eds., *Rethinking Protestantism in Latin America* (Philadelphia: Temple University Press, 1993); David Stoll, *Between Two Armies in the Ixil of Guatemala* (New York: Colombia University Press, 1993); Timothy J. Steinenga, "Protestantism, the State, and Society in Guatemala," in Daniel R. Miller, ed., *Coming of Age: Protestantism in Latin America* (Lanham, Md.: University Press of America, 1994), pp. 143–172.

3. The term "popular Pentecostals" is used in this chapter to distinguish the marginal-sector evangelicals who emphasize charismatic beliefs and practices from other Protestants. Pentecostals themselves are not always precise about these definitions, relying on acceptance or rejection of their beliefs, practices, and styles to determine the groups' boundaries. Terms such as "classical" or "primitive" Pentecostals are also used to refer to the same groups and defining tendencies.

4. This is the essential thesis developed in David Martin, *Tongues of Fire: The Explosion of Protestantism in Latin America* (Oxford and Cambridge, Mass.: Basil Blackwell, 1990).

5. Tom Barry, *Inside Guatemala* (Albuquerque, N.M.: Inter-American Education Resource Center, 1992), offers an analysis of the political evolution of Guatemala.

6. Jim Handy, *Revolution in the Countryside: Rural Conflict and Agrarian Reform in Guatemala, 1944–1954* (Chapel Hill: University of North Carolina Press, 1994).

7. Bruce J. Calder, *Crecimiento y cambio de la iglesia católica guatemalteca, 1944–1966* (Guatemala: Seminario de Integración Social Guatemalteca, 1970). The term "Christ-opaganism" is often applied to these popular practices by outsiders. The Indian term is *costumbre*, the body of tradition that governs relationships and practices in the indigenous communities. Regarding these reforms, Jean-Marie Simon was told, "It was easier to be a Catholic before than it is now." *Guatemala: Eternal Spring, Eternal Tyranny* (New York: W. W. Norton, 1987), p. 40.

8. Virgilio Zapata Arceyuz, *Historia de la iglesia evangélica en Guatemala* (Guatemala: Génesis Publicidad, 1981), p. 110.

9. David Stoll, *Is Latin America Turning Protestant? The Politics of Evangelical Growth* (Berkeley: University of California Press, 1990), p. 196. See also Stoll, "Evangelicals, Guerrillas, and the Army: The Ixil Triangle Under Ríos Montt," in Robert M. Carmack, *Harvest of Violence: The Maya Indians and the Guatemalan Crisis* (Norman: University of Oklahoma Press, 1988), pp. 90–116.

10. Amnesty International reports placed the number of victims at 100,000, with the likelihood of there being 100,000 surviving widows and orphans. A detailed account is *La práctica de la desaparición forzada de personas en Guatemala* (San José, Costa Rica: Asociación Centroamericana de Familiares de Detenidos-Desaparecidos, 1988).

11. The U.S. Agency for International Development (USAID), reporting these casualties, set the homeless rate at one-sixth of the national population of 6 million.

12. Barry, *Inside Guatemala*, p. 197. USAID reported that 100 public and private agencies were involved in relief and reconstruction projects. Total U.S. public aid was reported as US$25 million, much of it in kind sold at reduced prices.

13. Lee Penyak, "Ríos Montt and Guatemala's Military: The Politics of Puppetry," *Revista de la Historia de América* 108 (July–December 1989), pp. 131–147. In Penyak's opinion, Ríos Montt was a pawn of the higher-ranking officers (not the junior officers who led the March 1982 coup) as well as a tool of the United States and a representative of the evangelical sectors in the years following his rise to power. His association with the North American Gospel Outreach, moreover, made him a kind of evangelical ayatollah. Developments since his overthrow in August 1983 have shown that the speculative treatment of Ríos Montt was misleading. The issue here is not whether the general was unjustly accused but whether he was functioning in large part as a representative or tool of the Guatemalan evangelical movement, of the North American religious right, or of reactionary U.S. foreign policy. All of these points have been modified or called in question.

14. Scholars who took at face value the statements of North American evangelicals as evidence of foreign designs may have simply played into their hands by giving them unwarranted credibility. Jean-Marie Simon reports that the US$1 billion promised to (or by) Ríos Montt never materialized, and small donations had fallen off prior to his ouster. Perhaps US$20 million, mostly in equipment and services, were actually received from all sources. *Guatemala: Eternal Spring, Eternal Tyranny,* p. 121. According to David Stoll, the agency created to channel funds to Ríos Montt's resettlement program (Foundation for Aid to the Indian People; Fundación de Ayuda al Pueblo Indigena—FUNDAPI) reported having received only US$200,000 before it wound down in 1984. Stoll, *Is Latin America Turning Protestant?* p. 201. In 1984 Ríos Montt was brought as a right-wing political trophy to the United States, where, according to some accounts, his statements were on at least one occasion mistranslated and misrepresented. He consistently referred to himself as a "Christian" rather than as a Protestant or an evangelical and maintained his independence, never allowing himself to become beholden to North American religious groups. The evangelical fortnightly *Christianity Today,* having run supportive articles about Ríos Montt previously, published an article with the title "Oh No! Anything but Central America" (*Christianity Today,* November 23, 1984, pp. 52, 53) in which readers were chided for their lack of comprehension of or interest in the Central American situation. Ironically, many of the groups that purportedly advanced Guatemalan Protestantism were able to carry on their work only through the existing nationally directed and sustained evangelical infrastructure.

15. After a quarter-century under Barrios's predecessor, Rafael Carrera (1838–1865), when the newly formed republic was dedicated to the Roman Catholic faith, the president was decorated by the pope for his service to the church, the clergy was restored many of the privileges taken from it at Independence and given control of education, and a concordat (1852) was concluded with the Holy See. Barrios's policies represented an abrupt break with the past.

16. Hubert Herring, *A History of Latin America* (New York: Knopf, 1955), p. 473.

17. Mary P. Holleran, *Church and State in Guatemala* (New York: Columbia University Press, 1949).

18. The principal source on the Presbyterian church in Guatemala is José Carrera and David Scotchtmer, *Apuntes para la historia* (Guatemala: Iglesia Evangélica Nacional Presbiteriana de Guatemala, 1982). The statistics include all members of this tradition, including those that have remained independent from the main body.

19. The official Central American Mission history is Mildred W. Spain, *And in Samaria* (Dallas, Tex.: Central American Mission, 1954), pp. 154–213. See also Zapata Arceyuz, *Historia.*

20. Zapata, *Historia.*

21. Kenneth G. Grubb, *Religion in Central America* (New York: World Dominion Press, 1937).

22. Grubb, *Religion in Central America,* p. 67. Grubb considered this effort a "relative success" in comparison with similar efforts in other Latin American countries and attributed its effectiveness to the political climate provided by Barrios.

23. Although the term is technically applicable, it is resented by popular Pentecostals, who consider it pejorative both in denying their groups' inclusion in the historical Christian tradition and in identifying them with the Jehovah's Witnesses, Mormons, and others whom they consider to be only marginally Christian.

24. According to the standard evangelical account, the organization of a coordinating synod was a "defensive act to hold back the incursions of the pentecostal missions." Zapata, *Historia,* p. 10. Zapata gives an extended discussion of the cooperation between the early evangelical missions that provided the backdrop for the rise of the popular Pentecostals and demonstrated the evangelicals' nationalistic posture. See also Barry, *Inside Guatemala,* p. 196; Dennis A. Smith, "Coming of Age: A Reflection on Pentecostals, Politics, and Popular Religion in Guatemala," *Pneuma: The Journal of the Society for Pentecostal Studies* 13, 2 (1991), pp. 133–139. Richard Waldrop ("A Historical and Critical Review of the Full Gospel Church of God of Guatemala," Ph.D. diss., Fuller Theological Seminary, Pasadena, Calif., 1993, p. 20) indicates that at the time of the arrival of Charles T. Furman and Thomas A. Pullin in 1916 (Furman and Pullin were the first practicing Pentecostals in Guatemala), the western areas had not yet been occupied by another mission. See also Carrera and Scotchtmer, *Apuntes para la historia,* pp. 96–98.

25. Estimates of total evangelical growth for this period are based on Zapata, *Historia.* Pentecostal reports for the Iglesia de Dios del Evangelio Completo (Church of God) are found in Waldrop, "Historical and Critical Review," p. 56. Those of the Asambleas de Dios (Assemblies of God) are reported in *Origen y desarrollo de las Asambleas de Dios en Guatemala* (Guatemala: Asambleas de Dios, 1987).

26. The most current published statistics are those available in Patrick Johnstone, ed., *Operation World,* 3rd ed. (Grand Rapids, Mich.: Zondervan, 1993), p. 252. According to

this source, the "affiliated" or adherents (as opposed to full members) of the Asambleas de Dios, the Iglesia de Dios, and Iglesia del Príncipe de Paz were, respectively, 224,000, 187,000, and 169,000, although other estimates, such as those given in the text, are somewhat less. The total Pentecostal inclusive community in 1993, according to Johnstone, was 1,457,000. Johnstone's Guatemalan evangelical profile of 23.3 percent of the population can be compared with a research sampling report by Timothy E. Evans, "Percentage of Non-Catholics in a Representative Sample of the Guatemalan Population," paper presented at the Latin American Studies Association, Washington, D.C., 1991. Evans's study placed the evangelical population at 30 percent of the national population.

27. David Stoll, "A Protestant Reformation in Latin America?" *Christian Century* 107, 2 (January 17, 1990), pp. 44–48. Stoll concludes that the US$20 million that the largest North American Pentecostal group is investing annually in Latin America fails to account for the denomination's reported 10 million members—that is, an investment of US$2.00 per member per year is not sufficient to account for a dynamic church. In fact, the missionary expenditure is largely in support of North American personnel, not all of whom are stationed overseas. Virtually none goes directly to Latin American salaries and operations, and the direct assistance for capital projects and, increasingly, for schools accounts for only a small fraction of the total amounts given for construction and school operations, most of which come from Latin American Pentecostal members themselves.

28. *Origen y desarrollo,* pp. 17, 18. Of twenty married couples or unmarried missionaries identified by a publication of the Asamblea de Dios in a review of its first half-century of work in the country, a half-dozen completed or returned after their initial four-year term of service, during which, usually, they were in effect probationers engaged in language learning. The Iglesia de Dios appears to have had even fewer foreign personnel. By comparison, Presbyterian personnel, many of them specialists rather than general missionaries, numbered almost two hundred over the period of a century. Carrera and Scotchtmer, *Apuntes para la historia.*

29. In the current terminology of missionary work, their efforts were "contexualized." The eulogy given at the funeral of a pioneering Pentecostal missionary described him as not having had "much formal education" but as having been "a child of the King, and therefore . . . equally at ease talking to beggars or generals. . . . ever so gentle, . . . ever so faithful." Waldrop, "Historical and Critical Review," p. 44.

30. See Handy, *Revolution in the Countryside.*

31. The 1961 membership for the Iglesia de Dios is taken from Waldrop, "Historical and Critical Review," p. 57. Asambleas de Dios 1961 membership was taken from Robert Braswell, "Assemblies of God Growth Rates in Central America, 1951–1992," manuscript, Division of Foreign Missions of the Assemblies of God, Springfield, Mo.

32. Zapata, *Historia,* pp. 192–194, citing the *Directorio de iglesias, organizaciones y ministerios del movimiento protestante: Guatemala* (Guatemala: Instituto Internacional de Evangelización a Fondo [IINDEF], PROCADES, and Servicio Evangelizador para América Latina [SEPAL], 1981).

33. Johnstone, *Operation World,* p. 252. These statistics, however accurate in terms of individuals who may have some relationship with evangelicals, are inflated with respect to the numbers of active members (in the sense used by the members themselves of assuming congregational responsibility). On the basis of the impressionistic estimates of Guatemalan Pentecostal leaders the figures should be lower, perhaps 2 million. Lower es-

timates than those current at the time were given in Everett A. Wilson, "Central American Evangelicals: From Protest to Pragmatism," *International Review of Mission* 77 (January 1988), pp. 94–106.

34. This estimate is based on the expectation that there are reasonably 200,000 family units or single adults in a reported active membership of 400,000 whose contributions are 5 quetzales (approximately US$1.00) per week, although the average contribution could be five times that amount. Considerably higher estimates of assets and income based on typical church budgets were provided by Douglas Petersen, director of the Assemblies of God missionaries in Central America. Responses to requests for similar information by several Guatemalan denominational leaders were in keeping with his higher estimates. Rodolfo Sáenz, a Central American Pentecostal executive leader, provided a tiered system of rural and urban real estate values (*catastro*) adjusted to church size as a basis for the appraisal of real estate holdings.

35. Information about ethnic composition and other aspects of Pentecostal church organization was obtained by interviews with church administrators and pastors and by observation of congregations in all regions of Guatemala since 1987.

36. Zapata, *Historia*, pp. 160, 161. The Elim church began when a medical doctor, Otoniel Ríos Paredes, formerly a member of the leading congregation of the Central American Mission, conducted religious services in his home. With significant growth in 1973, the doctor left his practice and devoted his efforts to the churches, which have become perhaps the largest of this genre in Guatemala. Ibid., pp. 151, 152. Another example of the "Pentecostalization" of a historical group is the Misión Evangélica "Betania," which began among Presbyterians in 1972.

37. Rodolfo Sáenz, president of the Consejo Ejecutivo Latinoamericano de la Asambleas de Dios (CELAD), personal communication, December 5, 1994.

38. An acknowledgment of these tendencies with a less favorable interpretation is found in Gordon Spykman, ed., *Let My People Live: Faith and Struggle in Latin America* (Grand Rapids, Mich.: Eerdmans, 1988), pp. 216 ff. Contributors to this volume were Guillermo Cook, Michael Dodson, Lance Grahn, Sidney Rooy, and John Stam.

39. Waldrop, "Historical and Critical Review," pp. 16, 76.

40. Waldrop, "Historical and Critical Review," p. 76. Although the meetings in time became structured, initially they were occasions for prayer and discussion, even if no one with the ability to give a sermon was in attendance. The meetings' religious purpose never prevented them from being social events.

41. The sometimes intense emotionalism of Pentecostals, besides being an opportunity for unrestrained expression, may reflect believers' subjective struggle to reconcile the objective conditions of their existence with their own passions, aspirations, and fears before returning to face a hostile world. The language of Pentecostalism, after all, is replete with references to power, and the preaching is intensely motivational, intended to incite the congregants to moralistic action.

42. For instance, the "Informe estadístico correspondiente a 1984, Las Asambleas de Dios en Guatemala, February 16, 1985," lists 53,436 proprietary members, 14,567 converts, and 14,801 reconciled (restored) members. Another category, *catechumens*, approximately equal to the number of converts, indicates the ongoing process of believer formation in the churches. Given the costs of membership for these converts, a commitment had to be demonstrated over time. The fact that demands were are least as high in the early years,

when there were few evangelicals and their efforts sometimes met strong resistence, suggests that the first-generation Pentecostals were assertive individuals whose efforts to reconstruct the world as they knew it were viewed with considerable seriousness.

43. Waldrop, "Historical and Critical Review," pp. 74, 100.

44. The proportion of 5 percent is the estimate of women with credentials submitted by the Guatemalan denominational leaders at a meeting of the Consejo Ejecutivo Latinoamericano de las Asambleas de Dios at the group's triennial meeting in Panama in November 1992. Although Waldrop mentions the roles played by women in the Iglesia de Dios, in that group, as apparently in Pentecostal groups generally, women are given considerable authority in local congregations, but relatively few become pastors and virtually none advance to executive positions in national organizations.

45. On the origins of the *Reglamento local,* see Everett A. Wilson, "Sanguine Saints: Pentecostalism in El Salvador," *Church History* 52 (June 1983), pp. 186–198, and "Identity, Community and Status: The Legacy of the Central American Pentecostal Pioneers," in Joel A. Carpenter and Wilbert R. Shenk, eds., *Earthen Vessels: American Evangelicals and Foreign Missions, 1880–1980* (Grand Rapids, Mich.: Eerdmans, 1989).

46. Walter LaFeber, *Inevitable Revolutions; The United States in Central America* (New York: W. W. Norton, 1983), pp. 256–261.

47. Calder, *Crecimiento y cambio;* José Luis Chea, *Guatemala: La cruz fragmentada* (San José, Costa Rica: Editorial Departamento Ecuménico de Investigaciones, 1988).

48. Barry *Inside Guatemala,* p. 199.

49. The close association of Guatemalan evangelicals with the political establishment is apparent in the centennial publication prepared by Virgilio Zapata (see *Historia*). References to forms of recognition and attendance at evangelical functions occur in respect to Miguel Ydígoras Fuentes, Kjell Eugenio Laugerud García, Fernando Romeo Lucas García, and José Efraín Ríos Montt, in addition to Arévalo and Méndez.

50. Virginia Garrard-Burnett, "Onward Christian Soldiers: The Rise of Protestantism in Guatemala, 1954–1984," *Southeastern Conference on Latin American Studies Annals* 21 (March 1988), p. 101.

51. Ibid., p. 102.

52. Zapata (*Historia,* p. 177) remarks that Pentecostal participation in the 1971 united evangelical crusade was reduced because Pentecostal leaders had not been included among the organizers.

53. Braswell, "Assemblies of God Growth Rates, 1951–1992."

54. For insight into respondents' reasons for evangelical conversion, see Luis Corral Prieto, *Las iglesias evangélicas de Guatemala* (Guatemala: Universidad Francisco Marroquín, 1980). Although large differences between evangelicals and Roman Catholics may be inferred from this study, the same comments support the thesis that evangelicals, whether previously Roman Catholic, Protestant, or uncommitted, believed themselves to be sufficiently informed on religious issues (presumably because of their religious instruction) to adopt an alternative position.

55. For North Americans who find some Latin American behavioral patterns difficult to understand, the key has often been simply recognition of the importance of *dignidad*— more than "dignity," a sense of the individual's inherent worth, the right to respect. Its relationship to Pentecostals is treated by Frank E. Manning, "Pentecostalism, Christianity, and Reputation," in Stephen D. Glazier, ed., *Perspectives on Pentecostalism: Case Studies*

from the Caribbean and Latin America (Lanham, Md.: University Press of America, 1980), pp. 177–187.

56. The issue of the "revolving door" of evangelical conversion is treated in John Maust, "Keeping the Faithful," *Christianity Today,* April 6, 1992, p. 38. See also Clayton L. "Mike" Berg and Paul E. Pretiz, *The Gospel People of Latin America* (Monrovia, Calif.: Missions Advance Research Center, World Vision International, and Miami, Fla.: Latin America Mission, 1992), pp. 129, 130.

57. The political assessment of the popular Pentecostals, who are just beginning to gain some recognition, should be distinguished from the personalities associated with the Neo-Pentecostals, especially former presidents José Efraín Ríos Montt and Jorge Serrano. Neither of these figures has the same relationship with his church that he once had. Internal divisions in Verbo have resulted in Ríos Montt's having much less visibility in that group's activities than before, and Jorge Serrano, who was associated with several groups before identifying with his most recent congregation, was disciplined by the El Shadai church prior to his going into exile in Panama.

58. Research on the Pentecostal school systems in Latin America provides insight into the social focus of these groups. Everett A. Wilson, "Latin American Pentecostalism: Challenging the Stereotypes of Pentecostal Passivity," *Transformation* 11, 1 (January–March 1994), pp. 19–24.

59. In Guatemala, as elsewhere in Latin America, the Pentecostals' apolitical stance has been widely recognized, producing surprise (or disappointment) when they have taken sides on some political issue. Which, one might ask, is the real Pentecostal posture, avoidance or activism? In fact, both stances are typical. Pentecostals tend to stay aloof, their independence ensuring their freedom of action until, with little risk of compromise, they can assert their influence. They may be expected to be cautious and tentative, hedging their bets (figuratively; gambling is prohibited), avoiding direct confrontation, and taking advantage of opportunities. Although popular Pentecostals are dedicated to specific objectives, notably religious conversions and the strengthening of their church institutions, and thus remain aloof from political involvement, in the interests of advancing their cause they may be tempted to accept help from an otherwise unacceptable source. The justification that Pentecostals give for this mixing in temporal affairs is that the state—and by extension politics—for these groups has always been legitimate, as indicated by Romans 13, the proof text frequently thrown up to Guatemalan evangelicals as evidence of their supposed unquestioning submission to the military. The state, moreover, is indispensable, as it is for all Protestants, because rather than being the servant of the church as in Roman Catholic theology, in Protestant dogma the state is the temporal guarantor of the church. Civil disobedience, however, is equally as legitimate, as is evidenced by a passage (Acts 4:19) that Pentecostals have frequently invoked during years of social rejection.

60. Despite the considerable early attention to President Ríos Montt and the Verbo Church as a representative—if not the cause—of the evangelical surge, this group has never enjoyed the importance in Guatemala assigned to it by some observers. Rumors of dissension surround the church, and Ríos Montt's role is ambiguous. Clearly his political base is not in the evangelical movement, which he apparently does not need, and, in turn, the evangelicals are not dependent on him for support. Although undoubtedly evangelicals play a part in Guatemalan politics, they are extremely divided and have limited influence as a grouping at the higher levels. Evangelicals, for example, were not given credit for

the election of the evangelical president Jorge Serrano. Serrano's comment was, "If I talk to the general public with the language I use with Christians, they might stone me, but if I use political language with the brethren, they question my Christianity." "An Evangelical's Bid for the Presidency Falls Short," *Christianity Today,* December 13, 1985, p. 69. Ríos Montt's election as president of the National Congress in December 1994, moreover, demonstrates his durability and popularity not as an evangelical icon but as a civilian political figure. David Stoll's interpretation, especially, along with Montt's subsequent activities, leaves the reader with the suspicion that the general was at least using the evangelicals as much as he was being used by them. David Stoll, "Why They Like Ríos Montt," *NACLA Report on the Americas* 24 (December/January 1990/1991), pp. 94–97. The standard sympathetic biography, Joseph Anfuso and David Sczepanski, *Efraín Ríos Montt: Siervo o dictator* (Guatemala City: Gospel Outreach, 1983), despite its favorable assessments, cannot conceal the fact that an astute, well-connected, and experienced Ríos Montt could hardly be manipulated by novice politicians or be placed in positions contrary to his own career interests.

9

Brincando el Charco/Jumping the Puddle: A Case Study of Pentecostalism's Journey from Puerto Rico to New York to Allentown, Pennsylvania

ANNA ADAMS

El hombre hispano va a la iglesia con todo el bagaje de sus problemas con la lengua, con el trabajo. La misión aquí es más difícil que en Puerto Rico (The Hispanic man goes to church with all the baggage of his problems with language, with work. The mission here is more difficult than in Puerto Rico).

—*Pastor Edwin Colón*

Scholars and practitioners generally acknowledge that Pentecostalism has its greatest appeal among the poor and marginalized. The work of Emilio Willems and Christian Lalive d'Epinay in Chile[1] and Renato Poblete and Thomas O'Dea[2] in the Puerto Rican community in New York suggests that to join a Pentecostal church is to seek a way out of the anomie, or lack of community, that many recently transplanted people experience. In 1971, Joseph P. Fitzpatrick wrote of Puerto Ricans in New York that "the phenomenon of the Pentecostal storefront church represented a search for community, for the satisfaction of knowing that one belonged to, was respected by, and had a function to fulfill within the group."[3] More recently, Virginia Garrard-Burnett and David Stoll concluded that because of its very personal relationship with the Lord Pentecostalism empowers believers on many levels, enabling them to thrive in this world as well as in the hereafter, and in this sense religion becomes a pragmatic strategy for survival.[4]

In 1960, Sidney Mintz noted the importance of the Pentecostal churches in
Puerto Rico in his classic study *Worker in Cane.*[5] Mintz concluded that Puerto
Rico's rapid transformation from an agriculture-based plantation economy of
family workers to wage working in an impersonal manufacturing setting caused
many Puerto Ricans to fill the resulting social and psychological vacuum by joining Pentecostal congregations. The churches provided an ideology, sense of community, and purpose that compensated for the loss of a traditional style of life. It
is not surprising, then, that displaced Puerto Ricans in the industrialized cities of
the U.S. Northeast, where even the language is foreign, also find solace and a sense
of belonging in Pentecostal churches.

This study examines the Latino Pentecostal churches in Allentown,
Pennsylvania, where the growing Latino community is poor and marginalized.
Allentown makes an important case study because it is typical of small dying in-
dustrial cities in the Northeast that are rapidly becoming populated with Latinos
from New York seeking safer neighborhoods and cheaper housing. In Reading,
Pennsylvania, for example, Latinos now make up 30 percent of the population.[6]
According to the 1990 census, 12,000 Latinos made up 15 percent of Allentown's
population. Ten years earlier the population had been only 5 percent Latino.
Seventy-two percent of the Latino population today is Puerto Rican.

To trace the migrations of Puerto Ricans from their island in the 1940s and
1950s to New York City and more recently to smaller cities such as Allentown is
to trace the migration of Pentecostalism. Each of these migrations has created a
more alienated and displaced population.

Puerto Rico, by virtue of its long political association with the United States, is
the most Protestant of Latin American countries, with a Protestant population of
approximately 33 to 38 percent, the majority of whom are Pentecostal. David Stoll
calculates that if we extrapolate the growth rates of evangelical churches from
1960–1985 for another twenty-five years Puerto Rico will become 75 percent
evangelical.[7] Surprisingly, given the high percentage of Puerto Rican Pentecostals,
there has been very little scholarly examination of them or their history. The
available material comes primarily from divinity students or from Pentecostals.[8]
Most national histories of Puerto Rico or, indeed, of other Latin American countries, which have for centuries been officially or at least predominantly Catholic,
make no mention of Pentecostals. Pentecostals' own histories of their churches
represent an official discourse and chronology of God's will that lack historical,
sociological, or anthropological analysis. Juan Lugo's autobiography, for example,
chronicles various encounters with the Holy Spirit and the guiding hand of God
in the building of Pentecostalism in Puerto Rico.

Because there are no national, legal borders between the United States and
Puerto Rico and because Puerto Ricans travel frequently between the island and
the mainland, Pentecostalism too travels back and forth. These journeys create an
important bridge in the study of Latin American Pentecostalism. I have found

that Allentown Pentecostalism is similar in character to Pentecostalism throughout Latin America: It is the fastest-growing religion; the churches are homegrown
independent entities, not foreign in doctrine or language; most churchgoers are
of low socioeconomic status; their religion offers them a strong sense of community; women's status within the church and within the family is high; and, for
many, church membership seems to improve the unity of the family. Despite
these similarities, however, Allentown's Pentecostals have the disadvantage of
being foreigners who often do not speak the language. Discrimination is a feature
of their daily lives. For that reason, Pastor Edwin Colón believes that his mission
in Allentown is more difficult than in Puerto Rico.[9]

The case of Puerto Rican Pentecostalism is also unusual in that, in contrast to
the situation in the rest of Latin America, it was not North American missionaries who brought Pentecostalism to Puerto Rico but Puerto Ricans. Likewise, most
Puerto Ricans on the mainland were converted not by North American missionaries but by insular Puerto Rican missionaries who made the slums of the First
World their mission field. Although Puerto Rican missionaries have been evangelizing on the mainland for decades, recently other Latin American missionaries
have begun work among their compatriots resident in the United States. David
Barrett, former editor of the *World Christian Encyclopedia,* estimates that more
than 16,000 full-time Christian missionaries from Third World countries, most
of them Pentecostals, are working in the United States.[10]

This study was undertaken in the summer of 1994. It is part of a larger study,
a history of the Latino community of Allentown. As part of my research I visited
several different types of Pentecostal churches—older, well-established churches
and newer, smaller storefront churches. I attended four churches on Sundays as
well as on Tuesdays and Thursdays for Bible study and prayer evenings. I interviewed six pastors and members of various congregations and conducted a written survey in four congregations to obtain data on socioeconomic status, religious
history, and church social/political activities.

Pentecostalism in Puerto Rico

Protestant missicnaries from the United States first went to Puerto Rico in 1899
when it became a U.S. possession after the Spanish-American War. A comity
agreement among the U.S. Protestant churches divided the missionary field in
Puerto Rico among nine churches: Lutheran, Presbyterian, Methodist, Baptist,
Congregationalist, United Brethren, Christian Church, Christian Missionary
Alliance, and Disciples of Christ. The agreement gave each church a certain geographical territory. For example, the north went to the Methodists, the center to
the Baptists, and the west to the Presbyterians. In some areas where a church was
weak—in the Lutherans' eastern central area, for example—the Disciples of
Christ spread out beyond their designated territory. Nevertheless, Dan Wakefield

claimed in 1959 that one could tell a Protestant Puerto Rican's birthplace by his/her religion.[11] Seventh-Day Adventists also established mission work in Puerto Rico.

Today, however, the flourishing churches are not the traditional Protestant churches that went to the island at the turn of the century. As in many areas of Latin America, it is the Pentecostal churches that are attracting the greatest number of worshipers. As early as the 1950s, when Henry Van Dusen, the president of Union Theological Seminary, traveled to Puerto Rico, he was surprised to encounter the growing popularity of "fringe sects," with their "life-commanding, life-transforming, seven-days-a-week devotion . . . to a living Lord of all life."[12]

There is little information on the history of the early Pentecostal churches in Puerto Rico and virtually no scholarly work. We know that in 1916 Juan Lugo, a Puerto Rican who had lived in Hawaii since his youth, was converted to Pentecostalism by missionaries from the Azusa Street Mission in Los Angeles. Lugo was seventeen years old at the time and, like many adults who have converted to Pentecostalism, was living "a life of sin"—gambling, drinking, and smoking.[13] After his conversion he returned to Puerto Rico to missionize among his compatriots. He began his mission on a street corner in the southern city of Ponce. In the chapter of his autobiography entitled "Let the Persecution Begin" Lugo describes the hostility he experienced from both Catholic and Protestant hierarchies. For one thing, the Pentecostals ignored the geographical limitations established by the other Protestant churches and evangelized all over the island. Lugo was warned by the Protestant pastors in Ponce that he lacked the training to perform enduring work and accused him of "putting the Gospel on too humble a level."[14] Despite the pastors' warnings and some harassment from the local authorities, within two years there were eight Pentecostal churches on the island, and by 1929 there were twenty-five churches called the Iglesia de Dios Pentecostal, associated today with the U.S. Assemblies of God.[15] (There is some debate among Pentecostals as to whether Lugo's Iglesia de Dios Pentecostal was associated with the Assembly of God at the time.[16])

During the depression years of the 1930s, there was a great expansion of Pentecostalism. By 1942, according to a study by J. Merle Davis,[17] the Pentecostal churches were first among the Protestant churches in number of churches, sixth in the number of constituents, first in the number of candidates for baptism, and first in the number of pastors. At that time, Pentecostals constituted 8.5 percent of Protestants in Puerto Rico. Ten years later this figure had risen to 25 percent.[18] Today almost every small town on the island has at least one Pentecostal church. The largest denomination after Roman Catholicism is the Iglesia Pentecostal de Dios, Misión Internacional, which is independent and self-supporting. It sends missionaries to Spain, Portugal, and nine other Latin American countries. Other Pentecostal churches are the Church of God Prophecy, the International Church of the Foursquare Gospel, the United Pentecostal Church, the Missionary Church of Christ, the Pentecostal Church of Jesus Christ, and the Church of Christ in the

Antilles.[19] Puerto Rican missionaries are well known in Latin America. According to Everett Wilson, the Puerto Rican Pentecostal churches are a model of independence, rapid growth, and appropriateness to the culture. Their appeal can be seen by the fact that even with the recent rapid growth of Pentecostalism in Puerto Rico, at least 85 percent of the island's Pentecostals are long-term converts or their descendants. The early churches, writes Wilson, "have persisted, developing institutionally and, despite the obvious social mobility, and perhaps because of the continued assimilation of new, poor elements, have largely retained their character."[20]

Pentecostalism in New York

In 1928 Juan Lugo sent Thomas Alvarez to New York to begin Pentecostal work there. He opened the first Puerto Rican Pentecostal church, the Iglesia Misionera Pentecostal in Brooklyn. Three years later Lugo came to New York to pastor that church and oversee the expansion of the work among Puerto Ricans. By 1937, of the fifty-five Hispanic Protestant churches in New York City, twenty-five were Pentecostal.[21]

After World War II, Governor Luis Muñoz Marín's rapid-industrialization program, Operation Bootstrap, failed to provide enough jobs for Puerto Rican workers. Increasing unemployment in Puerto Rico and the need for cheap labor in New York's garment industry and surrounding farms drove many islanders, who had become U.S. citizens in 1917, to migrate to New York. Between 1950 and 1965, 50,000 Puerto Ricans made their way to the mainland each year. Pentecostal missionaries followed them, and the rapid growth of their churches in Puerto Rico is reflected in a similar growth of Pentecostalism among Puerto Ricans in New York. Hundreds of new Pentecostal churches have been founded by Puerto Rican missionaries, some trained in the Discípulos de Cristo, who left the island imbued with the spirit of their homegrown version of this North American religion. By 1983 there were 560 Latino Pentecostal churches in New York City.[22] The pastors of these churches believed that the United States was ripe for evangelizing and that they could offer salvation to the hundreds of thousands of poor, marginalized Puerto Ricans struggling to make their way in the industrialized cities of the Northeast.

The Pentecostal theologian José A. Reyes believes that for poor recent immigrants to the United States the Pentecostals' message is particularly meaningful. He stresses for future missionaries the importance of evangelizing in Spanish and of acting within the context of Latino culture so as to provide comfort and guidance in strange and foreign surroundings. He cites one recent immigrant's comments on his experience in the Catholic church: "In the Catholic Church, nobody knows me. In the Pentecostal church each member is greeted warmly, if you get sick, they visit you. The unity of the congregation is one of the most important expressions of community found among the Puerto Ricans in New York."[23]

According to Eldin Villafañe, the mainline Protestant denominations have for the most part been unresponsive to the needs of Latinos. He cites a study by David Traverzo Galarza:

> If there is any growth and vitality within the Hispanic Evangelical church in New York City, it certainly is not due to the historical response of the mainline Protestant churches of the city.
>
> Rather it has been the emergence of a Hispanic clergy and church that has impacted the development of the Hispanic Evangelical church in the city. The initiative and follow-up has come from indigenous movements spurred under the guidance and power of the Holy Spirit.[24]

Pentecostals in Allentown

Allentown, Pennsylvania, is one of the "gritty cities" of the northeastern United States and the fourth-largest city in Pennsylvania. Located fifty-three miles northwest of Philadelphia and ninety-two miles southwest of New York City at the confluence of the Lehigh River and the Jordan and Little Lehigh Creeks and with rich deposits of anthracite and natural cement, Allentown until recently had a thriving manufacturing base. Allentonians have never been especially welcoming to new immigrant groups, and their response to the Latinos is no exception. Almost all the Latinos whom I interviewed claimed that they had experienced some kind of discrimination either in the workplace, in schools, or in stores. Several independently expressed the belief that Allentown was unique in the prevalence of discrimination and attributed it to the dominant Pennsylvania Dutch culture. One man who had been in the United States since 1949 and had lived in New York, Chicago, Pittsburgh, Lancaster, and several small cities in Florida reported that he had never experienced such hostility as in Allentown.[25] Several prominent events serve as evidence for this perception. A popular member of the city council falsely asserted that 99 percent of Allentown's crime was committed by Latinos and blamed most of Allentown's troubles on the recent influx of Latinos who had "no values."[26] The night before the opening of the 1994 fall school term, the city council passed an English-only ordinance. It was largely a meaningless gesture, as the state mandates that certain materials be published in Spanish, but as a symbol it sent a clear message to the Latinos that their difference was not welcome.

Allentown's unwelcoming environment breeds precisely the conditions that might send outsiders to seek refuge in a Pentecostal church. Although 30 percent of Allentown's school population is Latino, less than 2 percent of the teachers are Latino. The dropout rate for Latino students is higher than for any other ethnic group, as is the number of suspensions and detentions. Teachers tell students not to speak Spanish even among themselves, and those who do so receive detention slips. Recently some Anglo students formed a white student union to "offer students of European descent an opportunity to meet with like-minded students to celebrate western values and their European heritage."[27] A local radio talk-show host suggested on his program that Allentown shopkeepers charge non-English-speakers 5 percent more or that the city designate an area of town where goods would be sold to Spanish-speaking people at regular prices. To his surprise, very few people in his listening audience protested or even recognized the satiric tone of his comments.[28]

Even old-timers who have raised children and grandchildren in Allentown do not feel as if they belonged, and, despite the high percentage of Puerto Ricans living in Allentown, they remain on the margins of Allentown's social and political activity. The police force of 203 officers has 18 Latinos. There is one Latino on the city council. The courts do not provide Latino defendants with qualified translators and interpreters. Public housing is insufficient and too costly to meet the needs of the large majority of Latino families.[29]

A feature article in the *New York Times Magazine* in May 1994[30] brought the plight of Latinos in Allentown and other smaller U.S. cities to national attention. In the past ten years, drawn by the green parks, cheaper housing, and safer streets, Latinos have begun an exodus from the poor, deteriorating, and dangerous neighborhoods of New York. However, along with the safe and attractive neighborhoods comes a sometimes blatant discrimination that was generally not a feature of life in the diverse New York neighborhoods from which they migrated.

The majority of Latinos in Allentown identify themselves as nominally Catholic. The Sacred Heart Catholic church offers mass in Spanish and claims a membership of 3,000 Latinos, 500 of whom go to mass on Sundays.[31] The church also runs an active social action program for Latinos. The Lutheran, Methodist, and United Church of Christ churches also run Hispanic ministries, but their membership is relatively small. The Pentecostal churches of Allentown are the flourishing congregations. The twenty or so Pentecostal churches have an average of about 100 members who attend services three or four times each week.

The first Latino Pentecostal church was founded in Allentown in 1967 by Francisco and Miriam Vega. The Vegas came from Puerto Rico via New York, where they had studied for three years at the Instituto Bíblico Latinoamericano. After they had completed their training as pastor and missionary, "God called them to the city of Allentown to bring the good news to a place that was without faith and without hope."[32] The Allentown that the Vegas encountered had a Latino population of approximately five hundred, many of whom felt alienated in the midst of a predominantly Pennsylvania Dutch community. Felix Puente, a Puerto Rican navy veteran, claimed in a 1962 interview in the *Allentown Morning Call* that he was unable to find a job or housing because of racial discrimination.[33] Martin Velázquez Sr. reports that in the early 1960s Mack Trucks clearly stated that they did not hire Puerto Ricans, and he and his Pennsylvania Dutch wife were unable to rent an apartment in an uptown neighborhood.[34] Except for masses offered in the migrant labor camps by Spanish-speaking priests aided by seminarians, there were no worship services in Spanish until the late 1960s, when Pastor José Rodriguez of the United Church of Christ began to offer them. Fearful of losing parishioners, the Sacred Heart Catholic church also began to offer mass in Spanish to some fifty members. In 1969 the Catholic church opened Casa Guadalupe, a neighborhood center to provide help in obtaining basic services to the Latino community.

Allentown must indeed have seemed to the Vegas a place "without faith and without hope" for the Spanish-speaking population. They began their church, the Iglesia Pentecostal Betania, in their home with seven members. Francisco Vega was the pastor, and Miriam Vega went door-to-door as a missionary. As her efforts took effect, the membership grew, and the church moved several times into larger quarters. Within a few years the congregation was able to purchase an old church in downtown Allentown, where it has been thriving ever since. It founded a biblical institute for those who wanted to prepare for the ministry. Today the church has a new pastor and an active membership of approximately 160, many of whom have been members since the beginning. The church is completely self-supporting through offerings and tithing.[35] It runs a food bank and has sent missionaries to Costa Rica, where they have established a church with thirty-five to forty members.

In the past five to six years approximately eighteen new Pentecostal churches have opened their doors to the Latinos in Allentown. (It is difficult to be precise, as some churches appear and disappear practically overnight.) Approximately 16 percent of Allentown's Latinos attend the city's Pentecostal churches, which provide familiarity and a sense of community for people who have been assigned outsider status. At their exuberant services, held in Spanish, Latinos feel at home in a church where the prayer is spontaneous and intense, the music is loud and rhythmical, the other worshipers are warm and loving brothers and sisters, and the pastor is a caring father. The strict rules provide structure that is missing in the community at large. Church members cannot drink, smoke, or dance. In most of the churches women are not allowed to wear pants, jewelry, or makeup or cut their hair. Speech in and out of church is heavily peppered with "Amén" and "Que Dios te bendiga." My surveys show that 83 percent of churchgoers attend regularly at least three times each week. Clearly, religion plays a very important role in their lives. For many, social life also revolves around the church and church activities such as evangelizing crusades, Sunday-school teaching, retreats, and the planning of worship services.

Some of the congregations are large and well established, housed in buildings bought from older Anglo congregations that have since moved to other parts of town, and some are in small storefronts. All of them hold some type of worship service three to four times per week. Of the members I interviewed, 64 percent were unemployed, held low-paying, menial jobs, or collected unemployment or disability insurance. Congregations were divided just about equally between men and women (47 and 53 percent respectively). Although 53 percent of respondents were married (and another 5 percent divorced and 6 percent widowed, with many of the single persons being teenagers), only 24 percent attended church with their entire families. Each church had some recent arrivals, but 60 percent of the members were long-term (more than one year) residents of Allentown. About half had been members of a Pentecostal church before moving to Allentown. Approximately 25 percent had converted, mostly from Catholicism. Each church is involved in some kind of charitable endeavor, and all but one deny any involvement in "political" types of activities. All of them follow a discipline that prohibits drinking, smoking, dancing, and sexual relations outside of marriage, and to varying degrees they all control the appearance of women. In some of the stricter churches, such as the Vegas' Betania Church, men and women sit in separate sections. Most of the pastors belong to an organization of Latino pastors; none of them belong to the Protestant ecumenical Lehigh Valley Council of Churches.

On a hot summer day on Sixth Street in downtown Allentown, young men without shirts loll about listening to music and commenting in Spanish about the young women who wander by. Children run in and out of the Happy Dairy Spanish Grocery with dripping ice creams, begging the hot, tired adults to take them to the municipal pool. On this one block, there are two storefront Pentecostal churches, a Christian Spanish bookstore, the transmitting office of Radio Vive (a Christian Spanish radio station), and a women's shelter run by the Nueva Vida Pentecostal church.

Two devout recent converts, Miriam and Ramón Reyes, live in the shelter and run it as volunteers. Until three years ago, Miriam was a drug addict. As hard as she had struggled for twenty years, she had been unable to rise out of her life on the streets—drinking, buying and selling drugs, and stealing to maintain her habit. Ramón had killed his first man when he was nine years old and spent the next thirty years in and out of jail as the leader of one of Puerto Rico's biggest gangs. They both believe that God watched over them and kept them alive all those years while they were in Satan's grip. Now that they have found God, they have dedicated their lives to helping other addicts cure themselves through the Lord. Their faith is strong, and their lives are completely devoted to serving the Lord. They go to church four times each week, and (even though Ramón holds down two secular jobs) they both work full-time in the shelter, ministering spiritually as well as physically to the residents. Miriam's thirteen-year-old daughter lives in the shelter with them, and her two older sons attend church with them.

The Pastors

The six pastors I interviewed have similar histories and to a greater or lesser degree fit Peter Wagner's profile of the Latino Pentecostal pastor.[36] Many of them are older, working-class, and received their theological training "in the streets." As Wagner points out, "When all is said and done, the lack of skills in Hebrew, Greek, and epistemology may have been more than compensated for by the inherent ability to identify with the proletariat."[37] These pastors are in their forties and fifties and converted as adults, when each was seized with a "burning desire" to serve. They are not well educated, having received their training in Pentecostal biblical institutes that they attended part-time for two to three years. They are from poor families and worked in low-paying jobs.

Raul Ramírez, for example, is the pastor of one of Allentown's larger Pentecostal churches, the Iglesia Pentecostal de la Nueva Vida. Ramírez came to Allentown in 1988 in search of a safer, quieter life for his family than the one they led in New York. Brought up as a Catholic in Puerto Rico, he had converted to Pentecostalism in Chicago during a low period of his life and had studied to be a pastor at the Instituto Bíblico Latinoamericano in New York. Upon his arrival in Allentown he had opened a Spanish Christian bookstore and become the pastor of an eight-member congregation. His church, which now has some 120 members, is located in a modest downtown row house the first floor of which is a faux-wood-paneled sanctuary. The lively services are well attended by men, women, and children. Guitar and conga-drum music accompanies their worship.

Hector Rodríguez, the pastor of the Iglesia de Cristo Misionera, is a Puerto Rican who appears to be in his midforties with little formal education. He converted to Pentecostalism as an adult in 1974 while working as an ironer in a clothing factory. He trained for three years at night in a Bible institute and began his new career in Buffalo, New York. He came to Allentown in 1986 to visit family and stayed to start a storefront church in its center city. The church is a simple space with pews facing an altar at what was the back of the store. Hand-painted signs and drawings and postcards of Puerto Rico decorate the walls. The church was bought with contributions from its hundred members.

Víctor González, pastor of the Iglesia Asambleas de Jesucristo, also fits the profile of Latino Pentecostal pastors. He too converted in his forties, having found that "the vacuum in his heart could not be filled with alcohol or worldly pleasures." Besides pastoring his hundred-member church and overseeing the food and clothing bank, González works as the chaplain to the Allentown police and visits inmates in three prisons. He also teaches in his church's biblical institute for the preparation of future pastors.

Edwin Colón's church, the Iglesia Primera Corintios XIII, is a white clapboard church in a stable working-class neighborhood. His congregation shares the church with the Anglo Missionary Church. He began the church in 1992 with seventeen members, and it has grown in two years to more than eighty. Like the others, this church is self-supporting through tithing and donations. The members appear to be somewhat better-off than the members of other churches (my survey confirms that impression), but the worship is as fervent, the music as loud, and the fellowship as warm. Colón himself is from a middle-class Protestant family. In Puerto Rico he worked as an agent for the Federal Deposit Insurance Corporation, and his wife was a schoolteacher. When he was seized by a burning desire to work as a missionary, he and his wife gave up their jobs and all their possessions and moved with their three small children into an American biblical institute in Puerto Rico for two years to prepare for missionary work.

Pentecostal Women

There are no women pastors in these churches, but women play an active role in church governance and leadership. Each of the churches has women in elected positions and as deacons. In some, women are responsible for planning and leading the services on particular nights. At all the services I attended, women either led the group in prayer or song, preached, gave testimony, or led Bible study. This is not to imply that the majority of fervent worshipers are women. In contrast to what may be found in Pentecostal churches in Latin America, in Allentown there are just as many men attending church, and their participation is as active and enthusiastic as the women's.

Elizabeth Brusco's study of male/female relationships in a Colombian Pentecostal family indicates that women enjoy more equality and higher status in Pentecostal families.[38] The aspirations of men and women seem to coincide more where life centers around church and churchgoing. Pentecostal men spend their time at home instead of in bars and become devoted to religion and to their families. For many women, their husbands' conversion can mean literally the difference between life and death: The men stop drinking, stop beating them, and bring home a paycheck that puts food on the table. These changes frequently mean an improvement of women's status within the family, as well as an improvement of the entire family's economic status.

In Allentown's churches, for instance, family life is a theme in the testimonies of men in church. Often their testimonies describe the importance of the church and the family in their fight against Satan's temptations. Many spouses attend church together, sit together, and share the care of the children. Some pastors allow couples living out of wedlock to attend church whereas others discourage them. Single men attend church, and participation in services is not dominated by men or women. On a Sunday afternoon, several stylishly dressed young men greet each other at the door with a "God bless you" and a hug. One of them describes himself to me as a former "Satanist." Before the services begin, they prostrate themselves on the floor in front of the simple altar to pray. A thirty-four-year-old single man with a good salary from a concrete company converted from Catholicism three years ago; now he comes to church four times each week to serve the Lord who saved him from a life of drugs and alcohol.

Carol Ann Drogus's chapter in this volume reports that, whereas Colombian Catholic women are encouraged to become involved in political activity and work outside the home, among Pentecostals men are enjoined to become more involved in the private sphere—to be more engaged with their families and abandon the traditional public men's world of drink and women. Although they may remain household heads, their active participation in household duties creates a more egalitarian relationship between husband and wife. Similarly, many of the women I interviewed in Allentown work outside the home and believe that in "Christian" families there is less machismo and more cooperation between spouses.

The strong family orientation of the churches, the many hours that families spend together in church, and the public sharing of child care support the perception that men and women participate more equally in so-called women's work. One of my women respondents, who insisted that there was more equality between men and women in Christian homes, explained that the restrictions on women's behavior are not so much a question of church doctrine as of what women feel. These rules, she says, come from the Bible, not from men. Whatever the reality may be, it is significant that these women perceive that their religion provides a more egalitarian relationship between men and women.

Political Participation

The conventional wisdom with regard to Pentecostals and politics is that they do not participate in so-called worldly matters and that this nonparticipation lends conservative support to the political status quo. In 1980 Anthony La Ruffa observed of Pentecostals in Puerto Rico that they upheld the commonwealth status or saw statehood as the only alternative. Independence, they believed, would lead inevitably to another communist Cuba.[39] In three recent essays on Pentecostals' participation in Brazilian politics, John Burdick, Rowan Ireland, and Paul Freston[40] challenge the conventional wisdom. Their case studies show that to varying degrees Pentecostals have indeed become "political" in Brazil. The work of Kathleen Harder indicates that Pentecostals worldwide are involved in various forms of political activity. In her survey of fifty-six church leaders representative of thirty-two countries from all continents, forty-six confirmed that Pentecostals in their countries were politically active. The largest number reported Pentecostals voting in elections, universally the most common form of political participation, but nearly half said that Pentecostals were also engaged in working for political campaigns, supporting candidates, and attending political rallies. Twenty respondents even claimed that Pentecostals were publicly marching or demonstrating for or against certain public policies.[41]

My surveys and interviews indicate that although most churches are involved in some kind of charitable activity, such as food and clothing banks and visiting the sick, none claim official involvement in what they would define as political activity to try to influence public policy or to challenge the system. Beyond saving souls, the churches' perception of their role is to create a comfort zone and to provide and minister to basic needs. Nevertheless, government cuts in spending on social services have had a strong negative impact on Allentown's Latinos. The churches' response of actively collecting to provide basic services can be understood in political terms as providing a substitute for shrinking social services. Although they may not be doing "big" politics, they clearly have a stake in the community and are not uninvolved. Besides maintaining a food and clothing bank, the Nueva Vida church runs a treatment center for drug-addicted women, and another church is trying to establish a halfway house for recently released Latino prisoners. Although very few members are publicly involved in the various struggles of the greater Latino community, most of the people with whom I spoke were aware of the political issues and problems that confront Allentown's Latinos. All of them knew of the infamous councilwoman's public attacks on the Latinos and shared a negative opinion of her crusade against their community. Some protested to local authorities over the neighbors' complaints about their loud music in church and the city's denial of a permit to hold outdoor evangelizing campaigns. Many participated in the first annual Puerto Rican Pride Parade in the spring of 1994.

Only one of my interviewees took a traditional active role in Latino politics, as a member of the Mayor's Advisory Council on Latino Affairs. Only one pastor expressed a belief in the importance of political involvement for improving the position of Latinos in Allentown. He has invited political candidates to speak in his church and urges his congregants to vote. Several respondents from his church indicated that they did political work "when necessary." These were the only affirmative responses to that question of my survey. Despite the disclaimers, however, regarding participation in politics, respondents indicated that they had protested in some way when they perceived they were being treated unjustly because they were Latino. When the issue was injustice—being followed around in a store, not being served in a restaurant, being told to speak English or not to speak Spanish—they protested.

Comparing the political involvement of Latino Pentecostals in the United States and Latin American Pentecostals, Samuel Solivan notes that the Latinos see the roots of their oppression in racism whereas Latin Americans see them in poverty.[42] His analysis supports the perception of Allentown's pastors, who believe that a large part of their work is to build self-esteem and cultural pride. Allentown's Latinos know that they suffer discrimination not necessarily because they are poor but because they look different, speak Spanish, and hold different cultural values.

Conclusion: The Pentecostalization of Allentown

Since Pentecostalism has an especially strong appeal to the most destitute of a given society, its popularity is greatest in the poorest barrios of Latin America as well as among new immigrant groups in the United States. However, it would be incorrect to conclude that only the poor and alienated are Pentecostals. Anthony La Ruffa's description of Pentecostalism in Puerto Rico is germane: "One of the most striking aspects of Pentecostalism is its accommodating propensity—adaptability to changing socio-cultural conditions. Although beginning as a religion of the poor and oppressed, it can readily adjust itself to more affluent conditions. Some Pentecostal churches in Puerto Rico have a constituency which is part professional and fits into the middle and upper middle class."[43] Similarly, in Allentown, although the overwhelming majority of Pentecostals are poor, living on welfare or disability insurance, there are also solidly middle-class longtime churchgoers whose involvement in the church is steady and fervent.

Phillip Williams argues in this volume that individual anomie may not be sufficient to explain the growing membership in Pentecostal churches. Differentiating between social and individual anomie, he explains that second-generation inhabitants of a city may experience anomie for reasons other than social dislocation. Long-term residents of Allentown who have been attending Pentecostal church for many years are no longer uprooted and displaced, but Allentown's increasing hostility toward the growing Latino community makes all Latinos targets of discrimination, sometimes subtle and sometimes blatant. It is not surprising, then, that they continue to seek haven in the Pentecostal churches. They may not all be new to the city and they may not all be poor, but they are all Latinos who want a place where they can speak and sing and pray in loud Spanish without having to worry about conforming to Anglo culture. The added dimension that Allentown's Latinos are an unwelcome minority community creates a more demanding role for the churches. Indeed, the pastors agree that an important part of their work in Allentown is to build self-esteem by instilling pride in and trying to preserve Puerto Rican culture.

It is likely that the continued Latinization of Allentown will mean the continued Pentecostalization of Allentown. Because the character of the Puerto Rican Pentecostal community of this study follows the patterns of Pentecostalism in Latin America as described in the literature, it is also likely that Allentown's relatively new but growing population of Latino churchgoers will follow the trends in terms of numbers, political participation, and social influence. It is predictable that an increased hostility toward Latinos will send more Latinos into the Pentecostal churches. And with increased injustice toward this minority community more Pentecostals will become more publicly "political." Recently, an Allentown patrolman, Thomas Siteman, was suspended from his job for racially harassing Latino residents of the Cumberland Gardens housing project. When the Allentown city council moved to reinstate him, Pentecostal Pastor Gilbert Rivera led the public protest. As this book goes to press, the city council is about to vote on an extension of the English-only resolution that would make English Allentown's *official* language. Raúl Feliciano is an active member of Allentown's large Assembly of God congregation. In response to a councilmember's claim that the English ordinance was good for the Latinos because it would encourage them to learn English, he was quoted in the *Allentown Morning Call* as saying, "Telling Hispanics the resolution is for their own good is like breaking a person's leg so he can have some rest from work."[44]

NOTES

1. Emilio Willems, *Followers of the New Faith: Culture, Change, and the Rise of Protestantism in Brazil and Chile* (Nashville, Tenn.: Vanderbilt University Press, 1967); Christian Lalive d'Epinay, *Haven of the Masses: A Study of the Pentecostal Movement in Chile* (London: Lutterworth, 1969).

2. Renato Poblete and Thomas O'Dea, "Anomie and the Quest for Community: The Formation of Sects Among the Puerto Ricans of New York," *American Catholic Sociological Review* 21, 1 (Spring 1960), pp. 18–36.

3. Joseph P. Fitzpatrick, *Puerto Rican Americans: The Meaning of Migration to the Mainland* (Englewood Cliffs, N.J.: Prentice-Hall, 1971), p. 129.

4. Virginia Garrard-Burnett and David Stoll, eds., *Rethinking Protestantism in Latin America* (Philadelphia: Temple University Press, 1993).

5. Sidney W. Mintz, *Worker in the Cane: A Puerto Rican Life Story* (New York: W. W. Norton, 1974).

6. Lawrence Stains, "The Latinization of Allentown, Pa.," *New York Times Magazine*, May 15, 1994, pp. 56–62.

7. Garrard-Burnett and Stoll, *Rethinking Protestantism*, p. 9.

8. See, for example, Donald T. Moore, "Puerto Rico para Cristo: A History of the Progress of the Evangelical Missions on the Island of Puerto Rico," Ph.D. diss., Southwestern Baptist Theological Seminary, n.d.; Victor de León, "The Silent Pentecostals: A Biographical History of the Pentecostal Movement Among the Hispanics in the Twentieth Century," Master of Divinity thesis, Fuller Theological Seminary, Pasadena, Calif., 1979 (including a chapter on Puerto Rico); Juan L. Lugo, *Pentecostés en Puerto Rico* (San Juan: Gospel Press, 1951), the autobiography of the first Puerto Rican Pentecostal; and Anthony L. La Ruffa, "Pentecostalism in Puerto Rican Society," in Stephen D. Glazier ed., *Perspectives on Pentecostalism: Case Studies from the Caribbean and Latin America* (Lanham, Md.: University Press of America, 1980).

9. Interview with Pastor Edwin Colón, Allentown, Pa., June 7, 1994.

10. See Larry Tye, "Missionaries from Abroad Preach Message in US," *Boston Globe*, November 15, 1994.

11. Dan Wakefield, *Island in the City: The World of Spanish Harlem* (Boston: Houghton Mifflin, 1959).

12. Ibid., p. 78.

13. Lugo, *Pentecostés en Puerto Rico*, p. 9.

14. Ibid., p. 50.

15. Everett Wilson, "Early History of Pentecostals in Latin America," manuscript, p. 32.

16. I gratefully acknowledge the comments of Samuel Solivan of the Newton Andover Seminary, whose knowledge of Pentecostalism in Puerto Rico has been invaluable.

17. See La Ruffa, "Pentecostalism in Puerto Rican Society."

18. Ibid., pp. 50–51.

19. David Barrett, ed., *World Christian Encyclopedia* (Nairobi: Oxford University Press, 1982).

20. Wilson, "Early History," p. 33.

21. José Caraballo, "A Certificate Program for Hispanic Clergy and Lay Leaders in an Accredited Theological Seminary: A Case Study with Projections," D.–Min. professional project, Drew University, Madison, N.J., 1983, p. 66, cited in Eldin Villafañe, *The Liberating*

Spirit: Toward an Hispanic American Pentecostal Social Ethic (Lanham, Md.: University Press of America, 1992), p. 100.

22. Villafañe, *Liberating Spirit*, p. 93.

23. José Reyes, *Los Hispanos en los Estados Unidos: Un reto y una oportunidad para las iglesias* (Cleveland, Tenn.: White Wing Publishing House and Press, 1985).

24. David Traverzo Galarza, "A New Dimension in Religious Education for the Hispanic Evangelical Church in New York City," cited in Villafañe, *Liberating Spirit*, p. 14.

25. Interview with Radames Santiago, July 29, 1994.

26. Stains, "The Latinization of Allentown, Pa." p. 61.

27. *Allentown Morning Call*, May 29, 1992.

28. *Allentown Morning Call*, December 2, 1992.

29. "Report of the Governor's Advisory Council on Latino Affairs," Harrisburg, Pa., March 1993.

30. Stains, "The Latinization of Allentown, Pa."

31. Interview with Father John Bisek of Sacred Heart church, February 15, 1994.

32. *Despedida pastoral del Reverendo Francisco Vega,* pamphlet (translation mine).

33. *Allentown Morning Call*, March 6, 1962.

34. Interview with Martín Velázquez Sr., November 12, 1993.

35. Like most Latino pastors, the pastor supports himself with a secular job.

36. Peter Wagner, *Look Out—The Pentecostals Are Coming* (Carol Stream, Ill.: Creation House, 1975).

37. Ibid., p. 70.

38. Elizabeth Brusco, "The Reformation of Machismo: Asceticism of Masculinity Among Colombian Evangelicals," in Garrard-Burnett and Stoll, *Rethinking Protestantism,* pp. 143–158.

39. La Ruffa, "Pentecostalism in Puerto Rico," p. 60.

40. John Burdick, "Struggling Against the Devil: Pentecostalism and Social Movements in Urban Brazil," Rowan Ireland, "The *Crentes* of Campo Alegre and the Religious Construction of Brazilian Politics," and Paul Freston, "Brother Votes for Brother: The New Politics of Protestantism in Brazil," in Garrard-Burnett and Stoll, *Rethinking Protestantism,* pp. 20–44, 45–65, and 66–110.

41. Kathleen Harder, "The Expanding Politicization of the World Pentecostal Movement," in *Conference Papers 1992, Society of Pentecostal Studies,* pp. 6–7. See also Harvey Cox, *Fire from Heaven: The Rise of Pentecostal Spirituality and the Reshaping of Religion in the Twenty-first Century* (Reading, Mass.: Addison-Wesley, 1995).

42. Personal communication, Samuel Solivan, October 1994.

43. La Ruffa, "Pentecostalism in Puerto Rican Society," p. 60.

44. *Allentown Morning Call*, October 4, 1994.

10

The Sound of Tambourines: The Politics of Pentecostal Growth in El Salvador*

PHILIP J. WILLIAMS

On a typical Thursday evening in Mejicanos, San Salvador, *evangélicos* through-out the city are glorifying God to the sound of tambourines and electric guitars. Along Mejicanos's Calle Principal the *hermanos* of the Fuente de Vida Eterna Pentecostal church remind the congregation that "Jesus is there for us if only we seek him out. The blind man sought out Jesus and was healed. We too can get back our sight if we seek out Jesus." Beyond the Punto Dos bus terminal in Colonia Buena Vista, the local Asambleas de Dios is holding a evangelistic cam-paign, imploring residents to repent and accept Christ as their savior. Farther up the Calle Mariona, the pastor of the Luz de la Biblia church draws a distinction between plastic surgery and "divine surgery": "Plastic surgery brings only super-ficial changes, whereas divine surgery brings profound change, a total transfor-mation. Only God's divine surgery can cleanse us." Around the corner, members of the Catholic base community grumble about the Pentecostals' insults against the church and its saints. "The *hombres separados* try to hide from the world in their little groups. Instead of seeking unity, they only sow division." Outside, a group of *hermanos* from the Iglesia Elim peers in on its way to a prayer meeting.

During the past decade, the ground has been shifting under Mejicanos as in the rest of El Salvador. Beneath the civil war and economic disparity, a revolution of sorts has been taking place. This revolution has manifested itself not only in the dramatic growth of Pentecostal churches but also in the expansion of Catholic

*I thank Ed Cleary and Manuel Vásquez for their helpful comments on an earlier version of this chapter.

179

charismatic groups and the resurgence of base communities. The scope of the religious changes taking place in El Salvador is not without parallel elsewhere in Latin America. Not surprisingly, scholars of religion and politics in Latin America have been turning their attention to Pentecostalism.

As Cleary points out in his introductory chapter, explanations for the growth of Pentecostalism vary. From the pioneering work of Emilio Willems and Christian Lalive d'Epinay to more recent studies by David Martin and David Stoll,[1] scholars have debated the usefulness of the concept of anomie in explaining Pentecostal growth in Latin America. Simply stated, in societies experiencing rapid social change the resulting dislocation produces an erosion of norms and insecurity. The feeling of insecurity and uprootedness is particularly intense among poor migrants to urban centers. Pentecostalism offers these migrants a substitute community, providing new norms to confront their situation.[2]

Rather than rehashing the arguments, I want to make several points. First, the model of anomie may account for only certain Pentecostals and forms of Pentecostalism.[3] Secondly, it may be useful to distinguish between individual and social anomie. Second-generation inhabitants of cities may experience anomie for reasons other than social dislocation, for example, a personal crisis with alcohol or drugs. And finally, a situation of anomie, whether individual or social, is not a sufficient explanation for an individual's decision to convert to Pentecostalism. There is nothing inevitable about uprooted individuals' choosing a Pentecostal church over some other church or social organization.

Scholars also have disagreed over the years regarding the capacity of Pentecostals to subvert the traditional social order. Whereas Willems and, more recently, David Martin view Pentecostals as latent carriers of liberal-democratic values and practices, Ireland[4] and others are skeptical of such interpretations. Studies of Pentecostalism in Central America also dispute the view that Pentecostals are capable of moving from symbolic protest to a more structural challenge of the traditional social order. Roberts, in his study of Pentecostals in Guatemala City, found them reluctant to participate in community organizations and distrustful of political activity in general.[5] Churches counseled members to ignore social problems rather than to collaborate actively in resolving them. Stoll's study of the Pentecostal boom in Latin America and especially his chapter on Guatemala provide a necessary corrective to the notion of Pentecostalism as nurturing democratic values. The brutal dictatorship of the Pentecostal leader Gen. José Efraín Ríos Montt, with the open support of some Pentecostal leaders, raises serious doubts about any direct relationship between Pentecostalism and liberal democracy. Studies by Martínez and Valverde[6] of Pentecostals in Nicaragua and Costa Rica depict them as apolitical and hardly a force for structural change. Martínez does make a distinction between church leaders, who are more likely to seek relationships with political elites, and members, who are indifferent to political involvement. However, leaders' political participation, rather than challenging the traditional social order, tends to be supportive of the status quo.

Historical Overview of Pentecostal Growth

El Salvador, like its Central American counterparts, would seem an ideal candidate for demonstrating the usefulness of the concept of anomie in explaining Pentecostal growth. The dramatic increase in the numbers of churches and members since the late 1970s parallels the deepening conflict and economic crisis in the country. The relationship between social dislocation and Pentecostal growth seems to help explain even the early history of Pentecostal churches in the country. Pentecostal churches in particular sprang up originally in the Western coffee-growing regions. After the 1870s these areas experienced the dramatic expansion of coffee production. Government decrees abolishing Indian communal lands and ejidal land in 1881 and 1882 opened the way for coffee producers to increase their holdings. As coffee production expanded in the western region, the Indian population suffered increasing displacement, joining the growing pool of landless and land-poor peasants forced to work in the coffee harvest.[7] It was here that the first Pentecostal churches took root.[8]

Pentecostalism arrived in El Salvador around 1904.[9] Frederick Mebius, a Canadian missionary, began preaching among coffee workers in Las Lomas de San Marcelino, on the slopes of Volcán Santa Ana. After splitting with the Central American Mission[10] because of his Pentecostal beliefs, Mebius went on to establish some two dozen congregations with approximately 2,000 members by the late 1920s.[11] In December 1929 the churches split, about half of them remaining under Mebius's leadership and the other half following the Salvadoran Pentecostal leader Francisco Arbizú and the Welsh missionary Ralph Williams. The latter founded the Asambleas de Dios, affiliated with the Assemblies of God in the United States, in 1930. The other major Pentecostal denomination, the Iglesia de Dios, consisted of churches under Mebius's direction. It was formally endorsed by the Church of God of Cleveland, Tennessee, in 1940, following the arrival of the American missionary H. S. Syverson.[12]

Pentecostalism remained a largely rural phenomenon until the 1950s. In 1956, following an evangelistic campaign by the North American evangelist Richard Jeffrey, the Asambleas de Dios organized several new congregations in San Salvador. By 1960 the Asambleas reported twenty congregations with 1,200 members in the capital.[13] During the 1960s the Asambleas de Dios shifted attention to San Salvador, transferring its national offices and Bible institute there in 1965.[14] The evangelizing efforts of the Centro Evangelístico, a thriving congregation in the heart of San Salvador, contributed greatly to the steady growth throughout the 1960s and 1970s. Under the leadership of the American missionary Juan Bueno, members of the Centro Evangelístico initiated prayer meetings in their homes, inviting neighbors to attend. Once a core group was established in a particular member's neighborhood, the Centro Evangelístico offered support to form a new congregation. In this way, the Centro Evangelístico "mothered" dozens of churches throughout San Salvador.[15]

The other large Pentecostal church, the Iglesia de Dios, grew more slowly than the Asambleas and was less successful in establishing congregations in San Salvador. Soon after his arrival in 1940, Syverson founded a large central church in Cojutepeque, some fifteen miles southeast of the capital. In 1944 he established a Bible school and national offices in Santa Tecla, a small town just west of San Salvador. However, most of the churches founded during the 1940s and 1950s were located in isolated rural areas, which were deemed less hostile to the church's evangelizing efforts. After growing rather slowly during this period, church membership increased more rapidly during the 1960s and early 1970s. In 1976 the Iglesia de Dios claimed a total of 183 churches with a membership of over 8,000.[16]

Throughout the 1960s and the first half of the 1970s, the Asambleas de Dios and the Iglesia de Dios, along with other Pentecostal churches, grew steadily, surpassing the Central American Mission and the traditional denominations. By 1967 it was estimated that Pentecostals accounted for 70 percent of all Protestants in El Salvador, with a total communicant membership of 35,800.[17] The late 1970s saw very rapid growth in Pentecostal church membership. Although not wholly reliable, church growth data from the evangelical churches themselves do give an approximation of the trends during the 1980s.[18] A study by the Confraternidad Evangélica Salvadoreña (CONESAL) reports that the average annual growth rate for evangelical church membership was 22 percent from 1978 to 1982, 15.7 percent from 1982 to 1984, and 12.5 percent from 1985 to 1987, all well above the 5.5 percent rate for the 1960–1967 period.[19]

Estimates for evangelicals as a percentage of the total population during the late 1980s range from 12 to 23 percent. Not surprisingly, the highest estimate, 22.6 percent, comes from CONESAL. The CONESAL study draws on membership figures from the churches themselves. After calculating the total number of baptized members—estimated at approximately 315,000—this figure is multiplied by a factor of 3.5, resulting in a total evangelical population of 1.1 million. The factor used represents the average number of nonbaptized family members or friends for each baptized member; however, it is suspect given that most church growth studies use a factor between two and three (Table 10.1).

A private survey conducted for the 700 Club in San Salvador in July–August 1990, based on a stratified sample of 3,693 respondents over the age of ten nationwide, estimates evangelicals at 17.4 percent of the total population.[20] The survey also includes a breakdown for the capital, other urban areas, and the countryside (see Table 10.2). Of particular interest is the percentage of Salvadorans not claiming any religious affiliation, 32.1 percent.

Finally, one of a series of surveys by the Instituto Universitario de Opinión Pública (IUDOP) at the Universidad Centroamericana José Simeón Cañas, conducted in June 1988, was devoted to religion.[21] The survey of 1,065 respondents from seven of El Salvador's fourteen departments estimated an evangelical population of 16.4 percent and included a breakdown by department (Table 10.3). Coleman et al., analyzing twenty-two surveys conducted by the IUDOP during the 1980s, estimate the evangelical population at 12 percent.[22] This figure, which

TABLE 10.1   Religious Affiliation of Salvadorans According to Various Surveys (percentage of population)

Survey	Evangelical	Catholic	No Affiliation
CONESAL, 1987	22.6	n.a.	n.a.
IUDOP, 1988	16.4	64.1	14.7
700 Club, 1990	17.4	47.3	32.1

Sources: CONESAL: CONESAL, "Estudio del crecimiento"; IUDOP: Instituto Universitario de Opinión Pública, "La religión para los salvadoreños," no. 17, San Salvador, October 19, 1988; 700 Club: 700 Club, "Estudio sobre hábitos religiosos en El Salvador: Julio-Agosto," unpublished report, San Salvador, September 27, 1990.

is an average of the survey estimates, does not take into account annual growth trends and is clearly too low. From the available data it appears that a more accurate estimate would be in the range of 15–20 percent, with Pentecostals accounting for approximately 75 percent of the total evangelical population.

Explaining Pentecostal Growth

The dramatic growth of Pentecostalism in El Salvador after the mid-1970s is undoubtedly related to the deepening political and economic crisis that plunged the country into a unending cycle of violence and despair. The crisis enveloping Salvadoran society affected every Salvadoran family to some degree. Poor Salvadorans saw their sons dragged off by the military to become cannon fodder in the hills while the wealthy sent their sons and daughters abroad or retired behind their walls and barbed wire. The social dislocation resulting from the war and economic crisis created increasingly precarious conditions for the majority of Salvadorans.

The crisis manifested itself in the massive displacement of the population during the 1980s. Even before the conflict began in earnest, the increasing concentration of landownership associated with the expansion of nontraditional export crops (cotton, sugar, and beef cattle) had produced a growing number of landless and land-poor. In addition to increasing rural-urban migration, more and more Salvadorans crossed into Honduras in search of land. On the eve of the Soccer War in 1969, some 300,000 Salvadorans are thought to have migrated to Honduras. The expulsion of 130,000 Salvadorans by the Honduran government in the aftermath of the war only added to the increasing land pressures.[23] Between 1961 and 1975 the landless population grew from 11.8 to 40.9 percent of rural families. By 1981 landlessness affected approximately 60 percent of the rural population.[24]

Not surprisingly, the armed conflict greatly exacerbated these tendencies. By the late 1980s over 25 percent of the population had been internally displaced or forced to flee the country.[25] As a result of the huge influx of migrants from the combat zones, the population of San Salvador's metropolitan area swelled from

TABLE 10.2   Religious Affiliation of Salvadorans (percentage of population)

Area	Evangelical	Catholic	No Affiliation
San Salvador	21.0	47.3	28.4
Other urban areas	15.0	50.2	32.4
Rural areas	15.0	39.8	40.2 ·

Source: 700 Club, "Estudio sobre hábitos religiosos en El Salvador."

560,000 in 1971 to over 1.2 million in 1990.[26] The deepening economic crisis translated into unacceptable levels of unemployment and deteriorating conditions for the majority of the population. Open unemployment reached 24 percent of the economically active population in 1989, while the percentage of households living in extreme poverty stood at 64.1 percent in 1985.[27] Finally, the armed conflict and military repression produced a growing number of victims, to the point that by the end of the war few Salvadorans would not know a friend or family member victimized by the conflict.

As life conditions for the majority of the population became increasingly precarious, it is not surprising that a growing number of Salvadorans searched for solutions to their physical and spiritual insecurity. However, there was nothing inevitable about their looking for support to the Pentecostal churches as opposed to the Catholic church. The churches' differing responses to the crisis are essential for an understanding of the relationship between the crisis and Pentecostal growth.

During the late 1970s, under the leadership of Archbishop Oscar Romero, a significant sector of the Catholic church adopted a position of prophetic denunciation, speaking out against the military regime's human rights abuses and in support of far-reaching social transformation. In response, the regime stepped up its persecution of church leaders, pastoral agents, and members of Christian base communities. The increasing repression culminated (but did not end) with the assassination of Romero in March 1980.[28]

In the wake of Romero's death, the church leadership in the archdiocese began to distance itself from the popular movements with which he had sought a relationship of solidarity. That sector of the church most committed to his pastoral initiatives found itself in the most difficult of circumstances. Its pastoral work among poor Salvadorans had become increasingly dangerous to all those involved. Not surprisingly, in those parishes where Romero's message had resonated most, pastoral agents and base-community members were forced to go underground, closing their doors to new members.

An example of this kind of "tactical retreat" occurred in the San Francisco de Asís parish in Mejicanos, San Salvador. In the mid-1970s, a Salvadoran seminarian and a Belgian nun began organizing "initiation" courses in the parish. On October 30, 1976, the first meeting was held with the participation of some fifty parishioners who had completed the courses. Those who accepted a "Christian

TABLE 10.3   Religious Affiliation of Salvadorans by Department (percentage of population)

Department	Evangelical	Catholic	No Affiliation
Ahuachapán	9.9	59.4	24.2
Santa Ana	26.4	54.7	15.7
Chalatenango	5.0	73.3	13.3
San Salvador	16.0	67.3	11.1
Usulután	20.1	53.2	22.1
San Miguel	13.8	68.1	15.0
Morazán	12.8	79.0	4.7

Source: IUDOP, "La religión para los salvadoreños."

commitment" returned home to evangelize fellow parishioners. As more and more members of the emerging base communities began to participate in popular movements, repression against the parish increased. The parish priest, Father Octavio Ortíz, was killed in January 1979 while on a youth retreat in San Antonio Abad. His replacement, Father Rafael Palacios, was gunned down in Santa Tecla only six months later.

Although a group of Passionist Fathers took over the parish in late 1979, pastoral work was constrained by the climate of repression. Periods of reorganization and consolidation of the base communities were followed by periods of intense persecution in which pastoral work was forced underground. In response to successive waves of repression, the parish adopted a number of security measures. Instead of meeting in members' homes, base communities met in the parish hall. There was great apprehension about recruiting new members, as they might turn out to be *orejas* (informants). The priests were unable to visit parishioners in their homes or to organize masses in the countryside for fear of reprisals. In short, pastoral work became highly centralized, and the church lost a significant presence in the *colonias*.[29]

Other sectors of the church were not so receptive to Romero's pastoral line. In some parishes, priests and religious maintained a highly sacramentalist approach to pastoral work. Instead of organizing grass-roots initiatives intended to increase lay participation in the life of the church, some priests and religious were content to wait for parishioners to come to them. A good example is the Corazón de María parish in Colonia Escalón. Although the majority of the parish's inhabitants live in squalid conditions, the bulk of the active members are upper- and middle-class Salvadorans. According to the parish priest, poorer inhabitants *se automarginan* (marginalize themselves) because they feel uncomfortable in a parish dominated by the wealthy.[30] Only recently (in late 1991) did the parish begin to devise new strategies to reach out to the poorer sectors, largely in response to a survey that found that 22.3 percent of households located in the *zonas marginales* of the parish were evangelical.[31]

At the same time that the Catholic church was losing its institutional presence among poor Salvadorans through either tactical retreat or pastoral neglect, the Pentecostal churches were launching an offensive to win over converts for Christ. Churches like the Asambleas de Dios were well positioned to take advantage of the Catholic church's tactical retreat. During the 1960s and 1970s the Asambleas de Dios had laid the groundwork for a significant expansion of its presence in San Salvador. In addition to the Instituto Bíblico, the church began a Christian day-school program, the Liceos Cristianos, and was successful in attracting a growing number of middle-class converts through the activities of the Centro Evangelístico, a thriving congregation in the heart of San Salvador.

Throughout the 1980s, with technical and financial assistance from their counterparts in the United States, Salvadoran churches organized massive evangelistic campaigns aimed at saturating the airwaves and filling soccer stadiums with new converts.[32] In 1980, the visit of a Puerto Rican evangelist, who preached to a full house at the Flor Blanca stadium in San Salvador, signaled the growing strength of the Pentecostal movement and served as an important impetus for future growth. By 1992 some of the larger churches had developed the mobilizational capacity to fill the stadium on their own.

Even more important than the evangelistic campaigns and use of the mass media were the efforts of Pentecostal churches at the grass roots.[33] Members of local churches visited neighbors in their *colonias,* invited family members, friends, and coworkers to attend services, and organized prayer groups in their homes. Unlike members of Catholic base communities, Pentecostals rarely faced persecution by the regime, which looked favorably upon the growth of Pentecostal churches. Contrary to some Catholic leaders who spoke against the regime, Pentecostal leaders were careful to maintain congenial relations with the government.[34]

Also important in explaining Pentecostal success in winning over new converts was the appeal of the Pentecostal message. Pentecostal churches offered both a *reason* and a *solution* for the crisis afflicting Salvadoran society. The suffering of the Salvadoran people followed biblical prophecy. The war and economic crisis were a sign that the Second Coming was imminent. Conditions were going to worsen before the apocalypse. Secular solutions that sought to transform society were useless when the world was full of sin. The only solution was to prepare oneself for the Second Coming. Salvadorans must repent, stop sinning, give up their vices, and accept Christ as their savior. In addition to guaranteeing their salvation, accepting Christ might bring other positive benefits, including material improvements and a renewed family environment.

In other words, the Pentecostal churches provided a solution that was within the grasp of most poor Salvadorans. They did not have to risk their lives by joining a political movement or trade union. Instead, they had to put their own lives in order before using up their energy on more collective solutions. For many poor Salvadorans, whose life conditions had not improved during the past several years and who were tired of hearing the empty promises of corrupt politicians, the message was appealing. And for those poor Salvadorans who had grown increasing skeptical of the Catholic church's exhortations to struggle against structures of oppression and injustice and had seen so many Catholic victims of that struggle, the message was attractive. One Pentecostal described his own conversion as follows, "In the Catholic Church I wasn't able to satisfy my feeling of emptiness. I felt this emptiness, this need for something more in my life. The situation of the war created a certain fear. The only solution was Jesus Christ. It was a necessity. Now I feel the presence of God in my life."[35]

The Pentecostal churches were an especially appealing option for poor women. First of all, they offered women consolation and solidarity. Most churches organized women's groups that provided a mutual support system for poor women. In fact, for many women, attending services was therapeutic. One woman commented, "How many times have I come to church ill or with a headache after a hard day but always gone home feeling better (*más tranquila*)?"[36] The women's groups also provided opportunities for participation and possibilities for assuming leadership positions within the churches. Besides organizing their own activities, the women's groups usually were responsible for one of the weekly services, and women in general played a prominent role in most of the services. Finally, those women who succeeded in converting their spouses generally experienced a dramatic improvement in their lives. As one woman commented, "My husband used to drink. When he came home drunk all he wanted to do was fight. Now we have peace in our home. My husband no longer wastes our money on alcohol, and now he cares about our children. We're still poor, but at least our children are growing up in the Gospel."[37]

In the context of a crisis and the Catholic church's diminished institutional presence, Pentecostal churches took the offensive with a powerfully convincing but simple message. It was a message that was easily comprehensible to poor Salvadorans and contrasted with the Catholic church's more abstract message about "evangelizing social structures." As more and more Salvadorans found solace in the Pentecostal churches, word spread. The boom was under way.

Poor Pentecostals in Comparative Perspective

The data that follow are drawn from field research I conducted between 1991 and 1992 in El Salvador as part of a larger research project on grass-roots religious movements.[38] Although my survey of Pentecostals included members from both lower- and middle-class congregations, given the overwhelmingly "popular" composition of Pentecostal churches I will present data only on members of lower-class ones. Of the eleven congregations selected, five were located in lower-class neighborhoods and six in *zonas marginales* of San Salvador and Mejicanos. Seven were affiliated with large denominations (Asambleas de Dios, Iglesia de Dios, Iglesia Pentecostal Unida). In order to assess the relative impact of religious affiliation on political attitudes and behavior, I also include data from a survey of lower-class Catholic base communities located in the San Francisco de Asís parish in Mejicanos, where most of the Pentecostal churches selected were located. Two of the four base communities were located in *zonas marginales*.

The data in Table 10.4 are revealing with regard to the migrant status of Pentecostals and base-community members. Members of base communities were more likely to have been migrants to the capital (64 percent) than Pentecostals (45 percent), suggesting that base communities are at least as successful as Pentecostal churches in attracting migrants. Moreover, of those Pentecostals that could be classified as migrants, 32 percent had converted before arriving in San Salvador and another 45 percent had converted seven or more years after arriving in the capital. In fact, only three of the fifty-one Pentecostals surveyed had converted as recently arrived migrants. Although the data are in no way conclusive, given the small size of the sample, they are highly suggestive and raise serious doubts about explanations of Pentecostal growth based on theories of social dislocation (Table 10.4).

Personal crises and the churches' aggressive evangelizing efforts, as opposed to social dislocation and uprootedness, seem to be more important in explaining individual conversion. Twenty-seven percent of Pentecostals cited personal crises (with alcohol, drugs, prostitution) as the primary factor behind their conversion. Typical are the following:

> I liked to drink. I was a womanizer. My home was going down the tubes. I was destroying myself. I didn't even think about my kids. On June 12, 1979, God had mercy on me. He called me. I felt God's touch. I accepted Christ into my life. Afterwards I felt His strength.

❀ ❀ ❀

> I was a sinner. I wasn't a Catholic. I never attended mass. One day I was invited to an evangelistic campaign. I went to have a look. During the celebration I became aware of my situation, that I was corrupted. I understood the message that only the believers would be saved. God was offering me an opportunity, a way of escaping from sin. It was then that I accepted God.

❀ ❀ ❀

> I accepted Christ in 1986. It was a total transformation in my life. I lived in sin, dissolution, sex, pornography, thinking that I was a know-it-all. But one day God made me understand my true spiritual condition, and it was then that I felt ashamed of my life. I gave my life to Christ, and He broke all the chains that enslaved me. It was something indescribable.

Another 25 percent pointed to the evangelizing efforts of family members of friends as determinant and 16 percent to the efforts of the churches themselves.

TABLE 10.4   Background Characteristics of Members of Pentecostal Churches and Catholic Base Communities (percentage of respondents)

	Pentecostals (n=51)	Catholics (n=47)
Gender		
Female	47	53
Male	53	47
Age		
Under 21	8	13
21 to 30	24	26
31 to 50	54	41
Over 50	14	22
Place of origin		
San Salvador	55	36
Elsewhere	45	64
Family income		
Under 1,500 colónes	62	81
1,501–2,500 colónes	18	11
Over 2,500 colónes	11	5
Don't know	9	3
Formal education		
None	6	14
Primary (complete or incomplete)	43	41
Secondary (complete or incomplete)	31	32
Postsecondary	20	14

The context of the war and economic crisis was not unimportant. Eighty-two percent of those surveyed had converted to Pentecostalism between 1976 and 1990, paralleling the crisis. The data, then, tend to support the argument that both personal crises, aggravated by the increasingly precarious life conditions associated with war and economic decline, and the aggressive evangelizing efforts of church members contributed significantly to the boom after the mid-1970s.

Also important in understanding the growth of Pentecostal churches is the level of satisfaction among church members. Ninety-four percent of Pentecostals said that their life conditions had improved since converting. Respondents pointed to both spiritual and material improvements in their lives:

> With the Lord I feel sure of myself, more confident. Before I wasn't married, but with the Lord I married a Christian. Before I lived with bitterness, hatred, vengeance, and many other things which the Lord has eliminated from me.

❀   ❀   ❀

> I can say that what I earn is little but I never go lacking because God provides me with everything I need.

Before I used to drink a lot and waste my money on liquor. God has blessed me. Now
I have a small house that I was able to finance through a social fund.

Before knowing Jesus Christ we rented a house. Since converting we have our own
house and vehicle.

Pentecostals also expressed a high level of satisfaction with their churches' ability
to address members' needs. Whereas 67 percent of Pentecostals believed that their
local church addressed members' needs, only 43 percent of base-community
members thought so.

The data in Table 10.5 on political attitudes and behavior are also revealing. As
expected, Pentecostals were much less likely than base-community members to
participate in political parties, trade unions, and neighborhood associations.
Likewise, only 14 percent (compared with 94 percent of base-community members) believed that the church should denounce social injustice. Several respondents qualified this by saying that "the church shouldn't involve itself in politics."
Nevertheless, a low level of participation is not synonymous with political conservatism. Although Pentecostals were much less likely than base-community
members to support political parties on the left (FMLN-CD), only 2 percent expressed support for the right-wing ARENA party. The overwhelming majority of
Pentecostals (63 percent) said that *no* party was capable of resolving the country's
problems. Typical responses were that *sólo Dios* (only God) could resolve the
country's problems or that political parties and politicians served only their own
partisan interests. Equally surprising was that Pentecostals were not much more
likely to support the status quo than base-community members. Only 8 percent
of Pentecostals believed that the government responded to the people's needs.
And finally, 41 percent cited socioeconomic inequality/poverty as the principal
cause of the war.

What if anything can we conclude from these data? It seems clear that
Pentecostals' low level of participation in secular associations is a result of something other than political conservatism. Like base-community members,
Pentecostals were highly critical of the ARENA government and (albeit in smaller
numbers) cited socioeconomic equality/poverty as the leading cause of the conflict. However, unlike base-community members, Pentecostals expressed deep
skepticism about the ability of any political party to address the country's problems and saw little point in denouncing social injustice. Their overwhelming disillusionment with politics in general and their rejection of secular solutions help
to explain their unwillingness to participate in secular associations with political
agendas.

TABLE 10.5 Political Attitudes and Behavior of Members of Pentecostal Churches and Catholic Base Communities (percentage of respondents)

	Pentecostals (n=51)	Catholics (n=47)
Believe government responds to people's needs	8	4
Believe the church should denounce social injustice	14	94
Causes of the war		
Socioeconomic inequality/poverty	41	64
Lack of love/understanding	24	13
Political power ambitions	10	2
Lack of spiritual direction	10	0
Biblical prophecy	8	0
Social discontent	4	0
Others	4	8
No opinion	4	13
Participation in secular associations		
Political party	0	19
Trade union	0	11
Neighborhood association	10	36
Voted in last election	69	66
Party preference		
ARENA	2	0
PDC	0	0
FMLN-CD	0	44
Party of the people	0	15
Opposition party	2	0
Evangelical party	2	0
No party	63	26
No opinion	31	17

The degree to which Pentecostalism influences members' political attitudes and behavior is more difficult to measure, and the data presented here can only be considered suggestive in this regard. Although the data suggest a fairly strong correlation between religious affiliation and degree of political participation among Pentecostals and base-community members, they do not necessarily demonstrate a causal relationship between the two variables. It may be that Pentecostals were already skeptical of politics and mistrustful of secular solutions prior to converting. The religious content of Pentecostalism, which tends to shun participation in associations with political agendas and reject secular solutions, may simply serve to reinforce a predisposition toward nonparticipation. For base-community members there does seem to be a strong correlation between active participation in the church and political attitudes; however, further research in this area is warranted.[39]

The Political Impact of Pentecostal Growth

Despite most Pentecostals' disillusionment with traditional politics, the dramatic increase in church membership and the churches' growing institutional concerns have led some Pentecostal leaders to seek a more public role in the country's political life. This is especially true among the larger, more institutionalized churches such as the Asambleas de Dios. As its outreach programs have expanded over the years, the Asambleas de Dios's relationship with the state has assumed greater significance. Maintaining harmonious church-state relations can bring concrete benefits to the church. An example of this is the church's network of church schools, which receives financial support from the government's Fondo de Inversión Social (Social Investment Fund—FIS). More important, as I suggested early on, congenial relations with the regime in power guarantee the churches freedom to carry out their evangelizing mission. Not surprisingly, then, most church leaders have been reluctant to criticize government abuses.

Restraint in criticizing the regime is not simply the result of political conservatism. Although most Pentecostal leaders are conservative, they also hold to an eschatological vision that is radically different from that of the Catholic church. A missionary for the Asambleas de Dios explained: "We believe that things will get worse before the Second Coming. Meanwhile, our job is to prepare the people, attending to their immediate needs. We're not feeding the poor to change society. Why change the structures of society? We don't believe the Kingdom can begin here on earth. Even if 95 percent of the people converted, there would still be human failure and sin."[40]

Given this eschatological vision and Pentecostals' widespread distrust of politics, it may seem surprising that after 1990 two evangelical-inspired political parties emerged. Does the establishment of these two parties signal a new direction in the political participation of Pentecostals? What are their chances of success, given the experience of evangelical movements in Peru and Guatemala?

The first of the evangelical-inspired parties to emerge, the Movimiento de Solidaridad Nacional (National Solidarity Movement—MSN), was founded in February 1991 by a group of mostly evangelical businessmen and professionals, including the rector of the Universidad Evangélica and the director of Crusada Estudiantil y Profesional para Cristo (Campus Crusade for Christ).[41] Several of the founding members had been active in the Christian businessmen's organization, Hombres de Negocio por un Evangelio Completo. In fact, the MSN's president, Edgardo Rodríguez, had served as national party president for six years. In addition to evangelicals, the MSN also counted Catholic charismatics, including Rodríguez, among its founders.

The MSN received legal status in February 1992 after collecting the required number of signatures (3,000). During 1992 it concentrated its efforts on building organizational bases throughout the country and enhancing its public exposure through the media. Positioning itself as a party of the center, the MSN presented itself as an alternative to the traditional political parties. MSN leaders hoped that, as in Guatemala and Peru, the large number of voters disillusioned with professional politicians would be attracted to a party of Christian businessmen and professionals with no political past.[42] Despite their efforts, the party received only 1 percent of the national vote in the March 1994 elections and failed to win a seat in the Legislative Assembly.

One of the MSN's greatest limitations was its weak connection to the Pentecostal community. Most of its leaders came from non-Pentecostal churches. This was a severe limitation, given that Pentecostals account for at least 75 percent of the Protestant population. It seems also that the decision to organize the party was made without consulting leaders from the largest Pentecostal churches. Moreover, the fact that the MSN's president was a Catholic created a great deal of distrust in the Pentecostal community.[43]

A potentially more promising development for politically activated Pentecostal leaders was the decision of Jorge Martínez to found his own political movement in January 1993. Martínez, a prominent Pentecostal with close ties to the Pentecostal community, had served as vice minister of agriculture and of interior during the Alfredo Cristiani government. He is the first Salvadoran Pentecostal to occupy a cabinet position in the government. Martínez is well known in the Pentecostal community, frequently preaching at churches around the country. During his tenure in office he was able to travel extensively, making invaluable contacts for a future presidential bid. Up until the fall of 1993 Martínez and his party, the Movimiento de Unidad (Unity Movement), concentrated their efforts outside of the capital, avoiding the media limelight.[44]

Unlike the MSN, Martínez made no bones about his ties to the Pentecostal community and his efforts to attract support among churches. Several prominent members of the wealthy Iglesia Josué (affiliated with the Asambleas de Dios), including the director of the 700 Club, and a number of pastors from the Asambleas de Dios actively supported Martínez's candidacy.[45] Although Martínez believed that his party was well placed to tap Pentecostal disillusionment with the traditional parties, its performance in the March 1994 elections was not much better than the MSN's, only 2.4 percent of the vote nationally. It was, however, enough to guarantee the party one deputy in the Assembly.

The parties' poor showing in the elections raises doubts about their potential impact on national politics. Despite widespread disillusionment with traditional political parties, it appears that Salvadorans in general and Pentecostals in particular did not view the evangelical-inspired parties as a viable alternative. Such a conclusion is supported by the data in Table 10.5 showing that only 4 percent of poor Pentecostals expressed support for evangelical parties. Personal interviews with both members and pastors of Pentecostal churches also revealed little enthusiasm for Pentecostal participation in electoral politics.

Another factor worth considering is the impact of Jorge Serrano's political demise in neighboring Guatemala. The debacle of Guatemalan evangelicals' first foray into electoral politics may have influenced Salvadoran voters to some extent. Probably more important was the nature of the electoral campaign itself. Given that the elections had become something of a referendum on ARENA, small parties had little opportunity to make their presence felt. Not surprisingly, media attention focused almost exclusively on ARENA and its two principal challengers, the Christian Democrats and the FMLN. Finally, some voters inclined to vote for the evangelical-inspired parties may have switched their loyalties to one of the larger parties to avoid "wasting" their votes. Whatever the case, the evangelical parties' poor electoral performance should result in a reassessment of their continuing political participation.

Interpreting Pentecostal Growth: Some Final Reflections

As I have pointed out, interpretations of Pentecostal growth vary widely. Part of the confusion in the literature may be a result of the paradoxical nature of Pentecostalism. Droogers argues that although the paradoxical elements of the Pentecostal phenomenon often appear to the researcher as contradictions, from the perspective of the believer they may seem complementary. In fact, the religion's paradoxical character may add to its appeal, since it affords believers wider latitude to satisfy their needs.[46]

My own research on Pentecostalism in El Salvador revealed a number of elements that may appear contradictory to the outside observer. However, after many conversations with Pentecostals and after having attended numerous services, I came to realize that the very paradoxical nature of the religion may have contributed significantly to its growth in recent years.[47]

1. Spiritual refuge versus symbolic protest. To the outside observer, Pentecostalism seems to represent a spiritual withdrawal from worldly things and a rejection of secular solutions. Nevertheless, this spiritual withdrawal is not the same as conformism or total withdrawal from the secular world. As was made clear by the data presented in Table 10.5, although most poor Pentecostals do not support the status quo, they are unlikely to put their trust in secular solutions. Instead, they continue to live "in the world" but distinguish themselves by adopting a radically different lifestyle. Preaching against sin, they venture out into the world, denouncing worldly things and calling on people to transform their lives as they have. However, despite their denunciations and their rejection of secular solutions, most Pentecostals submit to secular authorities. As Ireland suggests, there are clear limits to Pentecostals' transformative capacity, making it unlikely that symbolic protest would evolve into a direct challenge of the traditional social order.

2. Authoritarianism versus democracy. Here again there are elements of both. On the one hand, Pentecostal churches provide important opportunities for lay participation often lacking in Catholic churches. Members typically lead church services and sometimes even preach. Personal testimonies also give services a participatory flavor. Moreover, Pentecostals are constantly reminded that their communication with God is direct and does not have to be mediated through an ordained minister. And finally, although some of the larger denominations now require that their pastors complete a minimum period of training and apprenticeship, in most of the smaller independent churches members can aspire to become pastors with little or no formal training.

Despite the egalitarianism evident in many Pentecostal churches, pastors are the highest authorities in the churches, and many behave in a very authoritarian manner. In some churches pastors make decisions in consultation with lay leaders, but in others pastors decide with little or no input from church members. At a minimum, pastors exert significant influence over which members are given positions of responsibility within the church. This tends to foster the development of patron-client relations whereby members are "rewarded" for their loyalty to the pastor. Maintaining these patron-client networks takes on increasing importance as aspiring pastors compete for members' loyalties. Often the result of such competition is a final showdown or split in which members' loyalties are manipulated by church leaders.

Pastors exert influence over their congregations in other ways. In many churches, pastors control church finances with little or no accountability to the membership. This may not present much of a problem in small rural areas, where congregations are small and tithes are barely sufficient to support the pastor and his family. However, in larger urban churches, members' tithes are more than adequate to support the pastor and his family. Not surprisingly, some pastors use church finances to reward loyal members instead of investing in church facilities and program development.[48]

Finally, despite members' "direct communication with God," pastors typically impose "correct interpretations" of biblical passages and are rarely tolerant of divergences. Members are reluctant to challenge the pastor's authority in interpreting the Bible, knowing that loyalty will increase their chances of assuming positions of greater responsibility in the church.

Pentecostals may experience emotional freedom during church services, but at the same time they must submit to a very strict code of ethics. Although spontaneity reigns during worship, Pentecostals' lives outside of church are highly regimented. Moreover, for those who stray from the path, sanctions can be severe; it is not rare for them to be denounced in church.

Elements of both authoritarianism and democracy also affect the relationship between local churches and national church structures. The balance between centralized authority and local autonomy varies between churches and within different denominations. In the larger, more institutionalized churches, such as the Iglesia de Dios and the Asambleas de Dios, the balance is often tipped in favor of centralized authority. In both churches I encountered younger pastors who were particularly critical of restrictions imposed from above. Even so, in the Asambleas de Dios, wealthier congregations with large memberships can exercise a great deal of autonomy from national leaders.[49]

Tolerating autonomy at the local level can reduce the likelihood of schisms within the churches. Whereas divisions within smaller independent churches usually lead to a complete break, in the larger denominations breakaway groups are often allowed to form a new congregation while remaining within the fold. A strategy sometimes used by the national leadership of the Asambleas de Dios is to offer upstart pastors support to found congregations of their own. This flexible approach has been successful in avoiding major schisms.[50]

3. Women's submission versus women's liberation. As was pointed out earlier, poor women can find new opportunities for participation and exercising leadership roles within the churches. Nevertheless, there are limits on the leadership positions to which women can aspire. In many churches women cannot serve on the church governing board, let alone become pastors. And in those churches where women can aspire to become pastors, they are prohibited from becoming ordained.[51]

Upon conversion, many poor women experience a dramatic improvement in their domestic environment. This is especially true where women succeed in converting their husbands. But, as Burdick points out in his study of Pentecostalism and Catholic base communities in urban Brazil, "this can happen without the man himself actually becoming a *crente* [believer]. . . . simple moral pressure from *crente* wives is enough to moderate men's drinking, smoking, adultery, and so forth."[52] Women are, however, expected to submit to their husbands, and sometimes this may mean that they have to wait patiently for their husbands to convert. And even when a spouse converts, he continues to act as the head of the household. However, as Brusco argues in her study of Pentecostalism in Colombia, "in Pentecostal households the husband may still occupy the position of head, but his relative aspirations have changed to coincide with those of his wife."[53]

4. Rupture versus continuity. In many ways, Pentecostalism represents a rupture with the past. Most important, it signals a break with a dominant culture infused with traditional Catholic rituals and practices.

Converts can no longer participate in patron-saints fiestas or other religious celebrations. Because of prohibitions on drinking and dancing, converts cannot attend many community celebrations organized by the local neighborhood committee. Conversion may also lead to ostracism on the part of other family members. Not surprisingly, because of the radical nature of the break, many conversions involve entire families.

Besides representing a rupture with traditional culture and with past lifestyles, as was pointed out above, Pentecostalism may break down certain barriers for women, particularly in the domestic sphere. Moreover, because of the high degree of egalitarianism evident in some churches, members may overcome traditional obstacles to assuming leadership roles. At the same time, however, Pentecostalism represents a significant degree of continuity with the past. Authoritarian decisionmaking, patron-client networks, patriarchal structures, and submission to secular authorities are all reproduced to some degree within the Pentecostal churches.

Clearly, the ground has been shifting in El Salvador. The religious arena has become increasingly crowded as a result of the Pentecostal boom. Catholic church leaders, aware that the church's traditional religious monopoly is no longer a given, have begun to encourage new pastoral strategies aimed at regaining lost ground. The resurgence of base communities in several parishes in the archdiocese and the spectacular growth of the charismatic movement are examples of Catholic responses to the Pentecostal "offensive."[54] It may be that the paradoxical nature of Pentecostalism will produce unresolvable tensions that result in its stagnation. Just as likely, though, is that Pentecostal churches will continue to incorporate apparently contradictory elements in a complementary fashion, contributing to their future vitality and appeal.

Back in Mejicanos, the tambourines can still be heard. At the Templo La Jordán, Brother Fidel tells the congregation of a sick man who didn't know Christ. When Brother Fidel persuaded the man to appeal to Jesus, he was healed, miraculously. "The power of Jesus can heal us, it can change our lives completely. Those of you who want to appeal to Jesus, come forward." Brother Fidel then asks the congregation to pray for those kneeling before him. Several minutes of intense, rhythmic praying follow: "Gloria al Señor, Aleluya, Amen, Gloria al Señor." Across town in the Iglesia La Hermosa, one of the "sisters" steps forward to preach: "Many people ask us: 'Who are you if you're not of this world?' No, it's not that we don't live in this world. Of course we're in this world. It's just that we don't live the way the rest of the world does."

NOTES

1. Emilio Willems, *Followers of the New Faith: Culture Change and the Rise of Protestantism in Brazil and Chile* (Nashville, Tenn.: Vanderbilt University Press, 1967); Christian Lalive d'Epinay, *Haven of the Masses: A Study of the Pentecostal Movement in Chile*

(London: Lutterworth, 1969); David Martin, *Tongues of Fire: The Explosion of Protestantism in Latin America* (Oxford and Cambridge, Mass.: Basil Blackwell, 1990); David Stoll, *Is Latin America Turning Protestant? The Politics of Evangelical Growth* (Berkeley: University of California Press, 1990).

2. André Droogers, "Visiones paradójicas sobre una religión paradójica," in Barbara Boudewijnse, André Droogers, and Frans Kamsteeg, eds., *Algo más que opio: Una lectura antropológica del Pentecostalismo latinoamericano y caribeño* (San José, Costa Rica: Editorial Departamento Ecuménico de Investigaciones, 1991), pp. 23–24.

3. Droogers, "Visiones," p. 27.

4. Rowan Ireland, *Kingdoms Come: Religion and Politics in Brazil* (Pittsburgh: University of Pittsburgh Press, 1991). See also Judith Hoffnagel, "Pentecostalism: A Revolutionary or a Conservative Movement?" in Stephen D. Glazier, ed., *Perspectives on Pentecostalism: Case Studies from the Caribbean and Latin America* (Lanham, Md.: University Press of America, 1980).

5. Bryan Roberts, "El Protestantismo en dos barrios marginales de Guatemala," *Estudios Centroamericanos,* no. 2 (1967).

6. Abelino Martínez, *Las sectas en Nicaragua: Oferta y demanda de salvación* (San José, Costa Rica: Editorial Departamento Ecuménico de Investigaciones, 1989); Jaime Valverde, *Las sectas en Costa Rica* (San José: Editorial Departamento Ecuménico de Investigaciones, 1989).

7. David Browning, *El Salvador: Landscape and Society* (Oxford: Oxford University Press, 1971).

8. Everett Wilson, "Central American Evangelicals: From Protest to Pragmatism," *International Review of Mission* 77 (January 1988), p. 96.

9. Charles Conn, *Where the Saints Have Trod* (Cleveland, Tenn.: Pathway Press, 1959), p. 140. Wilson uses "about 1915" as the date of Mebius's arrival in El Salvador (Everett Wilson, "Sanguine Saints: Pentecostalism in El Salvador," *Church History* 52 [January 1983], p. 189). Nelson uses an earlier date, "about 1912" (Wilton Nelson, *Protestantism in Central America* [Grand Rapids, Mich.: Eerdmans, 1984], p. 40). The date I use comes from an official church history of the Church of God's missionary work in El Salvador.

10. The Central American Mission was founded by Cyrus Scofield, pastor of the First Congregational Church of Dallas, Texas, and sent its first missionary to El Salvador in 1896. See Nelson, *Protestantism in Central America,* pp. 32–34.

11. Wilson, "Sanguine Saints," p. 190.

12. Ibid., p. 192.

13. Ibid., pp. 196–197, and Cristóbal Ramírez, *Obedeciendo la Gran Comisión* (San Salvador: Asambleas de Dios, 1984), pp. 16–18.

14. *Luz y Vida,* no. 2 (1988), p. 9.

15. Interview with Hno. Herminio Dubón, administrator of the Centro Evangelístico, San Salvador, November 26, 1991.

16. Leonel Bernal, "Hacia un ministerio en El Salvador," M. Div. thesis, Church of God School of Theology, Cleveland, Tenn., May 1990.

17. William Read et al., eds., *Latin American Church Growth* (Grand Rapids, Mich.: Eerdmans, 1969) p. 150–153.

18. Unfortunately, none of the studies distinguish between Pentecostal and non-Pentecostal churches.

19. CONESAL, "Estudio del crecimiento de la iglesia evangélica de El Salvador," unpublished report, San Salvador, 1987. The CONESAL study suggests that the evangelical

boom began to run out of steam over the course of the 1980s. During my field research, August 1991–August 1992, I noticed increasing concern on the part of pastors regarding future growth. During several services that I attended, pastors talked of "stagnation" and called on members to be more aggressive in winning over new converts.

20. 700 Club, "Estudio sobre hábitos religiosos en El Salvador: Julio-Agosto 1990," unpublished report, San Salvador, September 27, 1990.

21. IUDOP, "La religión para los salvadoreños," Working Paper no. 17, October 19, 1988, San Salvador.

22. Kenneth Coleman et al., "Protestantism in El Salvador: Conventional Wisdom Versus Survey Evidence," *Latin American Research Review* 28, 2 (1993), pp. 119–140.

23. For an excellent discussion of Salvadoran migration to Honduras and the origins of the Soccer War, see William Durham, *Scarcity and Survival in Central America* (Stanford: Stanford University Press, 1979).

24. Charles Brockett, *Land, Power, and Poverty* (Boulder: Westview Press, 1990) p. 75.

25. Mario Lungo, *El Salvador en los 80: Contrainsurgencia y revolución* (San Salvador: Editorial Universitaria, 1990), pp. 97–101.

26. Ministerio de Planificación, *Indicadores económicas y sociales, 1990–1991* (San Salvador, 1991).

27. FLACSO, *Centroamérica en gráficas* (San José, Costa Rica: FLACSO 1990), and CENITEC, "La eradicación de la pobreza en El Salvador," *Política Económica* 1, 4 (December 1990–January 1991).

28. For a discussion of this period of church history, see Phillip Berryman, *The Religious Roots of Rebellion* (London: SCM Press, 1984); Jorge Cáceres, "Political Radicalization and Popular Pastoral Practices in El Salvador, 1969–1985," in Scott Mainwaring and Alex Wilde, eds., *The Progressive Church in Latin America* (Notre Dame, Ind.: University of Notre Dame Press, 1989); and Rodolfo Cardenal, *Historia de una esperanza* (San Salvador: Universidad Centroamericana Editores, 1987).

29. This discussion is based on interviews with lay leaders active in the parish since the mid-1970s. They asked to remain anonymous.

30. Interview with Father Francisco Fierro of Corazón de María parish, San Salvador, April 21, 1992.

31. Parroquia Corazón de María, "Censo parroquial de las zonas marginales," manuscript, San Salvador, December 1991.

32. For a discussion of the relationship between U.S.-based churches and religious organizations and their counterparts in Central America, see Stoll, *Is Latin America Turning Protestant?*

33. The director of the local 700 Club admitted that the use of the mass media was effective only if local churches engaged in follow-up work at the grass roots. Interview with Lic. Alejandro Anaya, director of the 700 Club, San Salvador, January 28, 1992.

34. The general superintendent of the Asambleas de Dios told me that "the government doesn't oppose the churches as long as they don't get involved in politics." Interview with Hno. Julio César Pérez, San Salvador, December 13, 1991. The national supervisor of the Iglesia de Dios added that "the reason the Catholic church has had problems with the government is that its denunciations are excessive." Interview with Hno. David Peraza, Santa Tecla, August 27, 1991.

35. Interview with member of the Centro Evangelístico, San Salvador, March 12, 1992.

36. Interview with member of the Templo Evangélico Emanuel, Mejicanos, San Salvador, February 25, 1992.

37. Interview with a group of women at the Iglesia de Dios in Colonia Progreso, Mejicanos, July 25, 1992.

38. My field research over a twelve-month period combined semistructured interviews with church elites and members, self-administered questionnaires, and participant observation.

39. I found a highly positive correlation between years of active membership and support for parties on the left (Kendall tau $b = 0.81$, Prob > :R: $= 0.05$).

40. Interview with Delonn Rance, American missionary for the Assemblies of God, San Salvador, October 14, 1991.

41. These are Dr. José Heriberto Alvayero and Adonai Leiva, respectively.

42. Interviews with Edgardo Rodríguez, presidential candidate of the MSN, San Salvador, November 12, 1991, and July 17, 1992, and with Dr. José Alvayero, rector of the Universidad Evangélica, San Salvador, October 29, 1992.

43. Most of the pastors I interviewed had a negative or lukewarm view of the MSN. Only two out of fifteen were enthusiastic about the idea of an evangelical party. The president of the MSN, Edgardo Rodríguez, admitted that the massive support they had expected from evangelical churches had not been forthcoming. According to him, "most pastors are afraid of getting involved in politics."

44. Interview with Dr. Jorge Martínez, presidential candidate of the Movimiento de Unidad, San Salvador, July 13, 1993.

45. Interviews with Martínez and a campaign volunteer at the Movimiento de Unidad headquarters, San Salvador, July 13, 1993.

46. Droogers, "Visiones paradójicas," pp. 36–40.

47. These reflections are based on in-depth interviews, both unstructured and semistructured, with members and leaders in the churches where I conducted my survey.

48. Confidential interview with the pastor of a large Pentecostal denomination.

49. A case in point is the Iglesia Josué, where, despite the strict dress codes generally enforced in lower-class churches, wealthy Pentecostals arrive at Sunday worship dressed in the latest fashions.

50. There are limits to this strategy. In the case of the Centro Evangelístico, one of the largest and most influential congregations affiliated with the Asambleas de Dios, an ambitious young pastor and some five hundred members left the church in November 1991. Despite the church's offering the pastor his own church, his group founded its own independent congregation a few blocks away from the Centro Evangelístico. Interview with Hno. Herminio Dubón, administrator of the Centro Evangelístico, San Miguelitos, San Salvador, November 26, 1993.

51. This is the case in the Asambleas de Dios. "Ordained pastor" is the highest of the three categories of pastors allowed by the church. Interview with Hno. Julio Pérez.

52. John Burdick, "Rethinking the Study of Social Movements: The Case of Christian Base Communities in Urban Brazil," in Arturo Escobar and Sonia Alvarez (eds.), *The Making of Social Movements in Latin America* (Boulder: Westview Press, 1992), p. 178.

53. Elizabeth Brusco, "Colombian Evangelicalism as a Strategic Form of Women's Collective Action," *Feminist Issues* 6, 2 (Fall 1986), p. 6.

54. Catholic base communities have flourished of late in the San Francisco de Asís parish in Mejicanos, La Resurrección parish in Colonia Miramonte, and Santa Lucía parish in Colonia Santa Lucía. The charismatic movement claims over 20,000 adherents in the archdiocese alone.

11

Pentecostals and Evangelicals in Venezuela: Consolidating Gains, Moving in New Directions

BRYAN FROEHLE

*W*hereas the Catholic bishops have only recently proclaimed themselves committed to a "new evangelization" of the continent, the evangelical churches of the region have been conducting enormously successful evangelization programs for decades. Throughout the past twenty years, evangelical churches and members have been increasing rapidly, and their rates of increase show no sign of slowing. Data collected between 1967 and 1980 in Venezuela suggest that adherents of the evangelical movement in that country increased from some 47,000 to 500,000 members over that thirteen-year period.[1] Although no data are available, the evangelical community is believed to have grown even faster since the 1980s. By far the fastest-growing portion of the evangelical community is converts to Pentecostal churches. The notably increased social presence of the evangelical movement in Venezuela may be gauged by the increasing role of evangelicals in politics and the increasingly bold plans and projections produced by local evangelical umbrella organizations.[2] Venezuelan evangelical churches grew out of British and North American mission efforts dating back to the end of the nineteenth century, but the great majority of churches are now completely independent of the original missions and fully national in terms of their financial and personal resources.[3] They act independently within the local religious context and shape their future in terms of the constraints and possibilities of their local cultural and social backgrounds.

Ultimately, the best way to understand the potential prospects and pitfalls of the so-called new evangelization or to explain the success of the evangelical movement and the emergence of Pentecostalism without recourse to polemics is through a historical analysis. Such work must take into account the specific constraints and unique developments experienced as this religious movement took root in Venezuela and throughout Latin America. In the presentation that follows, I will place the origins of Pentecostalism in Venezuela in the wider context of the evangelical movement in general. Correspondingly, I will refer to Pentecostalism and its distinctive experience when the available data permit me to distinguish Pentecostal from non-Pentecostal evangelicals. Much of the time, the experience of Pentecostal and non-Pentecostal evangelicals in Venezuela is too entangled to permit fine distinctions. The central goal of this chapter is a comparative evaluation of the unique reality of Pentecostalism in contemporary Venezuela. To do that, however, this analysis must start and end with the wider experience of evangelical growth and development in general.

The Development of the Evangelical Community

Evangelical penetration began in earnest in the late nineteenth and early twentieth centuries throughout the continent, when U.S.-based evangelical organizations were ready to replace the British as the leading evangelical entrepreneurs. The once predominantly English-staffed and English-funded *sociedades bíblicas* (biblical societies) and groups of Bible hawkers became increasingly North American in staff and funding at this time. Mission groups expanded from a mere presence into a substantial enterprise. These evangelical efforts were funded, staffed, and promoted through the appeal to Northern European and North American imaginations of a not too culturally or geographically distant area dominated by a Spanish Catholic tradition that was considered both religiously wrong and socially backward.[4]

During the beginnings of the North American Protestant missionary enterprise in Latin America in the late nineteenth century, two key U.S. denominations involved in missionary work came to an agreement designed to avoid duplicating work and prevent sheep stealing. The Methodists agreed to concentrate efforts on the Southern Cone and Brazil and the Presbyterians on the more northern portions of South America. As a result, the first permanent North American missionary church set up in Caracas was Presbyterian. The first permanent native congregation, El Redentor (The Redeemer), was established by Dr. Theodore Pond in 1900, some three years after his arrival in Caracas.

Following the evangelical strategy pursued by mainline denominations throughout Latin America, El Redentor sponsored the Colegio Americano (American School), and that school came to consume most of the energy and resources of the local Presbyterian community.[5] As its name implies, its purpose was to introduce young Venezuelans to North American culture, including its language and science as well as values and religious beliefs. Both church and school continue to this day, although the Presbyterians have long been among the slowest-growing of all denominations in Venezuela. Their relatively more elitist and educated tradition, perhaps, made them regarded as among the more liberal and least "evangelical" of the churches in Caracas. This image persists in spite of the fact that they took a strongly conservative, charismatic turn some decades ago.[6] The high amounts of energy consumed by their school further explain such slow growth.

In the early twentieth century, distinct North American missionary efforts associated with the Scandinavian free-church tradition played an important role in the history of the expansion of evangelical churches. These efforts are today the basis of several important church organizations of non-Pentecostal evangelicals. By the early 1950s, the Baptists had also established themselves as an independent national convention. The Assemblies of God became incorporated as a national denomination soon after. The former is now the most widespread non-Pentecostal evangelical in Venezuela; the latter is the most potent Pentecostal denomination.

Often termed "ecumenical" Protestants because of their relative openness to collaboration with Catholics, the British Anglicans and the German Lutherans have never had a perceptible impact outside of their communities. Both, however, have been present since the early nineteenth century. They have never really undertaken serious efforts to promote conversions and instead have focused on nurturing their ethnically based religious communities. This situation became somewhat more complicated for the Lutherans when U.S.-based Lutherans of the Missouri Synod arrived in the late 1940s. These newly arrived Lutheran pastors had no particular allegiance to the Venezuelan German Lutherans but needed a base with which to begin their work. They first tried to work with the Venezuelan German ethnic community, which had lost its regular supply of German-trained pastors during World War II. Once German pastors again began arriving regularly after the war, the missionaries of the Missouri Synod turned to their school and radio work. Although they have had enormous, ongoing investments of U.S. personnel and financial resources, they have grown very little. Their evangelical strategy has been characterized by high visibility, ample funding, and well-trained personnel. However, they have never really targeted a local clientele or developed local leadership. Their work has been overly centralized and dominated by a well-funded, well-staffed organization of foreigners. This approach has not sufficiently allowed for local initiative, and the Lutherans have had no more success than the Presbyterians.

Members of the Plymouth Brethren arrived relatively early in the nineteenth century with the intention to win converts. The first member to arrive in the country was a Spaniard working with a railway construction company. Other members followed, sent by individual congregations rather than a centrally funded and coordinated mission board. The very simple ritual, basic organizational structure, fierce, millennial emphasis on the Bible, and humble manner won this group a loyal following, particularly in the central and western portion of the country.[7] Although their congregations were usually small, they multiplied rapidly. By the 1970s they had more congregations than any other evangelical group in Venezuela.

Although they share with the Plymouth Brethren a fundamentalist, dispensationalist theology with millennial overtones, Pentecostals have a religious style enormously different from the Brethren's quiet, almost Quaker-like style. Noisy, revivalist organizers, they have historically scandalized many members of the more traditional evangelical churches, but leaders within both traditions commonly insist on their mutual recognition as fellow evangelicals.

Pentecostals and the Venezuelan Evangelical Experience

Organized religion in any form is weak in Venezuela, particularly among the popular classes. Since dramatic reversals in its status during the nineteenth century, Catholicism has had to build alliances with social groups that could shield it from hostile forces and allow it to rebuild. Institutional investment in the emerging urban-based professional and managerial classes and other middle sectors was particularly concentrated in the field of education. As a result of this development, the presence of the Catholic church among the popular classes declined relative to other social groups throughout much of the twentieth century. Although the number of persons per parish rose significantly, middle-class access to Catholic institutions and religious personnel actually increased as private Catholic schools run by religious orders dramatically expanded.

In many ways, the evangelicals of Venezuela and of contemporary Latin America in general may be classified among the Calvinist or radical streams of reformed Christianity. However, evangelicals in Venezuela no less than the rest of Latin America today generally share a crucial dimension relatively foreign to the historic, Reformation-descended churches. Most show some degree of influence by the North American Pentecostal movement, whether officially Pentecostal or not. Many churches were planted in the region by North American revivalists from mainline denominations on "faith missions." These preachers often had a certain enthusiasm and experience of the spirit that led them to preach and promote kinds of religious experience different from that more typical of their sponsoring denominations.[8] Many of the individual churches or church organizations founded by these persons and their native associates eventually split from foreign mother churches or sponsoring denominations precisely because their latent Pentecostal-like practices and beliefs were opposed by the parent churches.[9] Some faith missions have been strongly linked to particular denominations, but many others have been the results of free-lancing efforts of independent congregations in North America or elsewhere.[10] In any case, the revivalist, charismatic orientation of the faith missions and other missionary efforts accounts in part for the strongly Pentecostal content of Venezuelan evangelical religion. The revivalist spirit and theology conveyed by many of the North American missions easily combined with local popular culture, which gives a central role to the supernatural and the miraculous in everyday life.[11]

For all their Bible-smuggling, street-corner preaching, and bold missionary work throughout the nineteenth and the early twentieth century, evangelicals hardly increased until they became open to Pentecostal religious meanings and practice. Although this shift was well under way by the 1930s, it increased dramatically during the 1950s and 1960s. Before the predominance of Pentecostalism, movements could be built and organizations established, but a broad culturally based appeal to potential members simply did not exist.

The relative shift to Pentecostalism was due to both external and internal factors. Externally, the mission agencies that had supported the evangelical movement were changing. By the 1960s, above all after the Second Vatican Council, it seemed as if the Catholic church had reformed itself on many of the issues that had brought Protestant churches in North America and Western Europe to support missionary work in Latin America in the first place. Bible reading was now encouraged by Catholic leaders. Ecumenism was strong internationally. In Latin America the ecumenical movement was producing many collaborative Bibles and Bible-based publications produced jointly by the *sociedades bíblicas* and the Catholic bishops' conferences. The central offices of major Protestant religious bodies were losing interest in focusing on differences with Catholicism and were becoming suspicious of traditional "missionary" work in a multicultural world. In short, the commitment of traditional, mainstream Protestantism to fund and staff missionary work declined rapidly.

As Methodists, Presbyterians, Lutherans, and the other mainline denominations that made up the World Council of Churches lost interest in earlier missionary efforts, North American fundamentalist and Pentecostal churches were gaining the strength, capacity, and interest necessary to create increasingly strong networks of churches, publishing houses, Bible institutes, and umbrella organizations. Most of these churches were opposed to ecumenical collaboration with churches outside the evangelical tradition and unaffiliated with the World Council of Churches. The new missionary spurt, which began in earnest after World War II and came into its own during the 1970s, is now being carried forward by a variety of groups other than the traditional mainstream denominations, including independent faith missions, the mission agencies of such Pentecostal powerhouses as the Assemblies of God, and a variety of evangelical parachurch organizations. Denominational ties are no longer a vital feature. Instead, a commitment to fundamentalist beliefs in the Bible and an enthusiastically millennialist interpretation of the Great Commission[12] have become the glue that binds this new wave of evangelization together.[13]

In spite of their importance in transferring ideas and practices, foreign missionaries and missionary resources have never been the key to increased membership in grass-roots religious organizations. The appeal that grass-roots religious organizations hold for the potential member ultimately stems from the degree to which the meanings and structures they offer make sense in terms of everyday life and cultural patterns. At this level, social factors behind the Pentecostal orientation of Venezuelan evangelicals take on their full importance.

During the past generation, Venezuela has undergone a period of dizzyingly rapid urbanization.[14] As the city became the defining feature of social life, rural cultural values and religious traditions were transferred. The immense, newly urbanized but resource-scarce population found itself in marginal urban areas where the Catholic church was simply unable to deliver religious services in any appreciable way. Although self-identified as Catholics, the urbanizing former peasants had typically been even less exposed to institutional Catholicism than their urban counterparts.[15] Their religious worldview was relatively detached from orthodox understandings of practice and belief yet infused with Christian symbolism derived from popular Catholicism.

Theirs was a folk Catholicism, open to the interventions of spirits and saints and demons in their lives. Such notions found little room in the modernizing Catholic beliefs and practices offered by priests and nuns during the post–Vatican II era. In many cases, the official institutional church of bishops and priests began to curtail and reshape popular, traditional religious celebrations in favor of more "purified" and rationalist approaches.

At the same time that modernizing Catholicism appeared to be fighting a small-scale holy war against folk Catholicism and its beliefs in interventionist spirits, saints, and demons, nature religions and Pentecostal Christianity were expanding dramatically. Nature religions, often based on native or African animist beliefs and practices, had begun for the first time to organize beyond the folk level, utilizing the wide networks that urban life permits.[16] For its part, Pentecostal religion found that it had plenty of maneuvering room in the social context of an expanding urban frontier full of potential clients with strong affinities for Pentecostal Christianity.

The Pentecostal belief in the fundamental role of the Holy Spirit in everyday life and the worship experience and a concrete willingness to "cast out demons in the name of the Lord" have proved to be strong assets in the propagation of the evangelical movement. Pentecostals, elites, and ordinary members alike, have no question that spirits can heal and harm. The issue is to discern and render the demon spirits harmless through the superior power of the Holy Spirit. Rather than struggling to reshape popular culture in the direction of indigenous liberationist movements or rejecting popular culture in favor of rational, modern orthodoxy, Pentecostals easily fit their beliefs and practices into the complex array of popular religious beliefs and practices.[17] Both Pentecostal religion and popular religious tradition assume supernatural, spiritual intervention in everyday life. Also, they both have an individualist religious orientation toward immediate gratification and claim to solve the pressing problems of everyday life, such as disease.[18]

The preferred evangelical "market" and source of most new recruits is among the poor.[19] This observation is nothing new; many of the preachers and missionaries themselves noted this relationship at an early date. Haymaker, a prominent evangelical missionary early in the century, pointed out that it was the lower classes who had nothing to lose who were the most likely to join. Significant, family-like ties among members no less than ties to the Spirit, as Birdwell-Pheasant shows in a study of Pentecostalism in Belize, can be a dramatically important feature of Pentecostal life and one especially favored by people from within the popular classes.[20] A researcher of Protestant growth in Colombia during the 1960s noted that Pentecostalism has a strong elective affinity with its targeted population. Its structures rapidly adapt to local conditions, and it tends to grow most successfully among the marginalized. As noted elsewhere, the insistence on immediate gratification of spiritual and personal needs through the powerful intervention of the Spirit and fellow believers is important to people in a vulnerable position and from a cultural background steeped in popular Catholicism.[21]

The particular form that Pentecostalism has taken is not so much a rejection of traditional religiosity as a systematization of it. Certainly, Pentecostal beliefs and practices are intelligible to popular religious thinking that emphasizes spiritual intervention in the problems of the present both as causes and solutions. Pentecostal churches emphasize the devil in their preaching and highlight the power of the Holy Spirit to save one from evil spirits and cure both physical and spiritual ailments. The personal encounter with Jesus so central to the evangelicals is often understood as a kind of spiritual possession by the Holy Spirit. Holy water is an important ingredient in Latin American popular Catholicism, often being used for informal, unorthodox home healing rituals or on other occasions of pressing need for supernatural intervention. Among Latin American Pentecostals, such ritual is not eliminated outright; instead, water is replaced with an oil of anointing that is considered even more efficacious and is justified by Scripture. Such oil is commonly used in healing ceremonies when praying for the sick or exorcising demons from the disturbed. Often even terminology and patterns of deference related to religious ritual may be carried over from popular Catholicism to Pentecostal religious life. Not uncommonly, the pulpit may be referred to as an altar and considered a sacred space through which only the most worthy—pastors and their closest associates—may pass.

In short, evangelical Christianity has been transformed from small groups of pious Bible readers to dynamically expanding communities fired by an urgent Pentecostal reading of the Bible and interaction with popular religious culture in the new, expanding settlements of the urban poor.[22] Today, building on fundamental, deeply rooted cultural conceptions of the sacred and the spiritual within a biblical framework, the evangelicals—above all the popular, Pentecostal variety—have changed within a generation from an unnoticed portion of the population to rising stars.[23]

Pentecostalism, Venezuelan-Style

Almost since they emerged as a distinct religious tradition within evangelical Protestantism, there has been a strong linkage between Pentecostals and the "electronic church" of the mass audience. More than other religious organizations, they are adept at the technological tools of the mass media and such techniques as the mass-crusade evangelization campaign style, which provide invaluable opportunities for mobilization and recruitment.[24] Their message and methods quickly became shaped to fit their target clientele, but control remains local and remarkably adaptable to different social and cultural contexts.

A longtime Pentecostal church organization in Venezuela was a product of one of the first mass ministries to employ new communications technologies. Aimee Semple McPherson's Foursquare Gospel Church (Iglesia Cuadrangular) continues to flourish in the western part of the country, where it was first established over forty years ago. Like these churches, most Pentecostal churches are the result of personal, independent efforts of church sponsorship rather than centralized denominational planning for growth and evangelization. This is true whether the church is itself independent or part of an extensive network of churches. The loose network quality of church organizations and the personal ties on which they are based tend to encourage rapid expansion as well as the development of splinter groups.

The Assemblies of God are an ideal example of these tendencies. They constitute at once both the largest evangelical organization in Venezuela and the one from which the most splinters have occurred. Assemblies of God now may be found throughout Venezuela, but their regional stronghold has always been the western portion of the country. Such a regional tendency is common for many evangelical groups, which often tend to be strongest in the areas where they were first established, often years after they have spread throughout the country.[25] Developing a strong base of support is important for gathering the strength they need for dynamic growth and expansion. This supports the observation that locally based churches that have invested their organizational resources, however limited, in projects of expansion have been notably more successful than more centralized and more heavily funded organizations based on outside support and personnel.

The traditional evangelical organization that most resembles the Pentecostals in dynamism is the Baptists. Although most Venezuelan Baptist churches generally trace their origins to the U.S.-based Southern Baptist Convention, Venezuelan Baptists have had a fully autonomous national convention since 1959. By the late 1960s and early 1970s they had the leadership, organizational infrastructure, and resource networks to begin a surge of growth that has shown no signs of slowing.[26] They are more common than Pentecostals in middle-income areas but much less common in less affluent ones.[27]

Table 11.1 illustrates the changing composition of the evangelical presence in Venezuela and the Caracas metropolitan area between 1970 and 1990. Most churches have been growing, but the leading Pentecostal organization (Assemblies of God) has been growing much more quickly than the leading non-Pentecostal evangelical organization (Baptists). Other Pentecostal organizations,

TABLE 11.1   Growth in the Number of Congregations of Selected Religious Groups for Venezuela as a Whole and the Caracas Metropolitan Region in Particular, 1970–1990

	1970		1990	
	National	*Caracas*	*National*	*Caracas*
Assemblies of God	110	32	590	128
Church of God	16	6	28	12
Baptists	66	13	130	63
Free Church	111	17	233	38
OVICE	93	0	166	7
ADIEL	18	17	67	31
Plymouth Brethren	94	36	76	35
Catholic parishes	743	281	1,045	207

This table is based on the records of the Biblical Society and of individual denominations and the field notes of the Caracas-based Evangelical Directory Project (1990–1991). The sources were up-to-date listings of congregations' names and addresses obtained from the denominations by the Biblical Society. Some listings may have been of the same denominations but acquired by different means. Problems of multiple sources were dealt with individually by cross-checking and interviews with experts. Verification of the figures is, however, impossible for any denomination, as much because of faulty records and difficult communications as because of the tremendous growth these groups have been experiencing. Great caution should be exercised in drawing any conclusions from such data.

such as the Church of God, increased at slower rates. However, such statistics are particularly difficult to use for Pentecostals, since churches founded by a Pentecostal denomination often leave that organization or the organization itself experiences subdivision. For purposes of comparison, the two different organizations of free churches are grouped together, since the major difference between them is really that they were originally based in different parts of the country. The number of congregations affiliated with these important non-Pentecostal organizations has doubled over the past twenty years.[28] These churches constitute another growth area, but individual organizations of the free churches are much smaller than the extensive, well-organized National Baptist Convention. Finally, many non-Pentecostal churches such as the Plymouth Brethren are actually declining as membership ages and the younger generation finds other organizations more appealing.

In addition to the dramatic increases in the number of independent congregations evident in these changes, many local churches may contain up to a dozen or more *campos blancos*, dependent congregations founded in selected areas that may later become the basis for new churches. Targeted areas are carefully selected for a relative absence of churches and church activity. Typically, members of the mother church live in or near the area or have connections with sympathetic family, friends, or acquaintances who live in the targeted area. These dependent congregations are carefully nurtured by selected leaders from the sponsoring church, who often settle in the area and spend most of their free time there. Successful leaders of *campos blancos* may later become pastors of the "daughter" congregations should they become independent and self-supporting. This structure is quite flexible; some groups exist for years and come together chiefly for prayer meetings during the week, and others quickly come to worship independently on weekends as well. It all depends on what works in the local situation. Not surprisingly, the groups with the most *campos blancos* are those that have expanded the fastest, such as the Assemblies of God. These groups are also most likely to expand considerably in coming years, since they can draw on these networks of related congregations that they have created for further development of independent local churches.

Pastoral preparation is based on apprenticeship more than on academic studies. In itself, this is an important source of much of the dynamism of evangelical expansion. Such leaders never leave behind the class identity and social networks they had when they were ordinary members. They enjoy an easy fit with the local community and have an expert salesman's sense of what works and what does not in the business of evangelization and church planning. Once aspiring church leaders are put to work within the local church, they must continually prove themselves as church builders in order to progress to positions of greater responsibility. Only after they have amply manifested their vocation in this way do candidates for full-time ministry go on to seminary-type training. In such a career, a pastor or prospective pastor may be asked to perform tasks or live under conditions that would be difficult for those of other class backgrounds—or national origins—to cope with.[29] Consciously comparing himself to Catholic church personnel who worked within the popular sector, one pastor put it this way: "We don't opt for the poor; we are the poor."[30]

Persons within the evangelical churches who aspire to be leaders or who feel called to do so find that they have clear opportunities within the structures of evangelical churches. Few doors are really closed to aspiring leaders provided that they can read and write and have a strong commitment. Additionally, a number of evangelical churches, particularly Pentecostal ones, have long had a tradition of being as open to women as to men on the grounds that anyone the Spirit calls is worthy.

In Caracas, as many as 7 percent of Protestant pastors are women. In some Pentecostal churches, women make up the majority of local leadership. Within one small Pentecostal denomination, three of its four Caracas churches are headed by women. Even in churches where women are technically barred from leadership roles if qualified men may be found (such as the Jehovah's Witnesses), there are considerable numbers of female leaders.

When authority is defined as charismatic in origin, power becomes more personal than structural. Successful pastors are religious entrepreneurs first, not bureaucrats or organizational team players. Baptists and other traditional evangelicals, particularly the Plymouth Brethren, have had a much lower rate of fission over the years. In these churches, church structures and alliances are different, authority is less charismatic, and the local church organization would be less viable outside of larger church networks.

In general, decisionmaking processes are not particularly egalitarian. Control issues can be especially important in evangelical churches, where authority is more charismatic and less hierarchical than in Catholicism.[31] Authority does not flow from the legal structure of the denomination but must be established by the pastor, and it often has no recognized limits. The pastor may exercise an enormous degree of patriarchal control in one church but not in another church of the same denomination. In some churches the governing board has the final say. Usually there is a powerful organizational structure and centralized leadership, whether power flows from a single pastor or from a group of elders.

In any case, decisionmaking power does not go beyond the pastor and the congregation. An authority outside the local church may be well respected, but decisionmaking beyond the local level must involve the local church and is made by consensus. In a sense, such practices are reminiscent of the traditional relationship between local caudillos, their followers, and extralocal networks.[32]

Many churches, particularly the larger ones, include a range of socioeconomic levels but tend to be made up of persons, as one pastor put it, between the "comfortable middle class and the desperately poor." Occupation is often related to status in the church organization. The committed core of members and leaders of evangelical congregations is typically made up of those who have stable jobs and good incomes relative to the membership of each local church.[33] As key people in the local church organization, these persons are often coordinators of the Sunday-school program, the choir, and the men's, women's, and youth groups. Such groups as these are common subgroups of the local congregation and are almost universally found in churches that have a sufficient membership base. Other positions include deacons and lay preachers, evangelists, ushers, and musicians. Often, local organization seems designed to give every member some kind of leadership responsibility.

Interwoven networks of local leadership affect the way in which members relate to the pastor. In poorer areas, where there are often not many members with the time, educational preparation, or interest to serve as leaders and coordinators, the pastor commonly exercises considerable control and is regarded as the key authority who must be consulted for everything. Such attitudes may spill over into private life as well, and the pastor may be regarded as a kind of father figure to whom all of life's crises and major decisions are brought.[34] This, however, is not an automatic feature of evangelical life and stems rather from concrete social circumstances.

Effects of Economic Crisis

Over the past decade, Latin America has experienced one of the most severe economic crises in its history. More people than ever go without the basic necessities. Earlier, less urbanized generations could perhaps find at least a certain amount of food and shelter, if not economic opportunity, on the land. Now, with its population largely urban, modest economic opportunity that could significantly benefit the popular classes seems unlikely, while food and shelter have become more uncertain than ever.[35]

In this context, the security offered by social support networks increases in importance. Outside of family groups, however, there are few viable grass-roots networks. Neighborliness is weak, and neighborhood associations in popular areas are generally even weaker.[36] Other kinds of linkages exist, including the party system, the state, and ostensibly independent movements such as unions, cooperatives, or local associations, but these remain largely vertically linked structures of limited access controlled from the top by the political parties and the state.[37] Although Catholic parishes often have well-structured organizations, pastors estimate that such organizations reach only about 250 persons per parish in Caracas.[38] In any case, Catholic parish organizations and activities do not necessarily stimulate strong solidary ties. Further, simply going to mass is unlikely to make one feel linked to a rich communal network. In contrast, evangelical church organizations and worship experiences are especially designed to create a strong, palpable sense of community.[39]

The solidary ties characteristic of the close-knit church group, reinforced by the pressing needs of the members for such a network, easily combine to produce a highly communitarian organization. This character explains much of the remarkable development of evangelicals during periods of extreme economic and social crisis and accounts for much of their appeal.

Contemporary Catholic-Protestant Relations

Within the past thirty years, relations between Catholicism and the denominations that once operated most of the missionary churches and institutions in Latin America have improved dramatically. However, relations with those that constitute the evangelical community are perhaps more strained than ever before. A formerly distant threat has now become a present danger, and the Catholic hierarchy no longer attempts to hide its discomfort as its traditional dominance of organized religious life in Latin America erodes.[40]

After the Second Vatican Council an immediate, dramatic change in official Catholic references to other Christian groups occurred on a worldwide scale. No longer "heretics," Protestants became "separated brothers." For the first time many Protestant denominations were described as "churches" rather than "sects." Collaboration increased at the level of Bible translations and other joint publications. Nevertheless, it is unclear whether many in the Latin American hierarchy had truly broadened their views on non-Catholics in their local context or had simply been muzzled by a Vatican policy to promote better worldwide intra-Christian relations.[41] The bishops' fears were confirmed as evangelical leaders linked the soaring growth of their churches in the 1970s to the increased tolerance and openness on the part of Catholics.[42]

Venezuelan Catholic clerics, not unlike their counterparts throughout Latin America, tend toward facile explanations of the dramatically increasing evangelical presence.[43] Not uncommonly, the U.S. government forces are seen as responsible. Evangelicals are accused of unfairly competing with the weakly financed Catholic church and said to be essentially buying converts. In so doing, the argument goes, foreign agents are thereby draining Latin America of a key unifying force, its religious heritage, and opening the door to more complete cultural domination by the United States. This interpretation is common throughout Latin America and may be heard both in left-wing political circles and conservative Catholic ones.[44] The explanations that evangelicals offer for their growth are no more useful. Instead of fear they reflect a kind of triumphal millennialism. Leaders and members alike commonly give no other explanation than that the hour the Lord has appointed has arrived at last.[45]

Although Venezuelan evangelical churches originally developed out of British and North American missionary efforts, they can no longer be described as "foreign." They are neither foreign-staffed nor foreign-controlled. When the foreign bases of Catholic and evangelical groups are compared, the explanation for evangelicals' success commonly cited by many leaders of the Venezuelan Catholic church loses merit.[46] In reality, foreign involvement is probably more significant for the continuing vitality of Venezuelan Catholicism, as it is for much of Latin American Catholicism in general.

Foreign-born evangelical pastors from outside of Latin America are typically from the United States and tend to be responsible for small middle-class churches or to provide support for locally based churches. Their numbers have not been large, although the pastor of one of the largest and most important evangelical churches in Caracas, Las Acacias, has been led by a person of U.S. origin and education, Samuel Olson, since its founding. Nevertheless, over the past decade the number of North American Catholic priests and lay missionaries in Caracas has not been very different from that of their North American Protestant equivalents. Each group numbers about a dozen at any one time, most of them engaged in support work and not principal leaders of a church, chapel, or congregation.[47] Significantly, one of the largest and most rapidly expanding Pentecostal denominations, the Assemblies of God, has no non-Spanish surnames listed in its national directory of personnel. Although headquartered in the United States, the denomination has learned the lesson of local leadership well and is perhaps the strongest, most rapidly growing church of any in Venezuela (or, indeed, in Latin America in general). The Venezuelan evangelical movement (both Pentecostal and non-Pentecostal) has in fact experienced its greatest growth since foreign parent churches began reducing their financial and personnel support relative to local contributions in the late 1960s.

The available data for Catholicism present a different picture. A 1984 study found that an astonishing 984 of 1,077 Catholic religious-order priests, or 94 percent of the total, were not born in Venezuela. Most originated in Spain, and almost all came from Europe or North America.[48] In Caracas, some 68 percent of all parish pastors—53 percent of the diocesan pastors and 90 percent of the religious pastors—are foreign-born. Forty-one percent are from Spain, and thirteen nationalities are represented in all.[49] Not surprisingly, local church leaders with such international contacts know how to seek foreign financial support. In part, the cosmopolitan nature of Catholic personnel may explain why so many local church projects have been funded by granting agencies based in Europe or North America. Contacts are frequently made through one's own religious order or congregation or on the basis of independent projects initiated and carried out by a single priest or nun with specific financial or institutional connections. Although the haphazard and uncoordinated nature of such funding makes exact figures impossible to obtain, it seems likely that foreign-originated support for Catholic projects easily exceeds foreign support of evangelical work.[50]

The emergence and dramatically increasing appeal of the evangelicals, both Pentecostal and non-Pentecostal, cannot really be explained by reference to powerful forces outside the region. Consideration must be given to cultural changes and continuities as Latin American societies have accomplished the transition from an agricultural economy based on large landed estates and subsistence farming to an urban service economy. In the new urban environment, traditional Catholic pastoral approaches no longer work, and newer ones have proved incapable of preventing the increasing consolidation of the religious alternative represented by the evangelicals.

Venezuelan Catholic leaders typically have not recognized the full implications of the profound changes that have taken place in social and religious life. For example, many commonly claim that when priests come into an area of evangelical converts people abandon their new-found evangelical faiths and seek out the priest as a representative of a religion that they had never really rejected.[51] In a similar vein, parish pastors often deride the new religion of their former parishioners, suggesting that evangelicals are no less likely than their nonevangelical neighbors to be at a site of supposed Marian apparitions or to participate in cultural events such as the traditional festivals of local patron saints.[52] Ultimately, institutional Catholicism still wistfully assumes that the problem is merely one of priestly vocations rather than a basic and permanent loss of credibility and clientele.

Cultural Changes and Continuities

Popular Catholicism has facilitated the transition to Pentecostalism among the lower classes. Although part of a worldwide religious phenomenon, Pentecostalism has thoroughly adapted its meanings, structures, and worship to its local environment. This ready adaptation results from the natural flexibility of congregational religion, but it is also a result of a belief in the legitimacy of flexibly following the Spirit. If a certain style wins more converts, this constitutes a sign in itself. If a charismatic church leader has considerable success in church founding, that style is legitimated. Venezuelan Pentecostalism enjoys distinct advantages over its competitors. It has a more flexible structure than traditional evangelicals and a belief system akin to that found in popular religion. Pentecostal churches are typically characterized by independent local church structures far stronger than the larger church organizations of which they are a part. For this reason, Pentecostal church organizations fission frequently, and unity is often maintained on the basis of charismatic leadership rather than long-term institutional commitments.

Discursive Shifts

The evangelical religious message has transformed religious culture in many important ways, often influencing formal Catholic practice in its wake. One of the most lasting effects of Catholic baptism and other sacraments in Latin America has been the *compadrazgo* relationship.[53] Those who commit themselves as sponsors, or godparents (*compadres*), to the baptized enter into a lifelong relationship with that person. They are expected to provide gifts, emotional support, social contacts, and even a roadside marker in the case of accidental death on a road or highway.[54] Traditionally, the ideal *compadre* was the owner or overseer of a large estate who would take on a religiously sanctioned commitment to be charitable to the offspring of a peasant or peon on his estate in return for being regarded as a father figure. Religion in this way legitimated and formalized economic and social relations and became a kind of glue that held the class system together.

In evangelical churches as well, baptism results in a lasting nonkinship-based extended-family tie. The baptized are *hermanos* (brothers and sisters) to other members of the congregation and to other evangelicals as well. This identity is not limited to a particular congregation or denomination. In fact, evangelicals, Pentecostal or non-Pentecostal, usually refer to members of any evangelical church as *hermanos*.[55] Mere organizational differences are a minor point when all belong to the same movement and recognize its solidarity.

This relation is considerably more horizontal than the fictive kin relationship characteristic of traditional Catholicism. Its more communal aspect also suggests an opening to congregational religious life. Contemporary Catholicism is by no means without forms of communal religious experience, however. In part influenced by their Protestant counterparts, members of some Catholic groups, such as the catechumens, charismatics, and many youth groups, also refer to fellow members as *hermanos*. However, in the Catholic context this term is not universal and ultimately contradictory.[56] Instead of referring to all the baptized members of even just one denomination, it is meant to include only those committed to one's specific subgroup or the values it represents. For those who use the term, both evangelical and Catholic, this change in vocabulary is reflective of a momentous change in thinking and organization with far-reaching implications.

Another change observable in Catholicism but characteristic of Pentecostals (and true of evangelicals generally) is the word used for "pray." The traditional word used in folk Catholicism, *rezar*, is supplanted by the exclusive use of *orar*. *Rezar* implies the mere rote recitation of formula prayers. *Orar* represents the fast-flowing, often emotionally expressive release of words and thoughts as praise or pleas. Contemporary Catholic groups often employ this term as well, but among evangelicals few words are quite as taboo as *rezar*, which is sometimes seen as neatly summing up all that evangelical religion opposes in Catholicism.

Political and Social Implications

A key feature of evangelical Christianity is its characteristically Reformed ethic of self-denial and right living, which in proper economic settings can encourage saving and a measurable degree of social mobility over time. However, in the contemporary Latin American context such mobility does not necessarily occur, and it is by no means a defining characteristic of contemporary evangelical Christianity.[57] For the most part, the contemporary economic situation of Latin America allows for very little room to "redeem [spiritually] and uplift [economically]" the new converts.[58] Instead, a common message is that the "last will be first."[59] There is little connection between Latin America evangelical Protestantism and upward mobility. This is even more true of Pentecostals than of non-Pentecostal evangelicals, since the former tend to be slightly poorer and to have less interest in the kinds of capital accumulation strategies for which Calvinists are allegedly famous. Politically, evangelicals (again, Pentecostals even more than non-Pentecostals) are neither inevitably conservative nor apathetic. Rather, these options need to be placed in their broader historical context. A religiously sanctioned withdrawal from politics usually occurs during the formation period, when believers perceive their political options as relatively few. Often, withdrawal follows from the strong millennial orientation that characterizes the beginnings of an evangelical movement. Once the movement is under way and has a veteran membership, life becomes more routinized and ordinary civic and political participation becomes more plausible.[60] The issue then becomes what form of political participation is most "evangelical" and "biblical" according to the situation. To describe the politics believers choose as simply "conservative" misses the point.

Contrary to widespread belief among liberationist Catholics and secular commentators, evangelicals (both Pentecostals and non-Pentecostals) are not apolitical. This perspective is too simple to explain their participation in politics in the United States and hardly serves in the Latin American context. Their agenda, strategies, and orientation may be different from those of liberationist Catholics, but their message cannot usefully be defined as "conservative" in a North American sense. So-called conservative social issues that have politically galvanized evangelicals in the United States, such as abortion and school prayer, are nonissues for Latin American evangelicals. Abortion is illegal, and secular schools are emphatically preferred without public prayer, catechism, or anything that would give the nominally numerically stronger Catholic church an advantage.[61]

The classical Latin American conservatives, in any case, are more often staunch Roman Catholic corporatists or integralists. Further, neoliberal economic and social policy, whether defined as "liberal" or "conservative," is also outside the interests of evangelicals. Along with most of the population, they have been on the losing end of these policies. Prominent evangelicals (including many of the most prominent Pentecostals) who do support such policies tend to be engineers and others who find such policies in keeping with their worldview and economic interest.

Evangelical politics is ultimately based on the same underlying principle as Catholic liberationist political engagement. Both evangelicals and liberationists want their values to be reflected in everyday political life, and both tend to espouse positions embraced by many outside their particular groups. If "politics" as currently practiced is widely regarded as corrupt, some conclude that for the moment it is too corrupting for them to take part other than as "prophetic witnesses," while others may find that people such as themselves are precisely those who therefore must take part. These two contrasting perspectives are similar to those found within the general population.

There seems to be wide agreement among evangelicals of many differing political and theological positions that if they *could* take a leadership role in public life, they ought to. Differences are over whether the time has arrived for activist involvement in politics. When the Unión Latinoamericana de Evangélicos en Poder (Latin American Union of Evangelicals in Politics) was set up in Buenos Aires in 1991, a central debate was whether the evangelical community should organize its own political parties or participate in existing ones. The issue is by no means settled. Most of the members of this organization, which represents evangelical politicians from some sixteen Latin American countries, including Venezuela, belong to long-established political parties. However, over the past decade there has been an increasing tendency to establish specifically evangelical parties, and it seems likely that virtually every major Latin American country will soon have one.

Venezuela was the first of Latin American countries to have such a political party. The Organización Renovadora Auténtica (Authentic Renewal Organization—ORA), formed in 1976, acts specifically for evangelical interests when it champions changes in legislation regulating church activity. At times it is also an important minority political player in the building of coalitions of support for various legislative programs. Significantly, ORA believes that modernization will begin only when Venezuelan legal and political structures are truly "reformed."[62]

Some of the party's rhetoric explicitly rejects Iberian models, holding them responsible for the collective national crisis. The party's explicit prescription for Venezuelan social ills is the complete adoption of U.S. and Northern European legal structures and social values, considered as more successful because they are fundamentally evangelical Protestant in nature. ORA's presidential candidate in the 1988 election, Godofredo Marín, advocated "democracy based on the Bible," a slogan that nicely illustrates the tenor of the politics practiced by the party.

By U.S. standards, ORA's political perspective may well seem more "conservative" than "liberal." However, as we have seen, these labels can be misleading in a Latin American context, since the party in fact advocates radical change. Indeed, there is precious little in Venezuela's cultural or legal heritage that it would like to "conserve." Aside from promoting its particular ideology, the party also serves as a pressure group for the legal needs and political representation of the evangelical movement as a whole. In this movement, as in many others, the boundaries between Pentecostals and non-Pentecostals are easily transcended via the much more powerful common identification as evangelicals.

Just as Latin American evangelicals in general are divided over the issue of confessional political parties, Venezuelan evangelicals are internally divided on the same issue. Most evangelicals in Venezuela do not support ORA, which they see as only one of many political options. Among evangelicals I interviewed, for example, as many voted for the Christian Democratic party, which has origins in Catholic social doctrine and the Catholic educated professional classes, as for ORA. By far the political party that receives the greatest support from evangelicals is the ruling Acción Democrática (Democratic Action) party, long identified with populist politics and representative of the political status quo. In general, the political agenda of ORA is seen as too ideological and too different from ordinary Venezuelan politics for most Venezuelan evangelicals to feel comfortable with it. Nevertheless, ORA has provided the evangelical community a model of political action and sparked a deep debate over the place of evangelicals in politics.[63]

Today, the evangelical community, once simply interested in breaking the Catholic religious monopoly, has an increasingly diverse agenda. Previously, it was common to hear pastors preach that the believer does not involve himself in politics. Now, evangelicals commonly say that "brothers vote for brothers." The future relationship of evangelicals (whether Pentecostal or non-Pentecostal) and politics is as yet uncharted territory.[64] In a way suggestive of future possibilities, recent elections throughout Latin America have shown that the nonevangelical population is disposed to vote for evangelical candidates, who often have an image of greater trustworthiness simply because they are evangelicals.[65]

Conclusion

Certainly, Pentecostals have had record success in evangelization—surpassing the already impressive record of evangelicals in general. The lessons they offer to Catholic leaders initiating the so-called new evangelization are many. The issues that their success raises are common to the study of social movements, particularly within the resource-mobilization framework. Techniques that evangelicals, particularly Pentecostals, have pioneered in the contemporary Latin American context demonstrate the shortcomings of Catholic approaches and call into question current Catholic structures and perspectives. It is as yet unclear if Catholicism will develop an effective response to its formidable new competitor. The social and cultural ramifications of numerous new, communal religious movements throughout the popular sector are profound and permanent.

NOTES

1. Jacinto Ayerra, *Los Protestantes en Venezuela* (Caracas: Ediciones Trípode, 1980), p. 26.

2. Their representatives and political party have been pressing publicly for changes in the legal structure governing religious activities and have successfully rebuffed an attempt to pass legislation that would make it more difficult for evangelical churches to grow. Projections call for evangelical majorities by the end of the next century, and bold plans for evangelical charitable and educational organizations to rival Catholic ones have been proposed for the first time.

3. See Ayerra, *Los Protestantes en Venezuela.* It must also be recalled that whatever foreign personnel or resources evangelicals had at their disposal could be matched by the no doubt far more considerable foreign-originated resources of the Venezuelan Catholic church. Unfortunately, both Protestants and Catholics are too decentralized to permit the gathering of data of this kind.

4. A major symbol of all that was seen as wrong with religion and society in Latin America was the fact that preconciliar Catholicism in Latin America effectively discouraged and marginalized the reading of the Bible by the laity. That is, the people were at once denied the direct, personal exposure to God's word that salvation requires, and their illiteracy and ignorance on a broader, social level were reinforced. Religious ignorance and other forms of backwardness were seen as related; both religious and social progress would occur with the introduction of Protestantism. The sheer force of such triumphalist notions of progress and manifest destiny were typical of the era and the related missionary activity.

5. For more discussion of this strategy, particularly in the context of Brazil, see Emilio Willems, *Followers of the New Faith: Culture Change and the Rise of Protestantism in Brazil and Chile* (Nashville, Tenn.: Vanderbilt University Press, 1967).

6. Ayerra, *Los Protestantes en Venezuela,* pp. 40–43.

7. Cyrus Ingerson Scofield of the *Scofield Reference Bible,* which details dispensationalist theology, was heavily influenced by this group, as were groups such as the Dallas Theological Seminary.

8. As Nils Bloch-Hoell, in *The Pentecostal Movement* (London: Scandinavian University Books, 1964), points out, the Pentecostal movement has roots in Europe as well as North America. However, Pentecostalism arrived in Latin America directly via the Pentecostal movements common to many denominations in the early twentieth century. See Walter J. Hollenweger, "Methodism's Past in Pentecostalism's Present: A Case Study of a Cultural Clash in Chile," *Goworth Review,* May 1979, pp. 33–47, for an account of how Pentecostalism came to Chile, D. Smith, "Coming of Age: A Reflection on Pentecostals,

Politics, and Popular Religion in Guatemala," unpublished report, Centro Evangélico Latinoamericano de Estudios Pastorales, Guatemala City, 1991, for a description of the first Pentecostals in Guatemala, and Ayerra, *Los Protestantes en Venezuela.*

9. The Chilean case is illustrative here. See Hollenweger, "Methodism's Past," and Christian Lalive d'Epinay, *El refugio de las masas: Estudio sociológico del Protestantismo chileno* (Santiago: Editorial del Pacífico, 1968).

10. Such churches do not establish denominational structures but rather engender networks of "daughter" churches, "sister" churches, and "allied" churches.

11. For descriptions of how Pentecostal or charismatic-"Spirit-filled" forms of religious experience gel with popular notions of the religious, see Franz Damen, "El Pentecostalismo en Bolivia," "El Pentecostalismo: Algunos rasgos," "El Pentecostalismo: Ruptura y continuidad," and "Cuestionario sobre las sectas," *Fe y Pueblo: Boletín Ecuménico de Reflexión Teológica* 3, 14 (1986), pp. 22–23, 31–39, 44–49, 50–56; *El desafío de las sectas* (La Paz, 1988); and "Sectas," in *Mysterium liberationis: Conceptos fundamentales de la teología de la liberación* (Madrid: Editorial Trotta, 1990), pp. 423–445; and M. Preiswerk and F. Damen, eds., "Pentecostalismo y religiosidad popular: Dos enfoques," *Fe y Pueblo: Boletín Ecuménico de Reflexión Teológica* 3, 14 (1986), pp. 40–43. This is by no means a new finding in the literature, having been developed by Lalive d'Epinay, *Refugio de las masas;* Cornelia Butler Flora, *Pentecostalism in Colombia: Baptism by Fire and Spirit* (Rutherford, N.J.: Fairleigh Dickinson University Press, 1976) and "Pentecostalism and Development: The Colombian Case," in Stephen D. Glazier, ed., *Perspectives on Pentecostalism: Case Studies from the Caribbean and Latin America* (Lanham, Md.: University Press of America, 1980), pp. 81–94; and Karl-Wilhelm Westmeier, *Reconciling Heaven and Earth: The Transcendental Enthusiasm and Growth of an Urban Protestant Community* (Bogotá and Frankfurt am Main: Verlag Peter Lang, 1986), among others.

12. The Great Commission is the part of the Gospel in which Jesus tells his followers to go and preach to all the nations.

13. The common interpretation of the Great Commission now became that all in some way had to have access to evangelical religion in order for the Second Coming of Christ to occur. See Sara Diamond, *Spiritual Warfare: The Politics of the Christian Right* (Boston: South End Press, 1989); David Stoll, *Is Latin America Turning Protestant? The Politics of Evangelical Growth* (Berkeley: University of California Press, 1990).

14. Differences between countries in terms of the evangelical experience cannot, of course, be explained by differences in the urban experience per se and must be explained by reference to the historically specific panoply of factors in each particular country.

15. In rural areas, evangelical religion spread similarly, through the effect of the cities. Greater ease of transportation and communication brought former residents of rural towns and villages and others from the city to the country. This process brought both new ideas and organizers to the countryside, and after a brief lag, rural areas quickly became as influenced by the new religious currents as popular neighborhoods in the city. Because the affluent classes are smaller than in the larger metropolitan areas, the changes wrought by the evangelicals are now perhaps even more palpable in the countryside.

16. For examples of how this has occurred in Venezuela and elsewhere, see Angelina Pollak-Eltz, *María Lionza: Mito y culto venezolano* (Caracas: Universidad Católica Andrés Belle, 1985) and *La religiosidad popular en Venezuela* (Caracas: San Pablo, 1994).

17. Of the latter two groups of liberationists and modernizers, neither is entirely made up of Catholics. There are some, albeit few, liberationist-minded evangelicals, and many traditional evangelicals are more rationalist in their beliefs than Pentecostals.

18. On gratifying immediate needs, see Flora, *Pentecostalism in Colombia* and "Pentecostalism and Development," and Judith Hoffnagel, "Pentecostalism: A Revolutionary or Conservative Movement?" in Stephen D. Glazier, ed., *Perspectives on Pentecostalism: Case Studies from the Caribbean and Latin America* (Lanham, Md: University Press of America, 1980). Damen, *El desafío de las sectas,* expresses this idea of complementarity very forcefully. The elective affinity between popular religious tradition and Pentecostal Christianity is probably stronger than any tie, potential or alleged, with any other organized religious form.

19. See Stoll, *Is Latin America Turning Protestant?*

20. Donna Birdwell-Pheasant, "The Power of Pentecostalism in a Belizean Village," in Stephen D. Glazier, ed., *Perspectives on Pentecostalism: Case Studies from the Caribbean and Latin America* (Lanham, Md.: University Press of America, 1980), p. 104.

21. See Flora, *Pentecostalism in Colombia,* pp. 84–85.

22. In part this evangelical "explosion" may be due to the rapidly increasing literacy rates of the past few decades, which allow for many more readers of biblical texts. However, in my fieldwork it is often hard to demonstrate which comes first; being committed to evangelical religion is often what leads people to become literate in the first place.

23. In most Latin American countries today, about 15 percent of the population is Protestant, and in some countries this percentage now exceeds 30. Those countries where evangelicals are particularly present, Guatemala and Puerto Rico, are by no means the countries where they are the most numerous. The regional giant Brazil leads in numbers of evangelicals, baptized Catholics, and practitioners of spiritist religions. For more details on percentages and members, see Stoll, *Is Latin America Turning Protestant?* His appendix is particularly helpful.

24. See Bloch-Hoell, *The Pentecostal Movement;* see also Liston Pope, *Millhands and Preachers* (New Haven: Yale University Press, 1971 [1942]), esp. chap. 7.

25. This tendency may be due to the fact that the first missionary efforts typically occurred in areas with no evangelical competition. Thus these groups were able to establish near-monopolies of evangelical activity in many of the areas in which they worked, perpetuating their regional strengths.

26. For a detailed description of Baptist development and strategy, see Ayerra, *Los Protestantes en Venezuela,* pp. 53–57, esp. pp. 54.

27. According to an ecological analysis of all the churches of Caracas, when neighborhoods are ranked from 1 (affluent) to 10 (poverty-stricken), Baptist churches average 5 and Pentecostal churches 7.

28. These offshoots of free-church-related missionary activity are the Organización Venezolana de Iglesias Cristianas Evangélicas (OVICE), which developed from evangelical efforts in the eastern part of Venezuela that may be traced back as far as 1927, and the Asociación de Iglesias Evangélicas Libres (ADIEL), which emerged in the central portion of the country and had its beginnings in 1903. Both denominations trace their history to historically Scandinavian churches based in the North American upper Midwest. As such they are heirs to the Pietist movement against state Lutheranism and are conservative, fundamentalist, and congregational in orientation.

29. Willems, *Followers of the New Faith,* p. 219 also cites sources on this issue, and I have seen it corroborated in my own fieldwork.

30. See Rolando Gutiérrez, "Nuestra evangelizacíon," *Latin American Evangelist,* October–December 1990, p. 7. The author is a Baptist pastor in Mexico City and was president of the Mexican National Baptist Convention in 1990.

31. Max Weber's discussion of different kinds of authority remains a classic and is helpful in understanding the differences between the churches (*The Sociology of Religion,* 6th ed. [Boston: Beacon Press, 1992]). Differences between individual churches of the same denomination may be as great as differences between denominations.

32. In the case of caudillos, extralocal networks typically included the state, a political party, and the military.

33. This varies, of course, with the membership. In small congregations in the barrios, bank tellers may be among the leading members; in large, citywide congregations such as that of the nondenominational Iglesia Evangélica Pentecostal Las Acacias, bank tellers and secretaries may be among the ordinary members and those of higher socioeconomic levels may include engineers and other professionals. I base this description on my interviews and a census of the approximately 1,500-member Las Acacias church.

34. Hoffnagel, "Pentecostalism," and Lalive d'Epinay, *Refugio de las masas,* describe this situation well, and Diamond, *Spiritual Warfare,* details such practices in terms of the "shepherding" movement and other developing charismatic forms of Christian discipline.

35. On migrants to Caracas, see Kenneth Kartz, Murray Schwartz, and Audrey Schwartz, *The Evolution of Law in the Barrios of Caracas* (Los Angeles: University of California, Los Angeles, Latin American Center, 1973); Manuel Castells, *The City and the Grassroots: A Cross-Cultural Theory of Urban Social Movements* (London: Edward Arnold, 1983). My own interviews, based to some degree on this study, produced similar findings. For immigrants, until the past decade the city really has offered a better future. Life in the countryside remains as undesirable as ever.

36. See Larissa Lomnitz, *Networks and Marginality: Life in a Mexican Shantytown* (New York: Academic Press, 1977). My own research corroborates this point, as does Kartz, Schwartz, and Schwartz, *The Evolution of Law.*

37. In most vertical structures, resources have to be offered in exchange for access, and when one is required to bid for access those with the fewest resources lose.

38. This is based on data for Caracas provided by a 1989 survey.

39. Again and again commentators have referred to this feature of Latin American evangelical religion. See, for example, John Landry, "Epic Changes Here to Stay," *Latin American Evangelist,* April–June 1991, p. 4. Even the Venezuelan bishops recognize this, as do Venezuelan Catholic writers in general. Secretariado Permanente del Episcopado Venezolano, *Instrucción pastoral del Episcopado venezolano sobre el fenómeno de las sectas* (Caracas, 1988); Juan Miguel Ganuza, *La renovación católica carismática: Documentos de la iglesia* (Caracas: Universidad Católica Andrés Bello, 1978); Juan Manárriz, "El desafio de las sectas: Una avalanche de sectas nos está invadiendo," *Familia Cristiana* 7, 4(1988), pp. 17–19.

40. The bibliography is too long to cite here. Samuel E. Escobar, *La fe evangelica y las teologías de la liberación* (El Paso: Casa Bautista de Publicaciones, 1987, is among useful references on this issue.

41. Stoll, *Is Latin America Turning Protestant?* seems to support this view.

42. See Charles Berg, "Memories and a Reminder," *Latin American Evangelist*, April–June 1987, p. 5.

43. Interviews with Fr. Nicholas Espinoza, rector of Holy Trinity Chapel, Caracas, November 15, 1990; Fr. Francisco Javier Alberdi, pastor of Jesus of Nazareth parish, La Carucieña, Barquisimeto, January 5, 1990; Fr. Ignacio Berecibar, pastor of Dolores, Puerto Nutrias, and Ciudad Nutrias, Dolores, Barinas, December 30, 1990; Msgr. Manuel Delgado Avila, secretary of the Secretariado Permanente del Episcopado Venezolano, Caracas, January 20, 1990; Secretariado Permanente del Episcopado Venezolano, *Misión permanente: Plan de pastoral de conjunto, 1986–1992* (Caracas, 1986).

44. Nonreligious left-wing activists have often led the fight to oppose such groups as the Nueva Tribus, a local branch of the Summer Institute of Linguistics described in Ayerra, *Los Protestantes en Venezuela*. Although this literature is largely produced by leftist intellectuals, it is often crudely extended to all evangelical groups by both conservative and progressive church leaders. See, for example, Secretariado Permanente del Episcopado Venezolano, *Instrucción pastoral;* Berecibar, interview; Delgado, interview.

45. See, for example, Arturo Diaz, "Análisis, diagnóstico y perspectivas de la obra evangélica en Caracas, Venezuela," unpublished report, Consejo Evangélico de Venezuela, Caracas; Arthur Johnson, "*Llanos inundados* (Flooded Plains): A History and Analysis of the Iglesias Nativas Apureñas of Venezuela," Master's thesis, Fuller Theological Seminary, Pasadena, Calif., 1978; Arturo Rios, *Presencia evangélica venezolana en la política:* (Maracaibo: Organización Venezolano de Iglesias Cristianas Evangélicas, 1977) and *De los pequeños principios a las grandes realizaciones* (Maracaibo: Editorial Libertador, 1976).

46. See Secretariado Permanente del Episcopado Venezolano, *Instrucción pastoral,* p. 16. Typical of the clergy's interpretation of the growth of evangelical Christianity in Venezuela are the comments of Espinoza, interview.

47. In fact, I know of only three evangelical pastors and three Catholic priests of North American origin who head local churches in Caracas. Many more North American Protestants than Catholics make brief visits of support for the local churches, but more European Catholics than Protestants can be found working in and with the local churches.

48. *Los religiosos en Venezuela: Levantamiento sociográfico* (Caracas: Secretariado Conjunto de Religiosos y Religiosas de Venezuela, 1984), p. 23.

49. In 1950, when clergy immigration began to increase, only some 12.5 percent of the population of the Federal District (which includes Caracas) was foreign-born and only 4 percent of the total national population had originated outside of the country. (I. Alonso et al., *La iglesia en Venezuela y Ecuador* [Bogotá: Oficina Central de Investigaciones de FERES, 1962], p. 141.) In 1981, well after the end of the period of migration of clergy, some 6 percent of those living in Venezuela were foreign-born (Diagnóstico Social Permanente, *Informe social 1981* [Caracas: Oficina Central de Estadística e Información, 1982]; Centro de Investigación en las Ciencias Sociales, Caracas, unpublished data on 639 ecologically homogeneous areas of metropolitan Caracas categorized and ranked between 1985 and 1990.) Thus, although the clergy has tended to originate in the same countries as the major immigrant groups, Catholic clerics have clearly immigrated disproportionately to other persons.

50. It is hardly an exaggeration to point out that most Catholic projects enjoy some form of foreign or state support, however modest, be it in the form of a jeep, a salary, or a building. This is not to argue that foreign support is "high" and is meant only to em-

phasize that it indeed exists for both groups. Evangelicals, of course, tend to use whatever funds they may receive toward further preaching and church founding, whereas Catholic groups typically apply their funds toward social ends. Catholics have little investment and few skills in the area of public relations or mass marketing, activities with which the North American–influenced evangelicals are very familiar. At the same time, evangelicals can point to nothing that rivals the Catholic network of schools, training institutes, and small grass-roots agencies found throughout Latin America. Both sides, in effect, feel threatened precisely because the strength of the other is in the area of their greatest weakness.

51. Delgado, interview.

52. Berecibar, interview; Alberdi, interview.

53. See Westmeier, *Reconciling Heaven and Earth,* pp. 113 and 228.

54. This latter obligation was brought to my attention by Alejandro Ortíz, a cultural anthropologist who has researched the origins of roadside death markers in Venezuela. I mention it to illustrate the responsibilities and obligations that *compadrazgo* traditionally implied.

55. This notion and a helpful bibliographic review are found in Westmeier, *Reconciling Heaven and Earth,* p. 217.

56. This stems, of course, from the church-sect distinction long ago explored by Weber and his disciple Troeltsch.

57. Flora, "Pentecostalism and Development," p. 90; see also Guillermo Cook, "The Evangelical Groundswell in Latin America," *Christian Century* 107 (December 12, 1990, pp. 1172–1178.

58. Cook, "The Evangelical Groundswell."

59. Flora, "Pentecostalism and Development," p. 85. This commonly reflects the thinking of evangelical religion among the poor in Latin America, and I frequently encountered it in my interviews. It is a kind of reversed notion of the Calvinist ethic, one that Norman Cohn, *The Pursuit of the Millennium* (New York: Oxford University Press, 1961) shows to be common in millennial religion. Those most successful were mostly going to be damned for being unbelievers while the (unsuccessful) believers would have eternal life. For a sense of the tradition behind this belief in evangelical Christianity, see Cook, "The Evangelical Groundswell," p. 24.

60. See Stoll, *Is Latin America Turning Protestant?* on common contrasts between first- and second-generation converts.

61. Unless, of course, government-supported religious training in schools could be evangelical, as some evangelical politicians argue that it should be. These, however, are minority voices. Most seem to prefer to leave well enough alone and do not have much interest in seeking out government subsidies for such activities.

62. So many of the founders of this party, as well as the leaders of major evangelical umbrella organizations, were trained as engineers or math teachers that one wonders if there is some relation between this profession and the potential likelihood of professing an evangelical faith.

63. Ayerra, *Los Protestantes en Venezuela,* and discussions with many members and observers of the evangelical movement in Venezuela.

64. See Jochen Streiter, "Reseñas," *Presencia Ecuménica,* December 1991, p. 57, citing the work of René Padilla.

65. See "Fe cristiana y política en el Perú," *Edificación Cristiana* 145–146 (1991), p. 3, which is based on many items in the media that appeared at the time of the election of Serrano in Guatemala and Alberto Fujimori in Peru. On the issue of the image of greater trustworthiness for being evangelical, many writers have shown this to be a widely generalized popular perception. See, for example, Willems, *Followers of the New Faith;* Flora, *Pentecostalism in Colombia;* Hoffnagel, "Pentecostalism"; and Stoll, *Is Latin America Turning Protestant?* 1990, among others.

12

Latin American Pentecostals: Old Stereotypes and New Challenges

HANNAH W. STEWART-GAMBINO AND
EVERETT WILSON

$\mathcal{F}$or many of us, old or new to the study of Latin American Pentecostalism, our frustration has been that old categories of analysis simply fail to illuminate. Even the most basic questions of the dimensions of the phenomenon—for example, how to measure the numbers of faithful and how to delineate numbers of churches—prove to be thorny problems for the researcher. For students of Latin American Catholicism, demographic or descriptive information is relatively easy to obtain. National surveys show that overwhelming majorities of Latin Americans traditionally identified themselves as Catholic. Actual participation in the rites of Catholicism (mass attendance, baptisms, marriages, and the like) can be estimated from church or civil records, surveys, or observation. But assertions regarding the size of the Pentecostal presence in any country must be viewed as more or less educated speculations. The lack of a single "church" with centralized parish, diocesan, or national records and the fluidity of church creation and re-volving memberships make precise national measurements difficult.[1]

In fact, much of the initial literature on Latin American Pentecostals focused on issues of size and growth rates. These are not arcane debates. A number of grand claims are made regarding the alleged explosion of Protestant, especially Pentecostal, membership. For example, the popular press, particularly the business press in both North and South America, trumpets that the Protestant Reformation has arrived in Latin America, promising at last to break the logjam of traditional cultural values inhibiting economic growth and capitalist development. Business leaders openly praise Pentecostal workers because they allegedly work harder and suffer from fewer vices. The Catholic church is redirecting substantial resources toward traditional pastoral policies in part because of the wide-spread perception of a loss of Catholic souls to Pentecostal conversion. At the Latin American Bishops Conference held in Santo Domingo in 1992, Pope John Paul II warned against the "invasion of the sects" and "ravenous wolves," launching a continentwide "new evangelization" drive designed to strengthen the church's religious claim to Latin American culture. In sum, key institutions of Latin American life are making far-reaching decisions on the basis of a flurry of speculation regarding the Protestant and particularly the Pentecostal phenomenon. We seek in this volume to contribute to the understanding of Latin American Pentecostalism, and it is appropriate to ask ourselves now what we know and do not know.

The preceding chapters clarify a number of issues regarding the size, theological positions, historical roots, and interrelationships of Pentecostalism across a range of countries. We discuss below the most widely known and persistent, though inaccurate, stereotypes about Pentecostals in Latin America, describing the contributions to a more sophisticated understanding made by specific chapters in this volume, referring to other recent studies that discuss similar themes, and suggesting likely avenues for future research.

Old Stereotypes: New Challenges

Pentecostals as Newcomers to Latin America

One of the most persistent of stereotypes, particularly in the popular press, is that Pentecostalism is only a recent arrival to Latin America. Virtually every account of Pentecostalism employs the imagery of an "explosion" of recent growth. Each of the preceding chapters firmly puts this stereotype to rest. Although it is true that growth rates rose sharply in the post–World War II period, the roots of a number of national Pentecostal churches reach back to the early twentieth century—particularly in Brazil (1910), Chile (1910), Argentina (1910), Peru (1911), Nicaragua (1912), Mexico (1914), Guatemala (1916), and Puerto Rico (1916).[2] Some Latin American groups were in fact established prior to the formal organization of the North American denominations that are presumed to have brought them into existence.[3] The vast majority of Latin American Pentecostals (upwards of 80 percent) are found in denominational groupings that have existed a half-century or longer. Some Latin American movements have sufficiently aged, in fact, that observers purport to find the indifference and loss of intensity typical of second- and third-generation religious revivals.[4]

The early birth of Latin American national Pentecostal traditions is significant for at least three reasons. First, although a few North American churches have been exported to Latin America, the founding experiences of Latin American and North American Pentecostalism were occurring more or less simultaneously in a number of countries. Latin American Pentecostalism, then, is not simply another foreign invasion or expression of religious imperialism; it must not be studied as a derivative of something else or dependent on outside explanation. Latin American Pentecostals developed their character with virtually no North American influence long before the prototypical Elmer Gantry was created or before there was a Billy Sunday to imitate. What models of Protestantism that were available were most likely Lutheran, Episcopal, and Methodist, middle-class reproductions of European or North American mainline denominations. Moreover, twentieth-century Pentecostals are not very similar organizationally to their putative North American founders, and in fact the largest movements have had the least North American influence. The Chilean Pentecostals, with a reported membership of 2 million adults and a community of as many as 14 percent of the population, retain a Methodist episcopal polity and practice infant baptism, while most of their U.S. Pentecostal cousins, especially those that later sent missionaries south, organized around a congregational polity and baptize only adults. The Brazilian Assembleias de Deus tend to polities, styles, and customs that bear little resemblance to any of the major U.S. Pentecostal denominations, least of all to the Assemblies of God (Springfield, Mo.). Yet the Assemblies of God has done little to correct the false impression, resulting from their similar names, that it brought the Brazilian movement—the world's largest—into existence. In fact, Brazilian and other Pentecostal leaders in the region believe that they, not the North Americans, are the standard-bearers of the movement, experiencing rapid growth and accounting for an estimated following from six to eight times the number of North American Pentecostals.

Denominational names are generally unreliable for determining the affiliation—let alone administrative control—of a North American church with its supposed Latin American counterpart. The Assembleias de Deus was named in 1918 by Brazilians under the influence of the Baptist-trained Swedish pastor Lewi Pethrus of the Stockholm Filadelfia Church when the North American group was just four years old and was still known in some quarters as the Church of God in Christ. Moreover, the name under which the Brazilians registered was in the singular; the plural only later came into use.[5] Similarly, the large International Church of the Foursquare Gospel is known in Brazil as the Cruzada Interamericana de Brasil, offering no hint of its overseas denominational ties. In the case of Puerto Rico, the group of churches that affiliated with the North American Assemblies of God in 1916, the Iglesia de Dios Pentecostal, never used the name of its mainland counterpart even at its founding and, in fact, went its own way in 1953 without a backward look.[6]

What may be even more important is the strong influence Europeans have played in Latin American Pentecostalism. Brazilian Pentecostals trace their origins to two different sets of European "founding fathers."[7] Gunnar Vingren and Daniel Berg, Swedish immigrants to the United States, took Pentecostalism to Belém, Pará, in 1909 after having been introduced to the movement at the Chicago mission of William H. Durham the previous year.[8] Simultaneously, and without either's being aware of the other, Louis (also Luigi) Francescon, an Italian immigrant to the United States who had previously become a Presbyterian, introduced the movment to Italian communities in the south of Brazil.[9] Moreover, the Argentine Asambleas de Dios (which traces its origins to 1910, four years before the founding of the North American Assemblies of God) is a Swedish group that was reported in 1982 to have a membership two and one-half times larger than the Argentine group identified with its presumed North American namesake. Similarly, one of the largest Pentecostal movements in Mexico was pioneered in 1919 by Axel and Ester Andersson, supported by the Swedish Filadelfia Pentecostal Churches. "The heritage of much of Latin American Pentecostalism is generally to be traced to Sweden and Norway," concludes David Bundy. "The heritage of Latin American Pentecostalism is as much European as from the U.S.A.."[10]

In addition, today, at the same time that North American churches send missionaries to Latin America, Latin American churches are sending missionaries both to other Latin American cities and to major U.S. cities. Anna Adams examines Puerto Rican missionary activity in Allentown, Pennsylvania. Allentown is not only a microcosm of the postindustrial Northeast but also typical of U.S. urban centers targeted by Latin American Pentecostal missionaries. Thus, the cultural heritage of Pentecostalism is far more complex than a simple imperialist model suggests. In David Martin's words, "People travel, especially in search of work; ideas travel with people. An effective 'missionary' can be a domestic servant, a door-to-door salesman, or simply someone who goes to and from the urban center by bus."[11]

Secondly, as the historical record amply demonstrates, Latin American Pentecostalism cannot be explained merely as some imperialist conspiracy masterminded in the United States. As cynically political as some North American attempts in the 1980s to export Pentecostal churches have been, the common thread running through the foundational experiences of Latin American Pentecostal groups is their specifically and exclusively *religious* character. Indeed, what distinguishes Pentecostal churches and followers from other churches and groups of faithful is the vivid and palpable religious experience that marks the specific moment of transition from the old life to the new.

Yet, the fact that North American and European Pentecostal churches have long contributed funds and personnel to corresponding Pentecostal organizations in Latin America continues to reinforce the mistaken perception that Latin American Pentecostalism is dependent on outside, specifically North American support. Two considerations are vital in this regard: Do national leaders and churches receive salaries or substantial operational budgets from overseas sources, and is property registered in the name of the denomination or mission (or a proxy)? The fact is that few if any funds are given to the national churches by overseas groups beyond occasional projects of a capital nature, such as church and educational buildings and, less often, land. Moreover, the resulting assets, usually in urban real estate, are typically held in the name of the national church. An occasional Latin American Pentecostal has complained that affluent North American Pentecostal groups should be more generous with their help; however, there is little basis for complaining about foreign dependency or control.[12] In fact, as Bryan Froehle points out, it is likely that foreign involvement more adequately explains the continued viability of Catholicism in countries such as Venezuela than Pentecostal growth or vitality. For example, while no non-Spanish surnames are listed in the Venezuelan national directory of the Assemblies of God, the largest and most rapidly expanding Pentecostal denomination in the country, an astonishing 94 percent of the Catholic religious-order priests are foreign-born—helping to explain why so many local Catholic church projects have been funded by religious orders and granting agencies in Europe and North America.

More to the point, however, even national movements that have developed a fraternal relationship with some foreign agency depend little upon it for resources and assistance. The major Pentecostal groups, the Iglesia de Dios del Evangelio Completo (Church of God [Cleveland, Tenn.]), the Cruzada Interamericana do Brasil (Foursquare Gospel), and the Asambleas de Dios (Assemblies of God) maintain only a few dozen foreign missionaries, though the combined constituencies of these Latin American churches run into the millions of members. Nor do these foreign personnel, a substantial proportion of whom are second-generation missionaries to whom the culture and language are not foreign, exert direct administrative control or assume the financial support of the churches, as they are engaged primarily in educational and other support services.

In addition, as the descriptions in our case studies show, the Latin American Pentecostals' customs, styles, and practices are autochthonous (nationally governed, sustained, and extended), owing little to foreign influence.[13] The resources raised by these Pentecostals, their systems of polity, and their sense of ownership and control clearly indicate that stereotypes of foreign intervention in their operations are ill-founded. Ultimately, as our contributors all suggest, the region's Pentecostals possibly represent the most independent, self-initiated popular movement to be found in Latin America today.

Third, long-standing national Pentecostal churches' missionary efforts have paid off over time in the creation of a complex network of new groups. For reasons covered in the preceding chapters, Pentecostal churches tend to split often and easily, blurring the organizational lines between groups. The groups' development has been replete with defections by strong leaders and the proliferation of new Pentecostal organizations. Therefore, unlike the Catholic church or other mainline European Protestant churches, there is no one Pentecostal "church" with clearly defined organizational boundaries. Research opportunities will continue to abound in delineating local, regional, and national variants of the Latin American Pentecostal tradition.

At the same time, close observation also leads to the conclusion that the diversity of organizations is essentially a matter of the decentralization of similar if not identical groups that, should the constituents wish, could combine their efforts under one denominational administrative umbrella without damage to their beliefs and practices. As Guillermo Cook notes, the degree of doctrinal and organizational cooperation and agreement across broad lines within Pentecostalism belies the image of constant fragmentation leading to tensions between strong leaders and unbridled competition between churches. We are only beginning to understand the diversity and complexity of interrelationships of the Pentecostal landscape.

In the 1960s a penetrating study of Pentecostals celebrated their tendency to respond to local initiative, attributing their collective vitality in part to their diversity. Luther P. Gerlach found that these groups were characteristically "cellular, polycephalous and reticulate," semiautonomous and decentralized but interconnected segments. "Observers generally regard such a loose structure to be defective and seek to centralize it, tighten its command structure, terminate 'unnecessary duplication' and otherwise 'rationalize' its organization and operation," wrote Gerlach. "Our research leads us to propose that such organization is highly adapted for exponential growth."[14] There is considerable reason to believe that Pentecostals readily cooperate on most issues and projects and freely move from one to another group when circumstances make such changes desirable.

Pentecostals as Apolitical

Another persistent stereotype is that Pentecostals are always and inherently apolitical. This image is both grounded in reality and wildly misleading. Typically, Pentecostals are portrayed as concerned only with matters of private morality, participation in church activities, and intragroup identity/solidarity. Some observers note that Pentecostals espouse a "render unto Caesar what is Caesar's" justification for eschewing political activity.[15] But recent research including the preceding chapters indicates that there are numerous examples of Pentecostal participation in local and even national politics. Edward Cleary and Juan Sepúlveda note that a set of Chilean Pentecostal groups previously organized around a *pinochetista* line in the hope of gaining privileges from the state. Bryan Froehle points out that the Venezuelan Organización Renovadora Auténtica was one of the first explicitly evangelical political parties in the region, and although it does champion specific evangelical legislative interests, it also serves as an important minority member of legislative coalitions of support for larger, national interests. Philip Williams describes new evangelical-inspired political parties in El Salvador founded in an explicit rejection of traditional Salvadoran parties. In fact, new political parties that count on Pentecostal support now dot the region. If it is true that Pentecostals are apolitical, are these examples simply idiosyncratic?

First, let us look at what it means to be "apolitical." Pentecostals typically view their conversions in religious terms. Manuel Marzal's excellent research in urban Peru underscores this point. His respondents gave as their primary reasons for conversion "encounter with God and Christ," "experience of rebirth" (which brings redemptive changes in personal morality such as quitting drinking), experience of healing, and discovery of the Bible. Far less frequently cited were instrumental reasons for conversion such as the possibility of social mobility through the church, access to Pentecostal social networks (especially for newcomers to the cities), or support (moral or economic) from other members. All of these reasons are intensely personal with a focus on intragroup interaction; none of the reasons suggest that individuals convert because of Pentecostal groups' larger political agenda or vision for society.[16] Pentecostals themselves do not view their conversions or church memberships as in any way relating to the world of politics.

A few Pentecostals are quite self-consciously *anti*political. For these, a focus on personal salvation and redemption is gained only through a *rejection* of the things of this world, which obviously includes movements based on necessarily false ideologies or belief systems. These groups, analogous historically to similar movements within mainline European religious traditions, draw rigid distinctions between spiritual and temporal matters and build strong intragroup identity through rejection of all worldly affiliations.

But Pentecostals often reject politics as a matter of compromises and deals struck between elites, those whose positions of power and wealth are viewed in Latin American society as inherently corrupt. Typically in many areas, elites are also seen as completely intertwined with the Catholic church. Many Pentecostals feel excluded from the interlocking networks of civil elites and Catholic officials whose relationships are continually reinforced by participation in activities not open to or rejected by Pentecostals. Moreover, historically the Catholic church has been (at times brutally) opposed to Protestants and Pentecostals, making Pentecostals reluctant to enter into organizations in public life considered to be enmeshed in Catholic social policy.[17]

At the center of Pentecostals' church membership is the shared experience of the Holy Spirit, not a shared vision for society at large. Thus, most Pentecostals view themselves as apolitical in the sense that their lives and social networks are committed to and built around their religious faith rather than other (particularly partisan) commitments. Moreover, there is a shared view that individual faith should be placed in God, not in social or political movements that promise temporal transformation on the basis of man-made ideology. In these senses, then, Pentecostalism is inherently apolitical.

As the preceding chapters show, however, Pentecostals' faith often leads to substantial local community and even national social service involvement, which can easily have political implications. "Pentecostals can be heard as often as anyone else decrying bad drinking water, dangerous buses and roads, unstable tenure of house plots, and the lack of electricity," reports John Burdick about *crentes* in a town just north of Rio de Janeiro.[18] Typical programs created and funded by Pentecostals include rehabilitation programs for substance abusers, educational projects, and women's and children's assistance programs. Michael Dodson points to El Salvador's Liceo Cristiano, a twenty-five-year-old Pentecostal school system with thirty-four campuses and over 24,000 students, as a good example of the kind of commitment typically made by Pentecostal churches, although it is far more extensive than most. The Liceo Cristiano is affiliated with the international Programa Integral Educacional de las Asambleas de Dios (PIEDAD), which has affiliated schools throughout Latin America and provides schooling and many social services to 125,000 students. It is the largest private, non-Catholic network of educational facilities in the region. The vast majority of these schools can be found in the most economically distressed areas, and most of them offer meals, uniforms, and medical and dental assistance.[19]

The foregoing chapters underscore the degree to which Pentecostals involve themselves in social service networks, both locally and nationally. Adams's chapter further demonstrates that this tendency travels with missionary activity in the United States. Pentecostals are *not* inherently passive social separatists divorced from the social issues and demands that surround them. In fact, resignation, whether personal resignation in the face of one's sins or addictions or hopelessness about the condition of others, is not a central attribute of Pentecostal believers. Carlos Rodrígues Brandão, a Brazilian sociologist, asserts that Pentecostals' "active belief in supernatural forces is not escapism, but a source of hope in their struggle to change their environment."[20]

Perhaps it is not surprising that the degree to which Pentecostal churches are involved in social projects was initially overlooked. The traditional clientelistic linkages between Latin American states and the institutions of civil society, among which the Catholic church was always prominent, diverted scholars' attention from the kind of local, autonomous, and often fragmented activity typical of Pentecostalism. In turn, until recently the apparent lack of Pentecostal attempts to link their mobilization potential to traditional institutions of civil society (for example, political parties or other national movements) led observers to overlook the degree to which Pentecostals were enmeshed in organizational work of their own. In the words of the Catholic ecumenist Jeffrey Gros, "the Pentecostals do not *have* a social policy, they *are* a social policy."[21]

Pentecostals as Pawns of the North American Religious Right

A related stereotype of Latin American Pentecostals is that they are consistently linked to the North American religious right and likely to become tools of reactionary political regimes.[22] Observers who view Pentecostals as antipolitical, rejecting any involvement in worldly politics, have argued that the effect of Pentecostal growth has been an implicit acceptance of the status quo.[23] The progressive Catholics most inclined to support liberationist Christian base communities, for example, tend to depict Pentecostals as religious escapists who shirk their social responsibilities and allow governments to continue to oppress their peoples without challenge. Christian Lalive d'Epinay's groundbreaking study of Pentecostals in 1969 coined the phrase "haven of the masses" to convey precisely this notion of religious retreat for those most dislocated by the sweeping forces of economic, political, social, and cultural change.[24] Others who focus on the tendency in Pentecostalism to espouse what are considered conservative social and behavioral norms (particularly with regard to gender roles) argue that Pentecostalism reinforces traditional, patriarchal, and essentially authoritarian Latin American beliefs. Hence, it is asserted that Pentecostals, while not necessarily involved in politically right-wing or reactionary movements, serve as new conduits for traditionally conservative and antidemocratic values.[25]

Although it would be a mistake to view Pentecostalism as a political movement, several of the preceding chapters show us that some churches do enter the political fray in quite partisan ways. We are finding, however, that Pentecostals do not join partisan debates or electoral competitions rigidly or consistently. Not all Pentecostals are right-wing supporters of military or authoritarian rule, even though some Pentecostals have openly supported such regimes in countries such as Chile, Brazil, and Guatemala. Pentecostals have also supported reformist candidates or political "outsiders" in Peru, Brazil, and Venezuela. Rowan Ireland's discussion of the political implications of different kinds of conversion experiences in Brazil is especially suggestive here.

What seems to be consistent about Pentecostal partisan activity is not its ideological bent but its tendency to seek avenues for creating and making heard its own, unique "voice" in politics. Since most leaders are accustomed to working as part of a little-respected religious minority in the face of resistance from the political establishment, they tend to keep a low profile and choose skirmishes that they can win. In the meantime, Pentecostals are wary of confusing their perceived real interests and concerns with passing issues, and they sometimes avoid even participation in national evangelical organizations because of their concern for losing control. They are reluctant to deal away future advantage or to be used as conscripts in other people's wars—literally as well as figuratively. This posture was the basis of their opposition to the Sandinista government of Daniel Ortega in Nicaragua, where they adopted a not necessarily consistent position of pacifism, refusing to send their sons off to fight the Contras. Similarly, Cleary and Sepúlveda suggest that Pentecostals' support for the Chilean dictator Augusto Pinochet, like their support of his socialist predecessor Salvador Allende, can be explained in terms of their own logic as to what was best, given limited options, for their evangelical interests. This sense of independence, more than premillennial theology, anticommunist concerns, foreign influence, or any other motive attributed to them, may explain their particular political positions and policies.

At the same time, Pentecostals are highly skilled at mobilizing the marginal social sectors. As a result, increasingly other evangelical groups, which have often discounted these groups because of their humble constituents and lack of sophistication, are turning to Pentecostals for interdenominational leadership. For example, Pentecostals have been in the vanguard of negotiations with the Mexican government about the implementation of the recent constitutional changes, occupying positions that in former years would have been filled only by representatives of the historical denominations. Similarly, it may be expected that Pentecostal support will be courted by any number of other partisan national actors.

Pentecostal political activity is best explained, then, in terms of the nature of the political system in question and the obstacles to and opportunities for their participation. This shifts our attention away from inherent political beliefs toward questions such as the breadth and depth of a country's political party system, the degree of institutionalization of civil society, and the resources available to Pentecostals (wealth, historical tradition, political allies, strength of religious and political enemies or competitors, etc.) across national contexts. The key question is not which group of Pentecostals is "typical" or the "norm." The chapters in this volume show us that tensions over a range of theological and social-justice issues divide Pentecostals in a number of different ways. Rather, we need a framework for understanding the "space" that religions occupy in the different national political arenas.

To this end, we have discussed politics in terms of Pentecostals' own conceptions of their role in the communities or societies around them. But, beyond individual leaders' or churches' decisions, does widespread religious organization generally affect local or national politics? Typically, this question is posed by political scientists or policymakers interested in particular political outcomes such as democratization or stability.

For example, Michael Dodson argues that we must revisit the question first raised thirty years ago by Emilio Willems and Christian Lalive d'Epinay: Does widespread Pentecostal membership reinforce or undermine larger processes of modernization and democratization in Latin America? Dodson suggests that after three decades of dramatic economic and social dislocation, traditional aristocratic and paternalistic ties have been weakened in Latin America. At the moment, democracy appears to be more widespread, with deeper roots, than ever before in the region. Given the dramatic growth of Pentecostal membership precisely in those countries most ravaged by violence or economic crisis, Dodson argues that the question of whether Pentecostalism will serve to strengthen or weaken the associational ties of civil society that undergird democratic norms and processes is more salient today than ever before.

Dodson finds reason for cautious optimism. Along with Daniel Levine and David Martin, Dodson argues that the apparent surge in religious organization in parts of Latin America deepens democratic potential in the region. All three scholars suggest that Pentecostal growth rapidly expands new associational ties among believers that, over time, will challenge the traditional social order.[26] To the extent that the grass-roots organizing around participatory religious models strengthens civil society, thus improving the prospects for democracy, Dodson suggests that Tocqueville's characterization of Protestantism in the United States may now hold true for Latin America: "Freedom sees religion as the companion of its struggles and triumphs."

The contributors of the country chapters in the volume also find that Latin American popular groups, intent on bringing stability to their existence, have turned not just to religion but to organization. No other network of popular voluntary organizations outside the Roman Catholic church is as large and has so many resources. In the aggregate, Pentecostal churches have as many as 200,000 congregations, averaging per congregation probably no more than sixty in attendance but typically with legal recognition and ownership of real property. A closer look suggests that this process of institutional development—the creation of associations that they themselves own and direct—is one of the most important driving forces of these movements. Thus, Pentecostalism may also reinforce the cultural values, such as strong individualism, belief in at least the moral equality of all children of God, and access based on hard work and merit to avenues for social mobility, that are generally associated with Western liberal democracies.[27]

In the end, what do we know about Pentecostals and politics? First, far more diversity exists across groups than we originally imagined. At the very least, many Pentecostal churches are heavily involved in local community work in the delivery of vital social services that, in turn, links them with questions of public policy. Second, research shows that Pentecostals do enter partisan politics, both locally and nationally, in different ways. It may be that this should be expected. The decision to attempt to influence the larger, political debates of society can be supported biblically as well as by the call of the Holy Spirit. As Pentecostals grow in number and organizational strength, it is likely that their attention will turn beyond the immediate goal of missionizing and intragroup identity. Furthermore, there is no political agenda *inherent* in Pentecostal belief or official church policy, and this means that Pentecostals have a range of political options consistent with their faith. In fact, recent debate within evangelical circles centers precisely on the issue of "contextualization of the Gospel message," sometimes meaning the translation of one's faith into social responsibility. A number of writers have pointed out the vast transformative potential of grass-roots Pentecostal growth; however, it is reasonable to expect a range of diversity among Pentecostals themselves regarding the nature of the desired social changes.

It will be helpful to add one cautionary note at this point. As academic observers of Pentecostalism, we tend to look for the behaviors that our disciplines define as important—the political ramifications, sociological effects, or psychological motivations. However, we should learn from our mistakes in the 1960s–1980s, when we overestimated the (particularly political) influence of liberation theology by tending to ignore the fundamentally *religious* motivation of the vast majority of Catholics.[28] Moreover, it no longer makes sense to focus entirely on church-state relations except in the few cases where larger Pentecostal

churches have entered national politics or established Pentecostal groups have organized umbrella organizations to achieve specific ends, such as in Chile.
Certainly, established churches over time often develop linkages with the dominant culture and the political arena. But without new approaches we run the risk
of overemphasizing such phenomena simply because they are more accessible to
the researcher.

Pentecostals as Antifeminist

Common to most Pentecostal churches is a relatively traditional view of gender
relations. As Anna Adams points out among Puerto Rican Pentecostals in
Allentown, Pennsylvania, Pentecostals themselves often distinguish between "conservatives" and "progressives" on the basis of churches' positions on the proper
role of women, both in their homes and in their churches. For the most part, men
generally are conceived as heads of household, women as keepers of the home and
hearth. More conservative churches may also segregate church services by gender,
impose traditional dress codes on women, and explicitly prohibit women from
holding positions of authority within the church. Not surprisingly, critics of
Pentecostalism have argued that the spread of Pentecostal membership in Latin
America reinforces traditional machismo, further locks women into subordinate
roles that ensure their continued oppression at home and in national "development," and places God on the side of those who condemn empowerment for
women.

Carol Drogus's chapter demonstrates that scholars are taking a new look at the
implications of Pentecostal gender relations. Building on the work of Elizabeth
Brusco and others,[29] Drogus suggests that although Pentecostals' traditional gender divisions are intended to reinforce male dominance, the combination of emphasis on religious equality, new roles open to women in the life of the church,
and the equalization of work traditionally relegated to "women's sphere" all serve
to undermine hegemonic ideologies of machismo and *marianismo*.

Cecília Mariz and María das Dores Campos Machado's chapter on women in
Brazil underscores the notion that Pentecostalism can dismantle traditional
machismo; yet the authors argue that Pentecostal women choose to adhere closely
to traditional moral and social codes. The difference for Pentecostal women is not
that they reject traditional values regarding family, sexual codes, or gender roles;
rather, they see themselves as individuals responsible for their own liberation
from the oppression of evil, defined as natural passions and instincts. It is the
process of individuation, coupled with the assertion of a primary responsibility
to God rather than one's spouse or family, that transforms women into active, responsible agents in their own and their families' lives. These researchers assert,
then, that Pentecostal conversion not only "domesticates" male roles but also results in greater individuation and autonomy (if still traditional in social values)
for women.

Further questions remain, however, concerning the implications of Pentecostalism for Latin American women. As editors, we asked each contributor of a country chapter to examine the role of women in the churches they investigated. Not surprisingly, this proved difficult for most contributors; solid research is rare. As Drogus points out, even though the majority of active Pentecostal participants are women and women are often seen as having peculiar access to the ecstatic Pentecostal experience, little systematic research has been conducted on the role of women in Pentecostalism and its effects on them.

Some clues may be provided from the literature from other regions. For example, Elaine Lawless's work on women preachers in U.S. Pentecostal churches finds that even in traditions that explicitly bar women from positions of church authority, a number of women have become respected preachers and (albeit more rarely) church pastors. It suggests that women can transcend traditional gendered roles within Pentecostal communities by invoking God's insistent call (and their humble attempts to refuse) to serve Him as an instrument for His voice. Lawless's analysis of the preaching styles of female versus male preachers shows that women claim authority for their messages precisely by emphasizing that they are merely God's instruments, reluctantly obeying His command to serve—that is, displaying the very submissiveness and obedience traditionally assigned to women.

Scattered examples of women in leadership positions in Pentecostal churches do exist throughout Latin America. Historical studies of the institutionalization of North American religious groups give us reason to be cautious in our optimism, however. In the experience of other churches, growth and institutional "success" often led to a rigidification of traditional gender roles, resulting in the eventual prohibition of female pastoral leadership even in churches originally led by women. For example, Jean Soderland writes of early-nineteenth-century Methodism in the United States: "While female membership had grown considerably, the number of women leaders did not. Women lost the opportunities to preach and lead congregations when worship services moved from the fields and homes into churches that were built in the traditional Christian design with the pulpit situated at the front."[30] It cannot be clear yet to what degree Pentecostal churches will adapt to dominant social norms as they settle into established positions of authority with diffuse and multiclass roots.

The historical record of other religious institutions reminds us to focus on the "gendering" of Pentecostal churches over time. Borrowing from Joan Acker, "in this approach gender is a process, not a characteristic of persons, although, of course, the assignment of persons to gender categories is a central aspect of the process. . . . [This means that] gender is present in the processes, practices, images and ideologies, and distributions of power" in the institutions of social (or religious) life.[31] This focus shifts the central questions away from a snapshot description of women's roles toward the ways in which women are included in or excluded from positions of authority, the undermining effects of the Pentecostal religious experience on traditional male/female conceptions, and the extent to which religious institutions and the character of particular religious groups have been formed by and through gender.

Further research must explore more carefully the kinds of roles played by women, the religious justification for female participation in the gendered spheres of the church, the effects (if any) of female religious leadership on other women in Pentecostal groups, and the potential for empowerment in traditional "women's work" within churches.[32] Another issue that has been largely ignored is the role of single women in Pentecostal churches. Beyond suggesting that young women attend Pentecostal services in the hope of finding more egalitarian, serious, and faithful prospects for husbands, virtually all of the research on women focus on wives and mothers. What is the conception of women within Pentecostal circles beyond the categories of wife and mother?

Pentecostals as the Poorest of the Poor

The mission field for most Pentecostals is among the poor. According to existing studies, the areas of greatest growth among Pentecostals are urban shantytowns and, to a lesser extent, rural peasant communities. This has led to a general image of Pentecostals as poor, dispossessed, and marginalized. Statistically it is true that Pentecostalism has spread more rapidly in the lower classes, but the stereotype encourages faulty logic and poor methodology. Instead of asking what explains Pentecostal growth, observers often ask why poor people convert, and this question produces certain kinds of "answers." A representative list of reasons given for Pentecostal conversion includes the following:

1. The poor and uneducated do not understand the contemporary, particularly progressive, Catholic message.
2. Christian base communities "require too much," especially in countries where community commitment can be life-threatening, from the already socially and economically vulnerable faithful.
3. The poor and marginalized convert to Pentecostalism for instrumental reasons—for example, access to Pentecostal mutual aid or other social service programs.
4. Poor people are drawn to Pentecostalism, particularly in countries experiencing dire economic or political dislocation or violence, because the emphasis on taking responsibility for one's own life lends a sense of control to people otherwise subject to the vagaries of forces beyond their control.
5. Because authority and leadership in Pentecostal churches do not require years of study, celibacy, or approval through an international chain of command, aspiring young men are drawn to Pentecostal churches as possible paths to career and social mobility.

6. Pentecostal churches, led by strong, authoritative pastors who control access to the social service benefits of membership, reproduce the paternalistic patron-client relationships of traditional Latin American society and therefore provide needed psychological security to dislocated populations.

A few of these common explanations for Pentecostal growth have some merit, but there is significant evidence that Pentecostalism is not exclusively a lower-class phenomenon. In countries such as Guatemala, Brazil, and Venezuela, a substantial Pentecostal incursion into the middle to upper-middle classes is evident. Not surprisingly, explanations for middle-class conversion focus less on the ignorance or instrumentalism of converts than on the role of religions in the societies of different countries.[33] For example, Everett Wilson's chapter argues that the emergence of Pentecostal groups in Guatemala represents a new, national infrastructure of churches that, while made up largely of poor individuals, own their own buildings, have legal recognition, and are organized well beyond their local communities. Pentecostalism, then, fills a void both in religious terms and in terms of providing new organizational opportunities in Guatemalan civil society. As Wilson points out, this understanding of Pentecostalism in Guatemala shifts research attention away from arguments regarding the size of different groups or the importance of such highly visible figures as ex-president José Efraín Ríos Montt toward the more difficult issues of examining the strength and potential of popular religious groups and the space they occupy in local and national life. Such a research focus might offer new insights regarding why people of any socioeconomic group might convert to Pentecostalism.

Pentecostalism as Atheological

Pentecostalism's growing reach into the middle classes has another important ramification. One of the supposed attractions of Pentecostalism, especially for the poor and uneducated, is greater access to the authority of the Holy Spirit. Pentecostal churches are organized around the experience of the Holy Spirit, which is open to anyone. Many observers have concluded that because Pentecostal pastors usually lack seminary training and authority is conferred by the Holy Spirit rather than by scholarly bodies that define theological orthodoxy, Pentecostals lack firm theological foundations. But the image of Pentecostal services as simply "emotional happenings" is inaccurate. Some descriptions, such as Ireland's of Brazilian Pentecostals, emphasize just how routine and unexciting a Pentecostal church service can be, since permitting congregational participation in a public meeting is possible only because of considerable structure, stylization, and, ultimately, control.[34] However enthusiastic the Pentecostals' worship may be at peak intervals, spontaneity is kept within acceptable bounds.

One may point to the structure of the groups themselves to establish that they represent a fairly high proportion of dedicated, convinced members. The sociologist Bryan Roberts found in investigations of these groups in Guatemala that Pentecostals formed "effective moral communities" with a demanding code of conduct.[35] Pentecostals form close-knit congregations that require a postulant to demonstrate extraordinary commitment. New members must regularize their marital status, abandon what are considered personal vices, attend meetings regularly, support the group's programs, respect the group's purposes, and contribute regular financial support. The criticism that the Pentecostals are too "legalistic" about personal conduct is much more frequent than that they are too lax.

Although behavior does not speak to belief, the piety required of members of popular Pentecostal groups is tied to study, reflection, and values. Despite their vulnerability to tangential teachings, in practice these groups hew close to doctrinal lines. They are avid biblicists who tend to quote scriptures correctly and with meaning. They seem to know more about the differences between Mormons, Baptists, and Seventh-Day Adventists than their typical North American counterparts. The rote learning characteristic of Latin American elementary education and the thirst of the common people for information combine to make Bible studies sometimes interesting but almost always predictable.

Latin American evangelicals of any kind deeply resent the term "sect," understanding despite reassurances about the technical meaning of the term that its use makes their movements less than completely Christian. They aspire to emulate the primitive church of the New Testament Acts of the Apostles, empowered by the same spiritual impulses. Donald Dayton argues that we should understand Latin American Pentecostals as a renovating force within Christianity in an early stage of evolution. Like other now-mainline churches such as Methodism, "the new churches are born among the poor, and as they advance into the middle classes, they begin to assume the characteristics of a middle class church while continuing to be a force for renewal within the more traditional churches."[36] Dayton points out that North American degree-granting, accredited Pentecostal seminaries are only a decade or two old. As Latin American Pentecostalism becomes a more multiclass phenomenon, we might expect a similar trend in the codifying of a critical theology and systematic ethics. That prominent Latin American Pentecostal leaders have already achieved appointments to theological faculties is a sign of precisely this trend.

Moreover, most Protestant groups have in some measure become "Pentecostalized" by adopting such practices as prayer for the sick and belief in personal empowerment and miracles, let alone clapping and rousing coritos (repetitious and, critics claim, often theologically shallow choruses) in their meetings. "Since we all believe the same way about the work of the Spirit," says a Baptist lay leader in Central America, "why don't we non-Pentecostals simply acknowledge that the deep differences that separated us in the past no longer exist?" The vitality of the Catholic charismatic movement demonstrates that even the Catholic church can borrow elements of Pentecostal worship.

Conclusion

Few of the images usually conjured up to visualize Latin American religion accurately portray the Pentecostals. If traditional bell towers, ornate altars, votive candles, and street processions have little to do with the current Pentecostal religious enthusiasm, neither do the stereotypes of "Holy Roller" frenzy, nostalgic "old-time religion," and slick televangelism. The problem is that Latin American popular Pentecostalism, not without a rightful place in the spectrum of Protestant evangelical categories, is very much something of its own. But stereotypes, especially those that have to do with religious subcultures, die hard. The literature has been limited by the inadequacy of the available imagery and the lack of reliable definitions and statistics. This volume moves our discussion past easy stereotypes and fills in a number of the gaps in our knowledge with careful and systematic scholarship, but much remains to be accomplished.

NOTES

1. Harvey Cox, a long-time observer of Latin American churches, expresses similar frustrations in *Fire from Heaven: The Rise of Pentecostal Spirituality and the Reshaping of Religion in the Twenty-first Century* (Reading, Mass.: Addison-Wesley, 1995), pp. 161–184.

2. These conventional dates are given in David B. Barrett, ed., *World Christian Encyclopedia* (New York: Oxford University Press, 1982).

3. The Assemblies of God (Springfield, Mo.) was founded in 1914; the United Pentecostal Church was created by mergers of groups first organized in 1917; the Pentecostal Church of God was organized in 1919; the International Church of the Foursquare Gospel was created in 1923. Most of the remaining North American Pentecostal denominations, such as the Church of God (Cleveland, Tenn.) (1907), have earlier organizational dates because they existed as Holiness churches prior to their adopting Pentecostalism. See Robert Mapes Anderson, *Vision of the Disinherited: The Making of American Pentecostalism* (New York: Oxford University Press, 1979); Stanley Burgess and Gary B. McGee, eds., *Dictionary of Pentecostal and Charismatic Movements* (Grand Rapids, Mich.: Regency Reference Library, 1988).

4. John Kessler deals with the issue of evangelical attrition in "When Latin Americans Evangelize," *Christianity Today*, April 5, 1993, p. 73. Kessler's work is cited and discussed in Edward Cleary, "Protestants and Catholics: Rivals or Siblings?" in Daniel R. Miller, ed. *Coming of Age: Protestantism in Contemporary Latin America* (Lanham, Md.: University Press of America, 1994): pp. 223, 224.

5. In its official history the Assembleias de Deus (Brazil) claims to be the first organization to adopt this name, now found in more than one hundred countries. After initially calling itself the Missão de Fé Apostólica, the group registered its present name with the Brazilian government on January 11, 1918. Abraao de Almeida, *Historia das Assembleias de*

Deus (Rio de Janeiro: Casa Publicadora das Assambleias de Deus, 1982), p. 27. In emphasizing the distinctiveness of the name and the authenticity of the movement, Almeida writes, "On the 11 of January, 1918, [the church] was officially registered as the Assambleia de Deus, the first church in the world to assume [that name]." It was not affiliated with any foreign mission but genuinely Brazilian.

6. The account is given in Juan Lugo, *Pentecostés en Puerto Rico* (San Juan,: Iglesia de Dios Pentecostal, 1951). In the meantime, the North American Assemblies of God launched a new organization that is now reported to be the second-largest Pentecostal denomination in Puerto Rico.

7. An account in English of the founding of these churches is found in William R. Read, *New Patterns of Church Growth in Brazil* (Grand Rapids, Mich.: Eerdmans, 1965).

8. The standard biographies of Vingren and Berg are Ivar Vingren, *Gunnar Vingren, O diario do pioneiro* (Rio de Janeiro: Casa Publicadora das Assambleias de Deus, 1973), and Daniel Berg, *Daniel Berg, enviado por Deus* (Rio de Janeiro: Casa Publicadora das Assambleias de Deus, 1973).

9. Joseph Colleti, "Luigi Francescon," in Burgess and McGee, *Dictionary,* p. 315.

10. David Bundy, "Swedish Pentecostal Missions: The Case of Axel Andersson in Mexico," paper presented to the annual meeting of the Society for Pentecostal Studies, Guadalajara, Mexico, November 11–13, 1993.

11. David Martin, "Otro tipo de revolución cultural: El Protestantismo radical en América Latina," *Estudios Públicos* 44 (Spring 1991), p. 53.

12. For a different viewpoint, see Carmelo Alvarez, ed., *Pentecostalismo y liberación: Una experiencia latinoamericana* (San José, Costa Rica: Editorial Department Ecuménico de Investigaciones.

13. In addition to the case studies included in this volume, see Cornelia Butler Flora, "Pentecostalism and Development: The Colombian Case," in Stephen D. Glazier, ed., *Perspectives on Pentecostalism: Case Studies from the Caribbean and Latin America* (Lanham, Md.: University Press of America, 1980), pp. 81–94; Rowan Ireland, *Kingdoms Come: Religion and Politics in Brazil* (Pittsburgh: University of Pittsburgh Press, 1991); Barbara Boudewijnse, André Droogers, and Frans Kamsteeg, eds., *Algo más que opio: Una lectura antropológica del Pentecostalismo latinoamericano y caribeño* (San José, Costa Rica: Editorial Departmento Ecuménico de Investigaciones, 1991); and Virginia Garrard-Burnett and David Stoll, eds., *Rethinking Protestantism in Latin America* (Philadelphia: Temple University Press, 1993).

14. Luther P. Gerlach, "Pentecostalism: Revolution or Counter-Revolution?" in Irving I. Zaretsky and Mark P. Leone, eds., *Religious Movements in Contemporary America* (Princeton: Princeton University Press, 1960), pp. 680, 681.

15. For example, see Francisco C. Rolim, *Pentecostais no Brasil* (Petrópolis: Vozes, 1985); Judith Chambliss Hoffnagel, "The Believers: Pentecostalism in a Brazilian City," Ph.D. diss., Indiana University, 1978; Oneide Bobsin, "Produção religiosa e significado social de pentecostalismo a partir de sua prática representação," Ph.D. diss., Pontificia Universidade Católica de São Paulo, 1984.

16. Manuel Marzal, "Pentecostals and Migration in Peru," photocopy, Universidad Católica del Perú.

17. A good discussion of these concerns can be found in John Burdick, "Struggling Against the Devil: Pentecostalism and Social Movements in Urban Brazil," in Garrard-Burnett and Stoll, *Rethinking Protestantism,* pp. 24–28.

18. Burdick, "Struggling Against the Devil," p. 23.

19. See Everett Wilson, "Latin American Pentecostalism: Challenging the Stereotypes of Pentecostal Passivity," *Transformation* 11, 1 (January–March 1994), pp. 19–24.

20. Carlos Rodrigues Brandão, *Os deuses do povo* (Rio de Janeiro: Editora Brasilense, 1980) quoted in Guillermo Cook, "The Evangelical Groundswell in Latin America," *Christian Century* 107 (December 12, 1990), p. 1178.

21. Jeff Gros, "Confessing the Apostolic Faith from the Perspective of the Pentecostal Churches," *Pneuma: The Journal of the Society for Pentecostal Studies* 9, 1 (1987), p. 12.

22. Both David Stoll, *Is Latin America Turning Protestant? The Politics of Evangelical Growth* (Berkeley: University of California Press, 1990), and David Martin, *Tongues of Fire: The Explosion of Protestantism in Latin America* (Oxford and Cambridge, Mass.: Blackwell, 1990), describe the ties between right-wing political groups in the United States and their religious affiliates in both North and Latin America. For a more extreme picture, see "Evangelicals Target Latin America," *Resource Center Bulletin*, no. 15 (Winter 1988).

23. For example, Ireland's study suggests that while Pentecostalism does not *necessarily* lead to conservatism, it does tend to set limits to political activity, and this in turn tends to lead to an implicit support of the status quo. Ireland, *Kingdoms of God*, pp. 98–107.

24. Christian Lalive d'Epinay, *Haven of the Masses* (London: Lutterworth, 1969).

25. See also Judith Hoffnagel, "Pentecostalism: A Revolutionary or a Conservative Movement?" in Stephen D. Glazier, ed., *Perspectives on Pentecostalism: Case Studies from the Caribbean and Latin America* (Lanham, Md.: University Press of America, 1980), pp. 111–124.

26. Although writing specifically about grass-roots organization in the Catholic church, the strongest statement of the democratic, transformative potential of faith and religious association can be found in Daniel H. Levine, *Popular Voices in Latin American Catholicism* (Princeton: Princeton University Press, 1992), pp. 317–352. See also Martin, *Tongues of Fire*, pp. 284–288; Emilio Willems, *Followers of the New Faith: Culture Change and the Rise of Protestantism in Brazil and Chile* (Nashville, Tenn.: Vanderbilt University Press, 1967).

27. For a standard comparison of the linkages between religious values/culture and institutional and economic development in North and Latin America, see S. N. Eisenstadt, "Culture, Religions, and Development in North American and Latin American Civilizations," *The Americas: 1492–1992*, no. 134 (November 1992), pp. 593–606.

28. It is now generally recognized that U.S. scholars overestimated both the importance of such indicators of adherence to liberationist principles as Christian base communities and the political influence that liberationists, either within the ecclesial structures or among the faithful, had on Latin American politics. The strongest statement comes from W. E. Hewitt, *Base Christian Communities and Social Change in Brazil* (Lincoln: University of Nebraska Press, 1991). See also Edward Cleary and Hannah Stewart-Gambino, eds., *Conflict and Competition: The Latin American Church in a Changing Environment* (Boulder: Lynne Rienner, 1992).

29. Elizabeth Brusco, "The Reformation of Machismo: Asceticism and Masculinity Among Colombian Evangelicals," in Garrard-Burnett and Stoll, *Rethinking Protestantism*, pp. 143–158.

30. Jean R. Soderland, "Women and Religion," in Page Putnam Miller, ed., *Reclaiming the Past: Landmarks of Women's History* (Bloomington: Indiana University Press, 1992), pp. 187–188. See also Janet Wilson, ed., *Women in American Religion* (Philadelphia: University of Pennsylvania Press, 1980); Rosemary Radford Ruether and Rosemary Skinner Keller, eds., *Women and Religion in America*, vol. 2, *The Colonial and Revolutionary Periods* (San Francisco: Harper and Row, 1983).

31. Joan Acker, "Gendered Institutions: From Sex Roles to Gendered Institutions," *Contemporary Society* 21, 5 (September 1992), p. 567.

32. Although not about Pentecostals, Evelyn Brooks Higginbotham's book on women leaders in the black Baptist church could offer interesting parallels with women in Latin American Pentecostalism. Evelyn Brooks Higginbotham, *Righteous Discontent: The Women's Movement in the Black Baptist Church, 1880–1920* (Cambridge: Harvard University Press, 1993). Similar work has been conducted on women's participation in traditional Catholic organizations. The most obvious is the focus on the highly visible women of the Plaza de Mayo in Argentina. Marguerite Guzman Bouvard, *Revolutionizing Motherhood: The Mothers of the Plaza de Mayo* (Wilmington, Del.: Scholarly Resources, 1994); Marysa Navarro, "The Personal Is Political: Las Madres de Plaza de Mayo," in Susan Eckstein, ed., *Power and Popular Protest: Latin American Social Movements* (Berkeley: University of California Press, 1989), pp. 241–258.

33. See, for example, David E. Dixon, "Popular Culture, Popular Identity, and the Rise of Latin American Protestantism: Voices from Santiago *Poblacional,*" paper presented at the 17th International Congress of the Latin American Studies Association, September 24–27, 1992, pp. 16–24.

34. Ireland, *Kingdoms Come,* pp. 81–93.

35. Bryan R. Roberts, "Protestant Groups and Coping with Urban Life in Guatemala City," *American Journal of Sociology* 73 (May 1968), p. 767.

36. Donald Dayton, "Reflections on Latin American Pentecostalism," *Focus: A Bi-Monthly Bulletin of the Education for Communication Program of the Centro Evangélico Latinoamericano de Estudios Pastorales* no. 107 (May/June 1992), p. 1.

About the Book

*T*oday over forty million Latin Americans classify themselves as Protestant, of which the overwhelming majority belong to some form of Pentecostalism. The rapid dissemination of Pentecostal beliefs has produced vibrant alternatives to traditional dominant culture and changed relations within the family, locality, and workplace. This volume introduces broad issues in the Pentecostal movement, including gender relations, political power and organization, and inter-Pentecostal and ecumenical relations. These themes are then examined more specifically in the country case studies, which address the historical foundations of the Pentecostal movement, patterns of and explanation for its growth, and the consequences of its expanding presence, including increased political influence.

About the Editors and Contributors

Anna Adams is a member of the History Department of Muhlenberg College. She was exploring her own Puerto Rican heritage in the process of researching Latinos in the Allentown area.

Edward L. Cleary, O.P., is professor of political science and Latin American studies at Providence College. He is author of *Crisis and Change: The Church in Latin America* (1985) and coeditor, with Hannah Stewart-Gambino, of *Conflict and Competition: The Latin American Church in a Changing Environment* (1992), among other works.

Guillermo Cook has been a major force in the Latin American theological community as author, editor, and conference organizer. Born in Argentina, he has worked in Brazil and Costa Rica. Among his publications is *The Expectation of the Poor: Latin American Base Ecclesial Communities in Protestant Perspective* (1985).

Michael Dodson, a professor of political science at Texas Christian University, has pursued themes of religion and politics in Latin America in *Nicaragua's Other Revolution* (with Laura Nuzzi O'Shaughnessy [1990]), *Let My People Live* (with Gordon Spykman et al. [1988]), and many other works.

Carol Ann Drogus is associate professor of political science at Hamilton College. Her much-praised doctoral research on Brazil is scheduled for publication. She has written extensively on women in Brazil.

Bryan Froehle worked for two years at the Centro de Investigación en las Ciencias Sociales in Caracas, Venezuela, and has recently assumed a research position at the Center for Applied Research in the Apostolate at Georgetown University in Washington, D.C.

Rowan Ireland is senior lecturer in sociology and chair of Latin American studies at La Trobe University. His *Kingdoms Come: Religion and Politics in Brazil* (1991) was highly praised for showing the wide range of response to religion at the grass roots.

Cecília Loreto Mariz, after doctoral studies at Boston University, returned to Brazil to teach sociology at the Universidade Federal Fluminense. Her published works in English and Portuguese include *Coping with Poverty: Pentecostals and Christian Base Communities in Brazil* (1994).

María das Dores Campos Machado teaches sociology at the Universidade Federal Rural do Río de Janeiro. She has been an active researcher on religious subjects in Brazil.

Juan Sepúlveda edited *Evangelio y Sociedad* for some years before pursuing doctoral studies in England at Birmingham University. He has written extensively of Pentecostalism in Chile and Latin America and taught at the Comunidad Teológica Evangélica de Chile.

Hannah W. Stewart-Gambino is associate professor of government at Lehigh University. She returned in 1994 and 1995 to Chile to do extensive research on the contemporary religious situation. Her previous work includes *The Catholic Church in the Chilean*

Countryside (Westview Press, 1992) and, with Edward Cleary, *Conflict and Competition: The Latin American Church in a Changing Environment* (1992).

Philip J. Williams is associate professor of political science at the University of Florida and has taught at Universidad Centroamericana José Simeon Cañas in San Salvador. He is engaged in a multiyear research project on religion in Peru and El Salvador and among Hispanics in the United States.

Everett Wilson, a historian, directs the Centro de Investigaciones Culturales y Estudios Linguísticos in San José, Costa Rica. Formerly academic dean of Bethany College, he has published articles and chapters on Hispanic and Latin American Pentecostalism.

Index